74/

GENERAL
MONCK

George Monck: miniature by Samuel Cooper.
Reproduced by gracious permission of H.M. the Queen.
Photograph by A. C. Cooper Ltd.

GENERAL MONCK

Maurice Ashley

JONATHAN CAPE
THIRTY BEDFORD SQUARE LONDON

FIRST PUBLISHED 1977
© 1977 BY MAURICE ASHLEY
JONATHAN CAPE LTD, 30 BEDFORD SQUARE
LONDON WCI

BRITISH LIBRARY CATALOGUING IN PUBLICATION DATA

ASHLEY, MAURICE
GENERAL MONCK
ISBN 0–224–01287–8
941.06'6'0924   DA 407.A74
ALBEMARLE, GEORGE MONCK, DUKE OF

PRINTED BY BUTLER & TANNER LTD
FROME AND LONDON

Contents

Illustrations

AUTHOR'S NOTE
In the text all the dates are given in the Old Style, which was ten days earlier than the New Style prevalent elsewhere in Europe at the time. Occasionally both styles are given.

Acknowledgments

My first acknowledgment must be to the Mary Robson Lilburn trust for giving me a research grant without which I could not have written this book. Mr and Mrs Gavin Lilburn (Mr Lilburn is a descendant of Colonel Robert Lilburne) kindly arranged for this grant. The biography is dedicated to them. Professor W. G. Hoskins, Dr J. G. Simms and Professor MacDowell of Trinity College, Dublin, the Rev. J. R. Powell, Mr E. K. Timings and Miss Frances Dow, who has written a thesis on Monck's administration in Scotland, all helped me with various chapters on which they are specialists. I am indebted to the Rev. M. F. Glare, Rector of Holy Trinity, Landcross, and the Rev. R. F. Grist, Rector of All Saints, Merton, for facilitating my researches in Devon and to Mr and Mrs Lewis for twice allowing me to look round the house at Potheridge. Brigadier Peter Young generously lent me his copies of Gumble's *Monck* and Skinner's *Monk* which made the writing of this book much more comfortable. The present Duke of Buccleuch kindly provided me with a copy of Frances Monck's letter to her brother; my son-in-law and daughter, Mr and Mrs Finlay Wilson, amiably took me around Scotland when I was looking over the country where Monck fought and governed. Mr R. O. Swayne read through my manuscript and made valuable suggestions about a historical figure in whom he was himself interested. Finally, I am indebted to my young friends, Richard Smart and Frank Newman, who looked after me at their superb hotel, Springfield House in Chalford, so that I was able to complete this book in luxury and peace.

Maurice Ashley

15 September 1976

'The General ... has always had the
reputation of being a good Englishman;
if he be so, he and the King can never disagree.'

Charles II, 6 April 1660

I

Ancestry and Early Life

George Monck is a figure of distinction in British history, a man whose character influenced events. He earned a reputation as a soldier and a sailor, exceptionally capable in both services. In Scotland, where he became in effect the English governor for several years during the Cromwellian Protectorate and after, he proved himself to be a first-class administrator. Strong in mind as well as adaptable in spirit he declared that he was proud to obey the constitutional government of his country. During the civil wars he fought for both sides and was to carry out the orders of Oliver Cromwell and King Charles II with equal devotion. After the Protectorate ended, Monck was to lead the way in restoring the exiled Stuart monarch to the thrones of his ancestors in England and Scotland. That is the episode in his life for which he is best remembered, but it was the sole political action in a career largely concerned with soldiering. Fearless, and dedicated to his profession, he not only risked his life fighting on land and sea, but he also proved to be the most vigorous executive of the Government during the plague of 1665 and after the fire of London in 1666. In 1667 when he was nearly sixty he threw every scrap of his energy into trying to prevent the Dutch from capturing or destroying the biggest warships of the royal navy lying at anchor in the Chatham dockyards. He lived just long enough to witness the marriage of his only child. But though George Monck, first Duke of Albemarle came from a family of genuine antiquity, after his time the line soon died out. Never again was there to be such another.

All that is indisputable. What will be attempted in this biography is to probe beneath the surface. What shaped Monck's career? Where did his strengths and weaknesses lie? Was he indeed a simple, solid and rather slow-witted soldier always ready to obey the authorities? What was the reality about his relations with Cromwell and Charles II? Can one identify his contribution to the evolution of warfare? Could Charles II have returned to London after an absence of nearly twenty years without any shedding of blood if Monck had never lived? These are some of the questions that need to be answered. They are difficult questions. Monck left no memoirs or diaries and hardly any personal letters. He was a taciturn man. But we have a vast amount of his official or semi-official correspondence from which his attitude of mind may be deduced. We have the book which he wrote when he was a prisoner in the Tower of London but not published until after his death. We have the reminiscences of two of his chaplains and one of his doctors, though they have to be treated with caution. By delving into such material it is hoped to draw a portrait that will carry conviction.

George Monck's father and mother were married on 17 June 1601.[1] On Tuesday 6 December 1608 their fourth child and second son was born to them at Great Potheridge, the manor house of a small estate which stands by a road running from Torrington in north Devon to Okehampton. The house, though less grand than it once was, is still there; it is perched not far south of Torrington above the winding river Torridge in lovely fertile country. He was baptized at Holy Trinity church in the nearby parish of Landcross, close to Bideford, the smallest parish in Devon, on 11 December 1608.[2] Great Potheridge (a contraction of Puda's ridge—though who Puda was nobody knows)[3] lay in the parish of Merton, named after Walter de Merton, the founder of Merton College, Oxford. The house at Great Potheridge was rebuilt by Monck between 1660 and 1670, but was partly demolished in 1734 when Monck's daughter-in-law, the second Duchess of Albemarle died. However, there remain a splendid staircase, a painted plaster ceiling and a fine panelled room in which a sculpture in wood, showing the crown being bestowed on Charles II by cherubs, is to be seen above the fireplace. It is now a farmhouse.[4]

In Domesday Book the estate of Potheridge in the hundred of Shebbear was a virgate in extent (which was more than the thirty acres common in the Midlands) and was assessed at 1s. 3½d., the manorial lord's share being only 3d.[5] The Moncks dwelt at Potheridge since the twelfth century first as tenants and later as freeholders.[6] The family name was originally Le Moyne or Le Moigne and it is likely that the Moncks were of Norman descent. John Prince, the author of *Worthies of Devon*, has a story that one of the family was a medieval monk (possibly Roger le Moyne or 'the Monk'?) who after becoming heir to the estate wished to continue his house by dispensation of the Church and therefore returned from a celibate life to the normal temporal estate; that was how the family acquired the English name of Monk or Monck.[7] George's ancestry can with some degree of accuracy be traced back a long way.[8] Among his forebears was an illegitimate son of King Edward IV, Arthur Plantagenet, who was created Viscount Lisle in 1523 and married as his second wife a widow born Honor Grenville. She gave birth to a daughter Frances who married a Thomas Monck and was thus George's great-grandmother on his father's side.[9] More extravagant claims were asserted after he arrived in London in 1660 to show that George was of royal descent in case he fancied becoming King of England, though he never in fact had any such intention.[10] Exactly how much diluted royal blood flowed through his veins is not entirely clear, but he certainly belonged to an ancient and noble family.

Leaving the delicate if attractive mysteries of genealogy, one may affirm with confidence that Monck's paternal grandfather was Sir Anthony Monck of Potheridge while his maternal grandfather was Sir George Smyth of Maydworthy or Old Matford, now in the city of Exeter but then outside it, one of the three richest Exeter merchants of the time, sheriff of Devonshire in 1613–14 and three times mayor of Exeter, whose daughter Elizabeth was George's mother.[11] She was kept busy by her husband, Sir Thomas Monck, for altogether she bore him ten children of whom four died prematurely.

One or two of George Monck's earlier biographers have suggested that he could not have been born at Great Potheridge because if he had been, he would have been baptized in the Merton parish church, All Saints, instead of that of Landcross.[12] However, it is known that one of George's aunts, Margaret, his father's sister, had married Thomas Giffard, a member of another ancient Devonshire family, who lived in the manor house at Landcross.[13] It would hardly have been extraordinary if a christening party were held at his aunt's house in a nearby parish.[14]

Like the Moncks or de Moynes, the Giffards claimed (correctly) to have been of direct Norman descent and even to have been among the companions of William the Conqueror, but they did not acquire the manor of Landcross until the reign of James I. Thus it follows that the Moncks and the Giffards can be traced far back into Devonshire history and no doubt they were and remained intimate neighbours. Twice they intermarried and once they were buried in the same grave.[15] All this counted for a lot in Devon. Even in the twentieth century Devonians have been clannish and have not always taken kindly to strangers from elsewhere.[16]

Besides the Giffards, the Moncks were related to the Grenvilles; for George Monck's mother was a step-sister to Grace, the second wife of Sir Bevil Grenville, an able soldier, whose brother Richard was to be Monck's first company commander and was the son of Sir Richard Grenville, the naval hero and captain of the famed ship the *Revenge* that single-handed challenged the might of a Spanish armada. Bevil Grenville's son John, the future Earl of Bath, was to be a close collaborator of Monck in planning the Restoration. Another of his aunts (Frances Monck by birth) was the wife of Sir Lewis Stucley, vice-admiral of Devon, who though once a friend of Sir Walter Ralegh, arrested him on the King's orders when he returned from the Orinoco: the Stucleys (or Stukelys) lived at Farringdon in the hundred of Clyston.[17]

Thus the Moncks were an ancient Devonshire family, closely interrelated with other Devonshire familes such as the Giffards, the Grenvilles and the Stucleys. George Monck's father was a manorial landlord, a freeman of Exeter (an honour for which he paid no fine)[18] and the owner of property in a suburb of Exeter, evidently a gentleman of standing.[19] But he had inherited an encumbered estate and the upbringing of his children was costly. It was apparently because of this that Monck was for a time looked after by his maternal grandfather and godfather, the Exeter merchant after whom he was named. Sir George Smyth made himself responsible for the boy's upbringing and education; he is known to have attended a grammar school and it is likely that it was the one in Exeter.[20]

Nowhere in Devon or Cornwall lies far from the sea. Whether Monck was living with his grandfather in Exeter or visiting his parents at Great Potheridge or his aunt at Landcross he was near to the sea. Not only was fishing a profitable pursuit in south-west England — fishermen ventured as far as Newfoundland in search of

4

cod—but the Devonians furnished officers and men for the royal navy in time of war. Sir Humphrey Gilbert, soldier, explorer, navigator and educationist, who dreamed of finding the north-west passage to India and Cathay, was born at Dartmouth and became member of parliament for Plymouth. Sir Walter Ralegh was related to the Gilberts through his mother and was born near Budleigh Salterton. The Hawkins came from Plymouth and the Stucleys from Affeton in the hundred of Witheridge in central Devon. Francis Drake was born near Tavistock while the Grenvilles had owned property in Bideford since the reign of Henry II.[21]

The Grenvilles with their fighting traditions were, as has already been noted, kinsmen of the Moncks. Is it fanciful to suppose that George Monck visited the Grenville home on the quay at Bideford and became enamoured of the idea of going to sea? When he was sixteen he would have heard of the mobilization of large forces of sailors and soldiers who on the orders of Charles I were gathering at Plymouth in the autumn of 1625 preparatory to an assault upon Spain. This operation was modelled on the earlier expedition led by Queen Elizabeth I's one-time favourite, the second Earl of Essex, against the port of Cadiz in 1596, in which he sacked and set on fire the town and whence he brought back much booty. Angered and offended at the refusal of King Philip IV of Spain a year before to let him marry his blonde sister, Charles and his chief Minister, the first Duke of Buckingham, planned revenge. Nearly a hundred ships, mostly converted merchantmen, including coal-ships from Newcastle upon Tyne, assembled at Plymouth and at Falmouth in Cornwall, together with 10,000 soldiers, many of them ex-criminals and dregs of the earth, who were to be launched unwillingly against Cadiz or any other Spanish town the commanders decided to attack. In addition, the Dutch, who were officially at war with Spain, promised to send one ship to join the expedition for every four found by the English King, though they refused to return or exchange veteran English soldiers, who had been fighting for them in the Spanish Netherlands, so that they could take part in the campaign.[22]

Ten infantry regiments, each consisting of 1,000 men, almost entirely pressed into the service, were organized to go aboard the fleet. The ninth regiment was under the command of Sir John Burroughs, a gallant officer who had agreed at Buckingham's request to leave Germany where he had made a name fighting for

Charles I's sister, known as the 'queen of hearts', and her husband, who had lost their thrones, and try to mould the raw recruits into an effective body. Burroughs appointed Sir Richard Grenville as one of his company commanders and Grenville brought his young cousin, George Monck, along with him to Plymouth as a volunteer. There was nothing strange in a Devonshire lad of sixteen, imbued with the heroic stories of the Elizabethan sea-dogs, joining in such an expedition.[23] Indeed a Dutch boy of about the same age was to play a useful part in the coming campaign. Whether Monck was actually attached to Burrough's regiment or whether he was one of a group of gentlemen volunteers who were looked after and favoured by the commander-in-chief is not known.

The commander-in-chief, who was responsible both for the naval and military forces, was Sir Edward Cecil, grandson of Queen Elizabeth's chief Minister, Lord Burghley. It had at first been expected that the Duke of Buckingham would himself head the expedition but the King wanted him to go to The Hague to tie up details of a treaty of alliance with the Dutch. To popular amusement he retained the title of 'generalissimo' but Cecil was his 'shadow' with the less glamorous ranks of Lord Marshal and Deputy Admiral. Cecil was an extremely experienced soldier but had no first-hand knowledge of naval affairs; he had to consult his sea captains about the art of the possible. The King gave him a pretty free hand to decide, in consultation with his council of war, where he should attempt to land his army after weighing the intelligence that was collected. The broad purpose was to strike a blow at Spanish prestige, to occupy a port and to ambush the Spanish plate fleet which was due to return at that time of the year from the West Indies.[24]

After a false start earlier the English fleet sailed from Plymouth on 8 October 1625. The decision was taken, as soon as Cape St Vincent was reached, to storm Cadiz as the second Earl of Essex had done before. Cadiz lies at the tip of a finger of territory stretching out into the Atlantic and forming the southern side of the bay of Cadiz. It was tenuously linked to that part of the mainland known as the island of Leon by a bridge called Zuazo. The capture of this bridge would sever the land communications of the Spaniards; that is why Essex had at once seized it in 1596. Cecil resolved first to attack the fort of Puntal which guarded Cadiz from the sea. As only light vessels could get close enough in with their cannon, twenty of the converted Newcastle coal-ships were assigned to the attack. But the colliers sneaked away in the dusk and the fort defied the naval bombardment, such as it was, so Cecil decided to send in Burroughs, who was, in effect, his Chief of Staff, to land and assault the fort on the following day, Sunday 23 October. Burroughs first tried in the afternoon to storm the walls by ladders, but that was a failure; later he landed troops farther up the peninsula who were able to surround the fort. The garrison commander, who had only 120 men, then surrendered upon terms. Whether George Monck took part in the assault or whether he remained with a number of other gentlemen volunteers whom Cecil had gathered together on board his flagship the *Anne Royal* is uncertain, but one would hazard the guess that the second alternative is more likely; for it is known that Burroughs did not lead his own regiment into the attack.

The remainder of the story of this operation can be briefly told. After the capture of Fort Puntal, Cecil himself took charge of the army and marched from there towards the bridge of Zuazo since he had received intelligence that a Spanish contingent was on its way to relieve or reinforce the garrison of Cadiz. Cecil hoped for a battle, in which his land forces numbering some 8,000 men and double the strength of the Spanish reinforcements, might expect a victory. Unhappily Cecil had omitted to check that his soldiers had adequate rations in their knapsacks. When resting at a village on the road to the bridge, Cecil took pity on the half-starved soldiers sweating in the heat of the sun and ordered that a butt of wine should be served to each regiment. Casks of Spanish wine had been captured in the village. But, dissatisfied with this allowance, the soldiers got out of hand, broke into the casks, even though Cecil had put guards on them, and drank themselves silly. Cecil had to command men of his own regiment to fire on the drunken mutineers.

Meanwhile the Earl of Denbigh, the rear-admiral, who had been left in charge of the fleet, tried to destroy Spanish galleons and merchantmen which were anchored in a creek running out of Cadiz harbour. But the officer put in command by Denbigh learned from a Dutch boy, who had escaped from imprisonment on board one of the Spanish ships by swimming across the bay, that there were obstacles in the way. He therefore sent the boy forward in a ketch to sound the channel; he reported that four ships had been sunk to block the entrance into the creek, which was protected by shore

7

batteries. Thus the Council of War resolved that it would be best to abandon the assault on Cadiz and its harbours and return to England past Cape St Vincent in the hope of intercepting the Spanish plate fleet on the way. A few days after Fort Puntal was evacuated by the English, however, the Spanish treasure ships sailed unmolested into Cadiz bay. Thus nothing had been achieved except to give the Spaniards a fright. Hundreds of men were lost through sickness and starvation or killed in the assaults on Fort Puntal. No doubt Monck had marched with the rest of the army in its vain attempt to meet the enemy. It has been asserted — and it is probable enough — that he could never afterwards speak of this expedition without shame and sorrow.[25]

What lessons might Monck have learnt from the failure of the attack on Cadiz? One of them was surely that the general himself must ensure that his troops are properly trained, paid and equipped and furnished with adequate food and clothing. Cecil had in fact admitted even before he left Plymouth that he had not been allowed sufficient time for training.[26] Though the lack of provisions may have been partly the fault of the notoriously corrupt victuallers at home, and partly that of Admiral Denbigh, who had been ordered as a matter of urgency to dispatch rations for the use of the army assembled after the capture of Fort Puntal, the fact remains that in the last resort the commander-in-chief is responsible for deficiencies.[27] That became an accepted rule in war. It is as important for a general to make certain that supply dumps are available at the right place and the right time as to know when and where to hurl his men against the enemy.

Much criticism has been levelled both by Cecil's own sailors and by historians at the ignorance and folly not only of Cecil himself but of his vice-admiral, the third Earl of Essex, and his rear-admiral, the Earl of Denbigh, because none of them had previous experience of fighting at sea or engaging in amphibious operations. But this, one may imagine, was the least significant cause of the failure of the expedition. A successful combined operation demands a supreme commander and Cecil had many officers both among his own sea captains and his volunteers who could give him their advice, which he took, for example, in resolving to attack Cadiz rather than St Lucar, the port of Seville. Oliver Cromwell's decision not to nominate a supreme commander when he dispatched the expedition to the

Spanish West Indies in 1654 was a mistake which engendered confusion and disappointment and resulted in both the admiral and the general being thrust into the Tower of London on their return home. Furthermore, the essence of naval warfare in the seventeenth century was the handling of cannon which was identical with that used in battles on land. In the years to come, Monck was to be as considerable an admiral as a general. In spite of his limited experience at sea he did not think of refusing the offer of a naval command either in 1652 or 1666. What he discovered as a boy, watching the operations outside Cadiz and as he saw the fleet limping back through the November gales to their home ports, may well have taught him the requirements necessary for a victorious war at sea ranging from a plentiful supply of provisions to the maintenance of strict discipline.

Having had his first taste of warfare which, however calamitous, must have excited him, George Monck, two years later in the summer of 1627, again took part in amphibious operations, this time against France, no longer as a volunteer but as an officer holding the most junior rank of ensign. It was an instance of the political ineptitude of Charles I and Buckingham that though they had meagre funds and no trained army or efficient navy, they elected in that year to declare war on France while they were still fighting against Spain. The new war had arisen over squabbles at sea.[28] The English had seized a number of French merchant ships on the ground that they were carrying contraband goods to the Spanish Netherlands. On the other side, the French Government was blamed for using ships lent to it by Charles I at about the time he was negotiating his marriage treaty with the French princess, Henrietta Maria, for the purpose of keeping the restless French Protestants or Huguenots in order. Towards the end of 1626, the Duc d'Éperon, supposedly as part of a campaign to oust Louis XIII's leading Minister, Cardinal Richelieu, by embroiling him in a dispute with England, laid hold of a fleet of no fewer than 200 English merchant ships. These were peacefully carrying French claret from Bordeaux to England and English privateers retaliated by sweeping up French vessels plying on the Atlantic seaboard. Such was his annoyance with the French behaviour, and his disappointment over the conduct of his very young French wife that by the early summer of 1627 Charles I went to war with France.

Again an armada of over a hundred ships was mobilized at

Plymouth together with 6,000 soldiers, but now Buckingham took charge. Cecil, the commander of the previous expedition, who had been created Viscount Wimbledon in anticipation of victories that were not forthcoming, warned Buckingham that the King had 'but little means at the present to make war with', that his subjects were discontented, that he had no trained soldiers and that 'our mariners are out of practice'.[29] The plan was to effect a landing at La Rochelle on the west coast of France, which was largely inhabited by Huguenots who were unhappy under the government of Cardinal Richelieu. The cause was good, Wimbledon remarked, but the time inopportune and the resources inadequate. Nevertheless, Buckingham sailed from Plymouth on 27 June with Sir John Burroughs again in command of one of the foot regiments, Grenville, promoted to the rank of major, again as one of the company commanders, and young George Monck as its junior officer.

It is known that Monck took part in the campaign because Richard Grenville in his *Journal of the Expedition to the Isle of Rhé* — Rhé was one of two islands protecting La Rochelle from the sea, which Buckingham first aimed to capture — wrote:

> Mr Monck came from England through the Main[land] (passing the Army [i.e. the French Army] which lay before Rochel with great hazard of his life) and brought a Message by Word of Mouth from the King to my Lord Duke, with Intelligence of thirty or forty Sail of Ships, with three or four thousand men preparing in France.[30]

That was a force mobilized by Richelieu to enter La Rochelle from the land side while Buckingham was getting ready to assault it from the sea. It has justly been pointed out that it was strange that Charles I should have chosen so junior an officer, who lived not in London but in Devon, to be the messenger of these tidings.[31] It is possible, however, that Monck had been sent back to England with intelligence from Buckingham — having been recommended for the mission perhaps by his colonel, who was the senior officer in Buckingham's army, with the latest news from the battle-front and that the King not unnaturally ordered him to return to Buckingham to acquaint him with the latest news received in London about French movements and intentions. How proud the young officer must have been to be selected as the messenger boy between two such great men! But just as Wimbledon had been held up at Fort Puntal and again en route to Zuazo bridge, so Buckingham found his pressed, half-mutinous soldiers more or less useless, this time overcome by French instead of Spanish wine. He tried to capture the fortress of St Martin on the isle of Rhé which, together with the neighbouring island of Oléron, protected the approaches to La Rochelle from the sea. Like Wimbledon before him, Buckingham returned beaten, if not disgraced, to England.

But Buckingham was incorrigible; he planned to attack La Rochelle again in the following year. By then Richelieu and his friend Père Joseph, both of them pillars of the Roman Catholic Church Militant, had strengthened the defences of La Rochelle and built moles as a method of obstructing further assaults from the sea. However, when Buckingham was in Portsmouth supervising arrangements for the new expedition, he was assassinated by one of the many naval officers whose pay was in arrears. Distraught at the death of his favourite, and determined to avenge his honour, King Charles selected the Earl of Lindsey, who had little knowledge of naval warfare and was already saddled with an earlier failure at sea, to lead the second attack on La Rochelle, which was now in open revolt against Richelieu. Lindsey put to sea on 7 September 1628; among his infantry regiments was one which had previously been commanded by Sir John Burroughs, who had been killed in the isle of Rhé during the previous campaign, and now had Sir Richard Grenville for its colonel. There is little doubt that Monck was one of the junior officers serving in his kinsman's regiment at the time.[32] Lindsey vainly attempted to relieve La Rochelle by sending in fireships against some French vessles lying in front of the moles which guarded a narrow channel into the port. But the ploy was a failure while his crews proved lethargic and mutinous. In any case it was too late. On 18 October the town surrendered and a few days later Richelieu celebrated a victory Mass and then welcomed Louis XIII's arrival to the singing of the Te Deum. On the whole, the Huguenots were treated mercifully as the English fleet, which had been anchored nearby, slunk away.

So Monck had his third taste of war when he was nearing the age of twenty-one. As the youngest officer in Burroughs's regiment he had carried its colours in a vain attack on St Martin in 1627.[33] He had again witnessed the hazards of amphibious operations; he had learned the value of prompt and accurate military intelligence and, most important of all, he had observed that a victorious campaign could not be waged with unwilling and untrained soldiers and converted merchant ships, however brave were their captains. As his first biographer, Dr Thomas Gumble, wrote, 'he would often relate with grief the ill conduct of the Affair by which the English reaped nothing but Reproach and Dishonour and yet wanted neither Courage nor Gallantry.'[34]

2

The Rising Soldier

After the second failure of English arms at La Rochelle the next three years of George Monck's life are a blank. It is just possible that Grenville's regiment was not disbanded until peace with France had been signed at the Italian town of Susa in April 1629, or even until peace with Spain had been concluded in November 1630.[1] King Charles I was obliged to agree to these treaties because he was now governing without the support of a parliament; he dissolved his third Parliament in March 1629 after prolonged disputes over religion and taxation and no money was put at his disposal to pay for an army. Such money as he was able to collect without the consent of the House of Commons he needed to devote chiefly to the upkeep of his navy.

There were, however, prospects in the Netherlands for a young army officer. The revolt of the seventeen Burgundian provinces in 1568 against the bigoted rule of King Philip II of Spain, led by Prince William I of Orange, known as 'the Silent', enlisted English sympathies from the start. Following the triumphs of King Philip's man of blood and iron the Duke of Alva, over 'the men of butter' and the assassination of William the Silent in 1584, the cause of the rebels appeared to be desperate. It had not been until August 1585 that Queen Elizabeth I of England entered into an alliance with the seven northern provinces, which had banded together in the Union of Utrecht, and sent an army commanded by her then favourite, the Earl of Leicester, to fight alongside the Dutchmen. Elizabeth herself provided the money to pay this army, but with typical canniness insisted that the Dutch should place 'cautionary towns' under English garrisons as pledges that the costs of the war would be repaid to her when victory was won.

13

Leicester's campaign was more or less a fiasco. After he withdrew, the Dutch found means to hire English mercenaries while many enthusiastic young gentlemen volunteered to fight for the Dutch asking only that their food and billets should be paid for. Even though James I concluded peace with Spain in 1604 such English soldiers continued to serve with the Dutch against the Spaniards. Some 8,000 men, led by Sir Horace Vere, the scion of an ancient English noble family, and seconded by Sir Edward Cecil, were in the pay of the Dutch States-General. Furthermore, gentlemen volunteers seeking adventure continued to flock into the Dutch army commanded by William the Silent's son, a capable general known as Maurice of Nassau. Horace Vere fought in the Netherlands for fifteen years, was created Baron Vere of Tilbury by Charles I, and retired in 1632, but remained governor of Brill, one of the 'cautionary towns', until his death in 1635.[2]

The war consisted almost entirely of sieges in which the Vere family took a prominent part. A truce was concluded between the Spaniards and the Dutch which lasted from 1609 to 1621. After the truce expired (during it Horace Vere and Edward Cecil went to fight in Germany), the Spaniards began one last supreme effort to subdue the rebels. Ambrogio Spinola, a Genoese, proved himself a first-rate general in the Spanish service; he captured the strategically important town of Breda in 1625 where Henry Vere, the eighteenth Earl of Oxford, was killed. A kinsman, Sir Edward Vere, took over the regiment and Prince Frederick Henry, replacing his brother Maurice, who had died after the fall of Breda, riposted by conquering another strategic town, Bois le Duc or Hertogenbosch, from the Spaniards in 1630. Here Sir Edward Vere was killed, but his regiment remained in the hands of the Vere family, for Robert Vere, the nineteenth Earl of Oxford, took his place.

George Monck was commissioned an ensign in this Earl's regiment which had distinguished itself at Bois le Duc. Being a younger son he could not afford to serve as a volunteer as many English gentlemen were able to do, including Sir Thomas Fairfax and Sir Jacob Astley, who were destined to fight on opposite sides in the English civil war. An ensign was paid three shillings a day;[3] that was nearly five times as much as a private soldier received and of course there were always prospects of plunder when a town fell. Since Sir Edward Vere was not killed until September 1630 Monck presumably fought his first campaign in the Netherlands during 1631. Nothing much happened in 1631, but in 1632 the Dutch with their English and French auxiliaries laid siege to the fortified town of Maastrict, some sixty miles south of Bois le Duc.[4]

The siege lasted four months and was fiercely contested. The Earl of Oxford's regiment commanded one of the approaches, protecting itself with a powerful mortar against the enemy. Mining was met by counter-mining but eventually a breach was blown in the walls. The besiegers lost 900 men killed before the Spaniards surrendered in August. Among those killed was Monck's colonel, the nineteenth Earl of Oxford. That was the year in which Lord Vere of Tilbury retired and returned to England at the age of sixty-seven. Lord Goring, a courtier who had made a fortune as a monopolist, bought one of Lord Vere's infantry regiments for his son George, whose father-in-law, the Earl of Cork, an even wealthier man, contributed handsomely to the purchase.[5] They were both anxious to find harmless employment for this spendthrift and bibulous young man. Colonel George Goring arrived in Holland at the end of 1633 to take up his command.[6] Evidently he had heard well of the young Ensign Monck's conduct at Maastricht for he offered him promotion to company commander in his regiment in time to take part in the campaign of 1634.[7] Indeed Monck was put in charge of the biggest company in the regiment. Each colonel had his own company, just as each general had his own regiment, but they did not command them in battle. Monck, being responsible for his colonel's company of 200 men, was entitled to call himself captain-lieutenant and if he received a captain's pay must have been at least twice as well off as when he was an ensign.

After the capture of Bois le Duc, the war in the Netherlands languished to such an extent that one of the English volunteers, Thomas Fairfax, went off to travel in France and learn the language. Captain Monck was never to learn French and could not afford to travel so he had to stay in Holland.[8] His colonel, George Goring, who had earned a reputation as a gambler and a *bon viveur*, brought over his rather tiresome wife to The Hague and joined her there each autumn.[9] The exiled Queen of Bohemia presided over a merry Court where dances and hunts were held and George Goring was one of her favourites.[10] But Goring wrote to tell his father that he was bored; he said he would prefer to find employment of a more stimulating character.[11] No doubt George Monck, who was nearing thirty and was always pretty austere, was even more impatient over the lack of military action.

In 1637 the campaign in the Netherlands at last awoke into action. France declared war on Spain and in that same year young Philip IV, having discovered that his brother, known as the Cardinal-Infante Ferdinand was a much abler soldier than churchman, appointed him Governor-General of the Spanish Netherlands. Since Ferdinand was given a fairly free hand, he could either attack the Dutch or menace the French frontier. He decided to move boldly; he thrust over the border into France and reached a point only sixty miles from Paris. Understandably alarmed, the French Government, which also boasted an outstanding cardinal in Richelieu, begged Prince Frederick Henry to create a diversion. A plan to take Dunkirk by amphibious assault had to be abandoned on account of the weather, but later in the year the siege of Breda was undertaken. This strongly fortified town, guarding the route to Utrecht and Amsterdam, was manned by a garrison of 4,000 men and was reckoned one of the most formidable fortresses on the frontier of the United Netherlands.

But though Breda was a supreme example of military engineering, it was by no means impregnable. In 1590 Prince Maurice had captured it from the Spaniards by infiltrating a group of soldiers hidden in a peat-boat. In 1625 just before Maurice's death it had been retaken by Spinola. The fortifications were of a kind that was more or less standard in the first half of the seventeenth century. The outermost defences consisted of an earthwork known as a glacis sloping from the top of a parapet which was intended to frustrate the enemy's artillery and prevent a reconnaissance party from examining the interior except by climbing up it. Behind the glacis was a moat—in the case of Breda it was fifteen feet deep. On the outer side of the moat lay a counterscarp along which ran a covered way where soldiers could be assembled ready to counter-attack if the glacis was surmounted. On the inner side of the moat was a scarp, the revetted face of the main ramparts. These ramparts were strengthened with bastions—irregular pentagons usually at an angle to the main works; ravelins—outworks with two faces at salient angle before what was known as the curtain wall—and hornworks, consisting of two demi-bastions joined by a curtain wall. Breda was protected by fifteen bulwarks or earthworks, numerous ravelins and five hornworks. Prince Frederick Henry decided to use his English and French brigades to lead the attack on these hornworks.

The Dutch first of all constructed two lines of circumvallation and flooded the countryside by breaking down river banks. There were two reasons why lines of circumvallation were built: to prevent sorties by the garrison and to hamper attacks from any relieving force. The Cardinal-Infante, who had been obliged to withdraw from France, concluded after a personal reconnaissance that the lines of circumvallation were effective obstacles, and turned instead to attacking minor Dutch garrisons in the neighbourhood thus hoping to distract the attention of Frederick Henry from the siege.

But the siege was pushed forward swiftly.[12] The five regiments which made up the English brigade took it in turn each night to advance the approaches, that is to say the trenches leading to the glacis, by sapping. Sapping was dangerous work since it might be interfered with by gunfire from the top of the parapet. Goring's first turn to command the approaches took place on Friday 21 August when the Spaniards tried shooting at the sappers with little success, presumably because they were out of range.[13] On 26 August when it was again Goring's turn to advance the approaches, two of his sappers were killed just as Goring came back from inspecting them. Some Spaniards had crept out of the town and thrown hand grenades into the trenches. By 31 August when it was Goring's third turn of duty, the English sapped through the glacis and the counterscarp to reach the brink of the moat. Now the problem was how to bridge the moat running beneath the hornwork. Goring, related Henry Hexham the quartermaster of his regiment, 'Perceiving how desirous the Prince [of Orange] was that the work should be hastened ... gave the bold workmen of your nation 1,500 guilders and another 1,000 guilders to the bringers of the rise bushes.'[14] (The rise bushes were bundles of twigs used to help facilitate the crossing of the moat.) By six o'clock in the morning of 31 August the dam had reached a point within fifteen feet of the other side and next day it was completed.

The sappers nevertheless asserted that the dam was not yet passable. Goring, taking no notice, himself led the way across it to the foot of the hornwork. In doing so he was wounded by a bullet in his left leg. This rendered him *hors de combat*.[15] He refused to allow his leg to be amputated; instead he developed a limp which was said to add to his attraction for the ladies. His lieutenant-colonel, Sir John Holles took over, seconded by Captain Monck, the senior captain of the regiment. By Sunday 6 September when it was the opportunity for Goring's regiment to complete the sapping, everything was ready to breach the hornwork by mining. The French had also finished their task. A message was sent to Prince Frederick Henry and he, together with Charles Louis, the young Elector Palatine, and his brother, Prince Rupert, with other gentlemen of quality, came down into the approaches to watch the springing of the mines. Breaches in the hornwork were successfully made. The English officer to lead the way through the breach was Captain Monck with twenty musketeers and ten pikemen.[16] He was followed by a party of sappers who threw up a breastwork to protect their own men from a counter-attack. The noble volunteers and gentlemen of quality also forced their way through the breach and penetrated to the top of the hornwork, thus pushing back the enemy. It is legitimate to suppose that when thirty years later George Monck, Duke of Albemarle, and Prince Rupert of the Rhine were joint admirals in King Charles II's navy, they recalled how they had first fought together on the hornwork at Breda.

Monck's part is detailed by Henry Hexham who was there:

> The English mine being sprung [he wrote] and taking good effect Captain Monck ere the smoke vanished hastens up to the breach and with his commanded men fell up to the very top of it, where at first they were entertained by some musketeers of the enemies.[17]

These musketeers at once gave way and Monck with half of his men —half had slunk away—advanced into the hornwork to find a group of pikemen, over a hundred strong, ready to receive them. 'He fell pell-mell upon them and gave the word "a Goring, a Goring"' as a tribute of vengeance to his wounded commander.[18]

The capture of the hornwork enabled Frederick Henry and his Dutchmen to reach the main moat surrounding the town. On 6 October the Spanish governor asked for a parley and on 10 October surrendered on terms. The siege had lasted eleven weeks.

After the campaign ended, Captain Monck and his company were stationed at Dordrecht which was assigned as their winter quarters.[19] It has been described as a garrison town. Possibly this was so, but it was also an extremely prosperous place which was accounted after Amsterdam to be the senior of the eighteen towns in Holland. The burgomaster at the time was Jacob de Witt, the father of Johan de Witt and his brother Cornelis, who were for a while the heroes of the Dutch republic after the House of Orange was in temporary eclipse. The de Witts belonged to the Regent class (wealthy merchants who often gave up their own business to serve the community); their family had been associated with Dordrecht since the fifteenth century. Jacob de Witt not only was its burgomaster but represented Dordrecht both in the States of Holland and the States-General. He was rich and proud and believed that the small man should be kept small.[20] This made him a tough customer to deal with.

Goring's regiment, in which George Monck commanded Goring's own company, naturally contained a large number of reprobates since their colonel himself was a reprobate. Their behaviour did not commend itself to the populace of Dordrecht. When the English soldiers stationed there committed misdemeanours the burgomaster demanded that they should be tried before the city magistrates. That was understandable since all of them, including Monck himself, were in Dutch pay. On the other hand, it was customary in English armies for offenders to be tried and punished by court martial; apparently a precedent for this could be found in Holland. Monck appealed to Prince Frederick Henry as commander-in-chief, but de Witt referred the matter to the States-General which decided that he was in the right; after all, he was one of its leading members. Prince Frederick Henry, though no doubt in sympathy with Monck, felt he could not overrule the States-General. Monck's company was told to leave the city for other less agreeable quarters. Furious at his treatment, George took the first opportunity to return to England after having served with the Dutch army for seven years.[21]

'Upon his Return into England', wrote Monck's first biographer, 'there was but too much Employment for men of his Profession, when the Scottish Nation entered into the unhappy war for the pretences of Religion.'[22] This was a foreshortening of events. Monck must have returned home in the spring of 1638 and it was not until a year later that King Charles I decided to declare war on his Scottish subjects. Since King James I's accession it had always been the intention of the Stuart monarchy to establish political and religious union between the two kingdoms. James had proceeded cautiously; but he had failed to persuade the House of Commons to accept his plans for political union, while, though he had induced the Scots to tolerate the reintroduction of episcopacy, these new bishops had nothing like the authority exercised by bishops in England; they were virtually cold-shouldered by the rich Presbyterian Lowlanders.

Charles I acted more provocatively than his father.[23] With the assistance of his archbishop of Canterbury, William Laud, he promulgated a set of canons drawn up by the Scottish bishops which insisted that the King was the head of the Scottish Church (just as he was the Supreme Governor of the Church of England) and that the services included in a new liturgy or prayer book, then being prepared in London to replace John Knox's long-used *Book of Discipline*, must be accepted. Even more important, by an edict promulgated at the beginning of his reign the King had ordered that members of the Scottish nobility should restore land alienated from the former Scottish Church. Thus many of the leaders of the Scottish people, nobility (who were jealous of the bishops), Presbyterian clergy and ordinary church-goers were affronted by Charles's unwelcome commands. By the end of February 1638, a National Covenant had been drawn up whose signatories swore to resist all innovations in religion which were not freely approved by their own assemblies in Kirk and State. Though negotiations continued for months between the King's advisers on the one side and the Covenanters on the other, when a general assembly of the Scottish Kirk met at Glasgow in November 1638 it abolished the bishops and repudiated the new prayer book. Subscribers to the Covenant promised to uphold the authority of the Crown, but the resolutions taken by this assembly were an act of defiance, for the supremacy of the King over the Church was denied. Charles I insisted that he must be obeyed and prepared for war.

First he needed to raise an army. No difficulty was experienced about finding officers. The professionals, who had learnt their trade in the wars against France and Spain or in the Netherlands and Germany, competed eagerly for posts. For example, George Goring in spite of his gammy leg was appointed Lieutenant-General of the Horse under the Earl of Holland; his friend, Henry Wilmot, was chosen as Commissary-General. George Monck became the lieutenant-colonel in Mountjoy Blount, Earl of Newport's infantry regiment. Tradition has it that the Earl of Leicester, who was a relative of Monck,[24] and Leicester's sister, the intriguing Countess of Carlisle, procured the commission for him; but one would hazard the guess that George Goring, in whose regiment Monck had finished his career in the Netherlands, was more likely to have recommended him for the post. As it was, since the Earl of Newport also held the office of Master-General of the Ordnance,[25] Monck for the first time in his life became the effective commander of a regiment. As no war had been waged by the English Government since 1628 Monck had risen fairly rapidly from ensign to acting colonel in ten years.

The difficulty found by the King was not so much in commissioning competent officers, at any rate under the aristocrats who occupied the nominal posts at the top, as in collecting the rank-and-file. Since no parliament had met for ten years he had little money besides his hereditary revenues, so he had to exploit his almost obsolete feudal rights to extract funds or services from the nobility and to call up the militia or 'trained bands' which were not really supposed to operate outside their own counties. He also relied upon recruits from the north of England who were expected traditionally to be antagonistic to the Scots. Such recruits required to be paid; as Charles himself observed, 'moneys are the nerves of war'.[26] The Marquis of Hamilton, the King's principal representative and counsellor in Scotland, warned his master that he would 'find it a work of great difficulty and of vast expense' to curb the Scottish Covenanters by force,[27] while Sir Edmund Verney, the King's Knight Marshal of the Household, remarked 'Our army is but weak, our purse is weaker and if we fight with these forces and early in the year we shall have our throats cut.'[28]

Against such a scratch army inadequately paid and supplied, the Scottish Covenanters formed a far better army whose morale was high and pay regular and also contained first-class officers headed by Alexander Leslie, who had fought with the Swedes and had been knighted by the great Gustavus Adolphus. After crossing the Tweed the King's army was soon compelled to retreat simply because Charles had not the means to maintain it far from its base. He therefore preferred to patch up a temporary peace, known as the treaty of Berwick, by which both sides agreed to disband their armies while Charles undertook to call a parliament and general assembly in Scotland, and to accept the abolition of episcopacy there. Scarcely a shot had been fired in this curious campaign on the borders of Scotland. Such was George's first view of the Scots at war and also his first acquaintance with King Charles's propensity for vacillation.

Whatever he may have said and done, the King did not intend to submit permanently to the rebuff he had received from his Scottish subjects; in the autumn of 1639 he sent for Thomas Wentworth, Viscount Strafford, his Lord Deputy in Ireland, who also held the office of Lord President of the North and was his most determined Minister. Once an energetic member of the House of Commons, Strafford, thinking he knew how it would behave, advised the King to summon a parliament at Westminster and appeal to it patriotically to help him out of his difficulties by voting adequate supplies for war.[29] But when in April 1640 the Commons were asked to pay for the King's army to suppress the Scottish rebels, it refused to do so until domestic grievances, extensively accumulated during the eleven years when no parliament sat in England, were remedied. Affronted, Charles dissolved this Parliament and cast about for other methods of raising money. Perhaps the Spaniards would give him golden ducats in return for the loan of part of his fleet? His Privy Councillors were encouraged by Strafford to have a whip-round on his behalf. Maybe the Pope could afford a loan? Relying on such castles in the air, Charles ordered that preparations should be made for a second war against the recalcitrant Scots.

Who was to command this time? Applicants were not scarce. 'We were all ready to scratch each other's faces for the great posts', one of his courtiers remarked.[30] Algernon Percy, Earl of Northumberland, hereditary Lord Admiral and President of the Council of War, was selected for the supreme command, for it was thought that his influence upon the border of Scotland was paramount. But the Earl was conveniently taken ill and told the King he did not feel up to the job. So instead Charles appointed Strafford, who really was a sick man and had no military experience whatever, to assume the leadership of the expedition. Lord Conway, a tried soldier, replaced the Earl of Holland as General of the Horse. He was stationed at Newcastle upon Tyne and was in effect the army commander. George Goring, now a brigadier, Conway, Sir Jacob Astley and the

Earl of Newport were among the members of the Council of War; Monck, again the lieutenant-colonel in Newport's infantry regiment, was also at times invited to attend.[31]

By various means the King recruited a substantial army consisting of pressed men from the south of England and trained bands from the north. To show that he meant business Charles himself left London on 20 August and arrived at York on the 23rd. His army was partly stationed at York and partly at Newcastle, but it was not ready for what was coming. On the same day that the King left his capital the Scots crossed the Tweed. The Earl of Strafford was pleased about this — for surely every Englishman could see that the Covenanters were the aggressors?[32] But nobody else was pleased, least of all Conway. Strafford ordered Conway to hold the line of the river Tyne at all costs, for if the Scots got past Newcastle they could split the King's army in two; furthermore such a move would demoralize the half-trained and ill-armed rank-and-file.

Monck and his regiment were evidently stationed under Conway at Newcastle. When the Scots, who had by-passed Berwick, approached the Tyne on 27 August, Conway divided his forces, himself leading some 4,500 men towards Newburn, a village about ten miles west of Newcastle, where a ford that could be crossed at low tide was to be found, while leaving the rest of his men at Newcastle. Conway threw up some makeshift defences on the southern bank of the river, but the northern side was higher and the Scots commander at once erected a light cannon on top of Newburn church which created alarm among the raw English soldiers on the other side of the ford. At low tide on 28 August the Scots started to cross. The English cavalry under Sir Jacob Astley and Henry Wilmot did their best to resist. But the Scottish musketeers fired on them and the Scottish horse, once they had crossed the ford, counter-charged. Wilmot was taken prisoner and the English cavalry fled to Durham. The infantry also panicked and raced back to Newcastle. Only Lieutenant-Colonel Monck kept his nerve.[33] He had been ordered to bring off the ordnance which had been ineffective in stopping the Scots advance. Although he had only one bullet and one charge of powder for each man in his regiment, according to his biographer, Thomas Skinner, 'he so lined the Hedges with Firelocks, and brought off the Ordnance with that Bravery and Conduct, that none of all the Scotch Regiments had the Courage or Confidence to impede his Retreat.' Still it was a retreat. One fancies that Skinner somewhat embroidered the story, which is told a little less enthusiastically by Thomas Gumble from whom no doubt he lifted it.[34]

The rout at Newburn so shook the King that he decided to summon a council of peers to meet at York in order to consider the Covenanters' demands. Until it did so on 24 September a wave of optimism was felt at York. The Yorkshire trained bands were being drilled and paid for by the local gentry. They were soon joined by men from neighbouring counties who disliked the claim being made by the Scots for the financial support of their army so long as it was encamped on English soil. The remains of the King's army were being smartened up and disciplined. Sir Henry Vane, one of the King's two Secretaries of State, who was with him in York, informed his colleague, Sir Francis Windebank in London, that they had 'a gallant and sufficient army'. After Charles reviewed his troops on 10 September, Vane wrote: 'Braver bodies of men and better clad I have not seen anywhere, for the foot. For the horse, they are such as no man that sees them, by their outward appearance, but will judge them able to stand and encounter with any whatsoever.'[35] Just over a week later an enterprising professional soldier, Captain John Smith, beat off some Scottish marauders who had crossed the Tees; the King was delighted with his military success, but it was an isolated one and did not assuage the general feeling of depression which by then had returned to the army at York. Furthermore, Charles just did not have the resources to meet the expense of renewing the campaign. By October an armistice was signed at Ripon and the decision taken to summon another parliament in England pending a final agreement.

Lieutenant-Colonel George Monck—like John Smith, a dedicated professional—was, according to Skinner

> one of those few that earnestly urged a Battle, and gave very good Reasons for the Security of the Event: And was many times afterwards heard to discourse with a particular Indignation, that so brave a Force of Horse and Foot, able to reduce a better Army than the Covenanters could raise, and another Kind of Kingdom than Scotland, should be so basely betrayed and baffled by the Counsels of the late King [Charles I][36]

Can it be said that in purely military terms Monck was wrong?

In 1639 no fighting had taken place; in 1640 little more than a skirmish. The Earl of Strafford believed and indeed argued that the Scots could be driven back. But what Strafford knew and Monck could hardly be expected to know was that the crucial obstacle was scarcity of funds. For though the City of London had at last been persuaded to offer the King a large loan it was not intended to be spent on war but 'in the hopes of peace and a parliament'.[37] Had the campaign of 1640 been begun earlier, had sufficient time been allowed for the training of the royal army, had the fear and dislike of the northerners for the invading Scots been fully exploited, the King might have been able to put up a much better fight. All that had nothing to do with a mere lieutenant-colonel like George Monck.

3
Campaigns in Ireland

Following his humiliating concessions to the Scottish Covenanters, King Charles I summoned his fifth parliament to meet at Westminster in November 1640. The vast majority of the members were highly critical of his government partly because many of them were of a puritan frame of mind and objected to the religious uniformity imposed by Archbishop Laud, but mainly because they felt angry at the levying of irritating and burdensome forms of taxation by the exercise of the royal prerogative. They particularly objected to ship-money, which was a kind of local rate that affected every owner of property. John Pym, a skilful politician, concentrated his fire upon the Earl of Strafford whose policy of ruthlessness or 'thorough' had been successful in Ireland, though not in Scotland. The first six months of the session were therefore devoted largely to hounding Strafford to his death upon the scaffold for alleged acts of treason. His execution took place in May 1641, the King being compelled to sign the death warrant under threats of violence by organized mobs surging outside his palace. Then by the autumn of 1641, besides the rebelliousness of his subjects in England and Scotland, the King was faced with insurrection in Ireland.

The causes of the rising were many. Firstly, the natives or 'mere Irish', as they were called, resented the intensification of the English policy of establishing colonies for immigrants into their fertile, but poverty-stricken land. Fortunes could be and were made in Ireland by English settlers like Richard Boyle, Earl of Cork, or Strafford himself which were more easily come by than those from settlements in distant Virginia or the West Indies. At the beginning of the reign of James I, leading clansmen in Ulster including the heads of the O'Neills and the O'Donnells, who were incessantly at war with one another, refused to come to England to allow the King to settle their differences. They preferred exile to the acceptance of English authority, so their lands were forfeited and divided between English and Scottish settlers. The county of Coleraine was assigned to London guilds and renamed Londonderry. Here was an endemic source of grievances. Secondly, although the Roman Catholic religion, practised both by the native Irish and by most of the English families who had settled there since the middle ages, was tolerated and Irish Catholics allowed to sit in Parliament they had reason to fear that the rabid anti-Catholic prejudices then becoming dominant in England with the rise of puritanism would result in the proscription of all the 'papists' throughout Ireland. Lastly, the lifting of the firm hand of Strafford, who was replaced a month after his death by an absentee Lord Lieutenant in Robert Sidney, Earl of Leicester, meant that grievances accumulated in the past decade, or longer, bubbled to the surface. The Earl of Strafford had managed to govern with the aid of an almost tiny military force. He had, it is true, succeeded in enlisting an army of some 8,000 men intended for the King's service against the Scottish Covenanters, but it was demobilized as soon as he fell from power.[1]

The rebellion of the native Irish against oppressive English Protestant rule was sparked off by the triumphant example of the Scots' revolt against the King in defence of their Presbyterian religion. The indigenous Irish felt that their grievances 'both touching their estates and their consciences' went far deeper than those of the Scots. Thus, as Lord Castlehaven, one of the Anglo-Irish, wrote in his memoirs, 'the unexpected success of the Scots and daily misunderstandings between the King and his Parliament in England gave ... birth and life to the Irish rebellion.'[2] Because of the comparative smallness of the English garrison in Ireland and the emergence of a number of qualified Irish officers during the first forty years of the century, Irish nationalists nursed the hope of being able to enforce their wish to improve their status by means of guerrilla warfare. The soldiers enlisted by Strafford and then disbanded sought military employment. 'Not one in twenty of the Irish', wrote a contemporary historian, 'will go from the sword to the spade or from the pike to the plow again';[3] instead they either enlisted in the service of the King of Spain, for whom they fought in the continuing war in the Netherlands, or else against the Portuguese or remained in their own country to become the nucleus of brigand-like gangs.

The rebellion in Ireland was not a spontaneous outburst by down-trodden natives. On the contrary, a number of daring young men, some of them soldiers of fortune, plotted simultaneous risings on 23 October 1641 in Ulster and in Dublin, where they hoped to seize a large store of arms left by Strafford in the castle; then they counted on their example spreading throughout the Irish kingdom and even on receiving active help from France or Spain. Though the real rulers of Ireland at the time were a couple of elderly gentlemen, known as Lords Justices, who believed in letting sleeping dogs lie and were oblivious to rumours of unrest, an Irish Catholic informer betrayed to them the plan to surprise Dublin castle; the necessary precautions were taken; and two of the leading rebels were arrested and sent to England to be executed at Tyburn. That was during the third week of October 1641. The rising in Ulster was more successful. Thence two groups of guerrilla warriors, commanded by experienced officers, fanned out; Dundalk on the east coast was captured with little resistance, while Lisburn, south-west of Belfast, then occupied by English settlers, also surrendered to them. Other risings took place in Connaught and Munster. Soon the flame of rebellion spread throughout the whole island. A number of English settlers were killed and their houses set on fire but how many no one knows. It was enough to be called in England a popish massacre.[4]

As has happened so often in Irish history, the fighting engendered cruelty on both sides. Wars are usually won by decisive battles or by starving out the enemy. But by the end of 1642 the rebellion was so scattered throughout Ireland that the best that could be done by such English soldiers as were there was to inflict merciless punishment in local skirmishes and await the time when a well-drilled and seasoned army could be dispatched across the Irish Sea. That was not to happen for seven years. For Charles I was more concerned over the coming civil war in England than over rumblings in the distance. And in the House of Commons its acknowledged leader, John Pym, was reluctant to allow the King to enlist an army for service in Ireland unless he employed Ministers and commanders who enjoyed the confidence of Parliament. For Pym naturally feared that if such an army were once raised, it might be employed not in the civil war in Ireland but in a civil war in England.

Nevertheless, the second Earl of Leicester, who had become Lord Lieutenant of Ireland in June 1641, was authorized by the House of Commons to mobilize an army of 3,500 infantry and 600 cavalry which, it was estimated, would cost £200,000. Leicester was a ditherer who complained that neither King nor Parliament had much confidence in him and could not make up his mind whether to go to Ireland himself or stay in England.[5] He decided to stay, but appointed his eldest son, Viscount Lisle, to command the cavalry in Ireland; George Monck was a friend and kinsman of Lisle and no doubt for that reason was given the colonelcy of the Earl's own infantry regiment. Monck had earned a reputation by his conduct at Newburn. A commission must have been more than welcome to him. The regiment under his charge reached Chester by 21 January 1642, arrived at Dublin a month later, and by early April was actively engaged. Monck's care for his soldiers, the first mark of a good officer, was exemplified when he wrote to the slippery Earl of Leicester from Chester to tell him that twelve out of thirteen companies were already there and amounted to 1,200 men but that he needed money to buy arms, shoes and stockings, coats and caps for the soldiers and sufficient shipping to convey them safely to Ireland; he also asked for instructions about how much ammunition he should take with him. He was obliged to point out that the townsmen of Chester had refused to lend him any money 'by reason of the troublesome times'.[6] Money reached him from London by dribs and drabs.[7] Nevertheless the regiment soon distinguished itself.

The commander-in-chief of the English Army in Ireland was James Butler, twelfth Earl of Ormonde whom the King had appointed as his Lieutenant-General late in November 1641 but without the authority to choose his own officers; that was left to the Earl of Leicester until it became clear that he had no intention of visiting war-stricken Ireland himself. Ormonde was only thirty-one but had already held the chief command under Strafford. He belonged to the 'old English' or 'Anglo-Irish' but, unlike most other big landowners, was a Protestant. He had been one of Strafford's few friends and was devoted to his memory. Though loyal to the King, he was at first trusted both by the Lords Justices and by the English Parliament.

Ormonde conceived it to be his first duty to protect the English settlements that lay around the Pale (that is to say the area centred on Dublin where many Anglo-Irish families lived) from the pressure of the rebels. His expeditionary force consisted of 2,500 infantrymen whom he put under the command of Monck together with 500 cavalry and six cannon. One of the cavalry officers was Monck's old friend and cousin, Sir Richard Grenville. On 9 April, a week after leaving Dublin, Ormonde relieved Athy, some fifty miles south-west of the Irish capital, and Maryborough, another settlement ten miles farther west; the campaign gave a terrible lesson to the Irish rebels. 'In our march thither', wrote one of Monck's officers, 'we fired two hundred villages. The horse that marched on our flanks fired all within five or six miles of the body of the army; and those places that we marched through, they that had the rear of the army always burned.'[8]

Ormonde also determined to rescue other settlements farther west. As his supplies were beginning to run low he decided to send only his cavalry forward, leaving the infantry to guard the fords across the river Nore by which the horse would have to return. The Irish rebels managed to collect some 6,000 foot soldiers and a few cavalry-men to bar the expeditionary force from finding its way back to Dublin. Monck first tried to distract the Irish contingent from its intention by attacking a neighbouring castle on 11 April; when this ruse failed, his problem was how to prevent the Irish from entrench-ing themselves in such a way as to block both the fords. He resolved to concentrate his musketeers at one of the two fords (that of Port-nahinch), thus conveying the impression that it was over that ford the English cavalry would attempt to return. His manœuvre suc-ceeded, for the Irish uncovered the other ford and the English horse trotted safely along a dangerous causeway and over the ford without interference.

This action took place on 12 April 1642. Having crossed the Nore safely, Ormonde's army still had to negotiate the river Barrow where another Irish force tried to impede it. Three days later, as Ormonde's men were retiring to Dublin, a hastily collected but poorly armed body of Irish, about twice as numerous as themselves, assembled at Kilrush in Kildare on the east side of the Barrow. It was an encounter battle. Though facing a larger army, the English had all the advantages in weapons, training and equipment. They consisted, wrote the Irishman Richard Bellings,[9] 'of disciplined men disposed into regiments and companies under the command of

30

officers to whose direction they had been used, and under the conduct of one person.' The battle began with a cannonade by the English, followed by a cavalry charge. The Irish soon broke and fled to boggy ground where the English cavalry could not follow them. It was a minor affair. Such cannon as the Irish had were captured, a hundred of them killed, and no prisoners were taken. The precise part played by George Monck in the action is not known, but Ormonde commended him for his 'alacrity and undaunted courage'.[10]

One of those who was prominent at the battle of Kilrush was Sir Charles Coote, a ferocious and merciless soldier, who held the post of military governor of Dublin. Like Monck, he was a Devonian, but having first fought in Ireland during the reign of Queen Elizabeth I, he had settled there and owned much property in Connaught. Three months after the battle he was killed in a skirmish and George Monck, who had distinguished himself in the campaign, was nominated for the post on the recommendation of the Lords Justices and by the Earl of Leicester. Leicester wrote to Ormonde from London telling him that he had notified the Lords Justices to this effect, observing that as the commander-in-chief knew the gentleman, 'I shall not need to say any more, but that in assisting him your Lordship will oblige me.'[11] Monck was to have 'the same entertainment' as Coote and in addition twice his salary, amounting to forty shillings a day, substantial pay for that age. But it was not so easy as Leicester imagined. Charles I intervened and said that the post ought properly to be given to Coote's deputy, Lord Lambert of Cavan, the next old boy on the ladder of promotion. There is no basis for a supposition that, because of this disappointment, Monck was afterwards to become an enemy of Lambert's namesake, the Yorkshire general, John Lambert. One gets over such things in life.

During the summer of 1642 Monck was sent out upon a number of frontier raids, mainly in Kildare, south-west of Dublin. He must have been instructed to show no mercy to any rebels he found; for on one occasion he killed eight Irishmen and hanged others; later he was said to have done 'good execution upon the Enemy, and of Seventy which he had taken Prisoners, most of them murdering Rebels, were afterwards executed at Dublin'.[12] Perhaps it was thought that punishment by death would be a deterrent to other rebels. In fact it merely envenomed the war.

While Monck was engaged in skirmishing, killing and foraging around Dublin the character of the war was changing. Hitherto it had consisted of ill-co-ordinated attacks by native Irish from which most of the Anglo-Irish refrained and of which they disapproved. But in May 1642, leading members of the Roman Catholic hierarchy in Ireland headed by three archbishops, having met at Kilkenny, announced that the war had been justifiably undertaken in defence of religion; they were joined by a number of secular lords with whom they formed 'a Supreme Council of the confederate Catholics of Ireland'. All swore allegiance to King Charles I and his heirs while promising to uphold the true faith, 'the fundamental laws of Ireland' and 'the free exercise of the Roman Catholic religion' throughout the land; it was the Irish version of the Scottish Covenant.[13]

The Council first nominated four generals to divide the military command. The most important of these appointments were that of Colonel Owen Roe O'Neill in Ulster and that of Colonel Thomas Preston in Leinster. Both of them were well qualified officers though not on good terms with one another. O'Neill arrived from the Spanish Netherlands in July followed by Preston in August.

While all this was happening in Kilkenny, during the autumn of 1642 the situation in Ireland was complicated by events in England. Civil war had broken out in August so that both the parliamentary leaders and the King's advisers were mainly concerned over the possibility that English troops in Ireland would have to be brought over to intervene in the fighting in England. Even before the first big battle in the war, that of Edgehill, the House of Commons had sent two of its members, Robert Reynolds, a well-to-do barrister who represented one of the Wiltshire boroughs, and Robert Goodwin, a strong puritan who sat for East Grinstead in Sussex, to inquire into the state of the army and of the kingdom of Ireland; they were accompanied by Captain William Tucker, who was the agent of the English adventurers for Irish lands. One of the tasks of these commissioners was to ask English officers and soldiers in Ireland to accept part of their pay and arrears by guarantees that they would be given possession of lands confiscated from the Irish as soon as they were subdued. The acceptance of such promissory notes or debentures would obviously tend to make the soldiers loyal to the English Parliament. The King was too busy with the war in England immediately to attend to the problems of Ireland, but he was aware that he had loyal supporters there and that the Irish confederation, formed at Kilkenny, had unanimously agreed to maintain his rights and pre-rogatives. It was, therefore, to his interest to promote an armistice between the two sides so that most of the English soldiers could be released to reinforce his armies in England.

As the civil war had only woken into action in the autumn of 1642 it was not at first easy to decide which of the influential men in Ire-land were loyal to the King and which to Parliament. That was why, to begin with, the position of Ormonde as commander-in-chief was not challenged; but it was soon to emerge that he was a Royalist. The two Lords Justices, Sir John Borlase and Sir William Parsons, having spent most of their lives in Ireland, were not altogether familiar with the political situation in England, but they were inclined to sympathize with Parliament perhaps because it had hounded Strafford to death; Parsons at any rate had been double-crossed by him.[14] Borlase, the Earl of Clarendon remarked in his *History of the Rebellion*, 'had never been a man and was now a child again'; Parsons, as Charles I was later to discover, 'did him all ima-ginable disservice'.[15] Lord Lisle was definitely pro-Parliament, as was shown when later he intrigued to supersede Ormonde. Where George Monck as commander of the infantry stood no one was sure. But he was the friend of Lisle and he might also have been irritated by the King's refusal to confirm his appointment as governor of Dublin.

About this time, Monck is said to have received a verbal message from John Pym asking him to exert his influence with the army in Leinster to prevent it being employed to fight for the King against Parliament.[16] Whether that indeed was the case is hard to gauge. Why should Pym have known Monck? Why did he not write to Lisle who was a fellow member of Parliament? But if Monck was in fact approached in this way, it might merely have induced him as a professional soldier not to take sides in the English civil war until he knew more about it.

Monck was present at several meetings of the Council of War in Dublin which the Lords Justices had invited the two parliamentary commissioners to join. It was agreed that as the central army at that time consisted of only 6,000 men, most of them would have to be used to maintain the security of vital garrisons and communities in Leinster. Only in Ulster was there an adequate force capable of coping with the rebels. It was therefore considered whether it might be possible to withdraw 2,500 men from Ulster to strengthen the Leinster army. Cries for help reached the Council from Connaught, but it was decided for strategic reasons that the relief of Wexford, a flourishing port at the south-east corner of the island, should have the first priority.

The army was to be 'mustered' that is to say its total strength was to be officially registered; but the lay element in the Council of War insisted that at the muster every soldier should be required to take an oath of loyalty. A debate about the oath went on for a long time because the colonels in the Council including Monck were opposed to it.[17] They urged that 'where an army is not well paid, an oath was not to be imposed', for oath or no oath, such an army might be expected to mutiny. The army might have become even more mutinous if a motion had been carried in the Council of War to deprive soldiers of their weekly drink money. But on this question the parliamentary commissioners voted along with the colonels so that drink money was retained.[18]

While these debates were continuing, Ormonde ordered George Monck to march to the relief of Ballynekill, an English settlement which lay only eighteen miles north of Kilkenny, the Irish confederation's headquarters, and was therefore extremely vulnerable. The Earl of Londonderry had built a castle there. The town contained an iron mill 'which kept manie lustie men at work'.[19] It was watered by springs which were filled with fish and thus was amply supplied with food and water. Monck set out to relieve it in the early part of December. He accomplished his mission without difficulty. But Colonel Preston, the rebel commander in Leinster, was lurking at Kilkenny and determined as his first military exploit to cut up Monck and his men. Monck was overtaken by Preston near Timahoe, where a force of Irish musketeers was stationed, who had already lined the thick hedges through which the English contingent needed to pass on their way back to Dublin. Preston brought up a mixed body of cavalry and infantry and challenged Monck to battle. According to Lord Castlehaven, who was there, each side had 1,500 horse and foot, though no cannon, but he probably exaggerated the number of Monck's men.[20] Monck, having received early intelligence of Preston's approach, disentangled himself from the hedgerows and drew his men up on a plain where he placed his cavalry in the front and his infantry on higher ground to the rear. His intention was clearly to hold off the Irish if necessary with his cavalry, while his infantry sped away. In fact the Irish were easily routed by the English cavalrymen and were compelled to retreat to seek shelter under the castle there. At that point Monck received information that another party of Irish rebel soldiers was on its way to reinforce Preston.[21] The information was in fact inaccurate, but before that was discovered Monck had moved off. According to Castlehaven, 'had the enemy pursued ... we had certainly lost most of our foot.'[22] Nevertheless, Monck took fifty prisoners, some arms and a few cows. It was a fine example of his flexibility and adaptability in frontier warfare. 'This check at Timahoe made us pretty quiet till towards the spring following', observed Castlehaven.[23] Yet the inability of Ormonde's small forces to make any real headway against the Irish was shown by the fact that within three months of Monck's victory, Ballynekill was compelled to capitulate, though on good terms, to Colonel Preston.

George Monck got back to Dublin on 18 December where he rejoined the Council of War.[24] One of the questions that was discussed in January 1643 with the parliamentary commissioners, was the right of officers to try soldiers who committed offences by martial law. The civilians were always suspicious of courts martial thinking that they put the army outside the common law. In view of the way in which Monck had been angered about this question in Dordrecht, it is reasonable to suppose he took part in the debate which was left unconcluded.[25] That was no doubt because by the middle of February the parliamentary commissioners had heard of the Royalist successes at the battles of Edgehill and Brentford and decided that it was high time they returned to London. Moreover, they were by no means certain of their own safety if they stayed any longer in Dublin. For the King had written to the Lords Justices vehemently objecting to their presence at meetings of the Council and the Lords Justices had declared that they felt obliged to obey the King's orders.

Before the commissioners left, they tried hard to persuade Monck and other officers to accept promissory notes for confiscated Irish land in lieu of pay. The officers, however, naturally wanted a watertight guarantee that these notes would be honoured; in their view either an act of parliament would need to be passed at Westminster or, alternatively, the Lords Justices and members of the Council of Ireland would have to pledge their own estates as security. Neither of these guarantees was given; the most that was offered was that Reynolds, the senior commissioner, would give a written undertaking in the name of the English Parliament.[26] So the matter was left in abeyance.

The English civil war had now been in progress for six months. That meant that the divisions between Royalists and Parliamentarians were impinging upon the rulers of Ireland. Sir William Parsons, the more active of the two Lords Justices, was definitely committed to Parliament, as was also Lord Lisle, a more resolute man than his father who was still living in England. When, therefore, the Council of War had taken the decision that the most urgent need was to clear Wexford of rebels, Parsons aimed to put Lisle in charge of the operation, thus in effect replacing Ormonde, who was known to be Royalist in outlook. Before they left Ireland the two parliamentary commissioners had offered to advance money for Lisle's use in the campaign. When in January 1643, Ormonde received orders from Charles I to enter into direct negotiations with the rebels with a view to arranging an armistice, it looked as if the intrigue to undermine Ormonde's position as military commander would succeed. For Ormonde was assumed to be too occupied to take personal control of the expedition to Wexford while Lisle was his second-in-command.[27] However, Ormonde was too shrewd to allow himself to be outmanœuvred. He was in no hurry to negotiate and insisted that it was his right as commander-in-chief to direct the campaign. Colonel Monck accompanied him in command of the infantry with Lisle in charge of the cavalry. The army started out from Dublin on 1 March.

On the third day after the army left Dublin it reached Timolin in county Kildare, a village fortified by the rebels on the circuitous route south. Fifty musketeers had stationed themselves on the church steeple. Ormonde put Monck in charge of the artillery to cope with these rebels while he himself continued his march south. Using a culverin (a cannon weighing 4,000 pounds) Monck knocked down the steeple killing a number of rebels and taking a few prisoners. Other Irish rebels in Wicklow, south of Dublin, offered to exchange such English prisoners as they held for those captured by Monck at Timolin; but Monck replied grimly 'There be not many of them alive now'; such as there were they could have.[28] The principal interest in this episode is that it was the first time, so far as we know, that Monck acted as an artillery officer.

In the middle of March, Ormonde's force, consisting of some 2,500 foot and 800 horse, reached New Ross, an important town in the south-west of county Wexford, and began to besiege it. Colonel Thomas Preston, who had been put in command of Leinster by the Supreme Council at Kilkenny, came to its relief with 5,000 foot and 600 horse. On 18 March a battle was fought near Old Ross (west of New Ross) in a deep glen. Ormonde had six guns which were posted on hilly ground behind the infantry. Preston's men came down a narrow lane where they were subjected to cannon and musket fire from the English. When the Irish cavalry debouched from the lane, Ormonde sent in his own cavalry to fight them. Lisle panicked and withdrew his men in confusion; but Sir Richard Grenville, who was also there, rallied him and when the English cavalry returned to the battlefield they were able to complete a victory which had been largely won by the infantry and artillery.[29] It may well have been that as at Timolin, Monck was in charge of the cannon. Casualties were not heavy on either side and Preston and the remains of his contingent managed to retreat to Kilkenny.[30] Three times outfought by Monck, Thomas Preston was to have few successes in Ireland. Even before he returned there he had been nicknamed 'the Drum' because he was so often heard in defeat.[31]

Having cleared most of Wicklow and Wexford of rebels, the Lords Justices turned their attention to the area immediately west of Dublin. Towards the end of June, Monck was ordered to march with some 400 infantry and a few cavalry to Cloncurry, north of Kildare and about twenty-five miles west of Dublin, where other forces, chiefly cavalry, were to rendezvous with him coming from the neighbouring counties of Meath and Cavan.[32] Monck had just received news that his father was ill and had applied to Ormonde for leave to go home. However, he patriotically agreed to postpone his departure in order to carry out his mission.[33] But the number of men who reached him at Cloncurry was far fewer than had been hoped so that Preston with a larger force was able to secure Edenderry and Croghan (in the modern county of Offaly), two of the places which Monck had been sent to relieve. Preston then turned to besiege Castlejordan on the border of Meath where he was confronted by Monck with much inferior numbers. Stalemate ensued. Since his

38

supplies of food were running out and he could not live off the land, which was bereft of cattle, Monck was compelled to retire to Dublin without having accomplished anything much in this frontier raid, presumably because he had neither enough men nor victuals to overcome Preston.[34]

When Monck got back to the Irish capital he found that Ormonde was belatedly carrying out the King's instructions to obtain an armistice. Commissioners were dispatched to meet the Irish representatives at Trim in Meath, while Ormonde himself had one more shot at defeating Preston. Although Ormonde managed to recapture Edenderry and one or two other villages under Preston's nose, he was soon obliged, as Monck had been, to withdraw from the west owing to his scarcity of ammunition and supplies.

That August a kind of *coup d'état* took place in Dublin. On the orders of Charles I, Sir William Parsons was replaced by a Royalist as Lord Justice; and four Privy Councillors known to be friendly to the English Parliament were arrested and shut up in Dublin castle. Ormonde was convinced that because of insufficient manpower, money, food and ammunition he was in no position to put down the widely scattered Irish forces. So he concluded, as he had been empowered to do, an armistice with commissioners from the Supreme Council at Kilkenny. The treaty was signed at Sigginstown near Naas in Kildare at a fine country house built by the Earl of Strafford; two months later the King appointed Ormonde as Lord Lieutenant of Ireland in place of the absentee Earl of Leicester; Ormonde had already been created a marquis for his devoted and harassing work.

The terms of the armistice or 'cessation', as it was called, concluded on 15 September 1643, provided for a cease-fire for a year and agreed that meanwhile the English troops and the Irish rebels would respect the *status quo*. This meant that Ormonde was confined to the Pale and to an enclave around Cork to the south. North of Dublin a strip of coastline, which included Dundalk and Newry, was to remain in English hands, but throughout the whole of the rest of the island the Irish rebels were left as masters. Ulster was unique. For here the English Parliament had with the agreement of the Council of Scotland dispatched a sizeable army of Scots under the command of a hard-bitten professional, Colonel Robert Monro, to deal with the rebels there. By the summer of 1643, Monro had succeeded in driving Owen Roe O'Neill out of Ulster. The armistice treaty laid down that if the Scots under Monro chose to conform with it, they could share in its benefits; if not, Ormonde would stand aside and thus allow the Irish to continue fighting the Scots in Ulster.[35]

While the negotiations for the armistice were still going on, George Monck undertook yet another frontier raid this time into Wicklow, which was still unsettled in spite of Ormonde's earlier campaign there. It has been suggested that he went there to inspect his estates, but that does not appear to have been the case at all. Lord Castlehaven, who was dispatched by the Supreme Council to confront him, specifically stated in his memoirs that 'Colonel Monck ... marched into the county of Wicklow to take in the harvest and possess some castles there', while the Irish representatives at the armistice conference complained to Ormonde that Monck was garrisoning castles and was 'ravaging and destroying the county'—hardly the way to safeguard his own estates.[36] By the time Castlehaven had gathered his troops together, he learned that Monck had been recalled to Dublin whence he was ordered to Meath to reinforce Lord Moore who commanded there and was in difficulties.

The reason for this was that after O'Neill had escaped from Ulster under pressure from Monro and collected ammunition at Kilkenny, he had been asked by the Supreme Council to march through Cavan and Meath whence he threatened Trim near the Leinster border. By the time Monck reached the scene of the fighting, Lord Moore had been killed by Owen Roe O'Neill who had fired at him with a cannon. Although Monck managed to inflict a check upon O'Neill's men, he had insufficient weapons and ammunition to force his way through one of the passes. He reported to the Lords Justices that he was in desperate need of food and clothing, and if they were not speedily provided he would be compelled to return to Dublin, 'leaving the rebels in possession of the castles tending to the destruction of the garrisons in Meath and Louth' and endangering the survival of Lawrence Crawford's regiment, which Monck had been obliged to feed out of his own small stock of supplies. Monck sent this dispatch on 12 September, three days before the armistice was signed.[37] So Monck and his men were recalled.

What lessons did George learn from his two years campaigning in Ireland? Firstly, one may suggest, he recognized the problem, which has never been solved even in the present day, of how to wage war effectively against a determined guerrilla enemy. Monck realized that although he was at times handicapped by insufficient stores of food, his own soldiers were as a rule better armed, trained and equipped than the Irish. Thus the fact that he was liable to be outnumbered was by no means decisive. Furthermore, so long as he could rely on the obedience and discipline of his own men he could afford to act boldly. On the other hand, what could he hope to achieve by his raids around the Pale? He could temporarily relieve isolated garrisons and villages and he could try to frighten the Irish rebels by killing and burning rather than by taking prisoners. But when, having outstretched his communications, he was compelled to withdraw, the Irish simply resumed their guerrilla warfare.

Secondly, until then mainly an infantry officer, in these campaigns he found out a good deal about the advantages and disadvantages of artillery. Cannon in the seventeenth century had a limited range and a slow rate of fire; moreover, heavy guns were not easy to handle because they needed oxen or strong horses to move them about. But Monck discovered that if well-sited they could be employed to lower the enemy's morale and occasionally to break up attacks by superior numbers. His knowledge of artillery was to be extremely valuable in his subsequent military and naval career.

Thirdly, he saw that an army could not march on an empty stomach and that it was a military leader's duty to bombard headquarters with dispatches stressing the vital necessity of keeping up a continuous supply of food and munitions without which victories were not possible.

Lastly, Monck, who had previously fought either against a for-eign enemy on whom the English Government had declared war, or as a mercenary in the service of the Dutch came to realize from his experiences in Ireland the problems involved in the relationship between war and internal politics. Such evidence as exists indicates that he was determined to postpone, as long as he possibly could, definite commitments to either side — that is, to the King or to the English Parliament. Was that because as a professional soldier he disliked on principle mixing up service requirements with political partisanship or was it because he wanted to keep his options open? It can hardly have been the former reason because he was always to emphasize the necessity of a soldier knowing and believing in the cause for which he was fighting. This question will be examined in more detail in the next chapter.

4

In the
Tower of London

The armistice concluded by the Marquis of Ormonde had been accepted with reluctance by the English Protestants in Ireland, and it was roundly condemned by the Parliament at Westminster as constituting a pact with murderous papists. Ormonde had faithfully obeyed the King's orders to bring about a cessation of hostilities so as to release soldiers to fight for him in the English civil war; before the end of November the Lord Lieutenant had already dispatched five regiments from Dublin to Chester, only retaining enough troops to safeguard the Irish capital. But, as has been noted, he exercised no control over Ulster which was in the military grip of the Scots. The English parliamentary leaders became anxious to strengthen the Protestant hold on Ulster by sending reinforcements there to join Colonel Monro. For Ulster was the region where the Irish rebellion had started, where much of the damage had been done, where English interests (outside Dublin) were the largest and where a springboard might be erected from which the reconquest of the whole kingdom from the Irish rebels could be launched.

Apparently Lord Lisle, whose earlier attempt to supersede Ormonde as commander-in-chief had been thwarted, expressed his willingness to lead such reinforcements to Ulster; as a proof of his usefulness he had informed both the King and Parliament that he had great influence with the English officers fighting in Ireland, including Colonel Monck.[1] When this somewhat alarming news reached the King in Oxford—alarming because Lisle was known to be pro-Parliament—he instructed George Digby, a charming and supple politician who had recently been appointed Secretary of State, to write in his name to Monck 'taking notice of his good affection and encouraging him in the King's service'.[2] Ormonde, for his part, was suspicious about the loyalties of the English regiments that he was dispatching from Ireland to England and so, as Lord Lieutenant and commander-in-chief, he tendered to all officers and men before they left an oath. This required them to swear allegiance to the King and the Church of England and on no account to agree to fight under the Earl of Essex, who was the Parliamentarian general directing the military operations against the Royalists in the English civil war. The overwhelming majority of officers and men were only too delighted to get away from Ireland, where they had suffered much privation, and were in an obstreperous frame of mind; but neither George Monck nor Colonel Lawrence Crawford agreed to take the oath, thus risking dismissal.[3] Crawford as a Scot got away to Ulster where he joined Monro's army. Monck, on the other hand, was relieved of the command of his regiment, which was placed under the orders of his number two, Major Henry Warren, and was put under arrest by Ormonde.

Ormonde sent Monck as a prisoner over to Bristol (which had been captured by Prince Rupert early in 1643); he was accompanied by a letter written by Ormonde to the military governor, Sir Francis Hawley.[4] In the letter Ormonde said:

> I have found cause to send colonell George Monke under safe custody to Bristoll, where I must desire you in like maner to keepe him till you shall receave his majestie's pleasure concearning him, which I conceave you will in a short time after. In the meane tyme I must assure you that coll. Monke is a person that hath very well desearved in the service of this kingdome, and that there is noe unworthy thing layd to his charge; therefore I desire you to use him with all possible civilitie.

Obviously Ormonde as a responsible servant of his King had no alternative to doing what he did. It is unnecessary to seek recondite reasons for Monck's arrest. His refusal to take the oath of allegiance may, it has been suggested, have been owing to a high-minded objection to taking oaths in principle, but it is more likely that as he had friends in both camps (most of his kinsmen in Devon were Royalists, while he was certainly on very close terms of friendship with Lisle who, he must have known, was a Parliamentarian), he wanted to discover for himself which way the wind was blowing in

43

England. At any rate Hawley must have been satisfied with George Monck's explanation of his behaviour, while the tone of Ormonde's letter, which was forwarded from Bristol to Oxford, convinced him that Monck was an officer to be trusted. Therefore, after accepting his parole, Hawley awaited instructions from the King about what he should do with his prisoner.

Digby advised the King to send for Monck. He was introduced to Charles I in the gardens of Christ Church,[5] the royal headquarters in the city of spires. The prospect of being able to enlist in his service a professional officer who had won a reputation in the Netherlands, at Newburn and in Ireland was obviously attractive. Whether, as has been imagined, the King 'placated' Monck or not (if anyone did that it was more likely to have been George Digby),[6] it was natural that Charles should privately ask his opinion, as that of a fresh mind brought to bear on the subject, of the military situation in England. The remarks that Monck is said to have made are only known at second-hand, but they sound plausible.[7] Clearly he was unimpressed by the high command at Oxford. Even though, except for the failure to capture Gloucester and the defeat the Royalists sustained at the first battle of Newbury, they had done extremely well in the campaigns of 1642 and 1643, he thought that too many courtiers were lording it as amateur soldiers. He therefore ventured to say that what he thought was needed was not a number of disparate and semi-independent armies distributed in the north of England, in the south-west and in the Midlands, but a thoroughly trained and highly disciplined body of 10,000 picked men 'under such officers trusted to command as were known and experienced in the art of war'. That reads as if Monck was being a trifle ingenuous. But if he hoped he might be given an army of this kind to command himself— such as Thomas Fairfax was to be allocated by Parliament in the 'New Model Army' a year later—he was being unrealistic. For Charles already had Patrick Ruthven, Earl of Forth, a veteran soldier, whose propensity for the bottle did not cloud his military judgment, and Prince Rupert, his energetic young nephew who, since he had fought with Monck at Breda, had acquired first-hand knowledge of warfare. It is true that Monck was much younger than Forth and more stable than Rupert, but only time would reveal that. He had to be satisfied with a promise that he could recruit a regiment of his own for the King's service and that in time he might be put in charge of all the soldiers arriving from Dublin, as they knew him and trusted him.[8] Thus Monck became a Royalist.

The five regiments sent over by Ormonde were safely landed at Chester, the port from which Monck had originally sailed to Ireland. Cheshire and Lancashire were then largely loyal to the King, only the towns of Manchester and Nantwich (twenty miles south-east of Chester) being held by the Roundheads. Sir William Brereton was the senior Parliamentarian officer in Cheshire; he had made Nantwich his headquarters and had fortified it with earthworks. An active member of the local gentry, he was popular with his soldiers and did not merely sit in Nantwich but led raids around the neighbourhood and into north Wales.

As soon as the regiments from Ireland were in a condition to fight they confronted Brereton on Christmas Day at Sandbach, a town thirty miles east of Chester then famous for its ale. Brereton and his men made off leaving not a drop of ale behind them. Subsequently, however, Brereton was defeated at Middlewich to the north-east of Sandbach losing 300 killed as well as prisoners. The Royalist commander in Cheshire was John Byron, a tough and relentless character, called by his enemies 'an inhuman upstart', whom the King had created Baron Byron of Rochdale in the previous year. Though it was the depth of winter with snow lying on the ground, Byron laid siege to Nantwich, which he attempted to storm on 14 January 1644, but was repulsed. Nevertheless, he continued to press the siege, thus alarming the Parliament at Westminster which decided it must be relieved. Sir Thomas Fairfax, a Yorkshireman now in his early thirties, whom Monck had known in the Netherlands, was chosen for the task.

Fairfax — Black Tom who rode a white horse — had distinguished himself in battles in Yorkshire, but he and his father, who commanded there for Parliament, had been virtually driven out of the county except for holding Hull which, despite royal blandishments, remained under the authority of the Roundheads. It was for this reason that when Thomas Fairfax was called to the rescue of Brereton he was camped outside Yorkshire, in Lincolnshire, where he had been fighting alongside Oliver Cromwell who was making a reputation for himself as a commander in East Anglia. Thence Fairfax set out at the end of December 1643 riding through Derbyshire and Staffordshire to Manchester, augmenting his own force, which was chiefly cavalry, with fresh infantry enlisted on the way. Leaving Manchester on 21 January 1644, he moved towards Nantwich, which was surrounded by Byron's army. Byron had some 1,500 foot and 1,800 horse, while Fairfax, after he had joined Brereton, led 2,500 foot and possibly 1,200 horse.[9] But it was not cavalry country, being flat and lined with ditches and hedges. In any case horse were not much use in siegework, especially in freezing weather.

The troops which had arrived from Ireland to reinforce the Royalists were not, as even some later historians have implied, Irish papists. They were Englishmen and Protestants. But the war in Ireland had been cruel and exhausting; the English soldiers had not received their arrears of pay nor sufficient food and clothing but only empty promises of Irish land; they regarded themselves as professionals — 'mercenaries', to employ an opprobrious term — just like Monck. Furthermore, they appear to have thought too well of themselves because the ill-equipped Irish guerrillas had been fairly easy to deal with once they were located. With such newly arrived troops Lord Byron had completed the encirclement of Nantwich, but when he learned of Fairfax's approach, he abandoned the siege and formed a defensive line north of the town with five infantry regiments. These included that of Warren (formerly Monck's infantry regiment) and that of Major-General Earnley, his second-in-command, in the centre, while those under Colonel Gibson and Byron's own brother, Robert, were placed on the flanks; Sir Fulk Hincks's regiment acted as a reserve in the rear capable of withstanding a sortie from Nantwich.

On the day before the battle, 24 January, the snow and ice began to thaw.[10] Thus the river Weaver which ran through Nantwich overflowed its banks, cut the besieging army in two and neutralized Byron's slight superiority in cavalry. On that day George Monck arrived from Oxford; he was in no position to raise a fresh regiment of his own, let alone take over the command of all the men who had been shipped over from Ireland. He decided therefore to fight as a volunteer in his old regiment. His mere presence, according to Byron, 'added great alacrity to the soldiers'.[11]

Fairfax handled the battle skilfully; his cousin, Sir William Fairfax, was able to outflank some of the Royalist horse and then turn to the assistance of the infantry. But the battle was not at first one-sided; for the Royalist foot soldiers had begun by advancing on both flanks threatening to envelop the enemy. However, Lord Byron was at a disadvantage for three reasons: firstly, his men were sandwiched between Fairfax's relieving army and the Nantwich garrison; secondly, the flooding of the Weaver, with the only viable bridge washed away and ferries rendered unusable, had cut his army in two, compelling his cavalry to make a long detour to reach the infantry; lastly, the strength of the Roundheads had been underestimated.

After hot fighting the contest was all over in two hours. The two regiments in the Cavalier centre broke. Monck, who had led the original charge with a pike in his hand, vainly tried to inspirit the troops from Ireland.[12] When the centre caved in, Fairfax was able to attack. The flanking infantry regiments with superior numbers moved forward, while Sir George Booth, the governor of Nantwich (another Cheshire gentleman, who was Brereton's father-in-law), routed the Cavalier reserve regiment by assailing it from the rear with his musketeers. Though Lord Byron was able to escape with most of his cavalry to Chester, the infantry vainly tried to withstand the Parliamentarians in the church at Acton, a village to the rear of their line, which had been fortified as the Royalist headquarters. Here concentrated in the church they were caught in a trap and compelled to surrender. Monck, together with Warren and two other regimental officers, was among the prisoners taken.

Some odd comments have been written about the battle. For example, Fairfax's biographer stated that 'Warren's regiment, though led by the much-vaunted Colonel Monck, no sooner charged than it broke, was rallied by its officers, and at the next charge, broke altogether and ran away.'[13] That is an instance of how to mislead your readers; for, first, it is implied that Monck was in command of the regiment, which he was not, and, second, it omits to say that it was his courageous example that induced the regiment to rally. Monck must have been well enough aware of the strengths and weaknesses of the men whom he had commanded in Ireland. Facing the Irish rebels the regiment knew what it was fighting for; but when, in a pretty miserable condition, these soldiers were dumped on an inhospitable shore, deprived of their colonel, and thrust prematurely into battle in a different kind of war, and when their overall commander allowed himself to be outmanœuvred and forced to fight on unfavourable terrain, their morale was undermined. Fairfax, who was nothing if not courteous, at any rate to his equals, sent back George Monck as his prisoner to Hull where his father, Ferdinando Fairfax, was acting as governor.[14] Neither of the Fairfaxes can have had any doubts about the quality of their captive. Nor for that matter could George Booth. Fifteen years later both these Parliamentarian officers were to play crucial parts in Monck's life.

After the battle of Nantwich, George Monck was treated kindly as a prisoner of war in Hull where he remained for nearly six months. During 1644, Yorkshire became the scene of one of the most fiercely fought campaigns of the first civil war. At about the same time that Thomas Fairfax won his victory in Cheshire, a large Scottish army began crossing the border to fight as paid allies of the English Parliament. The Marquis of Newcastle, the King's general in Yorkshire, who marched north to confront them at Durham, was unable to stem their advance; so he was obliged to retire to York. The Fairfaxes then began a siege. Later they were joined first by the Scots and then by the army led by the Earl of Manchester so that the complete encirclement of the city was achieved. Yet York managed to hold out for over three months until it was brilliantly relieved by Prince Rupert. But immediately he had raised the siege, Rupert was defeated at the battle of Marston Moor on 2 July. Consequently, nearly the whole of Yorkshire came under the control of the Parliamentarians. The prisoners taken during the battle, together with Monck and Warren, were sent up to London.

It has been stated that Thomas Fairfax, having known Monck in the Netherlands, was anxious to induce him to change sides, informing the Council of Both Kingdoms, which now directed the war from London, that 'he was a man worth the making'.[15] But no firm evidence for this exists; it is not mentioned by Fairfax's biographers and since the tide of war had turned in Parliament's favour, it scarcely needed to enlist the services of Royalist officers. Together with Warren, Monck was brought to Westminster, six days after the battle of Marston Moor. When he was called to the bar of the House of Commons, the Speaker committed him to the Tower of London as a prisoner and ordered that he was to remain there during the pleasure of the House.[16] It is significant, however, that whereas Warren was committed to the Tower as 'a close prisoner' Monck was not, which may have been a mitigation of his sentence on account of his services in Ireland.

48

As a rule such prisoners in the Tower, if they were men of wealth and social standing, were not harshly treated.[17] They were expected to bring their own beds, to pay for their own food and creature comforts, or have them sent in by their friends, and were allowed to receive visitors. Charles I sent Colonel Monck £100 in gold,[18] while his elder brother Thomas, now the head of the family, managed to let him have £50; £150 was more than the annual stipend of a clergyman and four times as much as a skilled labourer could earn in a year. Yet after Monck had been in the Tower for only four months he was writing to tell his brother that his 'Necessities' were 'such that they enforce me to intreat you to furnish me with Fifty Pounds more'. He also asked his elder brother to try to have him exchanged for a Roundhead prisoner of equivalent standing, telling him rather bitterly 'I doubt all my Friends have forgotten me.'[19] Actually Prince Rupert had tried to negotiate an exchange, but it had fallen through. Whether that was because Parliament thought it would be dangerous to release such an able professional soldier, as Monck's admiring biographers have asserted, is mere speculation.

'Like many other active-minded men before and since,' wrote Julian Corbett, truly enough, 'having absolutely nothing to do, he [Monck] determined to write a book.'[20] It was to be published after his death under the title *Observations upon Military and Political Affairs*. Whether he revised it or added to it later in his life is not known—there is no internal evidence to that effect—but since he was about thirty-six when he wrote it and had been a professional soldier for the best part of twenty years, it is reasonable to suppose that it embodied the military ideas he had acquired by that stage in his career. The book is of interest because it has a broader approach than other military textbooks written in England during the first half of the seventeenth century.

Monck begins by observing that 'the profession of a soldier is allowed to be lawful by the Word of God and so famous and honourable among men, that emperors and kings do account it a great honour to be of the profession' though he admits that men are sometimes attracted to the army by a lust 'to do evil'.[21] After all, he cannot have failed to be aware that most soldiers, who were pressed into service either at home or abroad, were ruffians or criminals relying not so much on their pay, which was small and irregular, as on the opportunities provided for pillage and plunder. No doubt officers and gentlemen, who were better paid, were above that sort of thing, having nobler motives for enlisting, while in a civil war honourable motives might or ought to have existed.

Having fought in civil wars both in Ireland and in England, Monck was exercised about how they could be prevented in the first place.[22] He offered three suggestions: first, that 'good fortresses and rich treasure were needed to prevent civil wars'; in other words, he believed that a government should be capable of taking immediate action to put down such risings before they could spread, as they had done in Ireland; second, he thought that there should be only one religion in a country, a thought which must have derived from his own experiences since the divisions between Catholics and Protestants in Ireland and between Puritans and Anglicans in England were among the significant causes of the civil wars of his time. Last, he made the suggestion that 'an offensive war [abroad] will keep you from Civil War at home'.[23] That is an argument which has often been used by modern historians as an explanation of some wars, notably that of Mussolini in Abyssinia—but, on the whole, it is defensive not offensive wars that unite the people of a nation in the support of their government. But that it was religious differences which were the principal source of unrest, was an idea deeply embedded in Monck's mind. For when ten years later he was to become the military governor of Scotland, he constantly harped on the dangers presented by Quakers, Socinians and other disruptive sects, while in 1658 he was to advise Richard Cromwell that if he wanted to retain the throne of his father he must aim at religious unity in England.

Monck's experience of foreign wars, as distinct from civil wars, was limited and therefore his views about their causes and how they should be waged are broader and less precise. He thought that the causes of all wars were 'Ambition, Avarice, Religion, Revenge, Providence and Defence'.[24] If fighting began abroad it was his opinion that the first necessity was to capture a port with a convenient harbour. It was also, he believed, essential to land sufficient supplies of food since one could not count on being able to live off the country. On the other hand,

You may with good Fortresses and a good Army so tye up your Enemy in hindring him from Victuals and by intrenching always so near to him that you may now and then fall upon some of his Quarters and so hinder him from making any Siege of importance.[25]

During his seven years in the Netherlands, Monck had not been involved in any pitched battle. Consequently, he thought in terms of the kind of siege warfare that had prevailed and he realized that it was unlikely to result in either side exhausting the other. Monck was convinced that a 'sovereign prince' was more capable of conquest than a Commonwealth provided that he went to war in person and that in any case only one general was necessary to lead an army.[26] The last was a point that was only slowly grasped. At the second battle of Newbury, which took place in October 1644, while Monck was in the Tower, the Committee of Both Kingdoms had ordered that the Parliamentarian army should be directed by a Council of War, a direction which—although the Roundheads outnumbered the Cavaliers—resulted in their being virtually defeated; in Ireland in one of the many skirmishes in which Monck himself had been engaged the Irish fought without any recognized commander at all.

Like Oliver Cromwell and all experienced officers of that time, Monck laid heavy stress on the importance of morale and discipline. He thought that morale was most likely to be high if soldiers knew and believed in what they were fighting for. That was by no means a universal opinion. Sir James Turner, a contemporary professional officer, wrote of how he 'had swallowed without chewing in Germanie a very dangerous maxim ... that so [long as] we serve our master honestlie it is no matter what master we serve.'[27] But Monck insisted that 'Before you undertake a War cast an impartial eye upon the cause. If it be just, prepare your Army and let them all know they fight for God.'[28] Then God could be praised for victories. By way of a practical note Monck added that 'Chaplains could be used to settle an opinion of right in the minds of Officers and Souldiers.'[29] As to discipline, it should be 'mingled with love'.[30] If a general ensures that his men are fed and clothed, are adequately armed and supplied with sufficient ammunition (for instance, musketeers should have two bandoliers in which to carry their bullets),[31] if they are punctually paid and finally if their lives are not risked unnecessarily then 'your General can with Justice punish them severely' if they do wrong. But the general must set a good example himself; he must be careful 'not to measure the humour of his poor needy and undisciplined Souldiers by the garb of his own ambitious thoughts'.[32]

Monck discussed in some detail the way in which different kinds of warfare — battles, defensive actions, retreats and sieges — were best fought. Like other famous commanders — Frederick the Great, for example — Monck did not lay much stress on set-piece battles. Indeed he appears to have believed that they should be undertaken only in cases of extreme difficulty; then difficulties 'are never better cleared than by adventures and desperate undertakings'.[33] Everything must be done before a battle is fought to avoid muddles and errors. Orders should be given in writing; a field word should be fixed upon and men must wear some emblem (a scarf or paper stuck in their hats) to ensure that they can distinguish each other from the enemy. On no account must an enemy be despised, and no pillaging must be permitted before the field of battle is cleared.

In defensive warfare Monck thought that it was essential for forces to be kept together and not even divided to protect fords across rivers (Monck had certainly learnt that lesson in Ireland).[34] He also believed that it was wiser to take up a defensive position in trenches (sixteen feet broad and eight deep) than in villages, which were subject to infection. An entrenched force could subsist for three months in the summer, but only a fortnight even in the best villages. As to retreat, it should be along routes prepared in advance by pioneers. With regard to Monck's recommendations about how to conduct sieges, whether in attack or defence, it is unnecessary to go into detail, for — unlike Vauban — he added nothing to the normal practices of his age, as stated, for example, in Henry Hexham's book, *The Principles of the Art Military practised in the Warres of the United Netherlands*, which was first published in 1637 and reprinted in 1642.[35] Monck's most important contribution to the subject was probably the emphasis he laid on outworks; in defence they must be carefully covered from parapets and indeed commanded by the whole body of the fortifications; in attack they should be mined and stormed. No doubt he remembered clearly how Breda had surrendered soon after the mining of the glacis and the successful attack on a hornwork.[36]

Rather surprisingly perhaps but no doubt because his own experience in the Netherlands had been mainly concerned with siege warfare, Monck thought that the infantry was the queen of the battle — 'a more firm body to trust for victory than the horse'.[37] He laid down that in an army there should be two foot soldiers for every horseman, while the numbers of pikemen and musketeers in the infantry ought to be equal. Pikemen should be placed in the centre with the musketeers on their flanks to protect them against a cavalry charge. In minor actions musketeers could be employed to flank the cavalry, but in battle they should fight alongside the pikemen in ranks six deep. Thus Monck followed the tenets of Maurice of Nassau, a commander of wide experience during the first half of the seventeenth century, who reduced the number of infantry files and also the proportion of pikemen to musketeers; he reversed the Spanish army's methods of warfare, whose 'tercios' consisted of huge hedgehogs of pikemen, protected by musketeers, which could at times steamroller the enemy by their sheer weight.

About the artillery Monck did not have much to say other than that large field guns could be used to shoot at the enemy's infantry, but he thought that in sieges mines were more valuable than batteries because they could be employed to achieve surprise. Monck concluded his book by advising would-be commanders that reading was necessary to supplement experience and practice:

> For upon the variety of chances you shall meet withal in History, you meditate on the effects of other men's adventures that their harms may be your warnings and their happy proceedings your fortunate directions in the Art Military.[38]

Monck's book was first and foremost that of an infantry commander; for he had up to this time always served in or taken charge of a foot regiment. In enclosed country in Ireland, often full of thick hedgerows, where he had mostly fought, cavalry could not operate; while in sieges, which was the commonest form of warfare in the Netherlands, cavalry was not of much value except for reconnaissance and for scouring the country looking for food. Thus it might be argued in terms of the English civil war, which at the time he was writing was being largely determined by cavalry action, his book was anachronistic. For England had relatively few elaborately fortified towns — York was a notable exception, but Bristol twice capitulated to a besieging army in a few days — and military decisions were reached not by swapping walled cities but by set battles in fields or along river lines. The cavalry and not the infantry was being proved to be the then queen of the battle.

Though much technical teaching was included in Monck's book, it was not a purely military textbook as were Gervase Markham's book on military discipline, Robert Norton's book on artillery, William Bariffe's book on the postures of musketeers and pikemen or Henry Hexham's instructional treatise with its vast apparatus of diagrams and illustrations.[39] Monck thought a good deal about the causes of wars and how they could be lost, that is to say on strategy as well as tactics. That was why his book was fairly entitled observations on political as well as military affairs.

While Monck was in the Tower, he met his future wife, Anne or Nan.[40] Her father was of Flemish extraction and she had been married at the age of thirteen to a perfumer named Thomas Ratsford who lived near the Exchange in the City of London. She had been trained as a milliner and used to look after the linen of the well-to-do prisoners in the Tower. She has been treated rather unkindly by Monck's biographers (though Gumble and Skinner hardly mention her) who describe her as ugly, dowdy and ill-mannered. But it has to be remembered that these characteristics have been lifted from the celebrated writings of Samuel Pepys and the Earl of Clarendon, both of whom disliked Monck intensely. When Anne met Monck in the Tower she was twenty-five, whereas when Pepys and Clarendon wrote about her, she was in her forties. Monck at the age of thirty-six is not known to have had any sexual experiences; he was a lonely and disappointed man cut off from his friends and kinsmen in Devonshire by the lines drawn in the civil war. So it is likely enough that Anne Ratsford was 'kind' to him. In a permissive society one does not have to accept the Victorian view that Monck's conduct was discreditable and that 'the gloomy walls of the Tower were brightened with an unholy idyll'. Nor need it be assumed that at twenty-five Anne was not attractive nor even for that matter that she was 'not well bred'. At any rate her brother, Thomas Clarges, who was to be knighted by Charles II, was an educated man, as can be seen from his writings and letters. All through his life Monck was devoted to Anne and he was to marry her on 23 January 1653, eight years after he first met her. No breath of scandal was to hurt either of them at the bawdy Court of the restored Stuart king.

5

Ireland Again

What had been happening in England and Ireland while George Monck was writing his book and making love in the Tower of London? In June 1645 the battle of Naseby, in which King Charles I and Prince Rupert were comprehensively defeated by the Parliamentarian army under Fairfax, followed less than a month later by the victory of the same army over the Royalists in the west at the battle of Langport, virtually brought the first civil war to an end. But it was not until June 1646 that Oxford surrendered or January 1647 when the King, who had fled from Oxford to beg help from the Scottish Covenanters, was handed over by them to become an honourable prisoner of the English Parliament. By September 1645 the Marquis of Montrose, who had won astonishing victories for the King in Scotland, was at last beaten by a Scottish Covenanter army. So the only hope kept alive for the Royalists was in Ireland.

The situation there was incredibly confused and confusing.[1] Although the truce which Ormonde had concluded for one year with the Irish Confederacy at Kilkenny was renewed, fighting continued in most parts of Ireland. Meanwhile the Marquis, acting on instructions from the King, was attempting to reach a definitive treaty with the Irish leaders (the 10,000 men whom the Lord Lieutenant had shipped over to England after the armistice of 1643 had mostly been killed or taken prisoners). The truce had never taken effect in Ulster where the 'new Scots' and some English soldiers under the command of Robert Monro achieved supremacy for the time being. By the summer of 1644, Belfast had surrendered to Monro. In the south of Ireland Preston occupied the fort of Duncannon in Wexford in the name of the Irish Confederacy, while in the west Sir Charles Coote, son and namesake of the former Governor of Dublin, who had been appointed President of Connaught by the English Parliament, gained control over the county of Sligo.

Not only was the military situation fluid, but so also was the political outlook. For Charles I, instead of sticking to his able and loyal Lord Lieutenant Ormonde, decided to send over as his personal representative a Roman Catholic nobleman known, not entirely accurately, as the Earl of Glamorgan, with almost unlimited powers to unite the whole of Ireland in the royal cause. On the other hand, about the same time the Pope dispatched the Archbishop of Fermo, Giovanni Battista Rinuccini, to impress on the Irish Confederacy the importance of obtaining not merely toleration, but dominance for the Roman Catholic religion in Ireland. Glamorgan did more harm than good to the King's cause, while Rinuccini quarrelled with the Irish leaders in Kilkenny and engineered a *coup d'état* there. Thus at the end of 1643 Charles unscrupulously repudiated Glamorgan. In March 1646 Ormonde succeeded in completing a treaty which would have gained another 10,000 soldiers for the Royalist service in England, the peace, proclaimed in Dublin on 30 July 1646, proved abortive and in any case was reached too late.

Rinuccini denounced the peace treaty and aimed, with the help of O'Neill and Preston, to march on Dublin and drive the English out of Ireland. Meanwhile the English Parliament, having won the first civil war, sent over commissioners to Ireland, who arrived at the end of 1646, to discover, if they could, what was happening there. Ormonde, digesting the bad news from England and deciding that he had not the means either in men or in money to restore peace in Ireland, resolved to hand over Dublin to the English Parliament, hoping that if a settlement was finally reached between Parliament and the King in England, Charles would ultimately be restored to full sovereignty in all his dominions. On 28 July 1647 Ormonde handed over the military command in Dublin to Colonel Michael Jones, an Anglo-Irish Protestant officer. Ormonde left Ireland and on 2 August landed in Bristol, was allowed to visit the King imprisoned at Hampton Court, and afterwards went to France to consult Queen Henrietta Maria in Paris.

The English Parliament thereupon decided to appoint Philip Sidney, Viscount Lisle to succeed Ormonde as Lord Lieutenant of Ireland. The appointment was a natural one to make; Lisle was the son of the Earl of Leicester who had been named Lord Lieutenant in 1641 but had never got as far as Ireland. Lisle's sympathies had always been strongly in favour of the English Parliament; he had fought with some success as a cavalry commander in Ireland in 1642–3 and he knew many of the officers who had served under Ormonde after the outbreak of the Irish rebellion including George Monck. But Lisle had two disadvantages: first, he was only twenty-seven and second, when he had been in Ireland had shown himself to be too much of an ambitious intriguer. Parliament, perhaps because its leading members were uncertain of his qualities, appointed him to the office in April 1646 for only one year. By the time he landed in Munster in February 1647 he had barely three months' tenure left.

Lisle must have recalled that when he had fought in Ireland during 1642, George Monck had shown himself a proficient infantry commander who had learned much about Irish methods of fighting. Probably he had visited Monck in the Tower. At any rate he immediately asked that Monck should be released from imprisonment and re-appointed as a colonel to join his staff. Monck was asked to take the Covenant which meant he had to swear to uphold 'the reformed religion' in England, Scotland and Ireland, to extirpate popery, to preserve the rights and privileges of Parliament, but not to forget 'the honour and happiness of the King's Majesty and that of his posterity'. He was also asked to take 'the negative oath' by which he specifically swore neither directly nor indirectly to assist the King against Parliament. He took the Covenant without demur and said that he was ready to take the negative oath as well. Before he left the Tower, however, he is said to have received a blessing from Matthew Wren, the former high-church Bishop of Ely (one of Cromwell's *bêtes-noires*) and afterwards he told Wren that he was now 'going into Ireland against those bloody Rebels, but he hoped he should one day do his Majesty Service against the Rebels here.' Dr Gumble relates that he had this story from Wren himself before he died, but the concluding words sound like a piece of embroidery.[2] Whatever Monck said to Wren, outwardly he was all obedience. The House of Lords, such as it was, then agreed that he was 'a fit man to be employed in the service of Ireland, in regard to his abilities in martial affairs', consented to his being granted a commission for that purpose, and sought and obtained the concurrence of the House of Commons.[3] Once that was done the Committee for Irish Affairs speeded him on his way. It ordered two other colonels, selected by Lisle, to join him at Chester 'if Monck be not gone before'.[4]

In fact Monck waited for Lisle and together with reinforcements from England they landed at Cork in February.[5] But Ormonde had not yet left Dublin, and in Munster, Murrough O'Brien, Lord Inchiquin, another Irish Protestant, who had been appointed President there by the English Parliament in 1644 and made his military mark in that area, did not see why he should play second fiddle to Lisle. This personal squabble continued until Lisle's term of office expired in April. In this quarrel most of the English officers at Cork sided with Inchiquin, who, they thought, was a better soldier than Lisle and was Irish. Monck was one of the few officers loyal to Lisle; so in May he returned with his friend to England.

The Committee for Irish Affairs in London was displeased with the way in which Lisle had quarrelled with Inchiquin and refused to renew his appointment. In effect the Lord-Lieutenancy was put in commission. Michael Jones, who, after Ormonde left Dublin, became the senior English officer in Ireland, at once proved his quality by inflicting a decisive defeat on Preston at the battle of Dungan Hill north-west of Dublin, where 5,000 Irish or Anglo-Irish were either killed or put to the sword. Parliament voted £1,000 to Jones in recognition of his triumph. At about the same time it was resolved to send back Monck, who had been careful not to blot his copy-book in Munster, to take charge of all the English and Scottish forces in eastern Ulster with the rank of major-general.[6] This was in order to relieve Jones of the responsibility for establishing peace in northern Ireland while he was still holding the fort for Protestant England in Dublin.

Monck landed in Dublin on his third visit to Ireland on 5 September 1647, a month after Ormonde left. The Committee for Irish Affairs had ordered £7,000 to be sent over for Monck's immediate use.[7] He appears to have gone almost at once to Ulster which was the main danger spot for the English.[8] In Munster, Inchiquin was winning more victories, while Jones's defeat of Preston at Dungan Hill had ensured the safety of Dublin for the time being. The position in Ulster was that it contained three armies each with different aims. Robert Monro commanded 'the new Scots' who had settled there during the reign of King James VI (King James I of England); Sir Charles Coote was operating in north-west Ulster where Londonderry was an English settlement; Owen Roe O'Neill wanted to use Ulster as a base from which his guerrilla warriors could ravage the Pale. In June 1646 O'Neill had won the only big Irish victory of the war when he defeated Monro at the battle of Benburb. But although his army now swelled to some 8,000 men, it was not adequately armed so that he was unable to follow up his victory.

Owen O'Neill has been called an Irish patriot and a sincere son of the Roman Catholic Church.[9] Nevertheless, he was essentially a lone wolf and his army was a pack of marauders. O'Neill had sided with Archbishop Rinuccini against the moderate leaders of the Irish Confederacy; he had tried hard to menace Dublin from western Leinster; he had then moved towards Connaught; and finally with his headquarters at Charlemont in Ulster he had declared his purpose was to prevent the new Scots under Robert Monro from joining up with Sir Charles Coote.

Such was the position in Ulster when Monck took up his command. During the winter of 1647–8 nothing much happened except for raiding by both sides. Sometimes Monck collaborated with Jones in Dublin, sometimes he acted on his own. But when the campaigning season opened in the spring of 1648 the situation changed. The second civil war had broken out in England. Charles I had promised Scottish commissioners, who visited him in his new place of honourable captivity, Carisbrooke castle in the Isle of Wight, that he would agree to the establishment of Presbyterianism in England for three years and that he would confer privileges on his Scottish subjects; in return they engaged to restore him to his throne. Robert Monro decided to send over much of his Ulster army to Scotland under the command of his nephew George to reinforce the army of the Engagers, led by the first Duke of Hamilton, that moved down through Cumberland and Lancashire to fight for the king against Parliament only to be outmanœuvred and completely defeated by Cromwell in the Preston campaign.

So Monck had a comparatively easy time during the summer of 1648. Victorious in the second civil war, all that the English Parliament wanted was for the Irish to be kept in check until it could later send over a large army to reduce the whole island to obedience. Thus Monck's was essentially a holding operation which enabled him to reveal his administrative ability by acting, as it were, as the military governor of Ulster. As soon as Fairfax and Cromwell had won the second civil war in England the authorities in London sent Monck orders to arrest the officers under his command who ever since he arrived there had been disobedient and had been assisting 'the traiterous design' of sending over men for the invasion of England under the Duke of Hamilton. These arrests, Monck was told, were to be gradual and, if necessary, the prisoners were to be dispatched to England to be dealt with there. He was specifically commanded to arrest Robert Monro, who was known to be in Carrickfergus north-east of Belfast.[10]

George Monck immediately carried out these orders in the autumn of 1648. With the aid of some native Scots officers who were dissatisfied with Monro and his new Scots, Monck surprised the Scots commander in his bed and dispatched him to England where, like Monck himself earlier, he was incarcerated in the Tower of London. Monck followed this up by capturing Belfast. The English Parliament was delighted, promised him £500 for his 'extraordinary service' and named him first governor of Carrickfergus, which was to be garrisoned by his own regiment, and then governor of Belfast.[11]

Meanwhile the Marquis of Ormonde, acting under orders from the royal family, had returned to Ireland, landing at Cork on Michaelmas Day 1648 with the intention of defending Charles I's prerogatives, settling the religious question and upholding the privileges of Parliament and the liberties of the subject. This amounted to a very broad and somewhat contradictory programme. It can hardly be doubted that his main objective was to reconcile all sides in Ireland with a view to helping the King, whose fate, indeed whose very life was now trembling in the balance. With the Confederacy he came to an agreement pretty rapidly. By 17 January 1649 he was able to proclaim that peace had been concluded with the Irish leaders in Kilkenny. But O'Neill, who, under the influence of Rinuccini, was on bad terms with the Confederacy, refused to accept the peace, trying instead to come to a separate arrangement with Ormonde and Inchiquin. In return for non-interference in Munster and Leinster he asked to be given a free hand in Connaught, which was then the most prosperous and least fought over part of the country. Rinuccini, having failed to obtain dominance for the Roman Catholic religion or to prevent the revival of the Confederacy, sailed away fulminating against the heretical viceroy.

All this left much of Munster and Leinster under English Protestant control; Ormonde, who stayed near Cork, learned of the execution of King Charles I at Whitehall on 30 January and having proclaimed Charles's eldest son as king, assumed that he could now come to terms with Jones in Dublin and Monck in Belfast to secure peace in Ireland under the new King.[12] After all, Monck had fought for the late King in 1644 and had been imprisoned as a Royalist, while Jones was uncommitted. But neither of them could be shaken from obedience to the English Parliament. Jones maintained that it was not his business to intervene in affairs of state, but to carry out the work for which he had been appointed governor of Dublin. On 21 March Monck informed the officers of the regiments under his command that 'those who do not prosecute the rebels and particularly such as adhere to the late peace between Ormonde and the rebels' would be declared incapable of holding a command.[13] Such officers would be expected to resign. Furthermore, he required that all his officers and men should renew their adherence to the Covenant and sign a declaration of loyalty to the English Parliament. To some extent that was a bluff. For Monck had neither the arms nor the supplies which he needed to keep his men satisfied.[14] On 30 March officers under his command — mainly Scots — refused to sign the new declaration.[15] He was told by commissioners, whom he had appointed to treat with them, that though they had solemnly subscribed to the Covenant, they were opposed to Fairfax and Cromwell and were determined 'not to commit any violence but to secure themselves and carry on the service under the King and Parliament of England according to their first undertakings'.[16] Only if that were accepted, could they conscientiously continue under Monck's orders. They informed the Major-General that they would not obey instructions from the 'new prevalent powers in London' — that is to say the regicides — and they asked Monck to divide up the arms and ammunition which he possessed equally among all his troops and regiments and said that they would do nothing without the approval of the Council of War, which meant the commanders of all the forces, Scots and English, under him.[17]

Thus George Monck accepted the new republican regime in England and was as firm as he knew how to be with those who did not. But he was going through a difficult time. He was extremely short of money to pay his soldiers or clothes to give them to wear. The Council of State, which had taken over the executive government after the death of Charles I did what it could to help him. He was promised much, but received little; for example, he was told he could have £500 for his train and carriages.[18] Nevertheless, as winter drew towards its end he was writing to London about his 'poor condition' and all that the Council of State could do was to refer the matter to the truncated House of Commons — 'the Rump' — as the ultimate authority so that it might 'order payment of what was due to him'.[19]

About this time Monck wrote an interesting letter to Thomas Fairfax, the commander-in-chief of all the armies of the Commonwealth.[20] He began by thanking him for his favours and good opinion and gave him an account of affairs in Ireland. 'The Scots', he wrote, 'who were lately under my command are now involved into very high dudgeon among themselves occasioned by their dissension from this service.' He went on to describe how Sir George Monro had managed to return to Ireland after the second civil war in England and expressed the belief that some agreement had been concluded between him and Sir Charles Coote in Londonderry. Of himself he wrote that 'Colonel Jones is drawn into the field and I am joined with him ... we are in the way to stop Ormonde from advancing towards Dublin'. But he added that Inchiquin, since the King's execution an avowed Royalist, had allied himself with Ormonde which would make him strong in horse. He therefore expressed the hope that Fairfax would speedily be able to supply them with cavalry so that they could uphold the English Parliament's interest in Ireland.

If Monck was able to lend Jones some help against the threat from Ormonde and Inchiquin it could not have been for long. The position was that the Royalists were supreme in Munster and Leinster outside Dublin, while Monck, though he controlled much of Ulster, was in grave difficulties through lack of supplies and the desertion or cashiering of the Scots formerly under his command. Coote was holding out in Londonderry against a Scottish force under Owen O'Neill, who having been driven out of Leinster, had returned to Ulster. Here, he stationed himself with nearly 7,000 of his Irish followers some twenty or thirty miles from Dundalk, where Monck had set up his advanced headquarters.

Monck was fully aware that O'Neill might either be pressured or persuaded into coming to an agreement with Ormonde who would then be in an even better position to encircle Jones at Dublin and himself in Ulster. The danger of a deal between this independent-minded Irish general, who had not at any time fully committed himself to either English side (and indeed declared that he hated them both) and the Marquis of Ormonde, who was now eagerly searching for allies to invigorate the Stuart cause, was appreciated alike by Monck and Jones. Rinuccini stated after he finally left Ireland early in 1649 that if O'Neill should come to terms with Ormonde the future of the Catholic religion in Ireland would be doomed and 'we would have to recommend Ireland to the mercy of God'.[21]

So it was a question for Jones and Monck of how to hold on and hope for the best. For they knew that help was to be expected from England later in the year. On 23 March Lieutenant-General Oliver Cromwell had accepted the post of commander-in-chief of an expeditionary force and was already actively engaged in collecting an army, highly trained and with adequate supplies for the purpose of subduing the Irish and compelling their obedience to the Commonwealth which had replaced the Stuart monarchy in England. The embarrassing nearness of O'Neill with an army which had swollen since his return to Ulster from the south was one of Monck's immediate problems.

O'Neill was a pretty shrewd politician as well as a good soldier. He realized that if he and his men, most of whom had ancestral homes in Ulster, could extract good terms from the new Commonwealth Government in England, their own future and the causes for which they had been fighting might be assured. O'Neill is known to have sent over an agent to London who said that if the Irish general were given an indemnity for what he had done in the past, and if the future of his religion and his estates were guaranteed, he would submit and act for Parliament. The Council of State refused to see the agent, a Cistercian abbot named Crelly, but appointed a committee to hear what he wanted and offered. The committee decided that there could be no amnesty for the 'bloody massacre' at the beginning of the Irish rebellion and so O'Neill's proposals were turned down, though, in fact, he had not been responsible for the massacre.[22]

It was all very well for the politicians in London to be so high-minded, or bloody-minded, but both Monck and Jones believed that it was their bounden duty to prevent O'Neill, who was plainly a tricky character, from going over to Ormonde before Cromwell's army arrived.[23] Monck seems to have made a first approach to O'Neill at the end of March.[24] O'Neill took nearly a month to answer. Later he offered to send one of his officers, Captain Mac Mahon, to treat with Monck. Monck thought it was for the good of the service to play him along. The terms that O'Neill asked for were much the same as Abbot Crelly put forward in London. Besides the demand for an act of oblivion, the restoration of the confiscated estates in Ulster and religious freedom, he wanted to be promised 'a competent command' in Fairfax's army.[25] Monck cautiously replied in a letter dated 28 April[26] that he thought there were some things in the articles which Parliament 'may scruple to grant'; he therefore added some 'small changes' in the proposed treaty. What Monck wanted, as he made perfectly clear, was an immediate cease-fire and friendly co-operation between his forces and those of O'Neill until the answer of the English Parliament to O'Neill's requests, which, as has been noticed, had already been rejected in London, was received. It is evident that Monck was not fully aware of what was going on in London. Although the President of the Council of State had written to him on 23 April telling him that an expeditionary army was being formed to reduce Ireland to submission and ordering him 'to do his utmost to keep things in a good state until these forces shall arrive'. He never received the letter because it was intercepted.[27] So Monck was simply doing his best as the man on the spot. After negotiations lasting about six weeks a cessation of arms was agreed to between Monck and O'Neill on 8 May 1649.

It is doubtful whether either O'Neill or Monck was sincere in his behaviour. O'Neill was satisfied that if the treaty were kept secret for three months he need not commit himself either to the English Parliament or to the Irish Royalists; he could in fact come to a defensive agreement with whichever side looked like being victorious in Ireland. Monck was equally devious. He did not write to Cromwell to inform him of the reasons for these transactions nor furnish him with a copy of the treaty until nearly three weeks after it was concluded. He then stressed how vital it had been to prevent

O'Neill from joining up with Ormonde; therefore he had 'adventured by the advice of some special friends and wellwishers to this service' to treat with the Irish general. If he had not done so, then Jones and himself (Monck) would have been 'in a very great hazard of losing the Parliament's footing in this kingdom [*sic*]'. That was why the three-month armistice was necessary. He then told Cromwell, who had been made Lord Lieutenant as well as commander-in-chief and therefore was the proper man for Monck to address, that he had not thought 'it fit to signify this to the Council of State but do wholly refer the business to you ... since there was a great necessity for me to do it, I hope it will beget no ill construction, when the advantage gained to the Service, by dividing Ormonde and Mac Art [O'Neill] is fully weighed.'28

The only man to know of these negotiations from the first was Michael Jones, who wrote to Cromwell on 6 June saying that 'I have hitherto fomented (as I still do) the difference between Owen Roe and Ormonde, and am now on a design for taking off Preston also with his Irish army ... it will [he added] be of high consequence to the utter and speedy breaking of their whole powers.'29 In the same letter Jones told Cromwell that Monck, whom he had seen recently in Dublin, was only playing for time, though not by his treaty with O'Neill (which Jones did not mention) but by his dealings with the Scots in Ulster. They thought that if Monck could be persuaded to take the Covenant again he would be committed to going over to the side of the new King of England, Charles II, and disobeying the authority of Parliament. At one stage, he added, Monck had actually hoped to persuade two of the Covenanting regiments to come to the assistance of himself (Jones) in Dublin, though Jones doubted that he would be successful in this. Rather, he thought that Monck was doing the best service to the Commonwealth by persuading all the Scots in Ulster that his sympathies were with them. In fact, as with O'Neill and his Ulster Irish, Monck was only stringing them along.

All these elaborate intrigues, however, were soon to collapse like a castle of cards. Part of the agreement between Monck and O'Neill had specified that Monck would help to overcome a shortage of gunpowder. Early in June, O'Neill brought 3,000 of his men to within seven miles of Dundalk and then dispatched one of his officers, Colonel Ferral, with 500 men to collect six barrels of powder which had been paid for. By now Lord Inchiquin, who had proved to be one of the best Royalist generals in Ireland and had virtually subjugated Munster, had marched through Leinster and on 28 June captured Drogheda, afterwards moving on towards Dundalk. His intelligence must have been excellent, for he learned about Ferral's mission in advance and sent one of his officers to intercept the convoy, which he did successfully. Then Inchiquin himself prepared to lay siege to Dundalk. Monck's men were demoralized and hungry; but only one of them refused to fight on the grounds that Monck had allied himself with 'bloodthirsty Popish rebels'.[30] The rest, though promising obedience, also disliked Monck's dealings with O'Neill, which had become common knowledge after Ferral's arrival in Dundalk, while O'Neill's men, having no gunpowder but plenty to drink, failed to assist Monck and later marched off to north-west Ulster. Here, Sir Charles Coote, commander in Londonderry for the English Parliament, was able to supply O'Neill with the powder which he had been unable to collect safely from Dundalk. Londonderry had long been besieged by 'the old Scots' who were loyal to the Stuart monarchy. When O'Neill arrived there Coote fulfilled his part of the bargain; in return for powder, money and food O'Neill relieved the town.[31] Thus Coote achieved the result which Monck had hoped to gain by his treaty with O'Neill.

Without O'Neill's help or that of the Scots Monck held Dundalk for only a couple of days after Inchiquin arrived before its walls. The terms on which Monck surrendered to Inchiquin were that he and any of his officers who wanted to do so might return to England. In fact only a couple of captains and one or two junior officers elected to sail away from Ireland while most of the men enlisted in Inchiquin's army. Monck himself took ship for Chester, whence he travelled first to London and then to Milford Haven, where Cromwell was putting the final touches on his expeditionary force about to embark for Ireland. Here, Monck explained to Cromwell how and why he had allied himself with the Irish Catholics in Ulster.

No one knows what George Monck said to Oliver at their first meeting on 4 August 1649. When Cromwell had received Monck's letter of 25 May informing him of the reasons why he had come to terms with O'Neill, the Lord Lieutenant had laid the letter before the Council of State; the Council's minute book recorded that 'it was not thought fit for diverse reasons to return any answer thereupon to Colonel Monck, but enjoined secrecy upon the whole'.[32] In other words, realizing at the time how delicate the whole military situation was in Ireland, the Council had decided, perhaps on Cromwell's advice, to let sleeping dogs lie, even though the members disagreed in principle with such a treaty.

Cromwell ordered Monck to go up to London and report to the Council of State. He arrived in the capital on 6 August. The Council resolved that 'the secrecy enjoined upon the business of Monck's treaty with Mac Art O'Neill should be taken off'—obviously because its existence had now become generally known—and Monck was instructed to prepare a justificatory narrative and appear before the Council next day.[33] After hearing Monck's defence of his conduct, the Council voted that 'the treaty ... wholly against the judgment of this Council when they first heard of it' and the Council 'was still of the same opinion'.[34]

Three days later Thomas Scot M.P. reported from the Council to the House of Parliament and delivered there all the letters and documents relating to the matter. In the afternoon Monck waited at the door of the House before he was called to the bar. He was asked who were the 'special friends and wellwishers to the service' mentioned in his letter to Cromwell of 25 May who had given him the advice to treat with O'Neill. Monck refrained from answering the question; obviously he had no wish to get any other officer into trouble. Therefore he insisted that he had taken the step on his own responsibility, though he related that he had once had a conversation with Colonel Michael Jones, who had told him that 'if he could keep off Owen Roe from joining [with Ormonde] he would do good service'. He had therefore acquainted Jones with his intentions.[35] But his actions, he admitted, had been authorized neither by Cromwell nor the Council of State. Michael Jones's name should have been one to conjure with, for eight days earlier he had inflicted a crushing defeat on the Marquis of Ormonde and his army at Rathmines near Dublin.[36] After a long debate Parliament resolved that 'this House doth utterly disapprove of the proceedings of Colonel Monck'; but was 'satisfied that what Colonel Monck did therein was in his apprehension necessary for the preservation of the Parliament's interest in Ireland'; therefore the House decided that, as to George himself, the matter might be 'laid aside' and that it was 'content that the further consideration thereof shall not at any time be called in question'.[37] Thus he first received a reprimand and was then forgiven.

Five days later all the papers relating to Monck's treaty with O'Neill were published in London.[38] Nobody came very well out of the episode. In the first place, Monck himself, having concluded the agreement, should have tried harder to make sure it worked. Coote, as has been noticed, made a similar deal with O'Neill which resulted in the relief of Londonderry; but he was not publicly rebuked. In the second place, the Council of State should either have backed Monck to the full or, once it heard what had happened and disapproved of it, ought to have recalled Monck to England and dismissed him from the service of Parliament. Finally, Cromwell, who, if one may judge by his subsequent behaviour to Monck, accepted his reasons for concluding the treaty, should have told the Council of State that he did so instead of washing his hands of the affair. The result was that Monck was held up to the disapprobation of the puritans and when the officers of his regiment protested to the Council of State about their Major-General's treatment, their petition was ignored.[39]

There is a story which has crept into some recent history books that Cromwell and the Council of State had not only known of Monck's negotiations with O'Neill all the time, but that Cromwell had either initiated or encouraged them.[40] That was why the matter was kept secret from Parliament for so long. After Monck's return to England, Cromwell, it is alleged, advised the Council of State to make Monck the scapegoat for the conclusion of this treaty in return for a promise of future rewards and that he had found Monck inclined to fall in with such a scheme. In fact there is only one highly suspect piece of evidence for all that and the story was conclusively refuted by that great historian, Samuel Rawson Gardiner, ninety years ago. Probably, however, Cromwell was impressed by Monck's personality and military acumen when he met him for the first time at Milford Haven. That was why he was to employ this highly qualified and experienced officer in his army during the following year. Perhaps he felt that Monck had been harshly treated by the Council of State which had certainly acted in a rather hypocritical and illogical manner.

What lessons were learnt by George Monck during his third

tour of duty in Ireland? The first related to military administration. Whereas in 1642–4 his responsibilities had been chiefly those of an ordinary infantry colonel — and, after all, every good colonel was or is supposed to care for the welfare of his men — in Ulster he bore the title of Major-General and was recognized as the commander-in-chief in north-eastern Ireland. It was his duty to write to the Council of State in London stressing his needs in money and equipment, but during 1648 with the second civil war in progress, he was thrown on his own resources. The Council of State and the Committee at Derby House, which looked after the armies, were concentrating on suppressing the Royalist risings in south-east England and stemming the invasion of the Scots Engagers. It was not until May 1649 that the Council of State informed Monck that it was aware of his difficulties, that it was sending him money and that warships would be provided to scour the Irish Sea.[41]

In Ireland Monck had to carry out many different duties from administering martial law (always a sensitive subject with him) to writing to the censors (tax officers) within the island of Magee (north of Belfast) asking them for certificates of the monthly amounts paid by them to his army between May and November.[42] According to Skinner, he 'was not only a good Soldier but a good Husband also, so ordered the Tillage and Improvement of the Country, and providently disposed of all Booties taken from the Enemy, that he made the war support itself without much Relief from England'.[43] More picturesquely Sir Julian Corbett wrote about his hero happily combining 'the patient industry of the ploughman and the daring activity of the moss-trooper', but no doubt Corbett relied on Skinner for that view.[44] In any case Monck could see that there was a good deal more to warfare than winning battles, which was the end product of weapon drill, discipline, the possession of a war chest and a good commissariat. In Ulster he acquired knowledge of military government which proved invaluable to him later in Scotland.

In the second place, Monck's experiences in Ulster must have modified the idealistic and somewhat naïve opinions he expressed in his book about the relationship between the army and the civil power, and about how necessary it was for soldiers always to believe in the causes for which they were fighting rather than enlisting just to obtain pay and plunder. It was extremely hard then, and has been a difficulty for modern historians, to understand the objectives of the different generals in Ireland. Did the Marquis of Ormonde want to safeguard the English 'interest' in Ireland or to serve the cause of the Stuart monarchy? (Maybe he wanted to do both and that was why he lost out.) Was Michael Jones primarily devoted to holding Dublin for the English Parliament or did he aim at regaining Anglo-Irish supremacy in the Pale? Was O'Neill the exponent of 'Ireland for the Irish' or 'Ulster for Ulstermen' or was he a papal crusader or even a mere ambitious condottiere? What exactly did the 'old Scots' and 'the new Scots' want? Was it to avenge the execution of a Scots king, an act which was abhorred by all Presbyterians, or did these Scots intend to drive the native Irish out of Ulster altogether and convert it into a Scottish colonial settlement?

George Monck had to weigh all these different political interpretations. He found he had to break with the Scots officers, who were nominally under his command, when they insisted that they would not fight for Fairfax and Cromwell, who were the military instruments of the new republic, but only for King and Parliament. Monck had to retort that if they accepted Ormonde's pact with the Irish, concluded on behalf of the King, they must lay down their arms and resign.[45] It is a fascinating side-light on Monck's political views that at the end of 1649 when he was back at his home in Devonshire, he wrote to the colonel commanding at Lisburn, which had once been his own military headquarters, telling him that he must take care that certain officers never enjoyed their estates again and that Scots ministers did not ever preach again in Ulster. 'I doubt if this be not observed', he added, 'you will once more be slaves of the Scots and then none of your friends will pity you, being [that] it lies in your power to help it.'[46]

What Monck undoubtedly aimed at was to preserve Ireland under English rule. But the whole episode of the treaty with O'Neill, combined with his abortive negotiations with the Scots officers and his final dismissal of them, must have taught him that political means often have to be used to attain strategic ends; and equally that military pressure is the most potent weapon to effect political changes.

6

The Dunbar Campaign and After

After his condemnation by Parliament George Monck returned to his home in Devonshire where he stayed for nearly a year. It was the first real period of rest that he had enjoyed since the civil wars began. It is true that upon hearing news of his father's illness he had applied for permission to go to England in the spring of 1643, but he had agreed to postpone doing so. By the time he arrived back in England and was taken prisoner after the battle of Nantwich his father was dead. The estate at Great Potheridge went to his eldest brother, Thomas; all that Monck received from his father's will was the £100 a year which was rapidly spent when he was in the Tower. His mother and his grandfather, Sir George Smyth, who had brought him up, were also dead. Nothing was left to him in his grandfather's will.[1] Then his brother died in May 1647 after a fall from his horse while Monck was fighting in Ulster; so he succeeded to the family estates.[2] The younger Thomas Monck had been an active Cavalier, a colonel in the King's army and a royal commissioner in Exeter.[3] Colonel Thomas left two daughters. But the estate was entailed. The value of the inheritance was not large, being worth about £2,000 and it was heavily mortgaged.[4] Thus Monck became the owner of Great Potheridge and Squire of Merton.

As a Royalist or 'delinquent' Thomas Monck had been ordered to pay a fine compounding for the estate, but it had not been met at the time of his death.[5] Out of the estate Monck had to provide an annuity of £120 a year for his brother's widow and marriage portions for his two nieces.[6] He also had an unmarried sister, Frances, to look after, while it is not improbable that Anne Ratsford, who by then had left her husband, joined George Monck at Potheridge.[7] So his responsibilities were considerable. Furthermore, he had a younger brother another Royalist, Nicholas, who after taking a degree at Oxford, became rector of Plymtree, a small village near Ottery St Mary, which can hardly have been a valuable benefice. No doubt using all the administrative experience he had acquired in Ireland, Monck proved himself to be a better landlord and farmer than either his father or elder brother, but it must have been a struggle. He is known to have owned some property in Exeter[8] and it is highly probable that he had acquired land in Connaught and also perhaps in Ulster and Leinster.[9] But no doubt he had hopes of obtaining another commission, especially in view of the good impression he must have felt he made on General Cromwell when he saw him at Milford Haven.

Seasick, Cromwell arrived in Ireland on 15 August 1649 about the time when Monck was on his way home. Michael Jones's victory over Ormonde near Dublin and Charles Coote's success at Londonderry had already largely crushed the Irish Royalists before Cromwell's army was even deployed. By mid-September he recaptured Inchiquin's conquest of Drogheda, which Ormonde had confided to the care of Sir Arthur Aston, an old Royalist colonel with a wooden leg. Aston's refusal to surrender after he had been summoned to do so and a breach had been blown in the walls of the town, caused Cromwell to order that the entire garrison should be put to the sword. That was a legacy of the cruelty of Irish warfare which he had inherited. Though a number of the 2,300 Irish and English soldiers managed to escape or were even spared for lesser punishment,[10] the example that Cromwell set at Drogheda caused other Irish garrisons to capitulate without fighting. One of these was at Dundalk, the town lost by Monck. When Cromwell was in Dundalk he may have learned at first hand something more about the value of Monck's services in Ulster.

On 4 May 1650 the Council of State ordered Cromwell, even though he held the post of Lord Lieutenant of Ireland, to return to England. Three days earlier the young Charles II, who was exiled in Holland, signed the so-called treaty of Breda with commissioners sent there by the dominant Scottish Covenanters. In return for Charles II's promises to establish Presbyterianism not only in Scotland but also in England and Ireland, and to abide by the decisions of the Scottish Parliament and its executive body, the Committee of Estates, the Covenanters promised that he should be recognized and enthroned as King of the Scots and invited him to Scotland for these purposes. Charles's more sober advisers had been opposed to such far-reaching and embarrassing commitments (although Charles, an accomplished and inveterate liar, had certainly no intention of fulfilling them) but he wriggled and then succumbed to pressure.[11] For with England and Ireland subjugated to the new Commonwealth, his only hope of regaining his throne in Whitehall was with the aid of a Scottish army.

The intelligence received in London about these negotiations must have been remarkably good and prompt. For not only was Cromwell at once recalled from Ireland but during late June 1650, a day or two after Charles II landed in Speyside in response to the Covenanters' invitation, the House of Parliament at Westminster declared war on Scotland. They appointed Cromwell as Captain-General and commander-in-chief to lead an expeditionary force north and allowed Lord Fairfax, their former Captain-General, who adamantly refused to fight the Scots unless they committed an act of aggression, to resign all his offices and retire to his native Yorkshire.

Preparations for the invasion of Scotland had been going on ever since Charles's signature of the treaty of Breda was known. Fairfax proved right in thinking that the Scots had no immediate intention of marching into England as the Engagers had done two years earlier. All that the Scots wanted to do was to create a Covenanting King, obedient to their wishes. But the English Parliamentarians, remembering what had happened in 1648, had no intention of being caught napping. Wisely, they arranged that the bulk of Cromwell's army should be raised from regiments stationed in the north of England. So when Cromwell set out from London on 28 June along the Great North Road he had only a skeleton army consisting of some 4,000 officers and men; the rest of the army was to join him in the north. Among the officers whom he took with him from the south, bearing the rank of supernumerary colonel, was George Monck who had been sent for from Devon.

Monck's earlier biographers have speculated on flimsy or non-existent evidence whether or not he had searched his heart before thus shaking the hand of Cromwell stained with the blood of Charles I. These speculations were composed after the Restoration. It was urged that Monck disliked and despised the Scots whom he had fought against in 1639–40 and who deserted him in Ulster in 1649. It may have been so, but, like all good captains, he rarely underestimated his enemy and it is more likely that he joined Cromwell's army because he enjoyed the profession of soldier.[12] It also helped him to supplement his meagre inheritance with an officer's pay.

Cromwell rode out from London by way of Ware, Cambridge, Northampton, Leicester, York and Durham to Newcastle where the whole of the army was assembled. He was accompanied by Lieutenant-General Charles Fleetwood as his second-in-command, Major-General John Lambert, who was put in charge of the infantry and acted as his Chief of Staff, and by Colonel Richard Ingoldsby, all men who had learned their trade as warriors in the civil wars. Cromwell and Ingoldsby had signed the King's death warrant; Fleetwood, Lambert and Monck had not. It is not known whether Monck was asked to take the engagement to be loyal to the new regime which by an act of parliament passed that January had been imposed on all men in the community and could be construed to imply approval of Charles I's execution. Fairfax had refused to take the engagement and it is known that other officers were excused from doing so. Possibly Monck, fresh from the Royalist atmosphere in his part of Devon, was not required to do so either. At Cambridge the Vice-Chancellor met Cromwell at the Bear inn and specifically begged him to lend support to a petition that he and his colleagues should be permitted not to subscribe to the engagement.[13] At Leicester, Cromwell and his officers were entertained with wine and biscuits, beer and tobacco. At York they were dined and 'highly caressed'. Eventually when they reached Newcastle on 10 July dining was eschewed and a fast imposed on Cromwell's army.[14]

In York, Lambert's cavalry regiment joined the army. A regiment under the command of Colonel Robert Lilburne, the Leveller leader's brother, also came to Newcastle. These two regiments had been concerned for some time with keeping order on the unruly Scottish frontier. Other regiments which had been raised or were serving in the north also arrived at Newcastle. One of these, an infantry regiment, suddenly found itself without a colonel. For John Bright, its Yorkshire commander, had asked Cromwell for a fortnight's leave of absence to attend to his private affairs. As the Captain-General was in a hurry to get to Scotland where, it was rumoured, the enemy was massing on the border, the request was naturally refused. In fact Bright, like Fairfax, a fellow Yorkshire-man, was glad of an excuse to break with the regicides. Cromwell wanted Bright's regiment to be taken over by Monck. When the army, having left Newcastle, reached Alnwick, some thirty miles from the frontier on 17 July, Cromwell sent a number of colonels to inquire in a remarkably democratic way if the soldiers of the regiment would accept Monck as their commander. 'Colonel Monck!' exclaimed some of them, 'what! to betray us? We took him, not long since, at Nantwich, prisoner: we'll have none of him.'[15] Next day these soldiers were asked if they would have Major-General Lambert as their colonel whereupon all threw their hats in the air and declared that they would. Whether this incident rankled with Monck is unknown, but he and Lambert proved pretty effective colleagues once they were absorbed in active service. Not to be outdone, Cromwell formed a regiment for Monck by taking five companies from Colonel George Fenwick's infantry regiment, stationed at Berwick-upon-Tweed, and five from that of Sir Arthur Heslirige left behind in Newcastle. The Council of State approved the formation of Monck's regiment and on 30 July added it to the establishment: in years to come it was known as the Coldstream Guards.[16]

Cromwell's army amounted to some 16,000 men, with twice as many foot as horse, when it crossed into Scotland from Berwick on 22 July. What proved of vital importance to the expedition was that a naval squadron, consisting partly of frigates and partly of supply ships, sailed parallel with the army in the direction of the Firth of Forth. So long as Cromwell hugged the coast he could therefore be sure of assistance if his supplies ran out. For the Scots had no navy.

In effective charge of the Scots Covenanting army was General David Leslie, who had fought under Cromwell six years earlier at the battle of Marston Moor. He was a cautious commander. Far from massing his troops on the frontier, he had withdrawn every man of military age from the counties of East Lothian and Berwick; he had also given orders that all corn and forage were to be removed from the south-east and that cattle and sheep should be brought behind the walls of Edinburgh thus depriving the invaders of any chance of living off the country. However, on 26 July Cromwell quickly occupied the port of Dunbar, thirty miles east of the Scottish capital, where supplies could be disembarked. It was just as well for him that they could be, for the fertile fields lying north of the border were now desolate; all the English soldiers saw were 'streets full of Scotch women; pitiful, sorry creatures, clothed in white flannel in a very homely manner ... ' much bemoaning their husbands, 'who, they said, were forced by the lairds of the towns to gang to the muster.'[17]

Cromwell only carried field guns with him, not siege guns, relying for success upon naval bombardments from the river Forth. It appears that Monck was put in charge of the land artillery about which he had learnt much in Ireland. He became in fact acting Lieutenant-General of the Ordnance, though he was not officially confirmed in that rank until six months later. The Scottish cavalry beat up their enemy's quarters, but were quickly chased away. Leslie had planned defence in depth, fortifying a line which stretched from Leith, the port of Edinburgh, as far as the capital. The English naval squadron began cannonading Leith at the end of July while the English army occupied Arthur's Seat and Salisbury craigs, two high points lying to the south of Edinburgh. But as soon as the commander-in-chief recognized how formidable were the Scots defences he decided to retire to regroup his forces in the first instance at Musselburgh, a smaller port than Dunbar, which lay eight miles east of Edinburgh. From Musselburgh the English moved farther back to Dunbar, which was reached on 6 August, though the weather was so bad that difficulty was experienced in landing supplies there. Thus Leslie had won the first round in the fight.

Cromwell's original march westwards from Dunbar was in effect a reconnaissance in force.[18] Having decided that the defences southeast of Edinburgh were impenetrable, the Captain-General resolved to discover whether the Scottish capital could be attacked from the west. After several days' rations of bread and cheese had been allocated, the English army advanced into the Pentland hills. Colinton, a village to the north of the Pentland hills, three miles from Edinburgh, was seized without resistance, but Leslie was not taken unawares. His army also moved west, encamped on Corstophine hill with an outpost at Red Hall whence he could watch the movements of his enemy. Each side was manœuvring for position. Leslie's aim was either to cut off Cromwell's army from England or conceivably to march into England himself. Cromwell for his part had hopes of dissensions in the Scottish camp, for it was known that some extreme Covenanters were against supporting King Charles II, even after he had signed a declaration on 14 August deploring the misdeeds of his father and the idolatry of his mother. Once Cromwell knew that these dissensions had been temporarily smoothed over he had two alternatives: either to attack Leslie or to cut his communications across the Forth which ran through Queensferry towards Stirling.[19]

On 24 August the two armies ceased eying each other uneasily. That day Monck and part of his infantry regiment distinguished themselves by capturing Red Hall, whose garrison had resisted for two days. The Scots also evacuated Colinton House. But Leslie occupied high ground barring the route to Queensferry. In vain, Cromwell attempted to manœuvre past him. On 27 August the two armies were nearly within gunshot of each other in Gogar park, five miles west of Edinburgh. The English commander-in-chief called for a couple of guns, presumably directed by Monck, to fire at the sod walls protecting the enemy position.[20] An artillery duel was followed by a cavalry skirmish. Cromwell claimed that eighty Scots were killed while only four Englishmen were lost plus eighteen or nineteen wounded. But his stores were exhausted and he was cut off from the Firth of Forth where his supply vessels rode, while his army was demoralized by having had to encamp so long in inclement weather on the Pentland hills. So he was obliged to withdraw, taking with him the garrisons that had been stationed in Red Hall and Colinton House. On 28 August the English army returned to Musselburgh.

At Musselburgh a council of war met at which Monck must have been present. On 30 August the decision was reached to fortify Dunbar with the options of either, at best provoking Leslie into engaging in a pitched battle, or at worst embarking the army, already seriously reduced in numbers almost entirely through medical casualties (especially dysentery), leaving the renewal of the campaign in Scotland until the following spring. The first plan of inducing the Scots to fight, according to Lieutenant-General Fleetwood, was believed to be impossible[21] — for the Scots had hitherto left the English unmolested there — while the second was obviously un-desirable. We do not know what Monck thought, but if one may judge from his book, his belief was that when a military situation became desperate that was the time to stand up and fight.

It has been stated, though without proof, that Monck was responsible for fortifying the army camp at Dunbar. It is likely enough that he placed the guns. Meanwhile Leslie had led his army parallel with the route along which the English retired. Besides harassing the English rearguard, he sent a contingent to occupy the pass at Cockburnspath, ten miles south-east of Dunbar, through which his enemy would have to march if they retreated by land to Newcastle upon Tyne. In fact there is little reason to suppose that Cromwell intended at any time to do so; what, however, he did hope for was that reinforcements and supplies would be sent to him by Colonel Heslirige from Newcastle. Now that way was blocked. Leslie drew up his whole army on Doon hill, part of the Lammermuir chain, roughly two miles south of Dunbar. Thence he could launch a flank attack on the English if, as he assumed, they attempted to retire home by land. He was confident that they were trapped, while the Presbyterian ministers who accompanied his army everywhere were sure that the Lord had 'delivered ten thousand of the Moab into their hand'.[22]

On Monday 2 September Leslie resolved to move his army down off Doon hill into the rich grasslands below. The wet and blustery weather meant that camping there would be extremely uncomfortable; on the other hand, the English were reasonably at ease in Dunbar whence their sick and wounded had been evacuated by sea and where supplies were accumulating. Cromwell now concluded that the Scots were, after all, going to fight a battle. Between the two lines ran a stream, swollen by the summer rains, known as the Brox burn. It ran through a long and narrow glen or clough and was more of an obstacle to the east than to the west. To the right of the new Scottish position ran the road from Dunbar via Cockburnspath to Berwick-upon-Tweed. Near to this road and half a mile from the sea lay Broxmouth house, the seat of the Earl of Roxburgh. Here, after supper, Cromwell and Major-General Lambert, who acted as his Chief of Staff, rode out to inspect the Scottish dispositions. They observed that Leslie had placed two-thirds of his cavalry on the right, 'shogging [shaking out] also their foot and train much to the right, causing their right wing of horse to edge down towards the sea'.[23] 'We could not well imagine', continued Cromwell in a dispatch to the Speaker of Parliament written after the subsequent battle

but that the enemy intended to attempt upon us, or to place themselves in a more exact condition of interposition. The

Major-General and myself coming to the Earl Roxburgh's House, and observing this posture, I told him I thought it did give us an opportunity and advantage to attempt upon the enemy, to which he immediately replied, that he had thought to say the same thing to me. So that it pleased the Lord to set this apprehension upon both of our hearts, at the same instant. We called for Colonel Monk and showed him the thing ... [24]

Two points arise out of the dispatch; firstly, it proves that although Monck did not yet hold the rank of general he was already one of Cromwell's leading officers and closest advisers after Lambert and Fleetwood. Dr Gumble somewhat rhapsodically called him 'Cromwell's darling'. Secondly, one has to deduce 'the thing' that was shown to Monck. [25]

The main authority for what happened besides Cromwell's pious dispatches are the memoirs written by Captain John Hodgson, a company commander in Lambert's regiment of horse. [26] It is true that his book was published thirty years later, but most of what he says is plausible enough. He attended a council of war which was held at nine o'clock in the evening of 2 September. There, he wrote, Lambert gave two positive reasons for taking the offensive against the enemy: the first was that 'if we beat their right wing, we hazarded the whole army, for they would be in confusion, in regard they had not great ground to traverse their regiments between the mountain [Doon hill] and the clough [the ravine through which flowed the Brox burn]'. Second, he added, was that 'they had left intervals in their bodies, upon the brink of the hill, that our horse might march a troop at once, and so the foot.' Negatively he observed that it would be foolish to ship away their infantry and in any case it was too late. Dr Gumble, after remarking on Cromwell's cowardice — he 'would have given his Hopes of the Protectorship to have been safe at *Whitehall*' — claimed that 'Monk urged Battail and in that place where they were to assault the Enemy.' What Monck must have meant, if that was what he said, was that since the English soldiers had that day been brought out of Dunbar and were being lined up along the north bank of the Brox burn with two field guns assigned to each foot regiment because they were expecting to be attacked by Leslie, they were equally in a position to advance if they could surmount the ravine. Indeed, Leslie was also intending to attack partly under pressure from the ministers but mainly because he himself thought that his enemy had been delivered into his hands. So both armies stood ready to engage on the next day.

The Scots outnumbered the English by two to one. Neither side had an agreeable night for they were all drenched by a storm of rain accompanied by bursts of thunder. According to Gumble, Monck 'undertook the Work [of leading the offensive'].[27] According to Hodgson, 'honest Lambert ... ' was asked in the Council of War to 'have the conduct of the army that morning which was granted by the General freely.'[28] What probably happened was that Lambert, as Cromwell's Chief of Staff, was responsible for drawing up the troops in their attacking positions, while Monck was singled out to take full charge of the infantry in the centre. Lambert and Fleetwood were to lead a cavalry assault on Monck's left. Cromwell himself took control of the battle in so far as any control could be exercised in those days, retaining a reserve of one cavalry regiment (his own) and three infantry regiments.

Monck was given three and a half regiments of foot with orders to cross the burn and attack the enemy centre, while Lambert and Fleetwood with six cavalry regiments dealt with the mass of Scots horse stationed on their right wing which stretched across the back of Broxmouth house and over the Berwick road nearly as far as the sea. A well-trained regiment of dragoons under Colonel John Okey was assigned to demonstrate against the Scots left wing cramped under Doon hill.[29] The battle began at four o'clock in the morning when the storms (which had concealed the English dispositions) subsided and the martial scene was illuminated by bright moonlight. The Scots, who had been expecting to attack and not be attacked, were undoubtedly surprised. Nevertheless, the English cavalry and infantry were at first repulsed. The horse had to contend with the Scots lancers, formidably armed. The Scots foot soldiers, however, were ill prepared for battle after a wet night tentless in the corn-fields; their officers — some of them at least — actually left their men and found shelter for themselves in neighbouring farmhouses, having first given orders that match (a length of cord soaked in saltpetre which burned slowly) needed by the musketeers to fire their weapons, was to be dowsed lest it betrayed their positions to the enemy. Monck was outnumbered, it has been estimated, by as much as three to one. However, the English soldiers were excellently disciplined and knew that they had to fight for their lives, while most of the Scots were raw recruits, wet, tired and hungry. Leslie blamed himself for drawing them up so close to the enemy along the banks of the burn—just as Rupert had been accused of stationing his men too far forward at the battle of Marston Moor six years earlier, where Leslie had fought against him alongside Cromwell.

At the crux of the battle Cromwell threw in the regiments that he had kept under his hand. Most modern historians have attributed the final victory—the battle lasted only two hours—to a brilliantly executed flank attack by these reserves. But if such an attack took place (the sole authority for the story is Hodgson's memoirs) it could only have been made by Cromwell's single cavalry regiment. John Buchan in his biography of Cromwell actually has a battle plan showing the English infantry assaulting the Scots lancers.[30] That is nonsense. What surely happened was that Cromwell used his reserve infantry to reinforce Monck, thrusting the men into the line on Monck's left and Lambert's right, while his cavalry was employed to reinforce Lambert. Both Monck and Lambert rallied their men to beat back the Scots in a second advance. 'After the first repulse given,' wrote Cromwell, 'the enemy's horse and foot were made by the Lord of Hosts as stubble to our swords.'[31] The rout was total. Four thousand Scots were killed and ten thousand prisoners taken while the English were supposed to have lost a mere twenty to forty men: it sounds incredible, but, if true, the Scots must in the end have been completely demoralized.

After the battle Leslie withdrew the remnants of his shattered army to Stirling—the area where some of the most famous battles in Scottish history have been fought such as Falkirk and Bannockburn —and the Scottish Government settled in Perth. Cromwell occupied Edinburgh, which except for its rockgirt castle surrendered quickly, and so did the port of Leith. By 14 September the English army had entered West Lothian and four days later prepared to lay siege to Stirling. But naval support was unavailable since the Forth was not navigable as far as Stirling; Leslie had collected some reinforcements; and the roads were so bad that it was difficult for the English to move the artillery. Cromwell and his officers therefore decided to abandon the siege for the time being and build a base at Linlithgow, not far from the river and half way between Edinburgh and Stirling. The young King Charles II visited Stirling to inspirit the garrison.

Cromwell hoped that the Scots would be divided among themselves, part of them being Royalists and others, the sterner Covenanters, blaming their defeat on the fact that a malignant, misguided and unsanctified prince had been acknowledged as their king. These extremists, who were known as Remonstrants or Protesters, moved off towards Glasgow where they aimed to raise another Covenanter army that repudiated the new king. Cromwell himself marched into the west with the intention of either cajoling them or crushing them.

Meanwhile, it was necessary to clear the line of communications first between England and Edinburgh and then between Edinburgh and Stirling. For although the Scots had abandoned Cockburnspath, moss-troopers, that is to say guerrillas or freebooters, still interfered with the arrival of reinforcements and supplies from Newcastle along the Berwick–Edinburgh road. Monck, who had become Cromwell's artillery expert, was first employed in organizing preparations for reducing Edinburgh castle to obedience either by heavy gunfire or by mining—since as long as it was unsubdued it could make the lives of the English garrison in the city extremely uncomfortable—and after that mopping up the castles from which the moss-troopers operated.[32]

On 8 November Monck and Lambert together occupied Dirleton castle (west of North Berwick in East Lothian) where, finding that cannon fire made no impression, they used a mortar to launch grenades which tore open the inner gate. Then he and Lambert separated. Monck obtained the surrender of Roslin castle, which lay south of Edinburgh, and not long after reconnoitred Tantallon castle, three miles east of North Berwick, a stronghold belonging to the Earl of Angus; this was surrounded on three sides by the sea and the shell remains to this day. But he decided it could not be taken without better artillery and more mortars than he possessed. For although Cromwell had demanded the dispatch of siege guns, and General Richard Deane, a relative of Cromwell, who was acknowledged to be the greatest artillery expert in the New Model Army (he had handled the guns at Naseby), arrived in Scotland during September, there was not yet enough siege cannon to go round.[33] No doubt it was for this reason and upon the advice of Deane and Monck that Cromwell decided to abandon the assault on Stirling for the time being.

Instead, therefore, of concentrating against Stirling where Leslie was augmenting his strength, efforts were undertaken, probably under Monck's supervision, to mine into the rock on which Edinburgh castle stands. The attempt to do so failed completely; so Cromwell prepared to assault the citadel. But before he did so he tried to persuade the Governor, Sir Walter Dundas, to capitulate. Dundas was an extreme Covenanter in sympathy with the Remonstrants who deeply distrusted Charles II. He gave way. George Monck was one of the two officers appointed by the Captain-General to negotiate the terms of surrender, which were signed on 24 December.[34] Then Monck was appointed the English Military Governor of Edinburgh.

By now Cromwell had evidently come to rely on George Monck almost as much as he did on John Lambert, a younger man who had fought with him throughout the first two civil wars. It was just as well that he could do so because he himself was taken seriously ill during February and March 1651, though he tried hard to supervise matters from his sickbed. One of Cromwell's anxieties was to establish a military base on the north side of the river Forth because, if that could be done, it would be possible to attack Leslie in Stirling from the east as well as from the south. On 18 January Monck took charge of a force of 1,500 picked men, embarked in boats at Leith to capture the useful port of Burntisland in Fife, which lay immediately north of Leith on the other side of the Firth of Forth.[35] But the coming of the expedition was spotted well before it could arrive, beacons were lit summoning the men of Fifeshire to the rescue, the weather turned stormy and Monck had to give up the idea of landing there in the face of an effective cannonade.

In February and March Monck returned to the task of subduing isolated castles some of which still interfered with the English lines of communication. On 21 February he compelled the governor of Tantallon to surrender after he had besieged it for eight days following up the employment of mortar fire with that of heavy artillery. This was an amphibious operation since Monck's soldiers were supported by Deane's warships. At the end of March Monck captured Blackness castle, like Dirleton and Tantallon, lying on the southern shores of the Forth, but situated in West Lothian uncomfortably near to Linlithgow. In view of this string of successes it was scarcely surprising that at last on 6 May Monck was officially appointed Lieutenant-General of the Ordnance.[36] No doubt to avert the jealousy of his other artillery expert, Richard Deane, Cromwell on the same day named him Major-General and gave him the command of a vacant foot regiment.

By June 1651 Cromwell's health had recovered, the weather had improved and it was thought high time to resume major operations against the Scots. By now it was generally recognized by the commander-in-chief and his officers that the most feasible way of shifting Leslie from the Stirling area was by outflanking him. (In the early summer Leslie had moved his front line forward and by reaching Falkirk had made the English garrison at Linlithgow uncomfortable.) On 17 July Colonel Robert Overton had been more successful than Monck (who, after all, had tried his luck in the middle of the winter). After crossing the Forth with 1,600 men in boats, he established himself at North Queensferry. But Leslie had not been unduly disturbed since Overton had so few men and they were a long way from Stirling. Three days later, however, Cromwell dispatched Lambert over the river with 3,500 men. Now Leslie was alarmed. While Cromwell himself demonstrated against Leslie's front, the Scottish general detached a force of about the same strength as that commanded by Lambert to beat back the enemy. In a fierce battle at Inverkeithing, twenty-five miles east of Stirling, Lambert won a superb victory. Four days later on 24 July Monck crossed the Firth to take the castle of Inchgarvie, which had long been a nuisance to English shipping in the river; the garrison escaped, but left behind sixteen guns and much ammunition. After another five days Burntisland, which Monck had twice vainly attempted to capture both during the winter and the spring, at last surrendered to him.[37]

Cromwell now himself carried the bulk of his army over the river and advanced on Perth, the seat of the Scottish Government, which capitulated on 2 August. King Charles II, who had been crowned at Scone on 1 January 1651 and later been appointed commander-in-chief of a united Scottish army, containing Royalists as well as Covenanters, had to decide between three courses. Either he would have to withdraw into the highlands since the communications of his army between Stirling and Perth had been cut; or he could move north and challenge Cromwell to battle; or he could take the road that had thus been opened to him and march from Stirling by way of Glasgow into north-west England, aiming to pick up recruits as he went. Cromwell was well aware of this possibility; he had taken all necessary precautions; he wrote to the English Parliament telling its members to keep cool; Lambert was sent ahead after the Scots with a cavalry army, Cromwell himself following later with the bulk of the infantry. George Monck was left behind to capture and garrison Stirling and subject Scotland to an English military occupation.

7

Subduing the Scots

After the surrender of Perth General Cromwell returned to Leith where he assembled most of his infantry and some of his cavalry, which had not gone ahead under Major-General Lambert, and prepared to follow King Charles II and his Scottish army into England. As he informed the Speaker in a dispatch on 4 August from Leith, he was leaving Lieutenant-General Monck with five or six thousand men to occupy Stirling; he expressed the hope that he had provided 'a commanding force' for Scotland.[1]

How big was this commanding force? Monck had at his disposal four cavalry regiments — those of James Berry, Edward Grosvenor, Robert Lilburne and John Okey. Okey's regiment had formerly consisted of dragoons (mounted infantry) who distinguished themselves at the battles of Naseby and Inverkeithing. In answer to Cromwell's request the English Parliament had consented to its conversion into a cavalry regiment. Besides that, Cromwell left behind five 'loose troops' of dragoons. Monck wanted these troops to be embodied into a regiment under the command of Thomas Morgan, a Welsh professional soldier who was to become one of his most faithful adjutants. Cromwell agreed to that; by October Morgan had eight troops in his regiment.

Monck also had no fewer than ten infantry regiments in his service: his own and those of Alured, Ashfield, Cobbett, Cooper, Daniel, Deane, Fenwick, Overton and Reade.[2] If the figure given by Cromwell to the Speaker was correct, all these regiments must have been greatly under strength, although it is possible that Cromwell did not include a number of men scattered around on garrison duties, for example at Perth. Even before Charles II's invasion of England was halted Cromwell told the Council of State that Monck needed 2,000 more men.[3] Although the Captain-General reiterated Monck's want of reinforcements it is doubtful if any were sent to Scotland before Charles II was conclusively defeated at the battle of Worcester on 3 September. Reinforcements were then hastened to Scotland by sea. It is known that by the beginning of January 1652 Cobbett's and Cooper's regiments each consisted of nearly 1,200 men, which was almost up to establishment.[4] So by then Monck had a sizeable army amounting perhaps to 12,000 officers and men.

Monck experienced no difficulty over taking the town of Stirling. At Kinross, twenty miles away, he gathered together four cavalry regiments, three infantry regiments, dragoons and an artillery train. This was a formidable force when it is remembered that most of the garrison of Stirling had marched with Charles II into England. When Monck threatened to storm the city, the town clerk hastened to capitulate, while such Scottish soldiers as remained there retired into the castle. In the city Monck found the Chair of State, the royal robes and public records, all of which he dispatched to London. The subjection of the castle took longer. Monck straightaway ordered platforms to be raised on which to place his batteries; four guns and two mortar pieces were brought to Stirling mainly by water. Monck had on his staff a German engineering expert, Joachim Hane, from Frankfurt-on-Oder, who first came to England in 1649.[5] According to a diary which described the siege of the castle,

[On 13 August] the mortar peeces were planted, and Mr Hane the engineer plaid with one of the mortar peeces twice. The second shot fell into the middle of the castle, and did much execution. Afterwards he plaid with the other great mortar peece and did execution.

Thereupon the Governor, who the day before had told Monck that he would keep the castle as long as he could, was compelled to surrender since his men, who were unaccustomed to mortar fire, threatened to mutiny.[6] The Governor and his soldiers were allowed to march out to beat of drum with lighted matches and such baggage as they had and go where they liked except to places garrisoned by the English army. They had to leave behind, however, all their guns and powder, thirty or forty barrels of beef and beer, 'and as many rundlets and vessels of claret wine'.[7]

Monck remained at Stirling for a week. Then, having appointed

Colonel Reade, whose regiment had taken part in the assault, to be governor of the castle and the town, Monck went to Perth. Here, with the best part of two infantry regiments, three cavalry regiments, two troops of dragoons, a mortar piece (one mortar piece was apparently lost when carried by boat on the Forth)[8] and three siege guns, together with food sufficient for ten days, he summoned St Andrews, a port lying fifteen miles to the south of Dundee, to surrender. On 25 August he and Colonel Overton crossed the Firth of Tay; next day Dundee was called upon to capitulate. Dundee was crowded not only with its own citizens but a number of people from Edinburgh and Stirling who had fled there with their valuables. As a rumour reached Dundee that the Scots in England had won a great victory, bonfires were lit and prayers of thanksgiving recited. The Governor of Dundee, Robert Lumsden, saucily answered the summons by commanding Monck to lay down his arms and enlist in the King's service.[9] Once again Monck ordered his artillery to fire and Hane plied his mortar. Before the Lieutenant-General prepared to storm the town — he was awaiting the return of Colonels Okey and Grosvenor who had been on a mission of reconnaissance forty miles north of the beleaguered city[10] — he accepted the surrender of St Andrews which was completely cut off from north and south. He fined the town £500 for refusing his first summons, and distributed it as a gratuity to his own soldiers.

On 1 September all was ready for the storming of Dundee. Breaches were made by the cannon both to the west and east of the city. It appears that it was also attacked from the sea; at any rate it is known that 200 English sailors took part in the assault.[11] Eight hundred Scottish soldiers and townsmen were killed by the English assailants who cried out as their watchword 'God with us', but when the market place was reached, quarter was given to the enemy. Five hundred prisoners were taken including the former Governor of Stirling. Monck allowed his men to plunder the town all day and night for twenty-four hours and they acquired substantial booty. But Monck's officers were annoyed because they learned that the ships which were lying in Dundee harbour were going to be sold by commissioners for the benefit of the English Commonwealth. These officers, so Monck informed the President of the Council of State, 'had no other prize, though their soldiers had booty by the plunder of the town'. Monck recommended that at any rate the officers who

were required to garrison the town should 'be given the encourage-
ment they need to stay there'.[12] Presumably they were pacified. The
day after Dundee had been stormed Monck ordered that all plundering must cease, that no houses should be rifled of their contents and
that the inhabitants were to be permitted to bury their dead. Ten
days later he had to publish another proclamation declaring that the
inhabitants of Dundee were in future to be protected from plunder
and violence and allowed to resume their normal lives. Three days
afterwards Monck signed yet a third proclamation forbidding
plundering and warning both soldiers and sutlers (camp followers
who sold food and cooked for the army) not to remove beer and wine
and other goods belonging to the citizens of Dundee, on peril of
being court-martialled and severely punished.[13]

Even before the siege of Dundee Monck had sent out various
parties to scour and reconnoitre other parts of the country. Major
Scott was sent south to Dumfries, an important town which lies on
an outlet from the Solway firth and is roughly equidistant from
Glasgow and Edinburgh; he killed and captured a number of
Scottish soldiers and occupied the town. Colonel Okey and Colonel
Grosvenor were ordered into the highlands. They reached a point
roughly forty miles north of Dundee whence they chased a contingent of Scottish cavalry commanded by the Earl of Balcarres into
the mountains. Earlier than this, Monck had sent two of his colonels
with a small but highly mobile force of troopers and dragoons into
the west of Scotland where, it was rumoured, a new army was being
raised for the king in Lanarkshire and Renfrew. In fact though they
got as far as Glasgow and Paisley and swept the neighbouring
countryside, they met with little resistance. They reported that they
had 'totally broken [the enemy's] levies'; taken the royal commissioners as prisoners; and also bagged fourteen Presbyterian ministers,
who were released when they swore that all they were intending to
do was to seek the Lord's advice as to whether or not they should
obey the orders of the General Assembly.[14]

After the loss of Stirling and Perth, members both of the Com-
mittee of Estates and of the General Assembly foregathered at
Alyth, fifteen miles north-west of Dundee. But these eminent
Scotsmen had carelessly failed to protect themselves with a military
outpost; consequently, during the night of 27 August Colonel
Alured, who had been sent there by Monck with 800 cavalry,

surprised the entire committee including the veteran General Alexander Leslie, Earl of Leven, the Earl Marshal of Scotland and the Earl of Crawford. They were taken prisoner and sent by Monck to London. With the capture of these noblemen and gentlemen and those that Cromwell had caught during and after the battle of Worcester most of the leading figures of Scotland were in English hands. The principal exceptions were the Earl of Loudoun, Chancellor of Scotland, his kinsman, the Marquis of Argyll, who could claim to be the uncrowned Covenanter king of the highlands, the Earl of Atholl, the Marquis of Huntly, the Earl of Weems, the Earl of Linlithgow and the Earl of Balcarres. The last five in time capitulated to the English commander-in-chief and disbanded their armed retainers. The Earl of Loudoun, whose duty it was to summon meetings of the Scottish Parliament, made conscientious and desperate efforts to rally a Scottish resistance movement. This was to be based on such members of the Committee of Estates, the Parliament and the General Assembly who had managed to evade capture.[15] But Loudoun, who first organized meetings in Angus, found that even the most patriotic Scotsmen were divided and dismayed after the English victories. The Marquis of Argyll, that squint-eyed pillar of his Church, was with difficulty persuaded to abandon the position of political isolation which he had wisely adopted, and joined Loudoun at Rothesay in the island of Bute off the west coast. They decided to call a meeting of Parliament at Finlarig at the western end of Loch Tay, where in the midst of mountains, woods and narrow passes, they believed they would be safe from surprise. However, the news of the defeat of the Scots army at Worcester caused the remaining Scottish leaders to lose heart; they refused to go to Finlarig, while Argyll attempted to make his own terms with Monck.

On 15 October Monck received a letter from Argyll in which he asked the Lieutenant-General 'as one having chief trust in this kingdome' if a meeting could be arranged between them.[16] Monck answered that he could not agree to such a conference without the permission of the English Parliament. It was clear enough that the governing authorities in Westminster, who had proclaimed a Commonwealth of the English, Scottish and Irish peoples, had no intention whatsoever of giving recognition to a Scottish Government, many of whose leaders, having fought for Charles II, were their prisoners. Argyll then said that he personally would submit to Monck, who sent him a pass to come to Perth with a retinue of not more than thirty armed servants to meet him there. But Argyll said he felt ill and never arrived; he was thought to be 'foxy'. Meanwhile, the meeting of the Scots Parliament, which Loudoun had summoned to gather at Loch Tay, was a complete fiasco. Monck handled the political situation gingerly; but it was clear to him that there was no prospect of the Scottish lowlanders and highlanders, who were at loggerheads with each other, raising a fresh army, as Loudoun had wanted to do, in order 'to stopp the prevalencies of the Enemie'.[17] The most he could hope to achieve was guerrilla warfare in the remoter parts of the north.

Gradually Monck extended his hold over Scotland. Aberdeen was occupied during the second week of September and Alured's regiment sent to garrison Montrose on the coast of Angus. After the battle of Worcester Monck was promised three more infantry regiments. One arrived in January 1652 and was used to garrison Dundee; a second did not arrive until June 1654; the third never reached Scotland at all.[18] So, broadly, Monck had to manage as best he could. One fresh infantry regiment was ordered at the beginning of October 1651 to leave Carlisle, where it was stationed, to join Monck; it was dispatched by him to Inverness under its colonel, Thomas Fitch, who found there were insufficient beds to go round. The regiment was accompanied by Joachim Hane who reported back to Monck that the town would be expensive to fortify and difficult to protect against the highlanders round Loch Ness. Nevertheless a garrison was kept there.[19] Okey's cavalry regiment was placed in the inland town of Forfar. From these points in Angus—Dundee, Montrose, Forfar—Monck felt sure that he could prevent any irruption from the highlands, but his men had to be on the alert all the time with their horses saddled at night ready to cope with any emergency. The gentlemen of Angus, not relishing the idea of a strong force of English soldiers being quartered on their county throughout the winter, offered to come to terms. Okey, acting on the authority of Monck, met the leading gentlemen of the shire at Brechin near Montrose. He promised them that if they would guarantee to be peaceable and pay their assessed taxes a substantial number of the English officers and men there would be withdrawn.[20] Soon after this Huntly and his Gordons and Balcarres, who had been responsible for the defence of northern Scotland against Monck, capitulated. By the beginning of 1652 most Scottish castles including Dumbarton, had surrendered while Colonel Overton successfully established a garrison in the Orkneys and later received assurances of tranquil behaviour from the inhabitants of the Shetlands. Thus within a period of six months Monck had subjugated, though he had not pacified, Scotland. He was also able to assure the Council of State in London that King Charles II, who escaped in disguise after his defeat at Worcester, was not back in Scotland. 'The young Lad', he wrote, might be in Holland or France, but he was certainly not in Scotland.[21]

During these months George Monck governed with a mixture of firmness and conciliation. It has been observed how after he had allowed one day's plundering of Dundee, he had published strict orders to protect the inhabitants from further rapine and violence. On the other hand, he insisted that they must notify the captain of the watch if any strangers came into the town being heavily fined were they to neglect this duty.[22] Courts martial were set up in Dundee by the middle of September to ensure that all Monck's instructions were obeyed. For robbing two Scotsmen near the town two soldiers in Colonel Berry's regiment were sentenced to thirty stripes each and were kept in prison on bread and water until they restored what they had stolen.[23] Two other soldiers were condemned 'to ride the wooden horse'* for a similar offence.[24] According to John Nicoll, a Scottish lawyer whose diary of those times has survived, fornicators were whipped and ducked into the sea and examples made of drunkards.[25] Proclamations were issued to protect native bakers and encourage native fishermen. As for the better-to-do Scots, Monck undertook to protect those who promised they would do nothing prejudicial to the Commonwealth of England. To give two examples: on 19 August Monck told his officers and men that Lady Carnigee of the Glem, together with her children, servants and tenants as well as her houses and her goods, were not to be molested.[26] On 21 October he gave similar protection to Sir Laurence Olyphant of Gash and his family, telling his officers and men that Sir Laurence might wear his sword while he and his family

---

* The condemned men were seated on a horse made of wood with a sharp ridged back, their hands tied behind them and muskets and weights on their feet.

were to be allowed to live and move about freely 'provided they do nothing prejudicial to the Commonwealth of England'.[27] He also permitted the Marquis of Huntly to take up residence in his house in Aberdeen and promised him that he would be put in possession of lands that had been taken from him by his kinsman, the elusive Marquis of Argyll.[28]

Consistently with his own earlier career Monck placed much emphasis on the necessity of using courts martial to discipline his own men; he set more store by them than by the imposition of oaths which, he said, should neither be tendered nor taken without specific orders from the English Government.[29] Though a strict disciplinarian, Monck looked after his men extremely well. A war tax or assessment of £120,000 a year was levied in Scotland — though it proved impossible to raise as much as that — out of which £20,000 a year was employed to provide necessities for the English soldiers.[30] To facilitate communications Monck asked that a wooden bridge should be constructed to span the Tay at Perth;[31] supply ships were ordered by him to come north from Newcastle in order to bring provisions to outlying garrisons, as, for example, Inverness.[32] He constantly badgered the authorities in England for money, food and clothing to keep his army in trim.

Clearly Monck did not care overmuch for the Presbyterian ministers who had been so powerful when the Covenanters under David Leslie were harassing Cromwell's army on the eve of Dunbar. It was said in a newsletter sent from Aberdeen in January 1652 that 'the Kirkmen', who were 'still stiffe' and spoke 'little for Peace and Truth from the Pulpits' regarded Monck and Overton as their 'great antagonists'.[33] When Sir Alexander Irvine, the Laird of Drum, was excommunicated on the ground that he was a papist serving a Scarlet Whore, he thought it worth his while to appeal to Monck for protection and fair treatment.[34]

Once Charles II had been defeated and Scotland had come under Monck's secure military control, the English Government appointed eight commissioners to examine the whole military, religious and economic situation in the country. This was with a view to bringing in an act of union between England and Scotland and, until this had been arranged, to settle the civil government of the country. Among the commissioners named were Major-General John Lambert, Major-General Richard Deane, Colonel George Fenwick, the new governor of Edinburgh, and of course Monck himself.[35] The civilians on the commission included Oliver St John and Sir Henry Vane the Younger, two of the most eminent members of the republican Council of State. The commissioners assembled in Scotland early in 1652. Lambert and Deane came to meet Monck in Dundee where it was decided that the war tax of 'sesse' should be reduced, presumably to sweeten Scottish tempers.[36] Then the officers journeyed to Burntisland where they joined other commissioners. Apart from the grievances over a high rate of assessment and a debased currency, the Scots suffered from the free quarter which had to be imposed to meet the needs of the army of occupation. Free quarter meant that the Scots were compelled to furnish food and billets for the English soldiers and that in return they only obtained promises that they should be paid for in the future. The commissioners insisted that money must be sent to meet these obligations at once; for were it delayed, they reported to the Speaker of the English Parliament, this would seriously impede the negotiations for union. Although Monck did not sign this letter, it can scarcely be doubted that it earned his approval. Finally, all the commissioners gathered at the Earl of Buccleuch's castle at Dalkeith, whence they published on 4 February a declaration on behalf of the English Commonwealth promising justice to the Scottish people provided that they repudiated Charles II as their king. Monck was among the signatories of the proclamation.[37]

Before they wound up their work at the end of April, the commissioners published on 12 February 1652 another declaration by the Parliament of England (which had been agreed to at Westminster on 28 October 1651 but kept secret since then) in favour of union with Scotland. This was proclaimed by beat of drum and sound of trumpet at the market cross in Edinburgh. It was announced that twenty-one Scottish deputies (fourteen from the shires and seven from the burghs) were to go to England to negotiate its exact terms. Four days later, Lambert and Monck left Scotland, though not together, Lambert because he had been appointed to succeed Cromwell's son-in-law, the late Henry Ireton, as Lord Deputy of Ireland; Monck, because he urgently wanted to go to Bath where he hoped the waters would improve his health.[38]

Monck had been taken ill immediately after the surrender of Dundee. A diarist who wrote about the siege stated that he had fallen very ill on 5 September. Writing to the Speaker a week later, William Clarke, a barrister who had become Monck's military secretary, said that his master had experienced 'a very desperate sickness' but by then he was hoped to be on the road to recovery. Later, however, he suffered a relapse, for he himself wrote to the Council of State at the end of October: 'the lameness in my knee doth continue, but I hope it will shortly go away'.[39] It was remarkable that with such bad health Monck was able not only to direct and conduct military operations but also to maintain order in his army and take part in the work of the commissioners. One can only speculate what might have gone wrong. Was it rheumatism or gout, as has been suggested? One would hardly have thought that they would have made him desperately ill. Possibly it was an attack of phlebitis which can disappear after a good rest. This would explain why he was 'cured' at Bath. Nothing very specific is known about Monck's movements after he left Scotland until he was ordered by Cromwell to strengthen the fortifications at Yarmouth during August after the outbreak of the first Anglo-Dutch war. He is known to have been in London during April because he was dining with a fellow officer, Colonel Edward Conway (Viscount Conway), who had served with him in Ulster, at his house in Kensington at the beginning of the month. Conway wrote to another friend of Monck's, Major George Rawdon, who was still in Ulster, to tell him that Monck was intending to go over to Ireland with Lambert, no doubt to inspect his properties there. Monck confided to Conway that he wanted to withdraw from the wars and to marry. Monck was thought by Conway to have some 'smackering' (hankering) after his uncle Edward Popham's widow, but there he must have been wrong; for next year Monck was to marry Anne Ratsford.[40] In May he seems to have returned to Scotland for a spell. At any rate a letter of his has survived giving instructions to all officers and men to allow a certain George Ogilvy to reside at St Andrews in Fife 'without molestation'.[41] If he did return to Scotland in May, he did not stay long, for in July the Council of State petitioned Cromwell to send him back to Scotland; but he can hardly have done so or been asked to do so by Cromwell, for Major-General Richard Deane, who had taken over Monck's duties when he left Scotland in February, is known to have been in charge there during the summer and autumn of 1652.

Although Monck's first tour of independent duty in Scotland thus lasted only just over six months, his administration must have impressed both General Cromwell and the English Council of State. His handling of the task of putting a rapid end to organized Scottish resistance had been masterly. His capture of key towns and castles deprived the remaining Scottish Royalists of viable centres in which they could rally their men. The Marquis of Huntly and the Earl of Balcarres, as has been seen, were obliged to recognize their own military impotence and to disband their followers. The only possible place left where operations against the English republicans might still be planned was in the extreme north of the highlands. But by his garrisoning of Inverness and the Orkneys Monck made that very difficult. Indeed as early as October 1651 the information he received at Dundee was that despite rumours the enemy was 'not stirring in the highlands'.[42] Monck's coup in sending a force to surprise the Scots leaders at Alyth bore witness to the quality of his intelligence service and his power of decision. The discipline that he imposed on his men was of a high order, though he sympathized with their needs when they were stationed far from their homes. Finally, he handled the Scots with both resolution and tact. All this was a presage of what he was able to do when two years later Cromwell, as Lord Protector, asked him to go back to become military ruler of Scotland. But before then he was to enhance his military reputation as a general-at-sea.

8

General-at-Sea

The first war between England and the Dutch Republic broke out almost spontaneously in the summer of 1652.[1] Its causes were quarrels over the right of search exercised by the English navy, which refused to accept the view that a neutral flag covered enemy goods moved by sea unless they were contraband; over the envy felt by some English tradesmen and merchants and all English fishermen about Dutch dominance in industry, shipping, marketing and commerce; and over Dutch annoyance that the Rump Parliament had in 1651 passed a navigation act deliberately aimed against their carrying trade. Questions of prestige were also involved. When in a confused conflict that arose near Dover in May 1652 an English admiral, Robert Blake, had clashed with a Dutch squadron under Martin van Tromp, shots were exchanged and two Dutch ships captured; the danger of war, about which neither side was enthusiastic, loomed up. Oliver Cromwell, who was by then the most influential figure in England, in particular wanted to avoid a contest between two Protestant republics; yet he upheld the action by Blake who was generally considered in England to have been the victim of unprovoked aggression. In the following month Blake was ordered to seize Dutch merchantmen and fishing boats as a reprisal; at the end of the month Dutch ambassadors, who had come over to London to negotiate a treaty of alliance, were withdrawn; and on 8 July war was officially declared.

The English object in the war was to weaken their enemies by attacking their merchant shipping; many prizes were taken, for although convoys protected by escorts were arranged, the Dutch were extremely vulnerable since ships sailing to France, Portugal and Spain or making for the Atlantic had to go through the English Channel

97

unless they took the long route round the north of Scotland. On the other hand, the Dutch who had a large navy of at least 150 warships, believed that the quickest way to win the war was to inflict a telling defeat on the English navy. It was feared in London that the Dutch might even try to land an armed force in East Anglia. That, no doubt, was why Cromwell as commander-in-chief instead of sending Monck back to Scotland ordered him to inspect and reinforce the defences of Yarmouth, a port likely to be attacked by the Dutch.[2] By then Tromp, who had sailed north with the aim of fighting Blake, who was lying in wait for the arrival of a Dutch mercantile fleet from the East Indies, had lost many of his warships in terrible storms off the east coast of Scotland. When he eventually limped back to the Texel in early September 'very melancholy, without shooting a gun or wearing a flag' he handed in his resignation and was replaced by Admirals de With and de Ruyter. But they were defeated by Blake at the battle of the Kentish Knock, after which Tromp was recalled and in turn got the better of Blake in the battle of Dungeness on 28 November whereupon the English admiral also offered his resignation. He knew by then that the Council of State had appointed two other generals-at-sea to command with him — Richard Deane and George Monck — and innocently observed that as 'two such able gentlemen' had been added to take charge of the navy he would like to 'spend the remainder of his days in private retirement and prayers for a blessing upon you and the nation'.[3]

However, Blake was not permitted to resign in order to devote himself to prayer, for the English Government was anxious to do everything it could think of to strengthen the navy. A new admiralty committee was set up in which the leading spirit was Sir Henry Vane, the former Treasurer of the Navy.[4] The rate of the property tax, or assessment, the yield from which had previously been assigned to the army was raised so that it could help support the navy as well.

Monck's biographers have sometimes thought that it was curious that at the age of forty-five he was suddenly transmuted into an admiral. But no one thought so at the time. Blake was admittedly one of the twelve children of a Somersetshire shipowner and may well have been at sea when young, but during the first civil war he had fought on land; it was not until he was in his forties that he was given his first naval command. Richard Deane's experience of naval warfare was also slight; and it may be recalled that as a boy George

Monck had taken part in two amphibious operations. But undoubtedly the main reason for his appointment was that, like Deane,
he had won a reputation as an artillery expert. The cannon employed
at sea was identical with that used on land. The days of grappling
and boarding were over. Warships were mobile artillery units, not
cavalry chargers. Finally, it is conceivable that the Council of State
had in mind the possibility of a landing on the coast of Holland in
which case Monck's military experience would be invaluable.

The admiralty committee established by the Rump Parliament
on 10 December was small, efficient and energetic; it consisted of
four members of parliament, two experts on naval affairs and the
three generals-at-sea, who in practice rarely attended its meetings.
Monck, however, took part in five sessions between 17 December
when the committee set to work and the end of the year.[5] It is
reasonable to assume that strategy as well as the provision of men,
money and supplies for the navy was discussed. In January 1653
Monck was at Chatham where he met Blake for the first time.[6] It
was agreed that a fleet should be put to sea as soon as possible with a
view to intercepting Tromp, who was known to be off the west
coast of France at La Rochelle where he was waiting to escort a large
number of merchant ships back to Holland. Everything was done to
recruit crews, collect beer and food and make good the damage done
off Dungeness. A new naval establishment was drawn up; Monck
and the other generals-at-sea were paid £3 a day.[7] The pay of able-
bodied seamen was increased from nineteen to twenty-four shillings
a week. That was essential because otherwise the best sailors preferred to serve on privateers or merchantmen. To help the sailors,
and possibly in the hope of being able to land a marauding force
somewhere in the United Netherlands, a thousand soldiers were
embarked on the warships. Originally, perhaps on Monck's suggestion, it was intended to enlist men disbanded from regiments in
Scotland. But it was thought wiser to use disciplined men from
Cromwell's and Richard Ingoldsby's infantry regiments, both
quartered in London, to act as marines. At the end of January 1653
the three Generals were ordered to put to sea; on 8 February they
foregathered at the Swin near the mouth of the Thames. Thence
they moved on to the Isle of Wight; Blake and Deane were in joint
command of the Red or central squadron, Vice-Admiral William
Penn was put in charge of the Blue or vanguard squadron, while

Monck commanded the White or rear squadron. Their aim was to fight Tromp and capture the Dutch merchantmen as they returned from France through the English Channel.

What followed in the third week of February 1653 was a game of hide-and-seek. Tromp, who was favoured by a wind blowing from the north-west, circled round the Scillies and then, instead of hugging the French coast, sailed along the English coast hoping that the advantage of the weather gauge and the size of his fleet and the numerous merchantmen it escorted would hamper the English from coming out of their ports to attack him. However, when he reached a point a few miles from Portland he was surprised to discover a formidable English fleet strung out westwards off the Isle of Wight. Tromp had seventy or eighty warships and some 150 to 200 merchantmen to protect. The English had fewer warships but many of them were bigger and better gunned. Having been caught out, Tromp had no alternative but to fight his way through. Penn's squadron was ahead of that of Blake and Deane while their Vice-Admiral, John Lawson, in the Red squadron lay about a mile to their rear. Monck with the White squadron was some distance to the south when the battle began at ten o'clock on the morning of 18 February.

Both sides prepared for battle.[8] Tromp hoped to annihilate the English fleet so as to get his merchantmen safely home; Blake and Deane, though at the beginning greatly outnumbered, refused to retire, since if they did, they would have had to leave it solely to their frigates to catch up with the convoy. The two Generals, therefore, determined to battle it out until their other squadrons could reinforce them. During the first phase of the action Tromp attempted to disable the English ships under Blake and Deane by firing broadsides at their sails and rigging, while their enemy was aiming at the Dutch hulls. When de Ruyter came up, the intention was that his squadron would cut off Lawson and thus help to grip Blake as in a vice. But the Dutch reckoned without George Monck. As soon as he heard the distant cannonade he made for the sound of the gunfire. Although the wind was against him, he forced his way forward and by noon was attacking de Ruyter from the rear. His fresh and undamaged ships were thrown pell-mell into the battle where the captain of his flagship the *Vanguard* and thirty of his crew were killed or wounded, but the Dutch losses were more severe. At four o'clock in the afternoon Tromp broke off the fight. The night was spent by the English in repairing the damage to rigging and masts and transferring men from weaker to stronger ships. Only one warship had been lost as compared with five Dutch. Blake, realizing that the fortunes of war had changed, sent out his fastest frigates to attack and seize the merchantmen that Tromp had left to his rear. Learning of this, Tromp resolved next day to push his convoy ahead while he fought a delaying action to safeguard them.

The battle was therefore resumed on 17 February, south of the Isle of Wight. But Dutch morale was low and their ammunition was giving out. They lost another five warships that day, but owing to a calm the heavier English vessels were slow to move into action. During the following night, Tromp steered up the Channel with his ships' lights aglow as he shepherded the convoy ahead. The wind blowing west-north-west, the English were able to give chase to Tromp. On 20 February a running fight took place; the English found themselves three and a half leagues from France and enjoying the advantage of the weather gauge. That night Monck and his colleagues were assured that as the tide and the wind were both against Tromp, he could not possibly round Cap Gris Nez to reach his home ports. They believed that their enemy was trapped and that the convoy could be annihilated. The night grew pitch dark and a gale blew up. The three English Admirals reported that

> if it had pleased the Lord in his wise providence who sets bounds to the sea and overrules the ways and actions of men, that it had been but three hours longer to night we had probably made an interposition between them [the Dutch] and home, whereby they must have been forced to have made their way through us with their men-of-war, which at this time were not above thirty-five as we could count, the rest being destroyed or dispersed.[9]

But Providence was on the side of Tromp; showing magnificent seamanship he reached home safely. Nevertheless, Monck and his colleagues could claim they had destroyed seventeen or eighteen warships (though no doubt this was an exaggeration) and that they had captured six prizes; they had also lost fewer warships and men than their foe.

Dr Gumble remarked that Monck had been asked 'to try his

Skill by Water, a new Trade for an old Commander to learn' and relates that on one occasion when his officers had advised him not to stand up to the enemy because of danger from fireships, he had retorted that 'the very powder of the guns of his ship would be able to blow a fireship from it'.[10] Possibly that was an invented anecdote, but undoubtedly his knowledge of gunnery stood him in good stead. He was blooded in the battle of Portland where he had instinctively marched to the sound of the guns. Blake's modern biographer has told us that George Monck, by leading his fresh ships straight into the thick of the fight, had turned seeming defeat into definite victory.[11]

After the triumph near Portland the English navy returned to home ports to lick its wounds. Until more sailors had been recruited, repairs carried out on warships, and stores and supplies collected it was not possible to send a big fleet to sea. Robert Blake had been wounded in the battle and was also taken ill probably with some kind of influenza. So Monck and Deane were in charge at Portsmouth. Monck at once showed his administrative ability; he told the Admiralty Committee firmly what was needed. The chief difficulty was over obtaining recruits to replace men who had been killed or wounded. Proper hospital facilities were lacking; many sailors had not been paid off, but merely given tickets (promises to pay); some of them went to London to badger the navy commissioners. Desperate measures were taken to find men; some were seized from merchant ships after they had come to port; the Council of State stopped granting licences to privateers; yet even the press gangs could find few or no able-bodied seamen on the Thames-side. That was hardly surprising when sailors were in arrears with their pay, poorly treated—even the beer was often undrinkable—and given no guarantee of continuous employment.

While delayed in Portsmouth Monck raised the question of naval tactics; he had been astonished by the fighting at the battle of Portland—*mêlée* fighting, as it was called, in which no real control over the battle was maintained and each ship's captain haphazardly picked out his own targets. On 29 March the three Generals published instructions for the better ordering of the fleet.[12] These stated that, 'on sight of the enemy fleet the Vice-Admiral and Rear-Admiral are to make what sail they can to come up to the Admiral on each wing ... As soon as they shall see the General engage they can engage with the enemy next to them.' When the general (i.e. admiral) hoisted a red flag at the main-top mizen of his flagship or was seen to be engaging the enemy, all ships of every squadron must try to get in line with him. In other words, the ships were to keep in a line bearing parallel to the line of the enemy before they fired their broadsides at the enemy ship opposite them. These instructions were by no means easy to carry out in practice, but they aimed at ordered instead of *mêlée* fighting.

Blake's latest biographer believes that these instructions originated in 'the alert and adaptable mind' of Monck who, unlike his two colleagues, had led an army in the field.[13] Although published under the name of all three Generals, only Monck and Deane actually signed them on board the *Triumph*, the flagship of the Red squadron, for Blake was ill ashore; but he may have been consulted. On the day after the instructions were issued Monck and Deane ordered Vice-Admiral Penn to lead his squadron to London where he could dispose of the prizes captured from the Dutch convoy, leave 'lame ships' for repair, and collect reinforcements and powder.[14] After that he was to patrol the North Sea looking for more Dutch ships as prizes and he was to arrange the escort of English coal-ships from Newcastle upon Tyne to London.

That was all that could be done immediately. Meanwhile, Monck and Deane continued to press the Admiralty Committee for urgent necessities. They protested against the idea of dispatching more warships to the Mediterranean, arguing that the Dutch East Indian vessels could be better dealt with after they had come through the straits of Gibraltar before being met by a Dutch escort. They complained because only two warships were available to reinforce Penn.[15] However, at length provisions and other supplies began to arrive at Portsmouth. As it happened, Tromp who had his own kind of difficulties, and Monck and Deane put to sea about the same time, in the first week of May. The Dutch admiral's plan was first to sail up the North Sea as far as Bergen in Norway in order to protect Dutch merchantmen coming home from the Baltic and then, when he had been reinforced by two of his vice-admirals, to try once again to defeat the English fleet.

Monck and Deane reached Dover on 2 May and then sailed north first to the Texel where, having missed Tromp, they continued north-west as far as Aberdeen on the Scottish coast and the Orkneys beyond. Failing to find the Dutch fleet, they turned back south, warning the Admiralty Committee *en passant* that they would have to return to port within two months unless supplied with more food and water.[16] Once again a game of hide-and-seek was played. While Tromp anchored near the North Foreland and his two vice-admirals remained within the Goodwins looking for a battle off the Downs, Monck and Deane had again sailed towards the Dutch coast. Then hearing that Tromp had been seen off the English coast, they doubled back across the North Sea to reach Southwold bay by 1 June.

Next day the Dutch were sighted.[17] Tromp had ninety warships, the English 105 divided between the Blue squadron under Vice-Admiral Lawson, the White under Vice-Admiral Penn and the Red under Monck and Deane; Blake, though still far from well, had reached the Gunfleet and thence sailed out with thirteen ships to join the others. The battle began at eleven o'clock on 2 June within two miles of the south head of the Gabbard shoal. Deane and Monck had resolved that instead of closing with the Dutch they would attack them with long-range broadsides since the English guns were heavier and could fire farther than those of the enemy. Many of the Dutch ships were badly damaged, but at three o'clock in the afternoon, Lawson, disobeying his orders, closed with the Dutch. Lawson's squadron was on the portside of Monck and after the wind had changed in their favour de Ruyter and Tromp tried to drive a gap between them. Here was the crisis of the battle. Seven of Lawson's ships were seriously damaged. When Monck and Deane, aboard the *Resolution,* came to Lawson's aid they were surrounded and fiercely fired upon. Deane, standing at Monck's side, was killed by chain-shot. Monck threw his cloak over the body and then ordered that it should be carried below so that the crew of the flag-ship should not be demoralized. So Monck was left in sole command. It did not take him long to turn the scales when he was joined by the White squadron under Penn. First he managed to regain the wind and counter-attacked. As evening approached the Dutch fleet drew off, chased as long as it was light by English frigates. Writing at six o'clock on the next morning, Monck reported that the Dutch had lost four warships at no cost to himself. He added that 'it hath pleased the Lord to take away Major-General Deane, an honest and able servant of the Commonwealth.'[18]

The battle was resumed at noon on the next day. Reluctantly Monck agreed to abandon his new tactics which might have accounted for the rashness of Lawson. It was ordered that the ships should sail abreast with Monck in the centre. On 3 June the action lasted for four hours and ended with Monck chasing the Dutch as far as Ostend. Blake was once again with him; but in a letter to Oliver Cromwell Blake gave Monck the honour of signing the dispatch before him, thus conferring on him the credit for the victory at the Gabbard.[19] The Dutch had lost some twenty ships in one way or another; the English lost no ships, but twelve were damaged. It was a telling battle.

Tromp had retired with the bulk of his remaining warships into the Wielings to the south-west of the United Netherlands at the mouth of the Scheldt where the English dared not follow them. It was therefore decided to institute a blockade while employing the faster frigates to harass the Dutch carrying trade. In this Blake and Monck were successful for about a month, but then inclement weather and shortage of food, munitions and other supplies compelled them to return to Southwold bay to repair and restock their ships. Here Blake was again taken ill; according to a Royalist story. Monck 'gaped after the absolute command'; that sounds fanciful as he and Blake had been on most friendly terms, but in all forms of warfare there is a lot to be said for a single commander. At any rate George Monck made excellent use of his opportunity. In mid-July he planned to set off again to renew the blockade of the Dutch coast, firing off as he did so a series of memoranda to the Admiralty Committee about his need for food and water and beer that was not defective.[20] At first, contrary winds forced him to anchor two leagues off the Texel, but by 27 July he had gathered his whole fleet before the Texel, no injury having been done to his vessels by the foul weather.

Two days before this Tromp at last led out his fleet from the Wielings, aiming to join up with another Dutch fleet under de With which was stationed in the Texel. At first a south-west wind was helpful to Tromp and as he had learnt from his scouts of the presence of Monck's fleet off the Texel he was intent on battle. On the morning of 29 July the wind changed and blew from the north-west which tempted Monck to move against Tromp, as he had been informed by his reconnaissance units that the Dutch admiral had come out from the shelter of the Wielings. After the wind changed Tromp tacked and turned back south, Monck following him. By doing so Tromp enabled de With to come out from the Texel. But as Monck's force outnumbered the combined Dutch fleets he welcomed the chance to fight. At about five o'clock in the afternoon his leading frigates had brought Tromp into action; the main fleets did not engage till six o'clock; then Tromp started to sail southward drawing Monck away from the Texel. When night approached, the engagement was broken off. Next morning the gales were so fierce that the fight could not be resumed — Monck himself described it as 'thick and dirty weather' — [21] but Tromp had taken advantage of the night to tack again turning back north so that he not only gained the advantage of the wind, but was able to interpose his warships between Monck and the Texel.

On 31 July the winds abated, but what there were favoured Tromp. He therefore decided to attack, himself falling upon Monck's van and right wing, de Ruyter assaulting the left, and de With engaging the rear. The battle began at seven in the morning, Tromp still having the weather gauge. Now again in sole charge, Monck insisted on 'line ahead' instead of *mêlée* fighting. He himself aboard his flagship the *Resolution*, tacked with the aim of penetrating the Dutch line and securing the weather gauge, but was unable to do more than cut off a few Dutch ships. Twice both sides tacked and passed each other firing their broadsides. A bloody battle developed which continued for five hours. During that time Tromp was killed on board his flagship by a musket ball; his last words are said to have been: 'I have finished my course, have good courage.'[22] De Ruyter drew off some of his shattered vessels to Goeree and de With retired into the Texel with the bulk of the remaining fleet, blaming the defeat on the poltroonery of his captains. The Dutch lost about ten ships, but many others were severely damaged. Casualties on both sides were heavy; Monck is known to have had about a thousand killed and wounded, apart from the sick. In reporting to the Council of State 'how great and wonderful the Lord hath been' he claimed to have destroyed eight out of the nine Dutch flagships.[23] When he wrote his dispatch on the evening of 31 July his frigates were still chasing the Dutch warships as they drew off into the Texel. He did not yet know that his great adversary was dead.

The price that Monck had to pay for his victory was considerable.

A council of war over which he presided after the battle decided that the fleet must return to Southwold bay so that damaged warships could be repaired, wounded men cared for and provisions obtained.[24] Monck continued to bombard the Admiralty Committee about the poor quality of the beer;[25] he also took an active interest in the treatment of the wounded and compensation for widows of his men who had been killed. He himself was rewarded by the Assembly of Saints with a gold chain worth £300 in recognition of his services.

While much of the fleet was still refitting Monck sent Vice-Admiral Lawson with forty-five ships, which were later reinforced, to the Texel with the object of seizing Dutch merchant vessels. He himself joined Lawson with eighteen ships on the last day of August hoping to surprise de With. Owing to a false report that de With had sailed to the Baltic and because it was thought that his own larger warships might be damaged by the autumn gales, Monck, on the advice of his officers, returned to the east coast leaving only frigates to interfere with Dutch commerce. Thus Monck missed an opportunity; for soon after he left the Texel, de With and his fleet came out to escort over 300 merchant ships to Norway.

When Monck returned to England he sent all his bigger ships to the docks as only the lighter ships (fifth- and sixth-rates) could be employed as a winter guard.[26] He concentrated his energies on arranging for the refitting of the other warships and for recruiting more sailors so that the whole fleet should be ready for action in the following spring. He complained about a decision that had been taken in London to remove an embargo that had earlier been placed on English merchantmen going to sea because it made it more difficult to man the fleet as mariners were better treated and rewarded on them than they were in the navy.[27] Since however the larger ships were being laid up for the winter and foreign trade was beginning to become part of England's lifeblood, Monck had not much of a case for retaining the embargo. Moreover, his own sailors were in a mutinous frame of mind because they had not been paid off at the end of their voyages, and because some of them had been kept at sea longer than was necessary so as to avoid their having to be given their due.

In October Monck travelled up to Whitehall to see Cromwell and to receive the thanks of the self-named Parliament. This was a critical moment in Oliver's life. For the Assembly of Saints (or Nominated Parliament) which he and his officers had chosen to rule the country, had proved a disappointment to him as being too radical and reformist, 'flying at liberty and property' as he claimed. Already John Lambert was planning a written constitution with Oliver as Lord Protector of the Commonwealth. George Monck had not shown any enthusiasm for the Assembly of Saints; the letter which he signed on 22 April together with General Deane and all the captains at Spithead, merely said that they thought it was their duty to continue their service at sea under the new regime.[28] Both he and Blake had been chosen members of the Assembly; Blake, who was now on the road to recovery after a spell of convalescence at Bath, certainly attended one or two meetings. On 1 October the Commons journals recorded that

> General Monck, one of the Admirals at Sea, came this Day into the House and took his Place as a Member. The Speaker by order of the House gave the thanks of Parliament for his great and faithful Services to the Parliament and the Commonwealth.[29]

No evidence has been discovered that he attended any other meetings although the House was then discussing union with Scotland on which his advice would have been of value.

When Monck was in London sailors stationed on the Thamesside demonstrated because their tickets had not been paid off. Monck met them in Whitehall, struck their leader with his sword and persuaded or forced them to retire. That did not mean that he was unsympathetic about their grievances, quite the contrary. Cromwell, who was with him at the time, must have admired his firmness. When he dined with Cromwell, according to Dr Gumble, the commander-in-chief placed the gold chain round his neck. It may be doubted if the ceremony impressed the poverty-stricken sailors when they heard of it.[30]

At that time Cromwell was receiving letters twice a week from Robert Lilburne, who since Monck and Deane had joined the navy, was acting as military governor of Scotland, to the effect that 'the Lord is exercising us with trials' and that 'the country was false to us' and complying with the Royalists.[31] It was plain that Robert had bitten off more than he could chew—his brother the Leveller leader, Freeborn John, would have been importuning Whitehall more vehemently—and was looking for sympathy and advice. On 2 December Monck and Blake had their commissions renewed and were joined by William Penn, now a proved naval commander, and John Desborough, an expert in administrative organization, as generals-at-sea. Since Blake had seemingly recovered in health, Oliver Cromwell, appointed Lord Protector on 16 December after a bloodless political coup, decided that Monck could be spared to return to Scotland. On 17 January 1654 George Monck left the fleet to prepare for his new and different duties.[32]

9

Monck's Defeat
of the
Scottish Royalists

What had been happening in Scotland while Monck was at sea? At first all had gone forward smoothly enough. Richard Deane was left with an army made up of eleven infantry and seven cavalry regiments. His main task was to pacify the country and to reduce the highlands to obedience. A certain amount of mopping up had to be done; for example, the island of Arran was occupied by a small garrison while on 26 May 1652 Dunnottar castle, which faced the North Sea roughly half way between Montrose and Aberdeen, contained Charles II's crown, sceptre and other treasures and was his last remaining stronghold, surrendered to Colonel Morgan. In the following month Deane sent Colonel Lilburne and Colonel Ashfield into the northern highlands 'to level ... those lofty montaneers'[1] and he himself visited Inverary where the Marquis of Argyll lived. An agreement was reached between him and Argyll who undertook to accept the authority of the English Commonwealth and in return received a guarantee of all his estates and properties.[2] When Deane left Scotland to join the navy at the end of the year it was said that 'all things at present are in a strange kind of hush'.[3]

But Robert Lilburne, who succeeded Deane as commander-in-chief, was soon to be faced with new problems. Lilburne, who came from a remarkable family of country gentlemen in Durham, can be described as a left-winger in politics. He had signed the death warrant of Charles I and was an enthusiastic Anabaptist. After acting as colonel of foot in the New Model Army he distinguished himself as a cavalry commander in the Preston campaign, for which he was awarded lands in Scotland valued at £300. He now had to cope with reviving Royalist activity in the highlands for which, he complained, he possessed inadequate resources.

Two reasons may be given for this, both deriving from the Anglo-Dutch war. The first was that the attention of the changing authorities in London was distracted from Scotland; the second was that Charles II hoped to induce the Dutch, since they were at war with the Commonwealth, both to occupy the Orkneys and to provide money and arms to stimulate a revival of the Stuart cause in the highlands. In June Charles received a message from the highland chieftains that they were willing to resume the war on his behalf.[4] The King appointed John Middleton to be his lieutenant-general in Scotland. While Middleton was scraping around for money, ships and supplies, Charles invited the Earl of Glencairne to take temporary charge there. In July the highlanders had virtually declared war on Lilburne; several leading Scottish Royalists, including the Earl of Atholl and Lord Kenmure, promised to take part in an insurrection, while Argyll's son and heir, Lord Lorne, also adhered to the Stuart cause, though his father kept to his undertakings, even though Lilburne suspected him of 'juggling'.[5]

By August 1653 Lilburne was convinced of the reality of the danger; he asked for cavalry reinforcements and for ships to guard the coast. Though he had an army of nearly 15,000 men, he did not have enough to invade the highlands, sustain the garrisons scattered throughout the land and to suppress the moss-troopers who again began harassing the lowlands. Worried by the fact that the Presbyterian ministers regularly offered up prayers for the King and regarding them as 'trumpets of sedition', Lilburne forcibly dissolved the General Assembly of the Kirk, which had met with his acquiescence in Edinburgh during July, because he feared that the ministers would resuscitate Scottish nationalism.[6] That may be described as an error of judgment, for it only provoked the lowlanders. By the end of the year Lilburne became extremely depressed, grumbling about shortages of troops and shipping and insufficient money to pay such men as he had. He more or less asked to be replaced by a new commander-in-chief and said 'Mee thinkes Monke's spirit would doe well amongst them.'[7] That was why Cromwell had ordered Monck to leave the fleet, although he was not to receive his official appointment in Scotland until 8 April 1654.[8]

During his last months in office Lilburne offered suggestions which were to bear fruit under Monck. He expressed his belief that once the Protectorate was proclaimed in Scotland and an Act of

Union and of Pardon passed, all would be well.[9] He thought that prompt pay for his soldiers and employment of honest Scotsmen for intelligence purposes might help to do the trick.[10] One cannot help but commiserate with this decent and conscientious man. He felt that he had been a pure drudge in Scotland for four years. All he was anxious about was that he should be given a less onerous post.[11] He was in fact to be appointed governor of York, in which capacity he was to be in opposition to Monck later in our story.

When April came Cromwell addressed George Monck as 'our right trusty and well-beloved colonel, lieutenant of the ordnance and one of the generals at sea', and named him 'commander-in-chief of the army and forces in Scotland', giving him 'full power to rule, govern and command against rebels and enemies of the public peace.'[12] He was instructed 'to inform himself of the state of the country', particularly the highlands; he was also

> to protect the preaching of the Gospel and true religion; to imprison the disobedient and to favour the friendly; to issue proclamations, to collect money from the Customs, prevent crimes and disorders, to levy fines, and order officers back to their duties if absent for three months; and not to allow more than two colonels to be absent at the same time.[13]

Thus his authority was more extensive than that of Lilburne; indeed it owed something to Lilburne's suggestions to Cromwell. When Monck was on his way to Dalkeith, where Lilburne had his headquarters, he was reported to have said 'that he could live with any but Remonstrants and Protesters in Scotland [that is to say the unrepentant Presbyterian nationalists] and that he had a commission to burn and destroy wheresoever the highlands are resettled'.[14] If that really was what he said, he must have changed his mind later when he discovered that the Remonstrants were more favourable to the Commonwealth than their opponents, the Resolutioners.

In fact while Monck was making for Scotland the situation for the English army brightened somewhat. Colonel Morgan advanced from Aberdeen and reached the head of the Cromarty firth, having crossed the waterline which flows south-westwards cutting off the northern highlands from the rest of the country. Here he routed a Royalist force commanded by Glencairne, killing about 120 of them and took 27 prisoners, while soon after Colonel Daniel caught another Royalist force farther south at Dunkeld in Perthshire, once the capital of Scotland, taking 119 prisoners. Argyll in Inverary refused to support the Royalist campaign and at the end of March the northern counties of Caithness and Sutherland were reported to be quiet. But Lilburne continued to harp on his need for more money and men. Putting Monck in the picture in a letter which he wrote from Dalkeith on 21 January,[15] Lilburne said that his soldiers were badly in arrears with their pay, that there was even some disorder in Monck's own regiment and because of this and that, more gunpowder, backs, breasts and pots were needed; in the same letter he recommended that William Clarke should be continued as military secretary, for he had served him and Deane well. He also served posterity well because owing to the careful way in which he collected and preserved his documents we know almost everything that was to happen during Monck's resumed tenure in Scotland.

Monck took over from Lilburne on 22 April, about seven weeks after Middleton landed in Sutherland to rally the highlanders on behalf of King Charles II. Apart from his own capacities Monck possessed several advantages which Lilburne had never enjoyed. In the first place the Anglo-Dutch war had drawn towards its close, the peace of Breda being agreed to on 5 April; Monck had understandably written to Lambert to say that he hoped the news of the peace would 'tame these wild people'.[16] Secondly, a week later Cromwell as Protector and the Council of State at last promulgated four ordinances affecting Scotland of which the most significant were an ordinance of pardon and grace and an ordinance for uniting England and Scotland in one Commonwealth. From the ordinance of pardon and grace twenty-four Royalists were excepted, their estates being confiscated while seventy-three other Royalists were fined. The ordinance for union provided that Scotland was to be represented by thirty members in the Protectorate Parliament at Westminster when it met. On 4 May Monck was able to publish a proclamation offering a free pardon to all Royalists who surrendered within twenty days and a reward of £200 to anyone who killed or captured John Middleton.[17] The Protectorate was proclaimed in Scotland at the same time; until these various proclamations could be issued political conditions remained rather chaotic; Lilburne had long stressed the need for such a settlement. Lastly, Monck benefited from the fact that Morgan had by the time of his arrival already defeated Glencairne and thus given discouragement to Middleton.

Immediately after he took over his command, Monck wrote to Cromwell saying that he found the insurrections more 'universal' than he had expected. He pressed the Lord Protector, as Lilburne had done, for the provision of more money to pay his forces, and to meet the arrears, for additional regiments — particularly cavalry — and for the assistance of warships and supply vessels.[18] He emphasized that fortifications cost money and that he needed not only trained soldiers but surgeons, farriers and saddlers.[19] He also sent Lambert a list of officers in England who were absent from their duties. As soon as the Proctectorate had been proclaimed, the ordinance of union announced, and the ordinance of pardon and grace published in Edinburgh, Monck informed Cromwell that it was his intention to take the offensive. Morgan had reported that Middleton had an army of 4,000 men, which outnumbered his own force. Monck's plan was to join Morgan and to prevent Middleton from marching south.

The strategy was, as Monck told Cromwell, first to prevent the Royalists either in the west or in the north from penetrating into the lowlands and then to advance into the highlands to deal with Middleton.[20] In a letter dated 25 April he told the Protector that his first step would be to go to Stirling and then 'to draw the forces from Glasgow up to the passes, to make little redoubts and block up fords' so as to prevent the enemy horse from penetrating between the highlands and lowlands. After that, as soon as the grass had grown sufficiently to feed his horses, he would move over the hills to fight the enemy.[21]

By the middle of May Monck was in Stirling ready to begin his campaign. First he advanced west to Kilsyth and then changed direction and made for Balloch to the south of Loch Lomond where he destroyed all the boats in the loch. That stopped Glencairne, who was now at Dumbarton, from moving north and establishing himself in Argyllshire. Like Lilburne, Monck relied on the Marquis of Argyll's neutrality to prevent Royalist activities developing in the west of the highlands. By the end of May Monck was back in Stirling whence he hoped to go first to Perth and then effect a junction with Colonel Morgan. Morgan had withdrawn from his most northerly position, partly because he believed that Middleton outnumbered him, to Dingwall on Cromarty firth.

114

Scotland when Monck was commander-in-chief

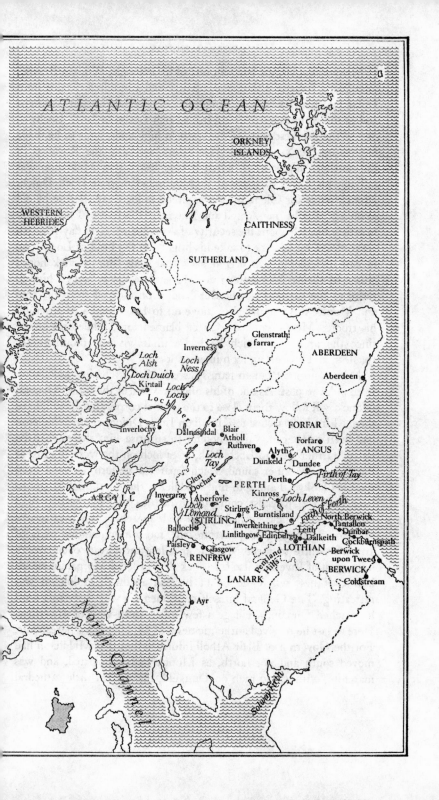

Meanwhile Monck had sent one of his colonels, William Brayne, to collect a force of a thousand infantry and a hundred cavalry from Ireland with a view to stationing it in Lochaber at the south-western end of the waterline stretching from Loch Leven to Loch Lochy—one of the loveliest parts of the western highlands, later to be made famous by the Young Pretender—thus hemming the Royalists in the northern highlands.[22] Then having heard that Middleton was rallying his forces of three or four thousand men at Loch Duich, Monck made for Glenmoriston eighteen miles away. Before he did so on 23 June he met Argyll and Brayne at the foot of Loch Lochy to satisfy himself about the security of Argyllshire. Next day Morgan was ordered by Monck to take his brigade to the head of Loch Ness in case Middleton was driven back that way. For Monck hoped either to thrust Middleton into Morgan's arms or oblige him to retire to the extreme north. But Middleton escaped from the trap and Monck was compelled to move on to Inverness to re-provision his troops. Monck could hardly be blamed for Middleton's escape since the area into which he had withdrawn was mountainous, roadless, and broken up by numerous lochs.

Monck now set out to harass his enemies by chasing Middleton from pillar to post. As one of his officers wrote at the time: 'General Monck will follow them close to the utmost corner, but he will have them.' First he marched to Kintail on Loch Duich where Middleton had been encamped, vainly hoping to surprise him there; then he moved farther west to Loch Alsh, a sea loch on the western coast at the foot of the inner sound which separates western Scotland from the isle of Skye. Failing to find Middleton there—though he got so near that the Royalist commander had to abandon powder and provisions—Monck turned back and marched north-eastwards somehow managing to penetrate the most mountainous parts of Inverness-shire to meet Morgan at Glenstrathfarrar, over twenty miles west of Inverness itself. Monck then ordered Morgan to march into Caithness where no doubt he had assumed Middleton was retreating. The General himself continued his way eastwards until he reached Dunain, a village a few miles south-west of Inverness. Here at last he received authentic news of Middleton's whereabouts. For the Governor of Blair Atholl informed him that Middleton had moved south and not north, as Monck had anticipated, and was marching with 4,000 men on Dunkeld, the ancient little cathedral city, only about a dozen miles north of Perth. In other words, like Charles II after the battle of Inverkeithing. Middleton had taken advantage of the road laid open to him by his enemy and was heading for the heart of occupied Scotland.

Monck immediately prepared to follow him, but before he did so he recalled Morgan and at Ruthven (south of Kingussie) on the northern end of the Grampian mountains, instructed him to advance south-westwards with fresh troops. Monck wrote to Cromwell on the following day (7 July)[23] that he believed Middleton was making for Loch Lomond, although after negotiating these vast distances his men were beginning to desert him. In the same letter Monck asked the Lord Protector to let the force from Ireland stationed in Lochaber remain there for at least another year, presumably in order to prevent the Royalists from establishing themselves anywhere on the west coast. Ten days later he again wrote to Cromwell asking that Argyll should be induced to fight against Middleton, offering to pay a hundred of his men at the rate of sixpence a day.[24]

As events turned out, this reinforcement did not prove necessary. Monck continued on his way south and stopped for a day at Weems castle, ten miles south of Blair Atholl, while he collected provisions. On 12 July he was at Loch Tay whence he marched west through Dochart glen. He had then been following Middleton for five weeks and claimed to have 'march't them from 3,000 to 1,200 men' and burnt parts of the highlands from which they had been operating. Middleton had retorted by burning parts of Argyllshire and then withdrew eastward into Perthshire. Monck pushed on westward through the twenty-five mile glen of Lyon, one of the most beautiful of the Scottish glens situated in richly wooded country. Here he received the welcome news that the day before the indefatigable Colonel Morgan had caught and routed Middleton's cavalry at Dalnaspidal, a lonely spot in the Grampian mountains near Loch Garry. Middleton had only 800 men left with him; he himself had been wounded; 300 prisoners were taken; and if it had not been for the bogs, Morgan reported, he could have destroyed them all.[25] Middleton's 1,200 foot were five miles away at the time and were beginning to disperse to their homes. According to prisoners captured at Dalnaspidal, Middleton was trying to make his way back to Caithness where he was expecting the arrival of supply ships sent to meet his needs.

It had originally been Monck's intention after Middleton's defeat, as he told Cromwell in a letter written at the end of July, to march to Loch Lomond and compel Glencairne to surrender.[26] Glencairne had never been happy since Charles II ordered Middleton to supersede him as lieutenant-general in Scotland. At first it was reported that he had only 200 cavalrymen under his command, although later Monck was informed that he had altogether 500 horse and foot. Evidently Monck decided it was hardly worth his while to search for him. Instead he resolved to devastate parts of the highlands so as to make it impossible for Glencairne or any other Royalists to maintain themselves during the coming winter. On 17 August he wrote to Cromwell from Aberfoyle, which is the gate to the Trossachs, saying 'We are destroying this place, which was the chiefe receptacle to the Enimy the last Winter.'[27] Colonel Morgan had dispatched a party in pursuit of Middleton, who had fled with the remnants of his forces into Caithness; some of them were killed and others compelled to abandon their horses. By 21 September Monck was able to tell Cromwell that Middleton was 'having a miserable life in the hills, hemmed in by garrisons and deprived of winter quarters'. Some of the prisoners whom Monck had collected were sent as indentured servants to the Barbados, a fate which induced others who had fought for the Stuart cause to give up fighting. In the same letter Monck wrote that 'the Enemy are coming in daily' and that another thousand had surrendered. He thought that 'This Countrye is now likely in a short time to bee in a setled posture.'[28]

Two facts are worth noting about Monck's skilful campaign of 1654. The first is that although he was largely ignorant of the geography of the country, this had not proved to be an obstacle to his operations. The mountainous and roadless character of the northern highlands even today would be suitable for prolonged guerrilla warfare. Yet Monck by remarkably swift marches with a mobile force eventually succeeded in cornering Middleton. Secondly, he had a strategic plan, which though it had had to be adapted to changing circumstances, worked exceedingly well. By careful siting of garrisons and the sweeping of the country by cavalry he cut off the highlands from the lowlands; and by sending Morgan from Inverness-shire into Caithness, while he himself advanced towards the waterline and by stationing his men from Ireland at Inverlochy in Lochaber, he was able gradually to shackle his enemies and then pursue them back towards the lowlands. It is astonishing that in such difficult country he was able on occasion to advance at the rate of sixteen miles a day, while in England it was thought exceptional for an army to cover more than ten miles in that time.

Monck's success in this campaign was owed partly to his excellent intelligence services. His object had been not so much to bring Middleton or Glencairne to battle as to deprive them of the means of subsistence, while promising that those Royalists who surrendered voluntarily would be pardoned and treated honourably. He also took great care of his own officers and men, never for one moment forgetting to remind the authorities in London of their various needs. As he himself was responsible for collecting the yield from taxes in Scotland, he was generally able to ensure that his soldiers received regular pay on campaign. Although he marched long distances, he usually encamped by midday, taking care that his sentries were well placed to prevent any surprise by the enemy and giving time for his troopers to collect forage for their horses. He would sit on the ground while he ate cold meats with his officers and in the evening invited them into his tent to share any food that had been obtained locally; he also made sure that his men were decently fed and billeted and helped to solve any difficulties that arose through sickness or exhaustion.

During the autumn of 1654 most of the chieftains and leading Royalists surrendered to Monck. In August he came to terms with the Earl of Atholl and by late September accepted the submission of the young Marquis of Montrose. In return for his giving up his arms and paying £3,000 as security for his good conduct, the Marquis himself was set at liberty to serve friendly powers abroad if he wished, his officers were permitted to retain their swords and horses, and the rank-and-file to return to their homes. The Earl of Callender received back his estate after he had given a bond for £6,000. The Earl of Tullibardine, who had persuaded the Earl of Atholl to give in, was recommended to Cromwell's special favour.[29] Those who still held out were more severely treated. When Lord Lorne and his men fell upon the guard of a vessel which, on Monck's orders was carrying biscuit, cheese and ammunition from Dumbarton to Inverary so as to supply an English garrison there and to relieve the necessities of the neutral Argyll, he was very angry; he told Cromwell that he would rather choose to let Argyll's county suffer through such depredations than hazard his own forces.[30] Lord Kenmure, who was taken prisoner in early September and was described by Monck as a resolute leader, was granted conditions 'as his fortune' was 'very broken'. On the other hand, Lord Cardross, who refused to agree to Monck's terms, was told he must dispose of all his horses above the value of £5 within six weeks;[31] for cavalry made the most dangerous enemies. Finally the Earl of Glencairne, using the excuse that he was ill and bed-ridden and had heard a report that Middleton was negotiating with Monck, agreed to terms at the end of August; his security was put at £5,000 in return for which he was to be allowed to enjoy both his real and personal properties. He was permitted to stay in Scotland for six months and if he wished to do so, during that period, he could raise a regiment of foot for the service of any government which was at peace with the English Commonwealth. Middleton, who had returned to Caithness only with his infantry, having left the remnants of his cavalry with Lorne, would, Monck thought, 'be able to doe [no] more than ruine his friends and people in the Hills, in which he will do us no disservice'. By the end of the year Middleton was seeking to conclude peace with Monck, but the negotiations broke down and by May 1655 Middleton had escaped abroad.[32]

Like his predecessor, Robert Lilburne, Monck pressed the Protectorate Government in London to send him more money and not to reduce his forces. But he was even more emphatic and tenacious than Lilburne and not afraid of tackling Cromwell himself. On 17 August he asked the Protector 'for the seasonable supply of these forces upon their return out of the field';[33] a week later he wrote: 'I cannot butt acquaint your Highness with our sad condition in relation to monie.'[34] On 7 September he was putting his case even more urgently:

> The pressing necessity of the souldjours here [he wrote] beeing upon theire comeing out of the field to pay for their provisions, and their clothes beeing worne out, and they having nothing to provide themselves against Winter, occasions mee to give your Highness this trouble, and earnestly to intreat that as your Highness was pleased to promise when I came to take charge of the forces they shal bee well paide, so that you will please to

give some effectual order that a speedy and sufficient supply with money may be sent downe hither without which the army must necessarily fall into free quarter suddenly.[35]

The position was that since the commissioners had visited Scotland at the beginning of 1652 the assessments—a property tax—levied on the Scots were fixed at £120,000 a year or £10,000 a month. The total amount needed for the upkeep of the army of occupation came to about twice as much as that. Monck told Cromwell that in view of the wasted lands and need for new garrisons the assessment would 'doe noe more than pay for contingencies'. Two days afterwards Monck wrote to the Lord Protector again entering into more detail. He notified him that the Army Committee (which was responsible for the assessments in England as well as in Scotland) had only assigned £134,155 for six months and fourteen days beginning on the previous 24 June, and that even allowing for the assessments raising as much as £10,000 a month in Scotland this meant that he would not receive enough money to pay for the army and the garrisons.[36] He told the Army Committee firmly that there was no possibility of obtaining £10,000 a month from the Scottish assessments and insisted that reductions of the rate had to be made on lands that were wasted or burnt.[37] Though he informed Cromwell in August that only £8,000 a month was attainable, by November he had changed his mind and stated that 'because of the great destruction and waste made by the Enimy, and of what wee found necessary to destroy that he might be deprived of sustenance, and the great decay of trade in all parts of Scotland', not more than £7,300 could be collected there.[38] At the end of September Cromwell nearly had a fatal accident when driving a coach and six horses through Hyde Park and was out of action for a fortnight. But the news of the accident, which Monck had received promptly from his Scoutmaster-General, George Downing (after whom Downing Street is named) did not prevent him from continuing to pester Cromwell about his monetary needs.[39] He told him that he had been reluctant to trouble him during his 'late retirement' but insisted that even though the lowlands were quiet and the enemy in the highlands had fallen out among themselves, he could not guarantee peace and security unless his army received regular pay.[40]

After his victories over the Royalists it was natural that Monck should be asked to reduce his establishment. For his army had swollen to fourteen infantry regiments, eight cavalry regiments (though much under strength) as well as eight troops of dragoons and 1,100 men from Ireland. Charles Fleetwood, who had been appointed commander-in-chief in Ireland after John Lambert had refused the post (sulking because Parliament would not confer upon him the title of Lord Deputy), asked that the force that had been posted at Inverlochy should be returned to Ireland and Monck agreed to this. Colonel Philip Twistleton's cavalry regiment, which, after following Cromwell into battle at Worcester, had been sent back as a reinforcement in Scotland during 1652, was ordered to leave its garrison duties in the lowlands and return to England. At the end of the year Lambert's cavalry regiment, which had reached Scotland in February 1654 in time to take part in the campaign against the Royalists, was recalled, together with two companies of Sir William Constable's regiment of foot, which had arrived in Scotland during the spring.[41] Monck protested vigorously to the Protector about all this. He had already demanded that Twistleton's regiment should be replaced. Of course most people object when their staffs are reduced; they usually want to see them expanded (Parkinson's law). Monck told Cromwell that there were 'many broken people' yet in Scotland and that he would not be able to prevent them from 'gathering to some kinde of heade againe without more force'; he would prefer to keep them down now they were down.[42] In a later letter he warned Cromwell that if more regiments were withdrawn from him 'even though the enemy are broken, many may take up arms to rob and steal'. Furthermore, they would be encouraged to recruit a new army in the following summer. Only if he retained his present strength would he be able 'to keepe both Scotts (and the English of our own army) in quiett'.[43] If reductions had to be made, he told Cromwell, he thought it would be wiser to lower the strengths of individual regiments and companies in them rather than withdraw regiments as such.

Monck possessed a useful weapon when he was insisting that he needed more money to pay his men and demanding that his establishment should not be reduced: that was his own value as commander-in-chief. Whereas Lilburne had been unable to keep the Scots in order and had allowed an insurrection to develop, Monck had swiftly outmanoeuvred and defeated Charles II's commanders in

Scotland and persuaded most of them to surrender on conciliatory terms. He had also proved himself a highly capable naval commander. Obviously it was to the interest of Cromwell and his Government to keep him in their service. During August and September Monck hinted that he had had enough. He wrote to Lambert on 20 August:[44]

> My present indisposition by reason of my continued lameness [evidently he had not been cured at Bath after all] the Countery not agreeing with mee, the unsetledness of my estate and familie in England, will I hope bee prevaileing arguments with your Lordshippe to move effectually for the granting the desires of your Lordshipps most humble servant.

A few days later he told Cromwell about his lameness and his anxiety to look after his estate in England and asked to be replaced, mentioning *en passant* that the Scottish assessments would barely cover his contingencies.[45] Three weeks later he again wrote to Cromwell complaining about not having enough money to meet his soldiers' arrears:

> This want here renders my condicion not soe[46] desireable, for pressing occasions for the settling my affaires in England do induce mee to renew my suite unto your Highnesse for appointing some other to take charge of these forces, and having once setled that little I have in England, I shall attend your Highnesse's commands.[46]

Later he thanked Lambert for reminding the Protector that he wanted to come to England on leave in the spring and added that little was left for his successor to do.[47] It was at this time that Cromwell was planning to send an amphibious expedition against the Spanish West Indies and it is known that he was considering Monck as its commander;[48] for after all, he had proved himself both as an admiral and a general. Whether Cromwell felt that he could not be spared from Scotland or whether the Lord Protector preferred to divide the command of the expedition is uncertain, but in the event Monck was not even allowed to go home on leave to Devon. Instead, his wife joined him in Scotland and he himself remained military commander there until after Oliver Cromwell's death.

10

Military Governor of Scotland

By the Instrument of Government, the first written constitution in British history, Oliver Cromwell had at the age of fifty-four been appointed Lord Protector of the Commonwealth of England, Scotland and Ireland and jointly with a parliament, which was to be elected by citizens possessing real or personal property to the value of £200, became the supreme legislative authority for this new united Commonwealth.[1] While parliament was not sitting, the Protector and his Council of State were empowered to issue ordinances on all matters everywhere. That was excellently succinct on paper, but the consequences which flowed from it so far as Scotland was concerned had still to be worked out.

For example, which shires and burghs were to provide the thirty members to represent Scotland in the first Protectorate parliament, destined to meet in September 1654? The decision was left to the Lord Protector and his Council. Eventually a list had been drawn up by John Lambert and promulgated on 27 June,[2] but only twenty-one, not thirty members went to Westminster in September 1654: those parts of Scotland which were most Royalist, mainly in the extreme north, refused to elect any members at all. Again, though, as has already been noticed, the ordinance of union between England and Scotland, which was agreed to by the Protector and his Council on 12 April, still required the ultimate approval of the united Commonwealth Parliament; that was not obtained until 26 June 1657. Meanwhile, since the royal Privy Council and the Court of Session had ceased to function, how was political order to be maintained and justice to be done?[3]

Obviously in those days when transport was slow and communications were poor, Scotland could not effectively be governed from London. In fact although the ordinance of union was brought before the Parliament at Westminster on 22 December and then received its first reading as an act, the members of the House, even after it had been purged of extreme republicans, were far too busy tearing the Instrument of Government to pieces to worry unduly about far-away Scotland. As to the executive, the Lord Protector took no action until well after he dissolved this Commonwealth Parliament in January 1655; then on 4 May he nominated a Council of State for Scotland to be presided over by Roger Boyle, Lord Broghill, and which of course included Monck, but its members did not assemble in Edinburgh until the middle of September.[4] Meanwhile Monck was really the supreme governor of Scotland.

Oliver Cromwell reposed the highest confidence in Monck whose abilities he appreciated. That did not mean, however, that he believed Monck's political opinions were identical with his own. For it was Cromwell's practice to pick out men of capacity regardless of past Royalist affiliations, or the misgivings that they had about Charles I's execution. One of the very first actions he took after he was chosen Protector had been to send Monck back to Scotland. After Monck's one attempt to get away from Scotland at the end of his successful military campaign of 1654, he attended to his administrative duties assiduously, while not being afraid of expressing in strong terms what he thought was best to be done. None the less he was aware on which side his bread was buttered. In March 1655 he wrote to Cromwell:

> I doe not know how I shall meritt all your Highnesse' favoures otherwise then by expressing my care and endeavours to serve your Highnesse faithfully and carefully soe long as it shall please God the Almighty to afford life unto Your Highnesse' most humble servant.[5]

He also knew how to trim his sails to the prevailing winds. It is noticeable that while his letters to Lord Lambert were written in very practical terms, he larded his dispatches to Cromwell with recognizable, if perfunctory, pieties.

Three big questions required Monck's attention, apart from disciplining his own army and ensuring that no revival of Royalist insurrections occurred: these were, reconciling the Scottish people to the union with England, providing for the proper administration of justice that had lapsed during the war, and looking after the exercise of religion and the pursuit of education. On 4 May 1654 the ordinance of union (which was followed next day by that of grace and pardon) was proclaimed at the mercat cross in Edinburgh. Monck, having ridden into the city in great military pomp, was flanked by the Lord Provost of Edinburgh and the Judge Advocate for Scotland. It was explained to the Scots that they were to enjoy free trade with England, were not to pay higher taxes proportionately than those paid in England, and were to be relieved of feudal obligations.[6] The occasion was celebrated first by a banquet and then by a magnificent display of fireworks that lasted from nine in the evening until midnight. Afterwards Monck did his best to fulfil his pledges. He himself saw to it that the Scots were not unreasonably taxed. Although the rate of assessment was nominally fixed at £10,000 a month, by 1657 he finally managed to have it reduced to £6,000. He had reminded John Thurloe, Cromwell's Secretary of State, that 'unless there be some course taken that the assessment may come to an equality with England it will go hard with this people.'[7] He himself thought Customs and Excise (not hitherto imposed in Scotland) were better means of raising money, but he was opposed to an excise on food or small (weak) beer.[8] To start with, the English Government had to find about two-thirds of the cost of the garrison in Scotland out of its own assessments or other resources.[9]

With regard to the administration of justice the Rump Parliament, before it was dissolved by Cromwell, had appointed seven commissioners, four English and three Scots, to undertake the task as well as to visit the universities. Scottish contemporaries, and later Scottish historians, commended the impartiality and efficiency of these commissioners. But Monck was concerned that the number of justices was at times insufficient. He complained to Cromwell in November 1654 that 'the course of justice to the people of this Nation' was 'something impeded' by the absence of several of the justices who were engaged on public affairs in England. He suggested that as Lord Hopetoun, president of the high court, first appointed to the commission in May 1653 and generally recognized as an able, honest and judicious man, had been removed from the commission, he should be replaced by another Scot, Sir Andrew Bruce.[10] Monck made two other positive proposals: one was that justices of

the peace, similar to those that carried on the work of local government in England, should be appointed in each Scottish shire. That
was agreed. Justices were duly nominated (Monck himself being
somewhat comically made a justice of the peace in every shire) but
some of the Scots refused to serve.[11] Their instructions were not
published until December 1655. Monck's other proposal was that
latitude should be given to the judges in their dealings with poor
debtors; that was in line with the policy advocated and promoted by
Cromwell in England. So that proposal of Monck's was promptly
accepted; on 16 May 1654 the Lord Protector promulgated an
ordinance, by and with the consent of his Council, to the effect that
the commissioners for the administration of justice in Scotland were
empowered to moderate decrees against debtors, who were unable
to meet their obligations at once, by giving them additional time in
which to pay.[12]

The religious question was perhaps the most difficult that Monck
had to face. Before he first left Scotland in February 1652, he had
been one of the eight commissioners appointed by the Rump Parliament to settle the affairs of Scotland with a view to its incorporation
into the Commonwealth. A declaration had been published at that
time in which the references to the organization of religion were
studiously vague, though they were in tune with their secret instructions.[13] The preaching of the Gospel was to be promoted, they
said, the power of 'true religion and holiness' was to be advanced, and
encouragement and protection given to those who served God
'according to his mind revealed in his Word'. But the fact remained
that the Scots were divided over questions of religion, though not to
the same extent as the English. The three parties in Scotland were
the Resolutioners, who, while adhering to the stiff discipline of
John Knox's Presbyterianism, were loyal to the Stuart family that
had governed their land for hundreds of years. Even after Cromwell
and Monck had conquered Scotland, the bulk of the parish ministers
continued openly to pray for that Christian paragon, King Charles
II, since prayers for the monarch had been laid down in Knox's
Directory of Worship and in the text of the National Covenant. On
the other hand, the Remonstrants or Protesters had consistently
rejected Charles as an unsanctified and perjured ruler, who, they
believed, turned the wrath of the Almighty against them. This party
in the Kirk had been courted by Cromwell and was for a short time

to be favoured by Monck. The third party were the highlanders, who with the exception of Argyll and his Campbells, were either Roman Catholics or of doubtful religious opinions. Finally, the English victories had stimulated the sects, which, having established themselves in England, set out to proselytize the Scots; soon the Baptists (or Anabaptists), the Quakers and the Fifth Monarchy Men began to achieve progress, while the Independents (or Congregationalists) made some slight headway. Monck took a particular dislike to the Quakers who, he thought, undermined the morale of his officers and men, while Cromwell, no doubt on Monck's advice, ordered the Council of Scotland three months before his death to see that 'no Baptist holds any office of trust nor practises at law nor keeps a school'.[14]

What Monck was most concerned about was not brands of Christianity but the political aspects of religion. Like Robert Lilburne before him, he first regarded most Presbyterian ministers as 'trumpets of sedition', while he feared that general assemblies of the Kirk would open the opportunity for conspiracies against the Commonwealth Government. For example, he discovered that when on the instructions of the English Council of State, he ordered a day of fasting and humiliation to be observed in Scotland on 11 October 1654 'for the guid and happy success of the Parliament of England', as one Scot put it, it was almost universally ignored by the Kirk.[15] The Kirk was also to refuse to fast as an act of thanksgiving for Cromwell's escape from assassination in September 1656. For the leading Presbyterians understandably took the view that it was the sole right of the Assembly of the Kirk to promulgate days of fasting and humiliation, not that of the civil authorities. When it did so later on, the Scots Presbyterians obeyed, but they defied Monck's orders. They also did not see why it should be regarded as 'a great treason' to name the King in their public prayers.[16] Furthermore, they resented the liberties now being given to the sectarians, especially the Quakers, who enjoyed disrupting services. Finally, they could not accept that lay commissioners, most of whom were English, should have the duty of supervising the universities, colleges and schools of learning in their land.[17]

Both Cromwell and Monck were adamant over the question of praying for the King. When the twenty-one deputies who came up to London to represent Scotland in the first Protectorate Parliament (though most of them were Monck's own nominees) took a formal farewell of Cromwell in February 1655, they expressed to him the deep grievance that they felt over having to support and accept the presence of a large English army in their country. Cromwell then retorted that the reason the garrison was there was 'because the Ministry did preach up the interest of Charles Stuart and did much inveigle against the present Authority'. In the following month Monck, in his capacity as one of the commissioners responsible for religion and learning in Scotland, signed a declaration, which was to be published by all the sheriffs and in every parish. It stated that any minister who continued to pray for 'the pretended King' should be deprived of his stipend and subjected to such penalties as the commissioners thought fit.[18] But this draconian decree had little effect. At the time that Lord Broghill and his Council set up shop in Edinburgh in the autumn of 1655 the ministers were still busily praying for the King, though sometimes they employed ingenious circumlocutions.

Immediately, however, Monck was confronted with trouble in his own army. After his victories over the Royalists and the submission of nearly all their leaders except Middleton and Lord Lorne, he had good reason to feel that the country was settled and all was well. The representatives or at least nominal representatives of Scotland, including nine of Monck's own officers such as Colonel Okey and Scoutmaster Downing, had gone up to London to attend the Commonwealth Parliament, which had been addressed by Cromwell in a skilful speech on 4 September. But although the Protector had a sizeable party of supporters in the House, there was a republican group, headed by Colonel Sir Arthur Heslirige, a wealthy man 'of morose and haughty temper', which vociferously demanded the right to debate and revise the Instrument of Government with a view to reducing the wide powers conferred by it on Cromwell and transforming him into a kind of ceremonial figurehead like the Doge of Venice. Many of the army officers, including Okey, were sympathetic to this movement against the Protector and his friends, because they felt that the good old republican cause for which they had been fighting against Charles II and his followers was in the process of being betrayed.

Cromwell was not the man to be defied in such a way; he was anxious to be conciliatory, but he insisted after an attempt at a compromise had broken down, that members of parliament must accept four fundamentals of the new regime: recognize that the Government should be jointly in the hands of the Protector and parliament, that parliaments must not perpetuate themselves, that control of the army must be divided between Protector and parliament, and that liberty of conscience in religion should be maintained. At least 300 members finally agreed to the recognition, but some 140 absented themselves. Those who remained in the House then assumed the right to revise the constitution except for its first clause. Cromwell felt increasingly frustrated; he was indifferent to dialectical niceties; he wanted to govern the country in peace and lead it to a New Jerusalem.

Monck was also a practical man though devoid of Cromwell's introspective idealism. He had as little sympathy with the parliamentary republicans as with the Scots General Assembly. When he heard of the stand taken by Cromwell he expressed his approval.[19] He wrote to the Protector on 21 September saying that he blessed God to 'heare that things are soe setled in Parliament' and that he hoped 'affaires will now goe on prosperouslie and without interruption'. In the same letter he reported that 'this Country is now likely in a short tyme to be in a setled posture'. He was right. For Scotland was a poor country, feebly led and exhausted by the military effort it had put out during the past fifteen years.[20] His trouble was less with the Scots than with his own army, for naturally some of the officers in the garrison of Scotland were in sympathy with Heslirige, Okey and other devoted republican politicians in London. One such officer was Colonel Robert Overton, a well-educated Yorkshireman who had distinguished himself in the army both before and after the establishment of the Commonwealth.[21] He was also ambitious, having an imperious wife and 'many pretty children'. After serving as a major-general in command of all the forces in the west of Scotland, he had, by the time Monck took up his appointment, returned to Hull where he held the post of governor. Dissatisfied with his prospects, he went up to London to ask Cromwell for a better job. The two spoke frankly to each other. Overton told the Protector that if he 'did only design the setting up of himself, and not the good of these nations', he could not serve him. 'Thou wert a knave if thou wouldst', retorted Cromwell. It may well be that Monck was told that he could find employment for Overton if he wished.

Glad to have such an experienced soldier at his disposal, he sent him to relieve Morgan who had done more than his stint in the inhospitable north.

That was arranged towards the end of September when Monck had learned more fully of the problems which Cromwell was having with his Parliament, even after it had effectively been purged of most of the republicans. Monck then wrote to Cromwell in his most pious vein:[22]

> It is noe pleasing thing to mee to heare of the troubles and difficulties that your Highnesse does meet withall in indeavouring to preserve the people of God and the peace of these Nations. My prayer unto the Almighty is to make you goe through soe greate a worke, and that he will unite the harts of all that looke towards him in promoting the Kingdome of his Sonne in these Nations.

He then told Cromwell of the command which he had assigned to Overton, after having first assured himself of his honesty.

> For Colonel Overton I finde upon discourse with him that his resolution was, that when he saw a setlement of government under your Highnesse, and could not with a good conscience submitt to it, he would deliver upp his Commission, but till then he would serve your Highnesse faithfully.

Monck, though no doubt acting on Cromwell's orders, realized that he was taking a risk with this serious-minded Yorkshire gentleman. Perhaps Monck felt that Overton's material needs would neutralize his political principles, but he could hardly say that to Cromwell, who was touchy about those whose minds dwelt on mundane things. At any rate by early November when Overton was on his way to Aberdeen to take charge of the forces in northern Scotland, Monck wrote again to Cromwell 'humbly entreating your Highesse' pleasure' for some allowance to Overton 'in consideration of his greate care and expences therein'.[23]

Meanwhile the republican movement in the army—and also in the navy—was being intensified and directed by conspirators in London. Okey, Alured, another of Monck's officers, and Saunders, a colonel who had served in Ireland, were in touch with Major John Wildman, who had succeeded John Lilburne, now in exile abroad, as the leader of the once influential Levellers; he was a saturnine man and proliferator of pamphlets, a kind of compulsive conspirator, eager to overthrow Cromwell at that time.[24] Wildman drew up for these officers a petition which was signed by them condemning the Protectorate, demanding the summoning of a constituent assembly and seeking to reinvigorate the Leveller principles of social equality and tempered democracy. But Thurloe's spies were fully aware of what was going on. Alured's rooms were searched and the petition discovered.[25] Whether other colonels except these dauntless three would have signed it or not is unknown. Okey was tried by court martial and acquitted of treason, but deprived of his command. His major, Tobias Bridge, promptly took his place so that the regiment continued to serve under Monck. Saunders was also dismissed, though not court-martialled; Alured was cashiered and for a time imprisoned.

Thus Monck was forewarned. As soon as copies of the three colonels' petition reached officers of Okey's regiment from London they were impounded. Another printed pamphlet critical of Cromwell entitled *Some Mementoes for the Officers and Soldiers of the Army* written by 'some sober Christians' was also seized.[26] Monck, who until then had been rather complacent about the loyalty of his army, realized that 'ill spirits' were at work.[27] He decided he needed every resource to keep both the Scots and restive officers and soldiers under his command 'in quiet'. But his intelligence was good. He soon learned that the main centres of discontent were at Aberdeen, where Overton was stationed, and at Hull where Overton was still titular governor. Major Bramston of Colonel Morgan's regiment of dragoons, Lieutenant Braman of Colonel Howard's cavalry regiment and Samuel Oates, father of the more notorious Titus Oates, who was the chaplain in Colonel Pride's infantry regiment, were all put under arrest and court-martialled; Major Style and Captain Hedworth in Sir William Constable's regiment, who, according to Oates, had agitated for a meeting of dissatisfied regiments, succeeded in escaping to England.

At this time there was a variety of scandalous and seditious papers circulating in Scotland; two, written by Major Bramston in Aberdeen, *The Reasons against Communion* and an *Epistle to the Church at the Glasshouse*, received the approval of Overton, another pamphlet written by Oates, who was an Anabaptist at that moment, and the papers and leaflets dispatched there by Wildman from London and by Overton's friends in Hull.[28] Monck reached the conclusion that Overton in Aberdeen was the most dangerous of all the army malcontents, though it has been contended that Thurloe thought he was a weakling cajoled by Wildman. Be that as it may, Monck sent for him following a command from Cromwell written on Christmas Day,' had him put under arrest and dispatched to London where he languished in the Tower or elsewhere in prison until the end of the Protectorate.[29] When he was arrested some verses were found on him which ran:

> A Protector, what's that? 'Tis a stately thing
> That confesseth itself but the ape of a King;
> A tragical Caesar acted by a clown;
> Or a brass farthing stamped with a kind of a crown.

Whatever Thurloe thought, it was hardly surprising that Monck and Cromwell were indignant.

Apart from Wildman the Leveller, and Overton the inspissated scholar, much of the unrest in the army both in Scotland and in England stemmed from the extreme sects of Fifth Monarchy Men and Anabaptists. The Anabaptists in Edinburgh, Leith and Perth sent an address to Monck vindicating themselves from having had any hand in plots against Cromwell and his Government.[30] In the same letter that Monck wrote to Cromwell informing him about this, he drew his attention to a certain trooper, Miles Sindercombe, who had served in Colonel Tomlinson's cavalry regiment in Scotland but had been discharged by Monck as being 'a busie and suspicies person ... who was forward to promote ... ill designs'; he therefore advised the Protector to have him arrested and examined.[31] Here Monck hit the nail bang on the head; for during the next year Sindercombe twice attempted to assassinate Cromwell. In Scotland at least six or seven officers were cashiered and made to swear that in future they would neither act nor speak against Cromwell. Most of them, like Overton, were then dispatched under guard to London.

The virulent opposition to the Protectorate shown in parliament, the machinations of Wildman and his friends, growing unrest in the navy, the propaganda against Cromwell distributed in Scotland, and the exertions of the extreme sects all combined to encourage the more adventurous Royalists to plan a general insurrection in the spring of 1655. Owing to the magnificent intelligence service organized by Thurloe, the Government was warned and prepared for such a rising. Fortunately for the Protector, at this stage no understanding existed between the Levellers and the more active Royalists. In February Wildman had been arrested in Wiltshire dictating to his servant 'the Declaration of the Free and Well Affected People now in Arms against Oliver Cromwell', a follow-up of the 'letter of the Three Colonels' which no doubt he also dictated, and was clapped into the Tower. His main ally, Colonel Edward Sexby, a former agitator in the army who, with Wildman, was ready to arrange the assassination of the Protector, managed to escape abroad. The Government took all the obvious precautions including summoning two regiments from Scotland, to Monck's open dismay.

Monck was evidently less perturbed about the subversion of his army by officers like Overton and Okey than he was about the discontent engendered in it by its arrears of pay. He had told Lambert at the end of January that even after £15,000 had been issued to satisfy the soldiers, they would still be fifteen weeks in arrears.[32] He could not even disband regiments unless he had the money to pay them off. He thought that the reduction of the assessment in England forced upon Cromwell by his Parliament, had animated the enemy in Scotland and that if a Royalist revival took place there, some of his cavalry and many of his infantry 'will probably run to the Enemy, who are in a low condicion at present', especially if they were threatened with demobilization.

The negotiations with Charles II's defeated commander, John Middleton, had by now broken down, but Monck was informed that he had decided to remain in Scotland. Thus Monck genuinely feared that if a Royalist insurrection took place in England, it would relight the smouldering embers in Scotland too. Nevertheless, when the Cavalier action party began its rising—it had been postponed from February to March 1655—Monck had to dispatch more troops into England, though he asked that Whalley's cavalry regiment should leave some of its men on the borders until it was certain that all was quiet in the lowlands.[33] For the last thing he wanted was a recurrence of moss-trooper depredations as well as renewed action led by Middleton in the highlands.

The Royalist rising in England was soon suppressed. Only in the west did the cavaliers have any success at all, temporarily occupying

Salisbury, but they were soon rounded up and nine of their leaders executed. In Scotland it had been a pretty dismal winter and spring. Three big fires broke out in Edinburgh; a drought in East Lothian damaged the crops, storms at sea interfered with fishing, raising the price of herrings; in mid-April the roads were so bad and the snow so thick on the hills that cavalry had difficulty in moving at all.[34] Monck continued to be alarmed over the shortage of money to pay his men. He constantly bothered Cromwell and Lambert, arguing that if the army remained unpaid, the men would be obliged to live on free quarter and that would arouse the latent discontent of the civilian population.

In spite of all these troubles Monck announced his intention of again taking the field when the campaigning season of 1655 could begin.[35] His plan was to march into the highlands and round up Middleton, while leaving cavalry behind to ensure the security of the lowlands. In informing Cromwell about his plans he did not omit to remind him again that 'the souldjours doe expect some monies before they goes into the feilds, and it weere well wee weere furnished for monies to carrie with [us]'.[36] But within three weeks he had discovered, as the Marquis of Argyll correctly told him earlier, that Middleton had now left the country; so Monck was able to assure the Protector that 'unless it bee the reduseing of some stubborn Clans in the Hills to obedience, heere is not like to bee any action this summer'.[37] By the end of June he was satisfied that Scotland was quiet and peaceful. For the remainder of the time he spent there as commander-in-chief he was concerned only with normal security precautions and with the discipline of his own army. Thanks to his brilliant campaign of 1654, Scotland had been subdued.

11

Monck and the Cromwells

As soon as the scare over Royalist risings had subsided and Monck had sent assurances that all was again quiet in Scotland — Lord Lorne, the last of the leading Scots to hold out, having come to terms with him during the early summer of 1655 — the Lord Protector and the Council of State in England were naturally anxious to reduce the size of the army there as it was a burden on the exchequer. Monck's army then consisted of fourteen infantry regiments, mostly engaged on garrison duties in different parts of the country, four cavalry regiments and eight troops of dragoons. The commander-in-chief's difficulty was that he had insufficient money to pay off any surplus men — he would, for example, have gladly disbanded some of the dragoons had he been in funds — while he also needed substantial sums for 'contingencies' particularly for maintaining forts and keeping them in repair. When he learned from Lambert that a total of £50,000 was all that was to be allowed him, he pleaded to be given an additional £1,000 a month for maintenance and £800 a month for the repair of forts.[1] In return he suggested that the strength of the regiments might be reduced; for example, infantry regiments could be lowered to two-thirds of their existing size and cavalry troops could be cut down from seventy to fifty men, which would mean a saving at any rate in the pay of officers, most of whom were not unwilling to be demobilized. He emphasized however that such of the officers who stayed with him would have to be paid at least as much as those serving in England, especially as many of them had left their wives behind and thus had to keep two houses.[2] By the end of August Monck was able to inform the Protector that the establishment was in the process of being reduced by demobilizing some of his men 'though we were much put to it to find moneye to repay them'.[3]

Disbandment, none the less, proved a slow business. Monck estimated in the summer of 1655 that the arrears due to his army came to over £80,000. The assessments in Scotland at that time amounted to £8,000 a month while the Customs and Excise, which Monck was told would supply the deficiency, were yielding little. Excise was not imposed until October 1655 while Monck thought that until peace was concluded with France—and he might have added Spain—the Customs would hardly be enough to cover the salaries of the Customs officers.[4] A later ingenious suggestion from London that a lump sum of £40,000 could be raised by fining Royalists in return for freeing some of their lands from sequestration did not prove practicable.[5]

It was not in fact until October 1657 that Monck was able to submit to the Protector detailed proposals for the redistribution of his army on the basis of three regiments of horse, six regiments of foot plus five companies, and two troops of dragoons which he thought would be sufficient to suppress disorders and be ready to march into England if needed. He also required that a cavalry regiment should be stationed partly in Carlisle and partly in Berwick where it could protect the garrison of Newcastle upon Tyne from Scottish incursions. Beyond the pay of his men, Monck also asked for a store of provisions in case of emergencies and enough money to buy stone and timber for repairing fortresses.[6]

The total cost of this reduced establishment was calculated at about £21,000 a month or £252,000 a year. The scheme was approved by Cromwell and his Council at the end of 1657.[7] To pay for it Scottish assessments, Customs and Excise were assumed to contribute about £118,000 a year while the contribution from the English assessments would be about £137,000 a year. But beyond this Monck had to find £12–13,000 for disbandments and nearly £50,000 to satisfy outstanding arrears of pay. This he hoped to obtain from English revenues other than assessments. Monck's own pay was £6 a day (plus £600 a year as a Scottish councillor of state). His major-general (Morgan) had to manage on ten shillings a day.

Monck did not depend solely on his garrisons for the internal security of Scotland. He also relied on a policy of severity and on the use of spies. In general, Monck insisted that when the Scottish Royalists capitulated, they should surrender all their arms except their swords and provide bonds according to their position. For

example, Lord Lorne was asked to 'give good Lowland security to
the value of £5,000 sterling', while a colonel had to offer £1,000
and a captain £100. But Monck wanted it to be clearly understood
that if any Scotsman who had submitted, afterwards took up arms
again or burned the houses of collaborators, he would be sentenced
to death. He told Cromwell more than once that if twenty or thirty
of his prisoners were hanged for committing murder in cold blood
'it would conduce much to the peace of the country'.[8] To Lambert
he expressed the hope that the ordinance of pardon and grace would
not prevent this drastic punishment. His officers pressed Monck
strongly that moss-troopers who were caught should be put to death.[9]

To get rid of subversive or dangerous Scots Monck advocated the
policy, previously urged by Robert Lilburne, of encouraging experienced Scottish professional officers to raise regiments to fight on
the side of powers friendly to the Commonwealth on the mainland
of Europe. Cromwell thoroughly approved of the plan. According
to the terms of the treaties of capitulation concluded with men like
Glencairne and Kenmure they were given permission to recruit
regiments for such service if they wished. Lord Cranston, who had
been taken prisoner by Lilburne in 1653, did actually raise an infantry regiment to fight for the King of Sweden. On the other hand,
a certain Colonel Thomas Lyon or Lyons, who was authorized by
Monck to enlist a regiment to enter the French Service (at the time
when Cromwell was preparing to attack Spain beyond the line),
wrote to King Charles II to explain that his real aim was to select
officers and men who would be available to fight for the Stuarts.
The exiled monarch might have liked that idea all right, but he
forbade other Royalists to take advantage of the concession.[10] Obviously he wanted all his own armed supporters to be readily at hand
when an opportunity arose for him to regain his throne.

An alternative to inducing Scottish soldiers to go abroad voluntarily or hanging prisoners taken in arms as a warning to others not to
rebel, a course pressed on Monck by Cromwell, who was an imper-
ialist, was that as many prisoners as possible should be transported
to the Barbados to work on the sugar plantations. When the campaign in Scotland of 1654 was at its height Cromwell (or his staff)
discovered two London merchants who were willing to transport
500 and 300 prisoners respectively to the Barbados at their own
expense. Cromwell even had the idea of collecting 'all masterless,

idle vagabonds and robbers, both men and women in Scotland' and pushing them off to the West Indies. The snag was that it was fairly easy for such hordes of Scottish prisoners to escape either by bribing the merchants to whom they were sold or once they had reached the Caribbean to get away from the plantations and board the next vessel homeward bound. Monck did not object to committing specific prisoners to be disposed of in the West Indies if Cromwell would not let him have them hanged; for example, he would have liked Lord Kinnoul, who after giving his bond, escaped from Edinburgh castle in order to fight again in the Royalist cause, to be 'executed for terror', but if that were refused, to dispatch him to the West Indies. But he was not in favour of rounding up 'pillaging rascals' and idle beggars because he believed it was not a secure method of dealing with them and, secondly, because he thought it was calculated to arouse widespread resentment throughout the whole country.[11]

Another policy which bears the stamp of Cromwell's and not Monck's inspiration was that of tolerating every kind of Christian sect in Scotland. The Kirk was naturally opposed to such liberality so that Monck had to use the weight of his authority to protect Congregationalists, Anabaptists and the like. But the Quakers, led by their founder, George Fox, who himself visited Scotland in 1657, proved an extremely disruptive influence, as were also the Fifth Monarchy Men (who believed in the imminent return of Christ to rule the earth); Colonel Rich's regiment, which had been stationed in Scotland since 1653, was full of them and because of this five officers belonging to it were court-martialled and cashiered in February 1655. Ashfield's and Berry's regiments were proved susceptible to evangelization by the Quakers. By the beginning of 1655 also the Presbyterian John Nicoll wrote:

> there rose up great numbers of that damnable sect of the Quakers; who, being deluded by Satan, drew away many of their profession, both men and women, sundry of them walking through the streets all naked except [for] their shirts, crying 'this is the way, walk ye into it.'

These Quakers were less peaceable than they became later; they burst into the Edinburgh churches, proclaiming that 'the sword of the Lord is drawn'. They achieved a number of conversions not only among the Scots but in the English army. Miles Mann, who was lieutenant-colonel in Colonel Fitch's regiment stationed at Inverness, was perturbed at their success with his troops; he thought that 'their errors' were 'of a very spreading nature' and were prejudicial to the discipline of the soldiers. Colonel Daniel, whose regiment was garrisoning Perth, was also alarmed when he learned that his captain-lieutenant, who had been under his command for nearly fourteen years, had been converted to Quakerism and had grown 'soe besotted with his notions that one might as well speak to the walls as to him'. Monck had warned Cromwell of the need to curb this 'growing eveil' and advised him that he ought to take action over it.[12] The lesson that Monck imbibed was that uniformity, not nonconformity, in religion was conducive to peace, discipline and order. But he was an Erastian; he would never have allowed the Church to rule the State.

In September 1655 Monck was relieved of some of the burdens of his office by the arrival of five Englishmen and two Scots (William Lockhart and John Swinton) who had been chosen to form with him the Council of Scotland, which had been promised eight months earlier. (Later a sub-committee of the Council of State in England, known as the Scotch Committee, was appointed to form a link between the Council in England and the Council in Scotland.) Basically, the instructions to the Council of Scotland were to preserve the union between the two countries, to secure peace and justice, to punish the obstreperous, to encourage trade and to cut down the expenses of administration.

Its president, Lord Broghill, an Anglo-Irishman, was paid £1,000 a year and seven other members were paid £600; it was provided with a clerk, Emmanuel Downing, the father of Scoutmaster George Downing, and a deputy clerk. The quorum was five. Its first declaration restored to the Scottish burghs the right to elect their own magistrates; the second abolished the severe penalties imposed on Scottish ministers who prayed for the King. This had the salutary result that the Reverend Patrick Gillespie, a Remonstrant who came from Glasgow, was the first minister publicly to pray for the Lord Protector, though the Resolutioners continued to pray for the King in their circumlocutory kind of way. The Council devoted its attentions to improving Scottish trade and freeing it from unnecessary restrictions. The principal Scottish grievances were the onerous taxation levied to support the army of occupation—the excise being heartily disliked—and the incursion of sectaries. The Council, however, insisted on toleration; even 'papists' were not interfered with so long as they behaved themselves.[13]

At the same time Broghill made a determined attempt to reconcile the Resolutioners and Remonstrants. He came to the conclusion that Monck's policy of threatening to deprive ministers of their stipends if they prayed openly for Charles II had only made them more obstinate. Broghill promised to annul the proclamation if they agreed to stop praying for the King in public. According to Robert Baillie, 'General Monck was irritated against us as if we had yielded to Broghill what we denied to him.' Be that as it may, Monck certainly changed his attitude, for he thought of the Remonstrants as republicans who might prove more loyal to the united Commonwealth than their opponents and bestowed on them his patronage.[14]

As the Council took over the administration of civil affairs, Monck was able thenceforward to devote himself primarily to the military task of building forts in strategic spots; despite the expense they were constructed at Inverness, Inverlochy, Ayr, Perth and Leith, all of them ports where an enemy might land from the sea. Monck was particularly concerned over the fortification of Leith and was anxious to promote its trade which, he claimed, was obstructed by the historic privileges of the city of Edinburgh. A number of other smaller forts were built, over-large garrisons weeded out and the new military establishment put gradually into effect. Monck had to overcome minor difficulties such as obtaining sufficient straw for his horses and fire-and-candle money for his more outlying garrisons. He actually ordered one of his most trusted officers, Timothy Wilkes, who was going up to London on leave, to visit Cromwell and explain these needs to him. The Protector duly gave his help.[15]

Monck did not enjoy the assistance of the Council of Scotland for very long. The members took up their duties in September 1655, but a year later all of them were elected to serve in the second Protectorate Parliament—all that is except for Monck and his deputy, Major-General Morgan, who could not be spared. Without them there was no quorum which was necessary in particular to deal with questions of finance, although Monck was empowered to authorize payment of his forces out of the assessments when the Council was closed down.

Englishmen did not much care for being sent to live in Scotland and embraced the slightest excuse to return to London. Broghill had stipulated that he should only be required to stay there for one year. In January 1657 while the new Parliament was still sitting, Monck wrote to one of the army treasurers in London to tell him that he wanted the councillors to make more haste to return to Scotland. He also wrote to the President of the Council of State that if they did not return quickly there would be confusions over the assessments and the excise. Two councillors, John Swinton and Colonel Adrian Scroope, were then ordered to return, but Scroope was rendered *hors de combat* by gout. Thereupon Monck wrote to the Lord Protector himself to ask him to send two more councillors immediately, for, as he explained to the President of the Council of State, without a quorum nothing useful could be done. When he wrote only two councillors besides himself were in Scotland. On the advice of the English Council the quorum was reduced to three by Cromwell which meant in effect that Monck had again become the virtual ruler of Scotland.

Not long after the quorum had been reduced the Council's commission expired[16] and six months later several of the councillors again trooped up to London to attend the Parliament summoned by Richard Cromwell, who succeeded his father on 3 September 1658. By then, however, Oliver's brother-in-law, Colonel John Desborough, was able to declare that as a result of the union (which was finally approved by Parliament on 26 June 1657) and, he might have added, Monck's achievement in the policing of Scotland, 'a man might ride all Scotland over with a switch in his hand and £100 in his pocket, which he could not have done these five hundred years.'[17] John Desborough was in a position to know the state of affairs in Scotland as his brother Samuel had been a member of the Council of Scotland since its beginning and had been appointed president of the bench of judges in June 1658. The first president, Lord Broghill, had got the Council off to a good start through his tact and sympathy and had been popular with the Scots. John Nicoll, who testified to that, observed in his diary that George Monck was 'no less beloved of this nation at this tyme for his singular wisdom and carriage to all that had address to him'.[18]

During the Protectorate of Oliver Cromwell, Monck had taken care to keep him fully informed on the situation in Scotland and

consulted him about how he should treat with members of the
Scottish nobility who, having fought for the Stuarts, were ready to
come to terms with the Commonwealth Government. Monck also
regularly notified John Thurloe about the fruits of his intelligence
service. Cromwell and Thurloe reciprocated Monck's confidence.
Timothy Wilkes, who occupied the key post of Governor of Leith,
was an Independent in religion, and was known personally to Cromwell under whom he had fought during the Dunbar campaign; he
received a letter from the Lord Protector after the exposure of the
so-called Overton plot, largely through Wilkes's own efforts, in
which Cromwell asked him to continue to show his fidelity 'in
standing by and sticking to your honest General Geo. Monck'.
This adjective 'honest' afterwards entered into the history books
along with the belief that Monck was 'simple-hearted'. Three years
later Thurloe was to aver that not a man 'in all the three nations
[was] more loyal and dutiful to his Highness than he [Monck] is
nor one to whom his Highness is more indebted for weeding out of
the army troublesome and discontented spirits'.[19]

Thurloe had reason for his commendation. It was Monck who
had promptly rounded up Overton and the other dissatisfied officers
at the end of 1655 by suborning a certain Major James Borthwick,
whose brother was a Royalist sent over by Charles II from Cologne
to Scotland; through James Borthwick, Monck was able to intercept
letters revealing the King's plans; it was through him that Monck
discovered Glencairne's whereabouts, was able to arrange for his
arrest and clap him into prison. He also intercepted letters to Middleton and to the Earl of Atholl; and he assured Cromwell that so long
as he had this double agent in his pay and the agent was not un-
masked 'there are no letters of Charles Stuart or others which come
into the hands of his friends but I shall know them'. Monck forwarded copies of the intercepted letters to Cromwell while the
intelligencer was sent up to London to obtain money and instructions
from Thurloe so that he could continue spying upon the exiled
King.[20] The Royalists were also not bad at intercepting letters. One
such letter was written to Thurloe about some 'seditious papers' that
he had discovered and assured him that 'Monck's care in all things is
inexpressible'.[21] Nevertheless, some Royalists remembering that
Monck himself had once fought as a Cavalier and been imprisoned
as such in the Tower, hoped to lure him back into their camp. Just

before Cromwell's death, Monck was the recipient of a letter from the exiled Royalists which was left for him with the officer of the guard. In it the assumption was that Monck would soon declare himself for the King. Again he dispatched a copy of the letter to Thurloe telling him that it must be 'a knavish trick of some Scotchman or other' and that he hoped God would enable him to make the Royalists 'smart for their roguery'.[22]

Monck, as has been seen, had approved of the expulsion of the Rump Parliament by Cromwell and the setting up of the Protectorate. Though he refused the opportunity to become an active member of either of the Protectorate parliaments himself, he followed the course of political events closely. After the Cavalier rising of 1655 he commended the Protector's decision to appoint major-generals of horse militia throughout the English counties for policing purposes. But he was also pleased when the resolution was taken to call a second parliament at Westminster in 1656, telling Thurloe that he thought the Protector had 'done very discreetly in it, for in case at their meeting they [the members of parliament] should not mind more the public good than their own ends, the fault will be theirs' — in other words, Cromwell could revert to the system of the major-generals who were in fact abolished by this very Parliament. Disliking the Quakers as he did, Monck approved of the severe punishment inflicted upon James Naylor, who had been judged to have acted blasphemously in Bristol. When in the first half of 1657 Thurloe informed him of the offer of the Crown being made by a majority of the sitting members of parliament to Oliver Cromwell — an offer which was resented by many republican officers — he did all he could to stifle demonstrations in Scotland. He wrote to the Protector to tell him he was confident that he could engage all the regiments in Scotland except perhaps one (Colonel Ashfield's maybe?) in loyalty to Cromwell and his Parliament and would see that he was not troubled by any petitions from his army; he did in fact strictly order his officers and men to take no notice of the antimonarchical literature in circulation. It has to be remembered that Lord Broghill, Monck's former colleague in the Council of Scotland, was one of the foremost members of parliament in trying to persuade Oliver to accept the Crown, while one of Monck's colonels, George Fenwick, was opposed not merely to the offer but to the Protectorate itself. Cromwell was not slow in removing Fenwick and replacing him by the trusted Timothy Wilkes. Fenwick had been governor of Edinburgh and represented Berwickshire in Parliament. The Protector rewarded Monck for his loyalty by giving him the governorship in Fenwick's place, which added to his already adequate income.[23]

Under pressure from the army — particularly from Thomas Pride, whose regiment had left Scotland at the end of 1655, Oliver Cromwell felt compelled to refuse the Crown in May 1657. As to the rest of the new constitution — known as 'the Petition and Advice', which had been drawn up with the intention of strengthening the Protectorate and making it more like the old monarchy — Monck expressed his approval, for he had evidently not wanted Cromwell to accept the title of king.[24] One of the rights given to the Protector by this constitution was that he was empowered to nominate seventy members of a new House of Lords or 'Other House'.

Monck was one of those selected by Cromwell for this honour, but he decided he was too busy to attend what proved to be a constitutional flop.[25] Indeed Broghill and his friends might have been wiser not to have tried to make Cromwell king nor to establish an upper house because these proposals stirred up republican unrest. No doubt Monck recognized as much when after he and the Council of Scotland had solemnly proclaimed the second Protectorate in Edinburgh, surrounded by trumpeters and magistrates dressed in scarlet robes, his own soldiers showed their restlessness and not a single Scotsman cried out 'God bless the Lord Protector!'[26]

Though Monck gave his general support to Cromwell, he was no sycophant. Indeed the exiled Royalists spread rumours that Cromwell was jealous of Monck, the wish no doubt being father to the thought.[27] Monck did not hesitate to badger the Protector about his many problems; unlike Lilburne, he made threatening gestures warning Cromwell that if he did not receive all that he thought was necessary, outlying garrisons would have to be withdrawn and 'free quarter' imposed elsewhere. He even bothered the Protector over the question of providing beds for the citadel of Ayr. Furthermore, he drew his attention to the treatment of individual Scottish noblemen who had proved loyal to the united Commonwealth. Writing about a laird's losses it was stated that: 'Although the General is sorry he should trouble your Highness with things of this kind, yet forasmuch as the gentleman has been really honest to the interest of the Commonwealth ... the General can do no less than present his sufferings.' In a later letter he asked that a fine of £1,400 imposed on Lord Montgomery, the son of the Earl of Eglinton, who had been 'very serviceable to the Parliament of England', should be remitted. Likewise he asked that the Earl of Lothian, a nobleman who had 'always lived peaceably' since Monck came to Scotland 'should be granted relief from his public debts'.[28] When it came to reducing the strength of his army Monck had insisted that his own plan for a new establishment should be accepted. Nor did he like appointments being made in the army without his being consulted. He even protested to Cromwell about the appointment of a Mr Fish as chirugeon to the artillery on the ground that the man was unqualified. In 1657 he vehemently objected to a draft scheme sent to him by Cromwell for naming magistrates and councils in Scottish burghs. He pointed out that on more than one occasion these burghs had, if only by implication, been confirmed in their ancient liberties. He even hinted that what Oliver Cromwell was attempting to do was contrary to the letter and spirit of the Petition and Advice, which had laid down that the Lord Protector should govern according to the laws of the three nations of England, Scotland and Ireland and not otherwise.[29]

As it turned out, it was the establishment of the new House of Lords that was to be the bone of contention between the Lord Protector and his second Parliament. The republicans had, after the acceptance of the Petition and Advice, been allowed to resume their seats in the Commons. Although their leaders, Heslirige and Scot, did not dare again attack Cromwell's own position directly, they persuaded the House of Commons not to recognize the Other House of which Monck had been named a member. By 4 February 1658 Cromwell's patience, rarely notable, was exhausted. He accused the members of the Commons of breaching the very constitution which they and he were committed to uphold. He ended an angry speech by declaring that he dissolved this Parliament and added 'Let God judge between me and you,' to which the republicans unrepentantly retorted 'Amen'.

During the last months of his life the Lord Protector was mainly concerned with foreign affairs and with ensuring the loyalty of his army, which involved the dismissal of some of its officers who disliked the Petition and Advice, so that it was a certain guarantee and protection against a Royalist invasion under 'the King of the Scots' as he called Charles II. A treaty of alliance had been concluded with France on 13 March 1657 which stipulated that an English contingent of six infantry regiments was to be sent to the Spanish Netherlands to fight the Spaniards along with the French army. The expeditionary force landed there in the spring of 1657 under the command of Sir John Reynolds (replaced after he was drowned at sea by Sir William Lockhart); it took part in a victory over the Spaniards at the battle of the Dunes which resulted in the capture of Dunkirk. According to the terms of the treaty of alliance this port, long the habitat of pirates preying on English shipping, was now to become an English possession. It was rumoured at one stage that Monck was to be given the command.[30] However, he was kept fully in the picture about the course of the campaign, receiving letters from Thomas Morgan who was in charge of one of the regiments (being replaced in Scotland by Colonel Daniel); from Richard Hughes, who had once been captain-lieutenant in Monck's own infantry regiment; and Lieutenant-Colonel Drummond who was acting commander of Lockhart's regiment.[31] The acquisition of Dunkirk was the last triumph of Oliver Cromwell's Protectorate.

But from a personal point of view the closing months of Cromwell's life were sad. He had already admitted publicly that he was a sick man when he dissolved his last parliament. His son-in-law, Robert Rich, the husband of his youngest daughter, expired only four months after their wedding. Then his favourite daughter, Elizabeth, slowly and painfully died of cancer. He was obliged to dismiss Major William Packer, who fourteen years earlier had been one of the first captains in his own original cavalry regiment raised at his birthplace of Huntingdon, because together with five other officers in the regiment, he refused to accept the new constitution. Finally, Cromwell himself was taken seriously ill and was brought from Hampton Court to Whitehall in a litter. A contemporary related that in his sleep Cromwell called out Monck's name,[32] possibly because he was worried over the danger of a Royalist invasion of Scotland aided by the Spanish, though Monck had assured him that everything was under control.

Thurloe kept Monck informed of what was going on and as Cromwell rallied for a while hopeful accounts reached him at Dalkeith. On 10 August he wrote to Thurloe from there saying how glad he was that the Protector had overcome 'a fit of colic' and that the Lady Elizabeth was 'in a hopeful way of recovery'. A fortnight later he was still optimistic, telling the Secretary of State that he thanked God for his Highness's recovery and prayed the Lord to continue it 'and preserve him from all dangers'. But after nearly another fortnight he realized that the end was approaching and dispatched orders to all his commanders that in case Cromwell should die — as a punishment by God 'for our sins' — they should be watchful and alert and take all necessary precautions. This instruction went out on 6 September 1658; two days later Monck received the expected news, he announced the death of Cromwell, and proclaimed the succession to his throne of his eldest surviving son, Richard.[33]

Richard Cromwell was a mild-mannered gentleman, though not devoid of strength of character. His father had brought him forward only in the last years of his life — Richard succeeded him as Chancellor of Oxford University, was created a member of the Protectoral House of Lords and appointed to the Privy Council. Before that he had enjoyed the life of a country gentleman at his father-in-law's house in Hampshire, where he was described by Royalists as being 'skilled in Hawking, Hunting and Horse Racing', though not so skilled as to avoid falling off his horse. He had never fought in the army and at first it was thought that such a blameless character would be a relief in Whitehall after the stormy times of his father. Thurloe was able to inform Richard's younger brother Henry, who was the Lord Lieutenant of Ireland, that Richard had obtained 'a very easie and peaceable entrance upon his Government'. 'There is not,' he added, 'a dogge that waggs his tongue, so great a calm are we in.'[34]

Richard's brother-in-law, Charles Fleetwood, was now *de facto* head of the army, though Richard assumed the title of commander-in-chief. On 20 September Fleetwood drew up a loyal declaration which he induced 220 officers, some from Scotland and Ireland, to sign; it was presented to the new Lord Protector on the following day. It told Richard that all would be well if he behaved himself, chose godly advisers and carried on the work of reformation. In return the army leaders undertook to uphold the Government according to the terms of the Petition and Advice, that is to say with a single person and two Houses of Parliament. A copy of the address was sent to Scotland and Monck did not quibble about accepting it. He persuaded the officers at his headquarters in Dalkeith to sign a similar address which he forwarded to John Thurloe.[35]

Monck's brother-in-law, the physician Thomas Clarges, brought the news of what was happening in London to Dalkeith. Monck recognized that the peaceful accession of Richard might merely be a lull before a storm. According to Dr Gumble, chaplain to the Council of Scotland, who was with Monck at the time, he expressed the opinion after Oliver's death 'that it was not possible for him to have held the Government much longer, if he had lived'. According to Dr Clarges, Monck also said he disliked a situation in which the nation was 'inthralled by the overruling tyranny of the soldiers who made themselves a divided interest from the rest of the people so that they consulted of a paper [presumably that of 20 September] to be drawn up to be presented to the Protector.' Nevertheless, the new Protector was acclaimed not only at the mercat cross in Edinburgh but at other towns and garrisons throughout the country. The English soldiers, however, failed to salute a man they hardly knew, while junior officers are said to have muttered 'Old George for my money; he is fitter for a Protector than Dick Cromwell.'[36]

When Dr Clarges left Edinburgh he carried with him a letter for Richard Cromwell from Monck.[37] As a copy of it is in Clarges's handwriting he was probably consulted about its terms. Monck had been impressed by the disruption caused in Scotland and in his own army by the Quakers, Fifth Monarchy Men and other sectarians. Also having been a member of the 'Assembly of Saints' himself, he knew how influential and disturbing the Fifth Monarchists could be. So the first piece of advice he gave to Richard Cromwell was that he should at the same time that he called his first parliament also summon an assembly of divines and give his countenance to moderate Presbyterian ministers. He also suggested that he should call back some members of the ancient peerage to reinforce the Protectoral House of Lords and rely upon leading gentry in the shires, men like George Booth in Cheshire and Edward Popham in Somerset, to back his government. Such men would form a makeweight to discontented elements in the army who had for the most part acquiesced in Cromwell's Protectorate, but except on paper, were not bound to Richard.

Another way in which Monck thought that Richard could

neutralize the army leaders was by amalgamating regiments. As has been noted, Monck had suggested that expedient to Cromwell in his lifetime. It had, in Monck's opinion, two advantages: first, it would save money; second, it would enable Richard to get rid of 'insolent spirits'. Monck assured the new Protector that 'there is not an officer in the army upon any discontent, that has interest enough to draw men after him, if he be out of place'. He might well have been thinking of Thomas Harrison and John Lambert, two of Cromwell's former generals, who had been dismissed from the army by Cromwell and thus made incapable of causing mischief because they had not a big enough following. Finally, Monck recommended Richard Cromwell to take moderate politicians like Oliver St John, Chief Justice of the Court of Common Pleas, and Lord Broghill, the former President of the Council of Scotland, into his Privy Council.

Richard did not follow Monck's advice or was not allowed to do so by his Privy Council. Soon junior officers and convinced republicans were planning to overthrow him. Charles Fleetwood, a weak man who thought highly of himself, had the impertinence to present to the Protector on 8 October a petition asking that he himself should be appointed commander-in-chief of Richard's army instead of Richard himself who held that title. The Protector was also asked to restore to their former commands officers who had been dismissed by Oliver. Richard would not agree to these demands, but when he summoned the officers in London to meet him on 18 October he stressed that Fleetwood was Lieutenant-General of all the army under himself, thus implying that he was Monck's superior. But agitation in the army continued uninterrupted. Officers like John Desborough and James Berry, who had exerted their influence to prevent Oliver Cromwell from accepting the Crown, took part in daily meetings; John Lambert emerged from the shadows and comforts of his country house at Wimbledon; junior officers, who followed in the footsteps of Major Packer and the other officers whom Cromwell had dismissed from his own regiment, wanted to be rid of a hereditary Protector and a House of Lords and revert to the 'Good Old Cause' of oligarchic or semi-democratic republicanism.[38] Dr Clarges drew a significant comparison between the conduct of the army in England and that of Monck's army where 'no officers and soldiers have any meetings to interpose in public affairs'.[39]

After Monck's army had acquiesced in the new Protectorate all remained quiet and peaceful in Scotland. For the moment, the exiled Royalists were too abashed by the easy way with which Richard had succeeded his father to plan any insurrection. Monck, who had advised Richard to call a parliament, exerted himself to send suitable representatives to Westminster.[40] He himself was summoned to the new House of Lords but told Richard that it was wiser for him to stay in Scotland, and Richard agreed.[41] Therefore, Monck remained in the Earl of Buccleuch's house in Dalkeith with his wife and members of the Buccleuch family, but as he was granted the custody of Holyrood Palace in Edinburgh the Council of Scotland met there.

When the House of Commons assembled at the end of January 1659, although two-thirds of its members favoured the Court, Heslirige and Scot, supported by other more cloudy republicans like Henry Vane and Henry Nevile, filibustered just as they had done in Cromwell's parliaments so as to bring about the destruction of the Protectorate. One of the constitutional questions which occupied the House for the best part of a fortnight, was whether the members elected in Scotland ought or ought not to sit there. Some of the filibustering republicans objected to their presence because they were foreigners, others because some of them, they claimed, had never seen Scotland before except on a map. Clarges, who represented Aberdeen in Parliament, asserted defiantly that the Scots had a better right to sit there than the English, on the grounds that an act of parliament had provided for the presence of thirty representatives of Scotland in the Commonwealth parliament, while no statute existed legislating for 400 members to be called in England.[42] In the end, after many complicated and irrelevant arguments, the Court party obtained the recognition of the members for Scotland by a majority of nearly two to one.

Monck was disturbed by the slowness of the proceedings in parliament, as he told Samuel Desborough, who was now President of the Council of Scotland, but had gone up to London as member of parliament for East Lothian. Monck thought that the members were standing 'uppon such little punctilios' when they ought to be attending to real business 'and settled [how] to keep us at peace'. While he trusted Clarges, he did not like the way some of his officers such as Colonel Ashfield were behaving—and tried to persuade or compel them to return to their regiments. He also had come to lack confidence in the Marquis of Argyll, another member of Richard's Parliament; he believed that 'no man in the three nations does disaffect the English interest [more] than he'.[43] Finally, this ill-assorted Parliament, which failed to pass a single act or to tackle the Commonwealth's finances was dissolved by Richard Cromwell on 22 April 1659 under pressure from the leading army officers in England, including his own brother-in-law, Fleetwood, and his uncle by marriage John Desborough. Too late Richard had tried vainly to call a halt to the meetings of the discontented army officers at Wallingford House, Fleetwood's residence in London. The Protector had counted on Parliament backing him against the army, as indeed it attempted to do, but this only further provoked both officers and men. When Richard ordered his bodyguard to arrest Fleetwood it refused, while such colonels as remained friendly to him were simply disobeyed.

The day after the dissolution of Parliament Fleetwood wrote to Monck justifying what had been done, assuring him that Parliament had not been 'forced', that all was now quiet and that it was the army's intention 'to serve his Highness in further preservation of the Good Old Cause'.[44] But since the 'Good Old Cause' was a republican government and not a Protectorate, Monck's initial reaction was to enquire exactly what 'the Good Old Cause' was.[45] It is clear that he did not like what had happened.[46] However, the Wallingford House party insisted that it was sure Monck would approve of 'the reviving and prosperity of the Good Old Cause in all its essentials in all three nations' that is to say the re-establishment of oligarchic republicanism.[47] That was a false assumption. Though the evidence is fragmentary, Monck might well have marched his army up to London had Richard appealed to him earlier.[48] The fact was that Monck's first reaction after he had assimilated all the news of what was happening in London was to ask that the Protector and his family should be cared for and looked after 'in view of the great services of that family to these nations', shows where his deepest loyalties then lay.[49] Afterwards Monck was credited with saying — and it is likely enough — 'Richard forsook himself, else I had never failed my promise to his father or my regard to his memory.'[50]

12
Monck Decides

Two officers, John Mason and Roger Sawrey, who were known to Monck and were in London during the critical weeks which followed the dissolution of Richard Cromwell's Parliament, wrote to tell him that 'the army here in England is very unanimous in the late action'.[1] It may have been unanimous about dissolving Parliament, but it did not agree upon what form of government was to be established afterwards. Some, including Mason and Sawrey, were enthusiastic Commonwealthsmen; Fleetwood and his closest associates, known as the Grandees, favoured retaining the Protectorate while ensuring that Richard Cromwell was no more than a figurehead; a third party would genuinely have liked to maintain the Protectorate as it was but without a parliament. Finally, after a meeting between the Grandees and some of the civilian republicans, such as Henry Vane and Arthur Heslirige, a firm decision was taken to reassemble the Rump, that is to say the members of the Long Parliament who had sat from 1648 to 1653, having been purged by the army leaders of the rest of the members who had wanted to negotiate with King Charles I even after the outbreak of the second civil war.[2] (These were known as 'the secluded members'.)

This solution was really a compromise. For while it could claim constitutional validity because the members of the Rump had been freely elected nearly twenty years earlier, it also represented a purely republican group which would be faithful to 'the Good Old Cause'. It was believed that over 200 members of this Parliament were still in rude health, but only 120 actually took their seats and the average attendance was fifty.[3] At the same time a Committee of Safety, consisting of only ten councillors—seven keen republicans and three army officers—was set up to manage affairs, but it was later superseded by a Council of State of twenty-one, most of whom were members of parliament and therefore could reasonably assume that their decisions would be approved by it. The majority of the Council was determined to keep the armies under control. Though Fleetwood was appointed commander-in-chief, he was not permitted to nominate or dismiss his own officers. A committee or commission was set up to recommend to the ageing Speaker which officers should be retained in Parliament's service; Cromwellians and others believed not to be loyal to the new regime, were dismissed or demoted and some officers who had been cashiered by Oliver Cromwell, such as Alured, Overton and Packer, were restored to their regiments.

To begin with, Monck signified his approval of what had been done. He expressed his joy to the Committee of Safety on its consisting of 'persons of soe eminent worth and integrity' entirely capable of managing 'soe weighty an affaire as the safety of the three nations'.[4] When the President of the Council of State, alarmed at rumours of renewed Royalist activity (though they were in fact premature), ordered Fleetwood to send an infantry regiment to the north of England, Monck promptly dispatched Ashfield's regiment, which had been engaged on boring garrison duties, to Durham, even though Ashfield himself had long been absent in London, absorbed in military politics and personal squabbles. Nevertheless, Monck thought it right to sound warning notes. Besides strongly recommending generous treatment of the Cromwells, he reminded Parliament of the need to fulfil civil and religious hopes and told Fleetwood that he was glad to learn he had 'a lively sense of his past failings and present duty', which was not the way one would normally write to one's superior officer.[5] He assured Parliament that he would defend it 'against the opposition of all arbitrary powers whatsoever'. Yet he refused to take any oaths, for he told the President of the Council of State that 'Government is an ordinance of God who bids us submit to every ordinance of man'.[6] Therefore, while he undertook to uphold 'the Good Old Cause', he refused to be fettered by iron oaths. Three weeks later he was telling the Speaker of the House of Parliament, whose duty it was to approve of all army commissions:

My conscience is a witness to and of my integrity (whatsoever men may judge) that I am none of those who seek great things haveing my education in a Commonwealth [the United Netherlands] where souldiours received and observed commands, but gave none. Obedience is my great principle and I have alwaies, and ever shall, reverence the Parliament's resolutions in civill things as infalliable and sacred ...[7]

Having struck this attitude, Monck clearly thought that as he had been so successful in imposing law and order on Scotland, converting the country into a haven of peace, as Fleetwood himself admitted, his army should be left alone to carry out its duties of protecting the ports, policing the big towns, ridding the neighbouring seas of pirates and seizing arms belonging to suspected Royalist sympathizers. Even before he wrote his eloquent letter to the Speaker promising to obey the Parliament in all things, he had on 2 June 'humbly requested' Parliament through the Speaker that they would not alter any of the officers under his command, since without exception they all freely assented to the re-establishment of the Commonwealth without a single person or House of Lords. Later the Royalists heard that Monck had refused to allow any of his officers to be dismissed until their arrears were paid and specific charges proved against them.[8]

The commission for nominating officers, which was also somewhat confusingly known as the committee of safety, started work early in June.[9] It consisted of seven members, four of the army Grandees, Fleetwood, Lambert, Desborough and Berry, and three consistent and unsullied republicans, Arthur Heslirige, Henry Vane and Edmund Ludlow; as Heslirige had formerly been colonel of a regiment and Vane had been Treasurer of the Navy and Ludlow still held a commission, they must have assumed that they knew what they were doing. The Commons journals for the summer of 1659 are largely filled with long lists of names of officers in the army, the navy and the county militias. The credentials of every man who had held a commission were carefully examined, then their names were submitted to Parliament which might or might not confirm them — sometimes the House divided on whether or not to accept the latest list — and finally all the officers approved or newly nominated were summoned before the Speaker to receive their commissions from his venerable hands. The leading spirit on the nominating committee was Heslirige who was convinced that this tight hold on the armed forces by the Rump Parliament was necessary in order to prevent any further *coups d'état*.

In spite of Monck's appeal to the Speaker, Heslirige had no intention of omitting the officers in Scotland from the scrutiny of his committee. The advisers to the nominating committee in regard to Scotland were two Anabaptist colonels, John Pearson, who was given Colonel Daniel's infantry regiment—Daniel being removed from it because he had been too enthusiastic a Cromwellian—and John Mason, a vigorous republican and patron of the sectarians. Both had served under Monck in Scotland, but neither of them returned there. Mason was appointed governor of Jersey and Pearson went over to Dunkirk in order to purge the garrison of ungodly officers. In reply to Monck's protest to the Speaker, Heslirige told him firmly that his officers' politics must be examined. 'It is of high concern', he wrote, 'that they will be faithful to Parliament and the Commonwealth', and added rudely that 'peradventure discoveries are known to the Parliament that are not known to yourself'.[10] The suggestion that the Rump knew more about his own officers than Monck himself did not go down at all well; he remonstrated emphatically, and to a large extent successfully, about proposed alterations in his regiments. Possibly for that reason relatively few changes were made.

The most noticeable alterations by the nominating committee were in the infantry regiments commanded by Colonel Talbot, Colonel Sawrey and Colonel Daniel. In Colonel Talbot's regiment, which Monck had personally vouched for (Talbot had replaced Alured in 1655), two field officers were demoted and three captains dismissed. The Anabaptist Pearson not only took over Daniel's regiment but replaced him as governor of Perth, while in Sawrey's regiment another Anabaptist, Major Abraham Holmes, was promoted over the head of its acting colonel. As late as the second week of August five changes were proposed in Monck's own regiment of horse which infuriated him and led him to protest vigorously to the nominating committee. Another cavalry regiment of which five troops were stationed in Scotland, was put by the Rump under the charge of the very Colonel Saunders whom Monck had arrested in 1655 and who had been dismissed by Cromwell. No doubt Monck was annoyed about that too, though Saunders wisely kept away from Scotland. Dr Gumble, who was in Edinburgh at this time, asserted that the aim of the committee of nominations was to give preference to 'Sectaries and Anabaptists' so as 'either to weary Monck out of his Command or else to tie his Hands'.[11] If their political criterion was, as it seems to have been, to demote or dismiss officers who had favoured the Cromwellian Protectorate, the first officer they ought to have removed was George Monck himself. As it was, few or no changes had actually been put into effect in Scotland when the Rump itself was forcibly dissolved for the second time in its history. Pearson never came to Scotland at all and when Monck broke with the officers of the army in England both Sawrey and Holmes fled the country.

The disagreement between the army and parliament which led to the downfall of Richard Cromwell had encouraged the Royalists both in England and abroad. Led by the young John Mordaunt, conspirators in England managed to persuade Charles II that the time was ripe for a national insurrection and for an invasion supported, it was hoped, by the Spaniards. The date fixed for the rising and invasion was 1 August 1659 when the King left Brussels for Dieppe aiming to land in eastern England. Although the Cromwells' Secretary of State, John Thurloe, had been dismissed by the new regime, the intelligence in London about the Royalist schemes was good. At that time Monck's loyalty to the Council of State was under suspicion for two reasons: first, because of the peremptory way in which he had resisted changes in the officers of his regiments; second, because he was less enthusiastic about the freedom given or offered to the sectaries in Scotland than was the English Parliament since he thought it conducive to anarchy and unrest, as exemplified by the disruptive tactics of the Quakers. He preferred a united Church and actually threatened to cashier some of his troopers if they refused to listen to the Scottish ministers preaching on Sundays. At the beginning of July a French representative in London reported home that Parliament was 'insensed against Monck' not so much because of his letter of 2 June, which some in the House said ought to have been burnt by the common hangman, as because he was uncivil to commissioners sent to him from Whitehall.[12]

But whatever suspicions they felt, the Rumpers had no alternative to trusting him since for five years he had been organizing the defences of Scotland and virtually no other commander was to be found by whom he could be replaced at short notice. Deane was dead and Lilburne had been a failure. Sir Archibald Johnston of Wariston, also known as Lord Wariston, a Presbyterian, was then, rather to his own surprise, president of the Council of State in England. He was much exercised about 'some strainge rumors of sturrings among Malignants' and wrote to Monck on 14 July to tell him that John Desborough had been sent to the west, where, among Monck's own relatives and friends in Cornwall and Devon Cavalier sympathies were strong, and that the Council was 'asking personal assurances from those on bond in the Tower of London'. He asked Monck to do the same in Scotland; Vice-Admiral John Lawson wrote to Monck about unconfirmed rumours that the Spaniards intended to ship men for England and draw forces before Dunkirk; officers at Dunkirk (including Ashfield and Pearson) informed Monck that a mutiny among the garrison there had 'Charles Stuart at the bottom of it'. Monck took immediate action. He ordered every one of his officers in charge of regiments or garrisons 'to prevent all horse races and other suspicious meetings, to seize arms of Royalists and horses above the value they have orders for; to get intelligence of intended meetings of Royalists planning risings and to keep in touch with adjacent garrisons and justices of the peace'. After consulting a council of war, he agreed to sending out a circular letter demanding an oath from all his officers that they would do nothing to help Charles Stuart, or disturb the public peace, or indeed do anything prejudicial to the Rump and the Commonwealth of England. So much for the story that he was inexorably opposed in principle to the exaction of oaths.

The Royalist stirrings were so widespread that the Council of State in England was understandably alarmed.[13] Besides dispatching Desborough to the west, where he had once been major-general of the horse militia, the Council sent Lambert to the north-west which he knew so well when fighting there under Oliver Cromwell. A foot regiment and a cavalry regiment were commanded to come over from Ireland; and Monck was ordered to dispatch two cavalry regiments and two infantry regiments out of Scotland. But he would not obey this order. That was comprehensible since his own recently reduced establishment was, he thought, barely sufficient for his own needs. For example, he had only three cavalry regiments (his own, and those of Saunders and Twistleton) which were available as a mobile reserve. That refusal must have made him even more un-

popular with the Rump. According to the memoirs of Edmund
Ludlow, 'he excused himself under colour of the Enemies Strength
and Inclination to revolt'.[14]

In actual fact the Royalist rising of 1659, like that of 1655, was
ill-concerted and badly executed. In one respect, however, it differed
from that of 1655, for the organizing body, known as the Great
Trust, consisted both of out-and-out Royalists and some Presbyterian leaders who detested the Rump Parliament. It was therefore
decided that a greater degree of decentralization should be permitted
'to solve the problems of co-ordinating simultaneous risings'. It was
intended to find in each area a leader to direct a semi-independent
revolt. In Gloucester, for example, Colonel Edward Massey, a
Presbyterian officer who had defied Charles I and Prince Rupert at
the siege of Gloucester in 1643, but was now an active Cavalier,
busily carried out a recruiting campaign in Gloucestershire and
Worcestershire in conjunction with Lord Herbert, grandson of the
most wealthy of Charles I's servants, the Marquis of Worcester.
But the authorities at Gloucester swept the countryside with
cavalry; both Massey and Herbert were arrested, though the former
at once contrived to escape.

In Lancashire and Cheshire the leader was another Presbyterian,
Sir George Booth, who had been the Governor of Nantwich at the
time when Monck was taken prisoner there in 1644. Booth had
been a member of the Long Parliament but was excluded by the
army in Pride's Purge. Rich and influential, he had later been
elected to both parliaments called by Oliver Cromwell; he had also
been trusted locally by the Commonwealth regime. But he was
alienated by the overthrow of the Protectorate and the recall of the
Rump in which he had not been allowed to take his seat, though he
tried to do so. After recruiting three or four thousand men he managed to seize the town of Chester without difficulty, though the
Governor defied him from the castle. Although Booth published
three declarations none of them mentioned the King by name. In the
first he condemned a corrupt and avaricious government and asked
for a free parliament; in the second he castigated both the army and
the existing parliament and sought either a new free parliament or
the recall of the old members of both Houses so as roughly to re-enact
the situation in 1640. In his last declaration, when he was desperate,
he appealed to everyone he could think of who had grievances

including the remaining Levellers. Logically what he was asking for was the restoration of the King and the two former Houses of Parliament. But he was gripped by indecision and his recruits were no match for the veterans of the New Model Army.[15]

Among the measures taken by Charles II's Court to help the rising on 1 August was a well organized attempt to suborn Monck himself. Lord Colepeper, a member of the King's Council, had several months earlier told Edward Hyde, Charles's Chancellor of the Exchequer, that an approach ought to be made to Monck, 'a sullen man that values himself enough', since it was only his personal affection for Oliver Cromwell and his pride in his profession as soldier which prevented him from resuming his ancient loyalty to the Stuarts. This idea was taken up and pushed forward by Monck's cousin, Sir John Grenville, whose father had been killed fighting for the King. As far back as 1653 Grenville had paved the way by installing Monck's younger brother, Nicholas, as rector of Kilhampton, which was in Cornwall but on the border of Devon. The benefice carried a stipend of £300 a year, remarkably high for those days; Nicholas was successful in persuading the puritan Triers, set up by the Lord Protector to vet new clergy, to confirm his incumbency. All that his patron, Grenville, required in return was that if he were asked to do him a service one day in the future Nicholas would do so. Grenville was in London and invited Nicholas to come up to see him urgently. For Charles II had written to Grenville empowering him to offer Monck £100,000 a year to spend as he liked and enclosed a letter for the General in which the King wrote, 'I cannot think you wish me ill, nor have I any Reason to do so: And the good I expect from you will bring so great a Benefit to your Country and to your self that I cannot think you will decline my Interest.' He left the way in which Monck should declare himself to his own judgment, promising to accept any advice that Monck gave him.[16] A messenger was needed to convey the offer to Monck in Scotland.

Nicholas Monck, a timid and honest man with Royalist affiliations had a well-to-do wife, but several children to support; thus he was the ideal person to carry out a secret approach, for his daughter Mary was staying with her uncle in Dalkeith and Nicholas gave it out that he wanted to consult his elder brother, now the head of the family, about her marriage. In London he received his instructions from Grenville, and also had an interview with Monck's brother-in-law, Dr Clarges, who himself refused to meet Grenville but used his influence to send Nicholas to Scotland on board a frigate, since the roads north were cluttered with parties of soldiers marching to quell the Royalist risings.[17] Grenville had received the commission from the King on 23 July; Nicholas Monck left Cornwall at the end of July on the very day when the drums were beating in War-rington to call Booth's recruits to arms. On 4 August, two days after Booth successfully occupied the port of Chester, Nicholas cheerfully sailed from London for Leith and on 8 August reached Dalkeith. He astutely refrained from carrying the King's letter to Monck with him, but he had learnt its contents by heart.[18]

When Nicholas arrived he found his brother extremely busy, no doubt redistributing his troops so as to prevent any invasions of the east coast of Scotland or a renewal of Royalist warfare in the high-lands. John Price, who was Monck's chaplain, was therefore deputed to welcome his brother and discover what messages he had brought from England. After Price had entertained Nicholas with a glass of wine he managed to extract from him the true purpose of his journey. Having heard what Nicholas had to say Price gave him encourage-ment by telling him that he believed Monck would be willing to close with any 'fair overture to redeem his country from the slavery of the army' (in England); that he objected to the way in which the Rump had behaved towards him since its recall, that he was annoyed by the committee for nominations's interference with his officers, which meant that he had to accept in his service new men 'of the most extravagant sort of principles', and that in general he was so disgusted by these affronts that he had been thinking of retiring to his estates in Ireland. According to Dr Gumble, rumours had already been circulating in England that George Monck might join the Royalists. At any rate as his headquarters staff and visiting officers included several dyed-in-the-wool republicans he dared not openly hold long interviews with his brother who came from the Royalist parts of Cornwall and so naturally was believed to be a Royalist himself. Indeed just before Nicholas arrived, John Price tells us, a certain Colonel Jonathan Atkins, who appears to have served with Monck in the campaign against the Scots during 1640 and was to become governor of Barbados during the reign of Charles II, visited Dalkeith when on his way to see relations of his in

Fifeshire: his object was to sound the commander-in-chief of Scotland about his willingness to support a Royalist insurrection in the north of England. Monck told Atkins that he could do no less than his duty by sending a force to repress rebels and promptly packed him off to northern Scotland. When Monck decided to meet his brother —which he could hardly avoid doing—he instructed his intimates to spread around the story that Nicholas had come merely to see his daughter and arrange about her marriage.

As soon as he understood the true purpose of Nicholas's journey Monck, according to Dr Gumble, was 'wary and reserved and did not seem to listen over-much'. Certainly he cannot have been surprised at a further Royalist approach to him in view of the letters that he had previously received in 1658. After reflection Monck discussed the question with the men in his entourage whom he trusted most including his adjutant-general, Jeremy Smith, his chaplain, Price, his physician, Dr Samuel Barrow, and Major Ralph Knight, who was in charge of his own cavalry regiment. The answer he received was that he ought to act at once and they would stand by him. Other officers in Edinburgh were sounded on the General's behalf. 'Why will not George do something?' they asked, 'it is not in our power.'[19]

George Monck was rarely impetuous. But the offer of £100,000 a year for life was not to be sniffed at. His wife, who had been brought up impecuniously, must have fancied the idea of becoming a really rich and titled lady. Although their second son, George, had died in infancy, they had an heir in Christopher (or Kit) and it may be stressed that dynastic considerations bit deep into seventeenth-century gentry. At any rate, according to Price, Anne was influential with her husband and favourable to the Royalist offer. When she put on her 'treason gown', it was said, Monck allowed her to say what she liked. Another factor was that Booth's rising had been largely engineered by Presbyterians; for General Monck as has been noticed, had come to prefer the Scottish Presbyterians, especially if the Kirk were united, to the numerous sectarian religions which contended with it; he believed profoundly that religious conformity was essential to permanent peace. His wife is also said to have been partial to the Presbyterians, as was his chaplain. Finally, Monck had reason to think that Lord Fairfax in Yorkshire and his friend and estate agent in Devon, William Morice, had now reached the conclusion that the political anarchy in England, which had prevailed since the overthrow of the Protectorate, must be brought to an end. Not only had Monck good cause to dislike the Rump's meddling with his army, but he also must have regretted that after he and the Council of Scotland had tried so hard to ensure that the Cromwellian ordinance and later act of union worked properly, the Rump had declared that act invalid and was now leisurely engaged in going over the whole business again including sending yet another commission to Edinburgh. Meanwhile administrative and judicial confusion supervened in Scotland.[20]

These were all persuasive considerations, financial, political and military. After deep thought Monck announced his decision to his most intimate advisers in the third week of August, more than a fortnight after his brother's arrival at Dalkeith, to throw in his lot with the Presbyterians and Royalists. He sent for Dr Gumble from Edinburgh who assured him that most of the officers there would follow him. Monck then authorized Gumble, who reached Dalkeith on the night of Saturday 19 August, and Price, both of whom had Cavalier sympathies, to draw up suitable declarations for publication; he instructed Jeremy Smith to go at once to Edinburgh and Leith to secure the castle of one and the citadel of the other. He ordered Knight, who was in charge of his cavalry regiment, to recruit each troop up to eighty men, 'well affected persons, preferably old soldiers'.[21] He asked the Receiver-General and the treasurer of his army to let him know how much money they had available and received from them a satisfactory answer. Gumble and Price burned the midnight oil drawing up a manifesto; next day (Sunday the 20th) Gumble offered to preach in Price's place while Price finalized their joint efforts. What they wrote and Monck approved was not directly in favour of the King in exile any more than Booth's declarations had been. The text was conciliatory, yet it gave warning to the Rump that unless Parliament now filled up its vacancies and agreed on rules for future free elections, the men in the army of Scotland would not or could not help to protect its authority since the supremacy of the Rump was not 'the Good Old Cause' for which they had fought.

The declaration was ready therefore on Monday 21 August which was five days after Major-General Lambert, dispatched by the Rump to the north-west, had with his trained soldiers easily defeated Booth's scratch army near Nantwich. Monck could have come into the open before that, but by what Gumble called 'Inspiration' he decided on that Monday to await the receipt of the next post. When Price protested at this delay, Monck retorted: 'What, Mr Price, will you bring my Neck to the Block for the King and ruin our whole Design by engaging too rashly?' The very next day the news of Booth's defeat reached Monck from his brother-in-law in London. (The post usually took about five days from London even when brought by a special messenger.) That was conclusive. Monck's army was neither big enough nor united enough to act without allies in England. Nevertheless, John Price recorded in his recollections of these events that it was from the time of his brother's arrival at Dalkeith that he dated General Monck's resolution to restore the King.[22]

So the whole scheme was called off. On 3 September, a fortnight after that fateful weekend, Monck submitted his resignation to the Speaker of the House of Parliament on the grounds that 'he was infirm in health, and had long continued in that remote Country; ... requesting that now all Insurrections, which threatened the disturbance of the Peace of the Nations were allayed, he might be permitted to return to his own Country, to end his Days in Quiet.' His brother-in-law thought that these pathetic words were simply intended, in view of the suspicions felt about him, to prevent his being 'wormed out' of his post or stultified in his command and that he had felt it wiser to resign of his own accord.[23] However, Clarges managed to get the Speaker to delay reading the letter to Parliament; Monck then changed his mind and asked that his letter should be withdrawn. By then he had become aware of the antagonisms developing between Heslirige and the oligarchic republicans on the one side and the army in England, directed by Fleetwood and Lambert, on the other. Though a thanksgiving dinner was held to celebrate the victory over Booth, in reality no doubt it was to commemorate the lucky escape of Monck and his friends from pressing the trigger too soon or despairing too early. When after two months stay Nicholas Monck with his daughter left Dalkeith on 8 October, Monck told him: 'I shall have a better game to play then I had before.'[24] Surely that meant that he intended to restore the King?

Though the story that has been outlined has been accepted by all Monck's previous biographers it has been delicately rejected by one or two modern historians as being intrinsically improbable. The late

Godfrey Davies in his excellent book on *The Restoration of Charles II* wrote that 'the complete absence of any of the kind of measures Monck took in the following October [that is to say presumably the purging from his army of unreliable elements] must render his biographer's account suspect.'[25] Did Price and Gumble then invent the whole story? Did Thomas Clarges, who confirmed it and was close in touch with his sister and brother-in-law, also make it up? If so, their purpose is far from clear while their words are remarkably circumstantial. Leaving aside what they wrote as meant to boost Monck's reputation after the Restoration, a possible but unlikely aim, can one not argue that the known and unchallenged historical evidence about the events of the summer of 1659 make his reported actions plausible? Monck was undoubtedly angry with the insolent way in which he had been treated by Heslirige and his Anabaptist friends and he is known to have been a personal admirer of George Booth, whose services he had recommended to Richard Cromwell after he came to the throne. As to the military preparations, it has been seen how Monck ordered Smith to secure Edinburgh and Leith, how he arranged for his cavalry regiment to be strengthened and how he had inquired about the size of his war chest when he was contemplating marching into England. When Price asked Monck what he would have done if the news of Booth's defeat had not reached them until later, he replied 'I would have commissioned the whole of Scotland to rise.'[26]

Thus it is scarcely true that no military precautions were undertaken. With regard to the loyalty of the army, it had been vouched for at any rate in Edinburgh by Gumble, while Monck by his persistence had been remarkably successful in partly preventing and partly postponing the infiltration of Heslirige's devoted republican nominees into his army instead of the men who had fought with him in the days of Oliver Cromwell. Finally, because of this very episode Monck could have realized that more elaborate arrangements would need to be carried out rather than hurried makeshift precautions if he and his army were to intervene effectively in politics. That must have been what he had in mind when after hearing of the beginnings of a rupture between the leaders of the army in England and the republican oligarchy directing the government of both countries, he told his brother that soon he would have a better game to play than before.

13

The Break
with the Army
in England

After the ending of that traumatic weekend in August which was
followed by Monck's offer to resign his command, an offer he withdrew a fortnight after he sent it, he concentrated for the time being
on trying to secure peace and order in Scotland. In view of the
Rump's delay in drawing up a new act of union, administrative chaos
prevailed there. Monck informed the Speaker at the beginning of
September that Scotland was 'in such a distemper that it's a miracle
of mercy that they [the Scots] are not running into blood'.[1] In response to instructions sent to him from London Monck demanded
from all the leading Scotsmen an engagement that they would
remain loyal to the Rump and arrested those who refused to take it.
He also asked that the committee for nominations would stop inter-
fering with his officers because at such an unsettled time 'men of
known courage and fidelity' were essential to him. The committee
referred his request to Parliament while the Council of State told
him on 20 September that he could release persons who had been
arrested on suspicion of being involved in the Royalist plot for a
general insurrection, provided that they took the engagement.
Monck had earlier reminded the Council of State that unless he was
sent more money from England, he would be forced to put his army
on 'free quarter'. It did so.[2]

The truth was that a state of anarchy practically existed in England and, to a lesser extent because of the firm hand of Monck, in
Scotland.[3] The army in England, flushed with its easy defeat of the
Royalist rising, was agitating for a complete reorganization of all
positions of authority and the people that held them, whether
justices of the peace, clergy or government officials, throughout the
Commonwealth, seeking a kind of universal purge, or, as a later

generation might have called it, a *Gleichschaltung*. A petition drawn up in Derby during September by a group of officers who had served under Lambert, also asked that Fleetwood should be given a permanent appointment with far-reaching authority, that Lambert should be his second-in-command, Desborough general of horse, and Monck general of foot. Fleetwood himself presented the Derby petition to the Rump on 22 September. The members were absolutely furious at the impertinence and threatened to send Lambert, recently awarded a jewel valued at £1,000 for his victory over Booth, to the Tower of London as a prisoner.

The officers at Derby had sent a copy of their petition to Monck in Scotland and had also written letters to some of his officers. Monck would have nothing to do with it. He at once told his commanders, 'Yow know it alwaies hath been against my way to signe any petitions at all, either by the Parliament or General [Fleetwood] from the forces heere, and I am still of the same judgement.' He added that no officers were to sign anything without his consent.[4]

Meanwhile in London, after Fleetwood had informed the Council of Officers at Wallingford House of the rejection of the Derby petition by Parliament, the Council refused to accept the rebuff and at once appointed a sub-committee to draw up another petition more moderate in tone but no less far-reaching in scope, omitting only the clause about the general officers. One of its nine demands was that no officer or private should be cashiered except by court-martial. Monck appears to have made the point that a commander-in-chief should also be given the right to cashier his men, but in any case he refused to endorse the new petition, which was presented by Desborough to the Rump on 5 October.[5] Monck immediately made up his mind to seize the opportunity he was thus afforded by the growing rift between the Rump and the leaders of the army in England, to purge his own army and stand ready to lead it into England. While the Rump was acrimoniously debating the second army petition for nearly a week, Nicholas Monck was leaving Scotland with a message for Dr Clarges (himself, as has been noted, a member of parliament), that Monck was ready and willing to march into England in support of the Rump. Monck knew that he was in the good books of Parliament because it had sent him a letter of thanks for his services on the very day when Desborough presented the second petition to the House. But did Monck really intend simply to defend the Rump, which had become increasingly unpopular both in England and Scotland on account of its incompetence and vacillations, as he said, or had he in mind to work for the restoration of Charles II to which he had virtually committed himself less than seven weeks earlier? The Anabaptists and other sectarians who sympathized with the Army in England (which ever since Cromwell's time had been the guardian of liberty of conscience) rather than with the Rump, believed that this was indeed his aim and would have meant the revival of Anglican supremacy. *A Declaration of Several Thousands in Westmorland and Durham* published on 12 October observed that they were 'greatly grieved to hear Malignant Spirits, some crying out Monk was always true to his old Master'. In the first week of November when it became known that Monck was planning a march into England the Anabaptists — so it was reported from London — were reproaching Monck and asserting 'he intends to bring in the King of the Scots and put out all the godly'. Two days later another newsletter received in Scotland reported that the Anabaptists were doing all they could to make Monck 'odious', saying that 'Charles Stewart is at the bottom of this his design.'[6]

In the middle of October the conflict between the Council of Officers in London, led by Lambert and Desborough, and the Rump Parliament, directed by Heslirige and Thomas Scot, reached its climax. On 11 October Heslirige showed to the House of Parliament a copy of a circular letter soliciting support from the regiments stationed in London for the petition which Desborough had presented; this was a copy sent by mistake to Colonel Okey, who was in fact loyal to the Rump. Next day Nicholas Monck having arrived in London, the Rump was informed — presumably by Clarges, that Monck 'was resolved if the Parliament would be resolute in asserting their own Authority against the Army, he would assist them in it; and if required thereunto, march into England in their Defence'. Thus encouraged, the Rump voted that the commissions of Lambert, Desborough and other leading members of the Council of Officers should immediately be taken away from them, while Fleetwood, Monck, Heslirige and four other officers including Robert Overton — a strange stablemate for Monck — should be appointed commissioners for the future government of the army.[7]

Next day Lambert and Desborough retorted by drawing up infantry regiments around the parliament house and Whitehall palace to prevent the Speaker and others from taking their seats. Colonel Ralph Cobbett, who had at one time been governor of Aberdeen and whose regiment was now in Glasgow, but had been himself playing a leading part in the Council of Officers in London, was on the same day dispatched to Scotland to explain the reasons for the latest *coup d'état* by the army in England. Colonel Robert Barrow was sent on a similar mission to Dublin. Both Cobbett and Barrow were among those officers whose commissions had been taken away the day before by the Rump.

The Council of Officers decided to set up a Committee of Safety to replace the Council of State as the executive government of the Commonwealth. It induced a number of civilians including Lord Whitelocke, who did everything he was asked to do perhaps because he had twenty children to support, the cloudy-minded Sir Henry Vane, and the Scot Johnston of Wariston to sit on it. On 18 October Fleetwood, who wobbled from side to side, was named commander-in-chief with Lambert as his major-general; the relation between these two men was compared with that between Fairfax and Cromwell ten years earlier.

The news of the *coup d'état* reached Monck on 17 October. Because Monck, even before this, had committed himself to the support of the Rump, his course was clear and his action rapid. On 19 October he instructed his colonels and garrison commanders throughout Scotland 'to be faithful to the Parliament of England which has been interrupted and broken'.[8] Any officers who refused to be so were to be displaced. On the next day he wrote letters to the Speaker, Fleetwood and Lambert telling each of them of his intention to assert the liberty and authority of Parliament as he profoundly condemned 'the force' put upon it.[9] On the previous day he himself left Dalkeith for Edinburgh to 'remodel' his own infantry regiment and to address the entire garrison there on its duty to serve and obey Parliament; those who refrained from doing so were to be cashiered, though he put it more politely. When Monck's letters reached London they were at once printed and published. On 22 October he ordered a day of fasting and humiliation to be held in Edinburgh four days later 'to seek the Lord for his blessing in this great affaire'.[10]

What was this 'great affaire'? It was George Monck's determination to march into England, whatever happened in London. He ordered the arrest of Colonel Cobbett as soon as he reached Berwick-upon-Tweed, which had been seized on Monck's behalf by Captain Thomas Johnson with a troop of horse and two infantry companies and purged of the Anabaptist officers in its garrison. Afterwards Berwick's governor and the inhabitants of the town protested their loyalty to the General. Monck was completely unmoved by the representations of two old friends of his, Colonel Thomas Talbot, whose regiment formed part of the Edinburgh garrison, and his crafty brother-in-law, Dr Clarges, sent to meet Monck and to exert their influence to restrain him from rash action. Talbot brought a long letter from Fleetwood with him, but Monck was adamant. He insisted that Fleetwood, Lambert and their friends were not really concerned about the government of the country but only about their own personal interests.[11]

In preparation for his march Monck purged his army, began a propaganda campaign and summoned the noblemen and magistrates in Scotland to meet him on 15 November so that he might persuade them to keep order while he began his march into England on or about 20 November.[12] Though originally Monck had announced that his officers who did not agree with him should be left unmolested, draw their pay and go home, he now began to employ rougher methods, putting recalcitrants under arrest. By way of propaganda he published declarations signed by himself and his officers as well as the letters he had written to the Speaker, Fleetwood and Lambert. He made his position crystal-clear when, after receiving a letter from the Committee of Safety empowering him to reinstate courts of civil and criminal justice, which had ceased to function when the Rump was considering a new act of union, he responded by saying that to do so would mean that the laws were being executed 'from an illegal foundation'. Nothing could be done until the Parliament was again restored. To Lambert he wrote on 3 November, 'It is much upon my spiritt that this poore Commonwealth can never bee happy if the army make itself a divided interest from the rest of the nation.'[13] But now a lull intervened. Monck realized that he was rushing ahead too fast. He needed time to complete the reorganization of the regiments under his command from which 140–150 officers altogether were to be removed and replaced, to persuade the Scots to behave themselves during his absence, and to allow his propaganda to make its impact. So, taking advantage of a sentence in one of Fleetwood's letters, he and his

Council of War agreed on 3 November to dispatch three officers to London, Colonel Ralph Knight, whom Monck had just put in command of his own regiment of horse, Colonel Timothy Wilkes and Colonel John Clobery, to seek an agreement with the Grandees of Wallingford House. All of them were trusted friends of Monck. Knight had been his confidant when he was thinking of supporting George Booth; Wilkes had been an intermediary between him and Oliver Cromwell; Clobery came from Devonshire and was a kinsman of Monck. Their instructions were detailed; among other things they were to arrange a temporary armistice between the two armies and to procure an act of oblivion. They were also to insist that officers whom Monck had dismissed in Scotland and at Berwick-upon-Tweed and had been replaced by others, were not to be interfered with until the Rump had been recalled and considered their position. But the most significant instruction (number 10) was, 'that noe forme of Governement be established over these Nations butt by Parliament, unless they shall refuse to sitt, or sitting shall refuse or neglect to establish the same betweixt this and the 6th of May next.'[14]

Before it became known in London that Monck was sending commissioners to treat with Fleetwood and his officers, John Lambert left for the north of England in command of an army of 8,000 men including 3,500 cavalry. He sent orders to Colonel Robert Lilburne, who was now the military governor of York and had approved of the English army's *coup d'état*, to collect reinforcements, raise the local militia and occupy Newcastle upon Tyne. Lambert's declared objective was to reach an understanding with Monck and his forces in Scotland; carrying an iron hand in a velvet glove he was cheerfully convinced that Monck would have to come to an agreement with him. For, after all, it was obvious that if the two armies were to clash it would be enormously to the advantage of the exiled Charles II and the Royalists everywhere. Moreover it was difficult for Lambert or anyone else seriously to believe that George Monck, who had accepted Oliver Cromwell's expulsion of the Rump Parliament in 1653 without protest, would regard the recall of this discredited group of extreme republicans as a matter of life and death. Indeed the French ambassador in London expressed at the time his view that if Monck had insisted upon the summoning of a free parliament instead of the return of the Rump he would have commanded more ready and general confidence.

However, it was clear enough to several impartial observers that Monck was playing for time since he was not yet in a position to confront Fleetwood and Lambert. They had all been comrades in arms under Oliver; surely they were not going to quarrel? Officers on both sides of the Tweed had their doubts. One of Monck's captains stationed at Dundee said he could not find it in his heart to fight against the army in England; Lambert's men asserted that they would not fight against Monck unless he declared for the King. So Monck dispatched soothing letters and messages. He wrote to Lilburne to tell him that the commissioners from Scotland were on their way to London 'to treat for unity' and that until a treaty had been agreed the various forces were to stay in their existing positions including those under Lilburne and Robert Overton at Hull; on the same day he wrote to Fleetwood observing that he hoped when his officers arrived the commander-in-chief would not have 'so severe an opinion' about their actions in Scotland; two days later he wrote to Johnston of Wariston, who was a member of the new Council of Safety, telling him that he (Monck) as a good Christian was sending up his three commissioners to see Fleetwood and 'heal breaches'. The letter to Lilburne had the desired effect; he promised not to move his troops nearer the border and not to raise any militiamen while the negotiations between the two parties were in progress.[15]

But in fact by the time Monck received this news Lilburne had ceased to be the key man in the north. For Lambert had just arrived and had taken over the supreme command and was empowered to negotiate with Monck. The three commissioners from Scotland saw Lambert immediately after his arrival, but when he discovered that one of their instructions was to demand the restoration of the Rump, he said he was in no position to consent to that and sent them on to London. On the same day Monck wrote to Lambert expressing his apprehension at rumours that 'great forces' were on the march and 'great preparations' were being made against him. He warned the Yorkshire general somewhat gratuitously of the 'sad consequences' of a civil war between them. Lambert would have liked to meet Monck at Berwick, but Monck did not respond to the invitation.[16]

On this same critical day, the beginning of the first week of November, when Monck was distributing conciliatory letters and his commissioners were on their way from York to London, a third highly significant episode occurred. Monck's most trusted commander, Thomas Morgan, who had distinguished himself in the Spanish Netherlands, was on his way to join his General in Scotland. He had been delayed by an attack of gout at York but had taken advantage of this to visit Lord Fairfax, the erstwhile Parliamentarian Captain-General, who had retired to his house named Nunappleton in Wharfedale to tend his roses and write bad poetry. Morgan also saw Lambert who speeded him on his way in the mistaken belief that he would wean Monck from his devotion to the Rump. When he reached Edinburgh about 8 November he brought with him a letter from Lord Fairfax's former Presbyterian chaplain, Edward Bowles. In this letter Bowles said that Fairfax would be willing to support Monck against Fleetwood and Lambert, but that he did not like the declaration of 22 October, firstly because it was restricted to upholding the Rump and secondly because it envisaged a republican government. After reading that letter Monck confided to Clarges, who had arrived in Edinburgh a few days earlier, that

> what was printed in his Name, was not (at that Conjuncture) to be regarded as the Result of his own Reason, because his Writings were drawn by other Hands; and till his Affairs had a firmer Consistency, and he more Power in his Hands, it was unseasonable for him to contradict what was done, since all that was writ could scarce prevail with the Army to believe he had not a Design to set up the King in his Government.

Monck then sent Clarges to see Fairfax and Bowles to give them assurances and to explain that he thought it expedient, 'to imploy all possible Care to amuse the Parliament and the Army till the General could get a Power in his Hands to justify other Counsels'. This remarkable and revealing admission by Monck about his future intentions was made only to Morgan and Clarges. It was concealed from Colonel Talbot and the other envoys sent to Monck by the Grandees in London. If this story is accurate (and it has not been questioned by those historians who are not prepared to believe in Monck's willingness to join Booth in August), George Monck had resolved on the restoration of the monarchy camouflaging his intentions by specious promises of undying loyalty to the Rump.

While the negotiations designed 'to amuse the Parliament and the Army' were going on and a standstill was in force, Monck was by no means idle. He was well aware that a fair number of his officers were searching their hearts to decide whether to follow their general if that meant having to fight other officers of the army in England with whom, in the past, they had been colleagues and friends. The loyalties of his officers had therefore to be put to the test. Thomas Morgan was immediately sent to Linlithgow, Stirling and Fifeshire to investigate the attitude of the garrisons there and to arrest and disarm any soldiers who refused to sign the declaration of 22 October on behalf of the Rump. In the case of defiant troopers he was to confiscate their horses.[17] On 15 November, as arranged, Monck met the representatives of the Scottish nobility, the Scottish sheriffs, justices of the peace and burghers and authorized them to keep order during his absence if and when he marched into England 'to assert and maintain the liberty and being of parliaments, our ancient constitution, and therein the freedom and rights of the people of these nations from arbitrary and tyrannical usurpations upon their consciences, persons and estates and for a godly ministry'.[18] In other words at the very time when his commissioners were engaged on peace negotiations in London Monck was still intent on himself leading an army, loyal to himself, into England. Why? Presumably because he was manœuvring politically until he could re-establish 'our ancient constitution'. What was that? Surely it was government by the King in parliament.[19]

Another thing that Monck did was to write a letter to the Mayor, Aldermen and Common Council of the City of London (dated 12 November) inviting them to support his programme of restoring the Rump and thus regaining the almost lost liberties of England. He said it would be dishonourable of the City if it did not help so worthy a cause. By that time it was well known that the Common Council was becoming tired of the anarchy that prevailed. So it did not relish Monck's letter at all and postponed answering it as long as it decently could. In fact the City was largely Royalist in its sympathies. Even the apprentices, so enthusiastically pro-Parliament at the outset of the civil war, started demonstrating in favour of a free parliament and the recall of the King.[20]

Such was the atmosphere in which the commissioners from Scotland quickly came to terms with Fleetwood's officers. It is said that Timothy Wilkes sold the pass by betraying his instructions to the other side, but it is not clear why there should have been any betrayal. For the object of the commissioners was to reach an agreement which would prevent an intestinal war. Among the terms accepted by both sides was that there should be no government by any single person, that Charles II was to be opposed, that a new constitution was to be drawn up, and (this was the fourth article) that a new parliament was to be summoned as soon as possible. Seven commissioners from each army were to form a tribunal to adjudicate on the cases of officers who had been dismissed or promoted since 11 October. While a new constitution was being drawn up, which would require the approval of a council of officers from the army and navy, the armies in England and Scotland were to move back their front lines. The commissioners from Scotland were pretty pleased with themselves; so was Lambert; on 21 November he wrote to Monck saying that he was sending him a copy of the agreement so that he and the Council of Officers in Scotland could ratify it.[21]

But George Monck himself was not at all pleased. As soon as he read the draft agreement he wrote to his commissioners in London to tell them that they had mistaken (or exceeded) their instructions. What he chiefly objected to was that they had not secured assent to the immediate recall of the Rump. He told his commissioners to return north, to arrange a meeting with Lambert either at York or Newcastle where they would be joined by two new commissioners. To these new commissioners they were to explain exactly why they had exceeded their instructions and they were to insist upon the restoration of the Rump.[22] The three original commissioners were not particularly contrite. They wrote to Monck on 24 November saying that they hoped 'there was nothing in the agreement ... but what is very consistent with your declarations and that the fourth article about calling a parliament was in no way inconsistent with recalling the Rump', but 'may as well be understood of that as any other ...'. They also told him that his writing to the Mayor, Aldermen and Common Council in London while the negotiations were in progress had astonished them; at first they had imagined that the letters must have been forged; Fleetwood, they said, was furious, while the two officers who had presented Monck's letter to the Lord Mayor had been imprisoned and had their papers confiscated.[23] Accompanied by Desborough, Bulstrode Whitelocke and Robert Tichborne, a former Lord Mayor of London, Fleetwood had (before Monck's letter arrived) visited the City authorities in order to explain the proceedings of Monck. Monck defended himself by saying that a stipulation had not been reached that no letters should be sent during the negotiations and that in fact during that time Lambert had written to the Provost of Edinburgh.[24] None the less Monck's letter to the City of London put the cat among the pigeons.

Nobody seemed to know exactly what Monck was up to. Fleetwood said that the General Council of Officers in London had naturally assumed that Monck's commissioners had full authority to conclude an agreement. Lambert told Monck that his decision not to ratify the agreement would merely be an advantage to the common enemy. A lot of other people thought that too. The French ambassador supposed that if Monck had not made a deal with Charles II then he must be hoping to become Lord Protector himself. Bulstrode Whitelocke, who had his feet in every conceivable camp, told the Common Council of London that 'the bottom of his [Monck's] Design was to bring in the King upon a new Civil War.'[25] Monck stuck to his guns in every sense of the phrase. He insisted that it was not differences between the two armies but the English army's expulsion of the Rump which had given so much advantage to the Stuart family. His answer to the argument that he had accepted without demur the expulsion of the Rump in 1653 was that at that time the Commonwealth was at war with foreign enemies and therefore needed the strong hand of Oliver Cromwell.[26] But his extraordinary devotion to the emasculated Rump was hard to explain or believe.

It was on the evening of 24 November that Monck received from London the information (which was sent to him by Clarges) about what the three commissioners from the army in Scotland had agreed to. The very next day Monck persuaded fifty-six of his officers gathered in Edinburgh to state that as delegates their commissioners had mistaken their instructions and that negotiations must be reopened in York, which was half way between Monck's headquarters and those which Lambert had taken up in Newcastle. That showed how persuasive Monck must have been or how much he was honoured and respected by the majority of his officers. On the same day Monck wrote to Fleetwood in the same sense asking that fresh negotiations at York should be opened as soon as possible. Lambert and Fleetwood were alarmed by his attitude, but could do no more than hope for the best. Outsiders thought that Monck was deliberately prolonging the negotiations in order to give himself more time to make ready to use armed force.[27]

Meanwhile Monck was pressed to be more conciliatory. For example, he received a long letter from Dr John Owen, who had been Oliver Cromwell's closest adviser on ecclesiastical questions, in which he argued that an agreement between the two armies was more essential to the maintenance of the Commonwealth and of religious liberty than was the restoration of the Rump. He explained that he had many friends who had been members of the Rump, but 'this I shall say, that it were better that both they and I and hundreds of better men than myself were in the ends of the earth, than that this cause [i.e. the preservation of the Commonwealth] should be ruined by the armies' contest about them'.[28] Later, ministers and officers—such as Joseph Caryl, an eloquent Independent, and Edward Whalley, Oliver Cromwell's cousin—came from England to Edinburgh to intercede with the General not to break with the army in England.

But far from being conciliatory Monck had become tougher. His answer to Owen was that Fleetwood must restore the Rump. He told Caryl if there were a breach it was Lambert's fault. He wrote an extremely sharp letter to Lambert denying that he had advanced to Berwick (he had not done so but ensured that the garrison and inhabitants were loyal to him) and complained about Lambert's presence in Newcastle. He was also angry that Lambert had stopped some packets of letters on their way to him, although he himself had opened packets being sent south from Scotland. He ended his letter by saying that if Lambert did not withdraw from Newcastle to York he himself would take up residence at Berwick; otherwise he would stay in Edinburgh.[29]

During the week when the commissioners from the army in Scotland, who were alleged to have disobeyed their instructions, were beginning to make their way back from London to Newcastle, the purge of Monck's army in Scotland continued and was extended. For example, on Monck's orders Captain Yaxley Robson dismissed six corporals and twenty-four privates in Colonel Sawrey's regiment stationed at Ayr; Sawrey and his family were obliged to escape to England. At Dunbar and Perth, which were both garrisoned by part of Colonel Pearson's regiment (Colonel Pearson, as has been noticed, had on the orders of the Rump replaced the Cromwellian Colonel

Daniel), Monck employed as his agent its senior captain, Joseph Witter. Witter succeeded in getting rid of a major, two captains, four lieutenants and six ensigns and was rewarded by his rapid promotion to lieutenant-colonel for his pains.' Morgan went about the country disarming, dismissing and arresting officers and men who did not approve of Monck's proceedings. Monck was assured of the loyalty of the garrison at Inverness and he himself went to Leith to make certain that the soldiers there would obey him.[30]

While Monck was reorganizing his army in readiness for a confrontation with Lambert, his three commissioners were lingering on in London. They had an interview in a Covent Garden tavern with members of the Council of State who had continued to meet in secret after the Rump had been closed down. These commissioners were told that the secret council had wider support than Monck might realize. Junior officers and privates in regiments around London were in sympathy with them because they did not approve of the tactics of the Grandees; Colonel Nathaniel Whetham, the governor of Portsmouth, was devoted to the secret Council; so were Vice-Admiral Lawson and Lord Fairfax. They added that if Monck remained true to the Rump he would be made commander-in-chief in England as well as in Scotland.[31] Naturally the commissioners did not risk telling Monck about their interview by letter, but Major Knight arrived back in Scotland at the end of November and no doubt conveyed this information to his General. At the same time Monck must have learned that the secret Council of State had in fact appointed him commander-in-chief with full power to take his army into England if and when he wished to do so. For by then the Council believed that Monck was also committed to its cause.

Outsiders were not clear what Monck was doing. The French ambassador thought that many people in the English capital wanted Monck to come there and arrange either for 'a free parliament' or the restoration of the King.[32] About the same time Fleetwood was writing to Monck to tell him of a tumult raised by the apprentices in the City of London in favour of a free parliament, a tumult which, he alleged, was managed by the malignant Cavaliers. Their cry, he informed Monck, was not for a Commonwealth, but to revenge the death of the late King. He reminded Monck of the danger of another rising like that of Booth and begged him not to delay any further in arranging an agreement between the two armies.[33] To Fleetwood Monck wrote soothingly, but to Lambert arrogantly. The exiled Royalists were told by one of their agents that Monck was irreconcilable with the army in England, that he would never reinstate the officers and men in his own army whom he had been busily cashiering, and that he could not endure Lambert's treachery and ambition. Though Monck's pretensions were dark and his designs ambiguous, he could hardly depend on the Rump, which was scornfully called 'the disunion'. Therefore, so ran the report, Monck had declared that he alone had ventured to stand 'in the Gap ... and will go on and leave the Event to God'.[34]

Monck's chaplains both paint a dramatic picture of what was happening in Scotland towards the end of November after the news of the commissioners' agreement with the army in England had been received. He was seen to be very melancholy, dark and despairing. Yet he had little trouble in persuading his officers gathered in Edinburgh at once to repudiate the agreement. The reason why they backed him was in part because several of them stood in danger of losing their commissions if that agreement were enforced and the officers cashiered by Monck were reinstated in their posts by the proposed tribunal of fourteen. As John Price wrote, they were afraid that the colonels would become captains, captains ensigns and ensigns would have to wield the pike again. So to conclude a theatrical scene, George Monck declared 'if the army will stick by me, I will stick by them'.[35] In defiance of Lambert, he first occupied Berwick and then on 8 December set up his headquarters in a village farther to the south-west near one of the fords across the Tweed; its name was Coldstream. He disposed most of his army to hold the line of the Tweed. It looked as if a battle between Monck's and Lambert's troops was not to be avoided. Yet it was.

14

The March to London

Before describing George Monck's final preparations for his march to London and the character of the march itself, the General's frame of mind will be examined as far as it is possible to do so on the basis of the available evidence, some of which was set out in the previous chapter. First, he had a Royalist background. His elder brother had been a prominent Cavalier in Exeter; his younger brother was a Royalist and an Anglican who rose to be a bishop in the reign of Charles II. Most of Monck's friends in Devon, particularly the Grenvilles, were known Royalists. He had never fought against Charles I; indeed he had fought for him not only before the summoning of the Long Parliament but afterwards when he was taken a prisoner by the Roundheads at the battle of Nantwich. It has even been suggested that when Lord Lisle enlisted his services while he was languishing in the Tower of London, he persuaded Monck that he would be fighting for and not against the King in Ireland. It has also been hazarded, though this is less likely, that the reason why Oliver Cromwell left Monck in Scotland while he himself moved south to follow and trap the young Charles II in England, was because he imagined that Monck would dislike the idea of fighting directly against the King in England.[1]

It may be argued on the other side that Monck had made no bones about faithfully serving both the Cromwells. That is perfectly true; indeed he established a special relationship with Oliver Cromwell, grounded on mutual trust, confidence and admiration. Even when he sent Cromwell a copy of a letter he had received from the Royalists the Protector treated it as a joke. It has also to be remembered that when Monck fought so brilliantly against the Dutch at sea during the Protectorate he was moved chiefly by the call of patriotism; and furthermore, though one is inclined to forget this, the Scots had been the national enemies of the English at least since the time of William the Conqueror. After the humiliations of 1639 and 1640, Monck must have derived some pleasure from taking part in victories over the Scots in 1650, 1651 and 1654. Admittedly, after the Scots had been subdued, Monck felt sympathy with their grievances over high taxation and the interruptions engineered by sectarians in the services of the Scottish Church. Moreover, after all the work he put into making a success of the union, first promulgated by Oliver Cromwell, he had reason to be angry that the Rump Parliament of 1659 sabotaged his achievement by repudiating the Cromwellian ordinance.

Monck could hardly have loved the Rump both for the above reasons and because of the way that it interfered with his army by demoting and promoting its officers without preliminary consultations with himself. As he was reminded more than once, he had not demurred when Cromwell forcibly ejected the Rump in April 1653; and he had accepted nomination to the Assembly of Saints which replaced it. By 1659 Monck knew perfectly well, whatever he professed, that the Rump had degenerated into a small, unpopular and unrepresentative coterie. He must also have realized that whereas the Cromwellian Protectorate had won positive benefits for the Commonwealth both at home and abroad, Heslirige, Vane and the rest were, for the most part, woolly-minded theorists who contributed to a growing anarchy, particularly manifested in the City of London, obliging the Common Council to meet daily during December in an attempt to maintain peace and order there.[2] As early as June 1659 a newsletter writer favourable to the Royalists asserted that 'the disorders in England seem more and more to thicken into a dark chaos of confusion ...' out of which the only road of course was monarchy.[3]

As has already been noticed, John Price, if one can trust his detailed account of the events that led up to the Restoration, selected the first week of August 1659 as the date when Monck made up his mind to restore the King. The demand that Booth put forward for the re-admission of the secluded members (including himself) into Parliament followed by arrangements for a free general election, was precisely the same as the course advocated by the City of London in December 1659 and by Monck himself in March 1660.[4] Yet even more significant than the Booth episode was Monck's correspondence with Lord Fairfax in which he had in effect acquiesced in the idea that they should work together to restore the 'ancient government'. Fairfax had pointed out what that meant.

The final point that deserves emphasis is this: Monck's deliberate dilly-dallying over the negotiation of an agreement between the two armies, and the many letters that he wrote demanding the return of the Rump to power after Lambert's coup, did not alone bring it about. Heslirige's success in winning over the garrison of Portsmouth to his side in December, and the efforts of Thomas Scot to secure the support of most of the navy, particularly the squadron commanded by John Lawson at Gravesend, for the Rump caused Fleetwood to lose heart altogether. For the navy could, if it wished, subject London to capitulation by strangling its trade. It was on 24 December, a week before Monck left Scotland, that Fleetwood told the Speaker 'that the Lord had blasted their Counsels and spat in their faces and witnessed against their perfidiousness ...' and then threw in the towel.[5] The Rump, which resumed its authority on Boxing Day, ordered letters of thanks at once to be dispatched equally to Monck and to Lawson.[6] Besides the letter of thanks the Speaker wrote another letter to Monck on the same day, 27 December. He informed him that orders had been sent to all the regiments in the north of England to return to their former quarters and to obey Parliament.[7] Neither of these letters said that the House of Parliament wanted Monck to march with his army up to London, as John Price noted in his memoirs.[8] On the contrary, they implied that he should stay in Scotland. Dr Gumble thought the first letter was 'as cold as night' with only a few words of thanks.[9]

George Monck received these and other letters notifying him of the Rump's triumph over the Grandees on the evening of 2 January 1660 after he and most of his cavalry had left Coldstream. But even before he was officially informed of the humbling of Fleetwood and Lambert and the resumption of rule by the Rump on 26 December, he had learnt about what had been happening. For in a letter dated 1 January 1660 which he wrote from Coldstream he told Sir Hardress Waller (in Ireland) that, 'all the forces in the south had submitted to the Parliament which is now sitting again at Westminster and there are none left to oppose us [in their march into

England] except Lord Lambert's brigade which lessens daily'.[10] In other words, before Monck himself moved out of Coldstream he was fully aware that the Rump—partly because of his own demonstrations in its favour—had triumphed. Neither on 1 January nor 2 January had he received orders from anyone to march into England. Fleetwood, he knew, had submitted to the Rump, though perhaps he could have argued that Lambert was still capable of carrying out another *coup d'état* unless he were brushed out of the way. Still the fact remains that it was on his own authority alone that he led an armed force into England.

Naturally he could not disclose at this time that his object was to replace the discredited oligarchy in London with a full representative parliament freely elected. For that might have meant that some of the soldiers, even in his own carefully remodelled army, would have turned against him, suspecting that he had betrayed their 'Good Old Cause' and fearing that he was 'carrying the King in his belly'; as Price remarked 'the silly fellows ... were near the matter, for the King "was in his heart" '. A declaration of his true intentions might also have meant that Fleetwood's regiments stationed in or around London would have resisted him and even beaten him. To decide how and when to take the decisive action he had first to test the market in the capital, while sounding the English gentry as he went there. All the indications are that George Monck was prepared to seize any occasion that presented itself to bring about the return to 'the ancient government'—meaning the rule by the King in parliament. That was his fixed principle. He was not just keeping all the options open.

To turn back to the month before Monck left Coldstream for London. During the first fortnight of December he continued to 'amuse' Lambert. They carried on a polite but stiff correspondence. Lord Wariston remarked that 'Monck's letters to Lambert' were 'fair in generals and sharp in particulars'.[11] Monck told Lambert that if he remained at Newcastle, then he himself would stay at Berwick-upon-Tweed. On 8 December, however, Monck was informed that Lambert had sent his dragoons to seize Chillingham castle in Northumberland, and had dispatched a party towards Morpeth near the Scottish border. But Lambert insisted that these were only reconnaissance patrols and gave Monck's officers returning from London a pass to Berwick.[12] Monck therefore concerned himself chiefly with final arrangements for the security of Scotland before he set out to confront Lambert.

On 13 December Monck received personal promises from the noblemen, gentlemen and justices of the peace in Stirlingshire that they would suppress any disturbances there during his absence, which he accepted with pleasure, though he was careful to tell the military governor of Stirling not to furnish the Scots with arms. Earlier he had considered various suggestions from Scotsmen that they should be allowed to raise horse militia in each shire and that 'watches' should be set up in the counties adjacent to the highlands or the English border. The second proposal he favoured, but not the first, for he was aware of the danger of tumults if the Scots got hold of arms and ammunition. He therefore limited the Scottish forces in these areas to a measly forty armed men apiece.[13] He did not intend to risk a rising in Scotland as soon as his back was turned.

A little earlier the trusted Major-General Morgan was ordered to bring cavalry and Monck's own infantry regiment to guard the vital pass across the Tweed at Kelsoe. On 16 December George felt strong enough to tell Lambert to withdraw all his forces from Northumberland, Westmorland and Cumberland (Monck himself had previously made an unsuccessful attempt to occupy Carlisle and Newcastle which stood on the two main roads from Scotland to London). Yet he continued to amuse Lambert by proposing that commissioners from both sides should meet at Alnwick, roughly half way between the two armies, in search of an agreement for a cease-fire.[14]

As Monck expected, by the end of the year Lambert's army was rapidly melting away. For he had no money to pay his distracted and mutinous soldiers, who had to manage with 'free quarter', thus alienating the inhabitants of Northumberland, and he had no clear cause for which he could persuade them to fight. Monck for his part had obtained a payment of £20,000 from London in the late summer and made it the foundation of a large war chest to which the revenues of Scotland contributed.[15] Monck also knew that Portsmouth was in the hands of Sir Arthur Heslirige acting for the Rump partly because its governor was a friend of Monck's; that the fleet was now entirely loyal to the Rump; and that the English officers in the garrison of Ireland, where Monck had exercised his not inconsiderable influence, had also declared themselves against Fleetwood and the Grandees. He therefore asked for a regiment to be sent from Ireland to Scotland to help guard the country as he made his way south.[16] Finally Lord Fairfax moved earlier than was planned. Though racked by gout he was carried in a coach to Marston Moor near York where local levies, raised mainly by Royalists, met him, while an entire brigade of Lambert's army, which had been brought over from Ireland to fight against George Booth, changed sides and joined him. On New Year's Day 1660 Fairfax was able to seize York without much difficulty. These actions of his old commander were the final blow to the hopes of John Lambert, who early in January said goodbye to his few faithful officers and disappeared into hiding.[17]

The expeditionary force under Monck's command consisting of four cavalry regiments (Monck's, Knight's, Morgan's and Clobery's) and six infantry regiments (Monck's, Morgan's, Charles Fairfax's, Lydcote's, Reade's and Hubblethorne's) marched out of Coldstream, formed into two brigades and by 6 January Monck himself was in Newcastle. An advance party of his took hold of Durham. Tyne-mouth castle was occupied. Overton as governor of Hull convinced Monck of his neutrality.[18] Thus the whole of north-east England was soon in his hands. Having satisfied himself that all Lambert's men had melted away or come over to his side, Monck felt it was safe to send Major-General Morgan back to Scotland. A week after Monck's arrival in Newcastle Morgan was ordered to take four infantry regiments, the brigade from Ireland, which had been given new officers, and a number of companies from other regiments so as to re-establish the military garrison of Scotland. In reply to a letter which Monck had written on 29 December to the Council of State from Coldstream, the Speaker of the Rump was commanded to thank him for his past services, to take care to ensure the security of Scotland during his absence and to come up to London as speedily as he could.[19] He had indeed faced the resuscitated members of parliament with a *fait accompli*.

Monck, who was not fussy about food and drink, had to put up with several discomforts when he was at Coldstream. His cottage bedroom had neither fire nor lights. At first no meat was available while the hastily brewed beer was warm, though outside the ground was covered with snow and ice. He had to sleep fully clothed with his body supported by two chairs. While he was there John Price ventured into the bedroom and asked permission to speak frankly to him. His chaplain then insisted that it was both Monck's duty and interest to re-establish the recognized laws of the land, that is to say the King's peace. Monck replied emphatically that he knew what Price meant and that if ever he had the chance he would do it. They spoke in conundrums but they understood one another. 'With God's aid,' Monck repeated, 'I shall do it.'[20]

On 3 January 1660 Monck was at Wooler in Northumberland whence he wrote to the Speaker and sent Dr Gumble with his letter to London, instructing him to find out all he could about the position there. The next night was spent in a village, which Price refused to name on the grounds that their lodgings were even worse than they had been at Coldstream. Morpeth next night was more agreeable. Here Monck received a letter brought by the Swordbearer from the City of London, a belated answer to his own of 12 November. From Durham he wrote to Sir Charles Coote, his old comrade in arms and now one of the commissioners for Ireland. His letter was carried by a special messenger across the sea to Dublin asking Coote to see that the forces there should declare for a 'free parliament', an ambiguous phrase.[21] At York Monck stayed for five days during which he listened to a sermon by Bowles and had an interview with Lord Fairfax. Fairfax reiterated what Bowles had told Monck in November, namely that he wanted the restoration of the monarchy as well as a free parliament. Satisfied by then that no remnants of Lambert's army were left to resist him, he said goodbye to Morgan. Charles Fairfax himself, who was an uncle of Lord Fairfax, was put in charge of the York garrison. Then Monck entered the Midlands, reaching Nottingham by way of Newark, Market Harborough and Mansfield on 21 January. Before that he had informed the Speaker of Morgan's return to Scotland, but had upon the orders of the Rump dispatched the Irish brigade with its new officers to Chester instead of Scotland; he also told the Speaker how Lambert's cavalry regiment had joined him and, stripped of its old officers, placed under the command of Colonel Hugh Bethel, who distinguished himself in Cromwell's time but had not before been in charge of a regiment. When the Rump told Monck to give the regiment to Colonel Twistleton, about whose politics Monck knew nothing, he refused to comply.[22]

At Nottingham Monck was joined by his useful brother-in-law,

Dr Clarges; thence he wrote to Chief Justice Oliver St John, one of the moderates he admired in London, telling him that he was glad to learn (through Gumble) of his resolution to settle the Commonwealth avoiding 'those two rocks of the malignant and fanatical interests'. That, he said, of course was his own aim, otherwise he would never have broken with his old friends in the army.[23]

From Market Harborough Monck wrote to his friends, the gentlemen of Devonshire, who had on 18 January petitioned the Speaker to admit into Parliament the members secluded in 1648. With his tongue in his cheek Monck asked one of these friends to persuade other Devonshire gentlemen to acquiesce in the proceedings of the Rump so that the common enemy might be disappointed and added that 'monarchy cannot possibly be admitted for the future in these Nations because its support is taken away'.[24] His letter was at once printed and widely circulated. He also appears to have had a talk with one of these secluded members, though what he said is not known.[25] At any rate he assured his Devonshire friends that the Rump has 'resolved to fill up their House' — that is by allowing elections in constituencies where the members elected in 1640 were now dead.

According to the French ambassador, Monck as he went through the Midlands was greeted everywhere with the ringing of bells; he treated everyone with civility, disclosed his feelings to no one and while he conferred appointments on persons suspended by Parliament, he assured it of his fidelity.[26] On 18 January Dr Gumble had rejoined him; his report was that members of the Rump did not altogether trust Monck, though they voted him £1,000 a year in lands, and that they were equally divided over whether or not a new oath, which had been introduced requiring all members of the Council of State to swear not to restore Charles II to his throne, should be taken; Gumble reported that Monck's friends were all against this oath. Later Monck heard much the same story from a busybody named John Collins, who had been chief butler and steward at the Inner Temple and had access to Monck because he was the uncle of William Clarke, Monck's secretary. Collins as he wrote at the time had the amusing conceit that it was he who was responsible for persuading Monck to restore the King.[27]

Clarges, Gumble and Collins were followed by two less welcome visitors who were members of the Rump, Thomas Scot and Luke

Robinson; both were notorious oligarchs who had been appointed commissioners to Monck's army, and their intention was to spy on him and compel him to take the oath repudiating Charles II. Monck answered blandly that he had heard that men of integrity had refused the oath and that he would wait until he reached London to make up his own mind about it. The two Rumpers would not let Monck out of their sight and they travelled with him in his coach as far as Barnet on the outskirts of the capital.[28] Monck was polite and silent. When they came to St Albans he wrote to the Speaker asking that all except two regiments should be moved out of London to make way for his army which now consisted of only three cavalry regiments and four infantry regiments, a total of about 6,000 men, too few to give the impression that he was arriving as a conqueror.[29]

During the month that was occupied in marching from Scotland to London, Monck was inundated with letters and petitions. The only outspoken one was that from the gentry of Devon who refused to accept his advice. He was sufficiently worried over this letter to write privately to his friend, William Morice, telling him that he hoped 'a settled condition of the Government' would free the Devonians from the 'phanatic humor which had held sway so long'. Therefore, he begged him to tell his Devonshire friends that they must acquiesce in the Rump's proceedings for the time being and he invited Morice, himself a secluded member of parliament, to come and meet him in London as soon as he could. Monck's letter to the Devonians disowning the idea of restoring the monarchy, encouraged the Rump to hope that they would be able to oblige their commander-in-chief to toe the party line. On the other hand, a counterblast to Monck's cold-shouldering of his Devonshire friends was the production of an ingenious forgery, circulated by the Royalists, of a letter which Monck was supposed to have written to Charles II from Edinburgh on 30 December 1659 saying that he had thoughts of going to London very suddenly and that he intended to keep his army ready until a fit time and opportunity should offer itself that he might employ for the greater glory of God and the good of his Majesty.[30] It was effective propaganda because it verged on the truth.

Among the petitions which Monck received either during his journey or soon after he reached London was one from the gentlemen of Oxford, headed by Lord Falkland, which demanded a full and free parliament; the gentlemen of Leicestershire told Monck that every freeborn person in England was supposed to be represented in parliament, but none of the counties in Wales and several in England, particularly Yorkshire, had a knight of the shire to look after its interests. The 'fundamental laws' should be defended, the true Protestant religion reinstated and the army demobilized or at least reduced in size. The citizens of London — both in the Common Council and the vociferous apprentices — waited hopefully for Monck's coming so that they could obtain through him a free parliament in which the City was fully represented, as it was not in the Rump. The gentlemen of Buckinghamshire told Monck: 'our credit abroad is impaired, our trade decayed, our laws violated, our religion endangered'. Therefore the secluded members should be restored to their seats and free elections held to fill the remaining vacancies in the House of Parliament. Then a stable government could be established which had not existed since the time of Pride's Purge. 'The voice of the people', they added somewhat gratuitously, 'was the voice of God.' The gentlemen of Warwickshire told Monck that it was scandalous that after all the blood and treasure that had been spent they were unrepresented in Parliament. The way to heal the country's wounds was to pass an act of oblivion, procure liberty for tender consciences and pay off the soldiers' arrears. The gentlemen of Cheshire, Shropshire and Staffordshire also attributed the present calamities to the 'force' of 1648; the gentry of Bedfordshire sought a full and free parliament; even some of the regiments in London were demanding a free parliament; while the London apprentices and young men of the City told Monck, when he was at St Albans and nearing the capital, that no taxes should be paid or laws passed until they received the consent of freely elected representatives.[31] How far there was collusion or copying between the various counties is hard to say. But it was a fact, as a contemporary noted, that during Monck's march every county in England asked him to secure a full and free parliament instead of the residue of some forty members of the Long Parliament elected nearly twenty years earlier.[32]

But Monck did not dare reveal his own intentions to anyone except his chaplain, whom he warned to keep his mouth shut. He pretended to be obtuse. A full parliament? Well, the Rump had promised to fill up its vacancies. A free parliament? Once Monck, always obedient to the civil powers, arrived in London while Fleetwood, Lambert and their friends were confined to house arrest, parliament would be free. However, very few people were convinced that Monck had come up to London simply to protect the Rumpers. All was obscure.

> Monck under a hood, not understood,
> The Citty pulls in theire hornes;
> The Speaker is out and sick of the goute
> And the Parliament sitts upon thornes.

So ran a contemporary verse.[33] The Royalists remained perplexed, their fears mingling with their hopes. Sir Edward Nicholas, one of the elder statesmen of Charles II's Council, wisely remarked in a letter to John Mordaunt, who was still at liberty in England, that while they awaited a declaration by Monck, they trusted that 'the moderate and discreet Presbyterians will judge it their best interest to advance His Majesty's from whom they will receive all reasonable satisfaction'.[34] While the letter to the Devonians had been a body blow and Monck had not yet committed himself either to the re-admission of the secluded members or to the calling of a free parliament, it was rumoured that he had told the Speaker that during his march he had observed that nothing would content the people but a free parliament.[35] Mordaunt himself had observed as late as 16 January that the new commander-in-chief was 'a black Monk and I cannot see through him'.[36]

At the very last stage of his journey when Monck was at Barnet on 2 February he learned that an infantry regiment on guard outside Somerset House, the residence of the Speaker, had mutinied, some crying out for Charles II and some for a free parliament. Many of these soldiers were said to have threatened to carry through an insurrection in the City that night in alliance with the tumultuous apprentices. Monck was thought to agree with them and it was believed by some of the Rumpers that he would set up a new and free parliament which would produce a king and liberty. In the utmost agitation the Council of State sent Thomas Scot to Barnet with instructions to tell Monck to come into the City immediately to restore order. Scot arrived wearing his nightshirt and nightcap. He woke Monck and asked him to have his drums sounded and march at once to London. But Monck was imperturbable. He had completed all his arrangements and refused to enter the capital until next morning.[37] His wife and son had arrived ahead of him towards the end of January and awaited him in Whitehall palace. On the morning of 3 February the General inspected his modest little army drawn up at Highgate. Thence on horseback he led his men along Gray's Inn Road towards Somerset House where the Speaker, William Lenthall, stood ready to welcome him; Lenthall had seen many changes during his long life and so greeted Monck's arrival with equanimity. It was his son who had been in charge of the regiment that had mutinied the previous night. Now all was quiet except for the ringing of church bells. With due modesty Monck did not wear elaborate clothes for the occasion but had a richly embroidered belt and a fine horse. He was accompanied by three trumpeters, three footmen and three grooms all dressed in red livery inlaid with silver lace. Then followed three or four coaches and a hundred gentlemen of the life guard. The Coldstreamers moved in procession down Chancery Lane, into the Strand to be met by the Speaker at Somerset House. Next day Monck was invited to attend the House of Parliament in order to receive the orders of the Rump and its thanks for 'his signal and faithful services'.[38]

15

The Restoration
of Charles II

When Samuel Pepys, the future clerk at the Admiralty, saw Monck for the first time (on 14 March 1660) he wrote in his incomparable diary: 'methought he seemed a dull heavy man'.[1] If that was the impression he gave, he was no mean actor. The truth was that ever since August 1659 he had been obliged to negotiate his way, as it were, along a river full of obstacles, some of them clearly marked, others hidden in the depths. His objective was clear enough: he wanted to re-establish a stable government; that, he had come to realize, required the return of the King, an undivided Church and a loyal parliament. But to have disclosed his intentions too soon would have been fatal. For many officers and soldiers loyal to the Good Old Cause would have turned against him including even some of the carefully picked men in his own army. As late as the middle of March 1660 several of his officers were discontented over what they saw was about to happen. They did not want either a king, a single person or a House of Lords. Monck had to insist ever since he left Coldstream that he had received his commission from Parliament, that his men must obey Parliament and not teach Parliament what it ought to do. So he became an opportunist awaiting his opportunity. Each step he took was a considered one. Thus until he reached London he had been obliged to remain, at any rate on the surface, the obedient servant of Parliament.

And yet as he had ridden south, he scarcely missed a trick. Though he knew when he left Coldstream that Fleetwood had been humiliated and the Rump had resumed its authority, he did not hesitate over moving on towards the capital; but until he faced the Rump with the accomplished fact he had received no orders to do so. When he got to York he had not committed himself openly to restoring the monarchy, which he knew perfectly well was what Fairfax wanted, yet he hinted to his chaplain that this was his ultimate aim. As the editor of Fairfax's correspondence wrote many years ago:

It must be conceded that Monck had a difficult game to play, but he played it like a trickster. He held back so ambiguously in his interview with Fairfax, even after the latter had avowed himself, that the old General, who was apt to be trustful rather than suspicious of others, entertained grave doubts of his honesty. He [Monck] wore his mask to the last moment, to the perplexity of his friends as well as his enemies, and [im]-perilled all interests by his impenetrable dissimulation.[2]

When John Weaver, a leading Rumper and formerly an eminent republican in Richard Cromwell's Parliament, who had become, along with his friend, Anthony Ashley Cooper, a member of the Council of State, wrote to ask Monck what had been going on in Yorkshire, he replied that he was sorry 'there should bee any jealousie uppon the Lord Fairfax in some mens spiritts, who assured mee in a private conference that hee would joyne with mee to the opposeing of Charles Stuart's family'.[3] In the light of what Bowles had told Monck in December and what Brian Fairfax wrote about his uncle, this must have been a lie.

Another fascinating sidelight on Monck's frame of mind is supplied by Major Robert Harley, uncle of the future Lord Treasurer, who saw Monck when he was at Mansfield on 19 January. Harley, who was a Presbyterian Royalist like George Booth, wrote that while no one could then fathom what were Monck's real aims, 'it cannot be said but Monck was in a great doubt whether the present time was fit to perform what he did intend'.[4] This convoluted sentence, which Harley's nephew would have been proud of, can be interpreted as meaning that while Monck was out to restore the King if he could, he had not yet decided when he should reveal himself.

Finally, when Monck's friends and relations in Devonshire wrote their embarrassing letter to the Speaker asking for the re-admission of the secluded members of parliament (the men who had been purged by Pride in 1648 because they favoured the continuation of negotiations with the Stuarts), Monck pressed his friend William Morice, himself a secluded member, to damp down their enthusiasm and acquiesce, obviously for the time being only, in the proceedings of the Rump. Openly he asserted that 'the monarchy cannot possibly be admitted for the future' and he ordered the cudgelling of a soldier who stated that the General meant to restore the King, yet Monck did not allow any council of officers to meet after he left York so that there could be no discussions on strategy and he refused to take an oath of abjuration against the Stuarts.[5] He played a lone hand.

The first thing that Monck had to do after his arrival in London on Friday 3 February was to ensure that the whole of the capital was fully under his military control. Fleetwood, Lambert and the rest of the Grandees were under house arrest. Though Heslirige had opposed them, the Rump had agreed on 30 January to Monck's requests about the dispersal of the London garrison. Only two regiments were retained. One was an infantry regiment that had just come up to London from Portsmouth and had a vacancy for a colonel. A Sussex gentleman, Colonel Fagge, had been imprisoned by the Wallingford House party because he had tried to help the Rump in southern England; on the restoration of the Rump he was released, thanked for his services, appointed to the Council of State, and was chosen by Monck to take over the command. The regiment was stationed at Southwark. The other regiment was that commanded by Colonel Henry Morley, another Sussex gentleman who happened to be Fagge's brother-in-law. Morley had been a member of the secret Council of State which had appointed Monck commander-in-chief during November. Both Fagge and Morley had been concerned with converting Portsmouth to loyalty to the Rump. It was no wonder that Monck trusted these officers, making Morley responsible for the Tower of London.[6] The other regiments which had formerly been posted in London were split up into companies or troops and sent away as far as possible from the capital so that they could do no harm. Naturally the men in these regiments, who were in arrears with their pay, did not relish their treatment. There were two mutinies before Monck arrived, one in St James's Park and the other at Somerset House on the night of 2 February, which was quickly suppressed by Monck's cavalry on the next day. By Saturday 4 February Monck's men took over in London peaceably and other soldiers were forced to depart with the consolation prize of a month's pay.

On that same day Monck was ordered to attend the House of Parliament on Monday 5 February. The Speaker then thanked the General and his army for their services, comparing it 'to the little Cloud which Elijah's servant saw upon Carmell, which in an instant spread to the refreshment of the whole Nation'. Monck, who modestly refused to sit in a chair provided for him within the bar of the House and removed his hat, had taken immense care over his reply which his friends called 'circumspect' or 'very wary'. He began by piously attributing the restoration of the Rump not to himself but to God. Then he went on to describe how during his march he had received many petitions and declarations asking for a full and free parliament, a gospel ministry, the encouragement of learning and the re-admission of the secluded members of Parliament without the imposition of oaths upon them. He told the Rumpers what his replies had been; that the English people were now about to have a parliament free from pressures, guarded by his own sword; that they had promised to fill up the vacancies in the House (a vote to this effect had been carried on 5 January and a sub-committee appointed to consider the necessary qualifications for new members and their electors), and that to admit any members without oaths or engagements 'was never done in England'. Then he expressed his view that 'the sober gentry' would support the members of the House so long as they were careful not to let either the Cavalier or the Fanatical Party have any share in power. After referring to the needs of Scotland and Ireland, he abruptly finished.[7]

This speech did not satisfy anybody. According to Dr Gumble, the majority in the House were far from pleased and in fact took no notice of it. The secluded members were upset that he had not supported their claims for re-admission. The Royalists found themselves repudiated so far as words went. The extreme republicans, like Heslirige and Scot, were annoyed because Monck had furthermore reiterated his refusal to take the oath as a Councillor of State abjuring the Stuarts; they were also offended because he had taken upon himself to speak for the officers in Ireland. Disappointment was felt by the authorities and others in the City of London that he had not declared for a genuinely free parliament; to describe the self-perpetuating Rump as such was a mockery. But, as when he was dealing with Fleetwood and Lambert four months earlier, he was clearly buying time.

Suddenly, but not unexpectedly, Monck was furnished with a golden opportunity to assert his will. Ever since John Lambert's coup of 11 October the situation in the City of London had been extremely unsettled. Trade was poor; the apprentices were unruly; after so many political changes the desire for a stable government supported by a full and free parliament at Westminster was prevalent. When early in December 1659 the apprentices presented the Common Council with a petition written to this effect and the Council postponed giving an answer to it, a riot broke out. Two regiments were sent into the City to quell it. Provoked by boys who threw stones at them, the musketeers killed two or more of the apprentices and although Fleetwood had promised to be accommodating, the council decided to take into its own hands the responsibility for public peace. On the eve of the restoration of the Rump six regiments of the City militia were called out and the officers assigned to command them were such as were welcomed by the Royalists.[8] The King's Secretary of State, Sir Edward Nicholas, even before he heard this news, wrote 'We know they talk of setting up a militia of their own and that some of them [the Londoners] say, as they helped to drive out the father, they will now help to bring in the son.'[9]

Even after the restoration of the Rump the City continued with its defensive measures. For the Rump was not the 'free parliament' it sought after all. The Londoners looked optimistically to Monck to assure them of a new deal. But their hopes had been dashed when in reply to the letter sent by their Swordbearer, Monck did not accept their wish to have the secluded members re-admitted and vacancies by death filled, but had replied that he and his army were resolved 'to stand by and maintain the present Parliament as it sat on 11 October' and that he hoped the City would concur. He adhered to this attitude when a deputation from the Lord Mayor, Aldermen and Common Council interviewed him at Market Harborough, though privately Dr Clarges had reassured them. The City authorities therefore had more faith in Monck than in Heslirige and the Rumpers. On 8 February the Common Council decided to send another deputation to congratulate Monck on his safe arrival and to express their thanks for the courtesy he had shown to the commissioners he had seen at Market Harborough.[10]

On the very same day the Lord Mayor and Common Council received a petition not from the apprentices, but from householders and freemen asking them to refuse to submit to any authority that could not rightfully claim the legislative power of the nation or to assess or levy any money on the petitioners unless it were voted by lawful authority; by lawful authority they meant a full and free parliament containing proper representation of the City which was lacking; these petitioners were thanked by the Common Council.[11] This petition was taken to mean—and has even been so interpreted by contemporary and later historians[12]—that the City intended to refuse to pay any taxes as long as the Rump stayed in power. That was not so. Nevertheless, the challenge flung down to the Rump by the City, which now obviously desired its overthrow and its replacement by a new and full parliament and which had called out its militia to forestall outside interference with its internal affairs, was as clear as crystal. On the advice of the Council of State the Rump commanded Monck to dissolve the Common Council, to quarter his troops in the City, to remove posts and chains from the streets, to take down the gates and to wedge down the portcullises, and to arrest eleven of the leading citizens.

Would Monck obey? Since his speech of two days earlier Heslirige and the Rumpers had become highly suspicious of him. So there arose not only a conflict between the Rump and the City but also a challenge from the Rump to their commander-in-chief. At first the Rumpers were exultantly confident. At daybreak on 9 February Monck entered the City as ordered. Though many of his officers protested, they did what they were told. The posts and chains were torn up under the supervision of junior officers and nine of the proscribed aldermen and common councillors sent to prison. When Heslirige heard the news he exclaimed 'All is our own, he will be honest.'[13] But was that indeed so? Were the orders given to Monck and insisted upon by the Rump a deliberate test of loyalty imposed upon him or were they simply the reflection of the Rumpers' angry reaction to the hostility of the City? One of the Rumpers, Thomas Scot, was to aver later that Monck himself had actually volunteered in the Council of State to pull down the gates and portcullises and to pluck up the posts and chains.[14] According to Edmund Ludlow, Monck went much farther than that.[15] He said that 'the disaffection of the City was so great that they would never be quiet until some of them were hanged; and that it was absolutely necessary for the present to break in pieces their gates and portcullises and to burn their posts and to carry away their chains to the Tower.' Monck is always said to have been an unimaginative man; but it did not require much imagination from him to realize that the City, already half-Royalist in its allegiance, would be further alienated from the Rump by such violent actions; and the City, even more then than now, was the heart of England. If what Ludlow wrote is true, Monck was a veritable Machiavelli. Monck's admiring chaplain described his tactics as a masterpiece of cleverness.[16]

Monck had taken up his headquarters at the Three Tuns Inn near the Guildhall. Here not only leading citizens but many of Monck's senior officers protested to him about the work of destruction. They had not marched up from Scotland, they said, in order to be city scavengers.[17] Some of them even wanted to resign their commissions. But Monck sat impassively chewing tobacco and listening to what Dr Gumble described as music in his ears. Having at first provoked the City by suggesting and carrying out the orders given to him by the Rump, he now back-pedalled. He decided to write a moderately worded letter to the Council of State at Whitehall. In it he informed the Council that he had seen the Lord Mayor and several of the aldermen and conveyed its orders to them. He observed that he had good grounds to believe that the assessments would be duly levied. Therefore, though he had seen to the removal of the posts and chains, he had refrained from taking down the gates and the portcullises because he was afraid that to do so would be further to provoke the City authorities and might make them abandon their good intentions. He therefore awaited fresh orders. In a postscript he asked that the House should accelerate its decisions about the qualifications for new members so that elections to fill up the Parliament could go ahead. Heslirige and his friends were furious. The reply was sent that not only were the gates of the City to be pulled down and the portcullises wedged but they were both to be destroyed. Furthermore, the present Common Council must be dissolved.[18]

Once again Monck reluctantly did what he was told by the Rump and by the evening of 10 February he was back in his quarters at Whitehall. Here he was subjected to pressures from all sides, particularly from his friends, who included Thomas Clarges and Dr Barrow; a rising and supple politician, Anthony Ashley Cooper (though he was no chicken and had been married three times); two of his cavalry officers, Colonel Thomas Saunders (the same Saunders who had been one of the three colonels that had disapproved of Cromwell's Protectorate), and his major, Nathaniel Barton. What arguments swayed him are not known but he saw that the crunch had come. The Rump had to be defied. Finally, late at night Monck took the decision to march back into the City to see if he could repair the damage he had done, while a long and pointed letter was drafted to be sent to the Rump, a letter that was agreed to by Monck's chief officers early the following morning. It was entrusted for delivery to two of his colonels as Monck himself was leaving White-hall.[19]

The letter, which was signed by Monck and fourteen of his officers, explained how grieved they had been to have to take forceful action against the City of London; they said that they feared that 'sober people' would be seriously upset if further compulsion was to be used against them. They would be satisfied only if parliament speedily filled up its vacancies. After complaining about the in-dulgence shown to men like Lambert and Vane and other dangerous and notorious offenders lingering in London or its neighbourhood, the letter stated that it was the desire of the signatories 'upon which we cannot but insist' that 'you would proceed to issue forth Writs in order to Elections'. These writs must be issued by the following Friday (17 February), less than a week ahead, to fill the vacant places in the House of Parliament and later it must be dissolved, as had been promised, to make way for a new one.

The letter was a thunderbolt, but the members of the Rump concealed their anger and dispatched a soothing reply which was to be delivered by the two commissioners who had joined Monck in the Midlands, travelled up with him in his coach, and believed that they carried weight with him. Yet that same afternoon the Rump showed its claws; instead of confirming Monck as commander-in-chief he was appointed one of five commissioners who were to con-trol the army while the discredited Fleetwood was resurrected as the executive commander-in-chief. The leading commissioner was to be Arthur Heslirige, the most rigid of all the oligarchs. Monck's friends tried to add an amendment that he was always to be a mem-ber of the quorum of three, but even that was rejected. The insult could hardly have been plainer. So Monck, hearing about all this, was not in at all a good humour when he met the Lord Mayor and

Common Council for dinner that afternoon. Still, after he had informed them that he was insisting upon a full and then a freely elected parliament everyone was absolutely delighted. Bonfires were lit, church bells were rung, the soldiers were stood drinks and rumps were roasted. 'Indeed,' wrote Pepys, who saw it all, 'it was past imagination, both the greatness and the suddenness of it.' Another diarist recorded somewhat misleadingly that 'many were drunk for joy when the news ran like wildfire that the secluded members would return whom Oliver had put out because they would not consent to the death of the King.'[20] In fact Monck had not yet committed himself to the cause of the secluded members.

Apart from this omission Monck's actions and decisions met with the approval of many other parts of the country. Lord Fairfax concerned himself with organizing meetings in Yorkshire not only in favour of a free parliament but also for the re-admission of the secluded members. The officers whom Monck had left there wrote to tell him that the county was so disturbed they needed reinforcements. In Bristol too, people were agitating for a free parliament and Monck even received letters from Dublin supporting the cause of the secluded members.[21]

From now on Monck and the Council of State dealt with each other as if they were negotiating at long range instead of being merely a few miles apart. Monck, who had originally stationed his army in Finsbury Fields so as not to cause offence to the City authorities, took up his own quarters at the Glasshouse in Broad Street whence he wrote a letter to the Council of State asking it to 'dispense with my absence for a week or ten days' while he restored peace in the City. The President of the Council of State had already written requiring him to return to Whitehall in order to give his advice about 'the outrageous disorders in the City' during the previous night and to ensure that a good guard was appointed for the protection of Parliament. Reluctantly the Council permitted him to stay where he was, but he was invited to come back to Whitehall on the 14th to attend a conference. Monck refused point-blank to do so and wrote another letter to Heslirige warning him not to try to draw together forces against him. He himself, he asserted mendaciously, had done nothing to infringe the lives, rights and liberties of the people's representatives in parliament; he had not attempted to seize power for himself; his aim was simply to maintain the three nations 'in a free state without King, Single Person or House of Peers'. He spoke of course in the presence of God.[22]

Heslirige, his principal opponent, began to crumble. He at once assured Monck that he had not sent for any forces to come to London; that he had had no meetings with Lambert or Vane; that he was 'in no design or plot whatsoever'. Monck replied sourly that Heslirige's correspondence with Lambert and Vane was 'a matter of fact', but, he added, 'seeing you deny it, I will be so just as to believe you'. On 15 February he virtually ordered Heslirige to report at his headquarters (which were now in or near to Drapers Hall) at six o'clock in the evening of Friday 17 February and to bring Scot and one or two other leading Rumpers with him. They were then, he said, invited to meet a number of the secluded members to work for a right understanding and a national settlement.[23]

Up to this time Monck, though he had pressed for the filling up of the House of Parliament and after that the holding of a general election, had not committed himself in favour of the secluded members. As late as 18 February, the day on which because of Monck's own actions a meeting had been arranged between some of the Rumpers and some of the secluded members the day after the meeting at Drapers Hall, Monck wrote to Lord Fairfax and the gentlemen of Yorkshire to tell them that as the Rump had agreed to fill up the House by a series of by-elections, in which the secluded members could be chosen again if the constituencies wanted to elect them, he did not intend to object; he concluded by saying that though this was not what Lord Fairfax and gentlemen of Yorkshire asked for, he hoped it was near to it and would give them satisfaction.[24]

According to one account, Monck had come to a secret agreement with Heslirige and the leading Rumpers that if they were to reverse their decision and re-appoint him commander-in-chief, he would allow them to proceed with their by-elections. That was also the impression received by the French ambassador who considered that Monck's primary aim was to consolidate the republic and make himself its general.[25] This sounds highly improbable. Heslirige and Monck had been at daggers drawn and did not trust one another. If Monck was not toying with the idea of re-admitting the secluded members, why did he arrange the conference at Drapers Hall? What is far more likely is that as Monck knew that if the secluded members were admitted, they would swamp the House of Parliament, he was not prepared to let them re-enter it except on his own terms. After all, he had made the point in his speech to the Rump after he reached London that it was unheard of for members to enter parliament without making a declaration or taking an oath. Monck's terms were that he should be appointed commander-in-chief, that the arrears owing to the armed services should be paid, that writs for a new parliament which should meet on 20 April must immediately be issued, and that the House should agree to a dissolution within a specified time. Yet in the speech in which he outlined these terms he managed to face both ways. While expressing his opinion that the restoration of the monarchy on its old foundations was out of the question and that although some of the old Lords had distinguished themselves 'by joining with the people', the situation of the nation was such that it could not bear their sitting as a separate House, he assured his audience that 'as to the Way of future Settlement, I desire you may be in perfect Freedom ... '.[26]

In his memoirs Anthony Ashley Cooper, who was on friendly terms with Mrs Monck, tells the story that it was not until the early hours of 21 February that Monck was persuaded by him, Clarges and two of his most trusted colonels to support the re-admission. Again this sounds unlikely. Monck was not a volatile man; he did not make snap decisions. What is more probable is that Monck had been impressed by the enthusiasm of his friends in Yorkshire, in Ireland and elsewhere for the re-admission, but that he was determined that the minimum force should be employed to achieve this end and that the secluded members would do what he wanted. The Rump had hoped to anticipate him by issuing writs for by-elections on 20 February. But the Speaker, William Lenthall, who was by nature a time-server, surprisingly objected to the writs being issued on the ground that the secluded members might sue him if this were done. Monck was a friend of Lenthall, later standing godfather to one of his grandsons. He may well have persuaded him to secure a day's delay. At any rate early in the morning of Tuesday 21 February seventy-three of the secluded members were rounded up (this could scarcely have been arranged at the last moment), agreed to Monck's demands and were then conducted by his adjutant-general to the House.[27] The Rumpers were paralysed, the army kept quiet and the City of London celebrated. They knew what it meant: the King would be recalled.

Monck's object was to prevent the army from mutinying once it heard that the secluded members had taken their seats because they would realize this presaged a Stuart restoration. So George summoned all the officers in or around London to meet him in St James's Palace (now his headquarters) on that same day, 21 February, where a letter was drawn up assuring their colleagues stationed elsewhere that the only reason for the return of these members was so that the existing House of Parliament could be speedily dissolved and writs issued for a new one. This Parliament, they explained, would not repeal any of the acts forfeiting lands to the State (many of which had been promised to officers as security for their debentures), would vote money to meet pay and arrears, and would see that anyone who attempted to disturb the peace in favour of Charles Stuart would be severely dealt with. The missive was signed by Monck and fourteen of his colonels; so many clerks were employed upon copying it that by nightfall letters were on their way to all the commanders outside London in England, Scotland and Ireland.[28]

The transformed Parliament, in which the secluded members were in a clear majority, carried out all the promises given to Monck. These members, Edmund Ludlow wrote caustically, 'were but Monkes Journey Men to make up what work he had cut out for them, he being a man void of all faith and honesty'.[29] He was at once appointed commander-in-chief in England, Scotland and Ireland, and unanimously named a member of a new Council of State. He was also chosen general-at-sea with Edward Mountagu. A bill was introduced to settle upon him the palace and manor of Hampton Court, but significantly he did not want to receive royal lands and instead was awarded a sum of £20,000 for his public services. Anne Monck, on the other hand, was deeply disappointed. She would have liked Hampton Court as her country house; for the time being she had to be satisfied with St James's Palace. Her husband took up permanent residence there whence he watched with eagle eyes the reactions of his army to events. Two decisions by Parliament showed which way the wind was blowing. Sir George Booth, who was imprisoned in the Tower of London, was released on bail, while votes condemning those who had advocated negotiations with Charles I in 1647 and 1648 were expunged from the records.

Those who were most upset by the manner in which things were moving were the sectarians, particularly the Anabaptists, Quakers and Fifth Monarchy Men, who had been such a trial to Monck when he was in Scotland. Colonel Nathaniel Rich, who commanded a regiment stationed in East Anglia and was reputedly a Fifth Monarchy Man, called a general rendezvous of his officers at Bury St Edmunds who were mostly antagonistic to Monck. The commander-in-chief promptly replaced Rich by Richard Ingoldsby, who managed without too much difficulty to take over from him, Rich meekly coming up to London to hand in his commission. The Anabaptist Colonel John Okey, who had earlier crossed swords with Monck, was posted at Bristol where soldiers in his regiment and some of the leading citizens were becoming restless, but he himself at first took Monck's letter at its face value and suppressed the disturbances; afterwards he came up to London to put his point of view which was against either a single person (Monck) or Charles Stuart governing. Okey demanded that the members of the reinforced Parliament should be sent for and compelled to pledge themselves in favour of a free Commonwealth without King or House of Lords. Bristol and East Anglia were the main centres of discontent, but the garrison at Hull under Colonel Overton was also agitated over the idea that the return of the secluded members would mean the restoration of the Stuart monarchy. Overton himself engaged in propaganda against the return of the King. Monck at once ordered Colonel Charles Fairfax to take over the command and Overton was told to come up to London to report to the Council of State.[30] A watch was kept on Colonel Lilburne, who after his supersession at York had retired to his country house in the North Riding. There also appears to have been trouble at St Michael's Mount in Cornwall where Monck ordered Robert Bennett, an Anabaptist colonel in command there, to hand over the house and all the ordnance to another more trusted Cornish colonel, John St Aubyn.[31] But broadly the army was quietened by Monck's assurances; in some places, including Durham, Newcastle and Carlisle and, above all, the City of London the news of the return of the secluded members and the promise of a new parliament were welcomed. Nor were there any signs of trouble in Scotland or Ireland.

Monck took every possible precaution to keep the army under control. Robert Lilburne was reprimanded, Lambert was arrested and sent to the Tower (the cell formerly occupied by Sir George Booth was put at his disposal) and on hearing that agitators were being sent into the regiments, Monck ordered their colonels to tighten discipline and offer a reward of £10 for the arrest of anyone trying to 'debauch the soldiers'.[32] But even before Parliament dissolved itself on 19 March the feeling was growing everywhere that either Monck would become Protector or King himself or that Charles II would be recalled or—though this was hardly on the cards—that Richard Cromwell (who was at that time pathetically asking Monck to help him to meet his debts) would be resuscitated. Few observers believed that a republic would be retained. That was why Monck was warned by Colonel Charles Fairfax and others of the dangers of assassination.[33]

On 7 March a number of Monck's officers, inspired by Okey after his arrival in London, drew up a declaration against the government by a single person which they asked Monck to sign. Monck at first found it hard to think of an answer when he met the signatories. Okey opened the proceedings with a lengthy speech in which he said that the best expedient that could be thought of in order to safeguard their civil and religious liberties was for the Parliament to be obliged to 'engage for a Free-State and Common-wealth without a King or House of Lords'. Perplexed Monck postponed his answer until the following day, meanwhile consulting his friends including Clarges, his secretary, William Clarke, and his chaplain. On the evening of 8 March another conference was held at St James's. Monck then told the worried officers that nothing was likely to happen before Parliament dissolved. The new Parliament, from which the Royalists were to be excluded, would, he was sure, give them satisfaction. A simpler version of his speech was that he told his discontented officers 'that they must obey Parliament and not teach Parliament what they ought to do'. Soon addresses of loyalty were reaching Monck from regiments everywhere in the land, as well as from Dublin and Dunkirk.[34]

The new Parliament or Convention, as it was later known because it was not summoned by the King, was due to meet on 25 April, five days later than Monck had originally intended. But a month before this a contemporary diarist was noting that the nation was very quiet for 'the famous City of London and Council of State and the Lord General Monck are all of one mind, as is verily supposed, to have a king, the right king, Charles the Second'.[35] However, in order to ensure that there should be no trouble when the new Parliament gathered in Westminster and a House of Lords made an unexpected appearance (much to his embarrassment for he feared that would provoke his army),[36] Monck was told by the Council of State to review in Hyde Park an army of more than 12,000 London militiamen called out as a kind of police force.[37]

Certainly the Royalists, although they were not supposed to stand, won a resounding victory in the election. A hundred acknowledged Royalists and their sons were among those who took their seats. The new House consisted largely of Anglican Cavaliers and Presbyterian Royalists. Only sixteen former members of the Long Parliament were re-elected. Monck was elected a knight of the shire for Devonshire and a member for the university of Cambridge. He chose to sit for Devonshire. It has been estimated that about ninety per cent of the members favoured the restoration of Charles II.[38]

So skilfully had Monck purged his army—he was still doing so in April—that none of the republicans left in the army put up any show of resistance. A momentary sensation was caused when John Lambert, who was more of an egoist than a republican, escaped from the Tower and tried to rally a force at Edgehill. Monck became rather agitated and at first wanted to march in person against him. However, he was dissuaded; Colonel Richard Ingoldsby with Rich's former cavalry regiment and some infantry, found it fairly simple to round up Lambert, bringing him back to London on the eve of the assembly of the new Parliament. Monck told Grenville earlier that if Ingoldsby were to be beaten 'he was resolved to put-off his Disguise, declare the King's Commission, own it for the Authority by which he acted, and commission the Royal Party into Arms ... '.[39]

Six days before the Long Parliament finally dissolved itself George Monck at last revealed his intentions to the Royalists and the exiled King. An optimistic move by Monsieur Bordeaux, the French ambassador in London, to act as a mediator between Monck and the King and to arrange that Charles II should return to England from France was ignored. Monck saw Bordeaux on 8 March but refused to discuss internal politics with him.[40] About a fortnight later, however, Monck at last agreed to a secret interview with his kinsman, Sir John Grenville, the same Royalist agent who had dispatched Nicholas Monck to Scotland in August 1659. It was William Morice who persuaded his friend Monck, with whom he was now living in St James's Palace, to see Grenville. Introduced to Monck in Morice's apartment, Sir John handed the General the letter from the King dated 21 July 1659 which contained the offer of £100,000 a year. After he read the letter Monck said: 'I hope the King will forgive what is past, both in my words and actions' and went on to explain that although he had always been faithful to him at heart, it was not until recently that he had been in a position to help Charles. Now he was prepared to obey the King's commands. As to the offer of a princely income, various offices and the right to name leading Ministers of State Monck said he would not tie the King's hands by asking for specific awards.[41]

A few days later Monck saw Grenville again. He now told his kinsman that in order to damp down the fears of his army the King must issue a general pardon, subject to such exceptions as parliament might think necessary; that he must promise to accept any acts parliament might pass about the sales of royal lands to soldiers and others and that he should guarantee liberty of conscience. He also advised Charles to leave Brussels in the Spanish Netherlands for Breda in the Protestant Dutch Republic. As Grenville was returning to Brussels Monck was receiving another more up-to-date letter from the King saying that he would 'take all ways he could to let the world see his entire trust in him'.[42]

Monck had not written to the King, but had asked Grenville to learn his advice by heart. Soon after Grenville reached Brussels the King departed for Breda where he arrived on 4 April. On the way he gave Grenville letters drawn up by Edward Hyde to be delivered to Monck: to Monck and Mountagu as joint generals-at-sea, to the two Speakers of the Lords and Commons (the Earl of Manchester and Sir Harbottle Grimston, a Presbyterian) and to the Lord Mayor of London. He also sent a declaration of his intentions in which he dealt with three subjects, the act of oblivion, the future of religion and the land settlement. The King promised a free and general pardon excluding only such persons as were excepted by a future parliament, to declare liberty to tender consciences, and to leave to parliament the decisions on land sales.

Sir John Grenville saw Monck for the third time on his return to London where he gave him, in his new capacity as royal commander-in-chief, another letter from the King, in which Charles wrote that he relied on the English army not foreign help for his peaceful restoration.[43] Grenville's meeting with Monck was on 27 April; next day Grenville visited the Council of State and on 1 May the Speaker of the House of Lords received the declaration of Breda which was read to both Houses of Parliament. At this joint meeting Monck spoke first expressing his happiness for the King's goodness. The two Houses then voted that government 'is and ought to be by King, Lords and Commons'.[44] That evening Monck read the King's letter to him to his officers in London and later instructed Colonel Knight to see that the royal declarations from Breda were communicated to all the officers elsewhere. The army as a whole was naturally concerned over the act of oblivion, religious toleration and the payment of its arrears. Monck promised to forward an address made to him in this sense to the King. A few of his officers vainly tried to avert the Restoration by pressing Monck himself to become king. But both Monck and his wife thought they would do better as king-makers.[45]

On 5 May Monck was in a position to write to the King with the permission of the new Parliament assuring him of the army's loyalty. Three days later Sir Matthew Hale proposed in the House of Commons that a committee should be set up to consider which of the clauses in the so-called treaty of Newport of 1648 should be presented to the King. Monck strongly opposed the motion. He warned the House that any delays might endanger a peaceful settlement and that commissioners should at once be sent across the North Sea to invite Charles to return to England. So warmly was Monck's speech received that Hale's motion was withdrawn.[46] Thus Charles II owed it to George Monck that his restoration was unconditional. On 10 May Monck wrote again to the King to tell him of the universal joy with which the royal rights had been proclaimed and that it would be to Charles's 'glory to advance the Crown and Sceptre of our Lord Jesus Christ and that under you all your people would be able to lead a peaceable life in all godliness and honesty'.[47]

The King also owed it to Monck that his restoration was blood-less. The purged army was made to assent to the declaration of Breda and only isolated disturbances took place. For example, at Hull a busy agitator named Lieutenant Merry was put on trial. Charles Fairfax, the new commander at Hull, then wrote to Monck to say that as 'this work has been hitherto—by your Excellency's sweet conduct—without any blood, [it was] not fit for us to begin the precedent'.[48]

Consistently with his speech in the Commons, deploring the imposition of conditions on Charles since any unnecessary delay in his return to England would be dangerous, Monck sent a message to his fellow general-at-sea urging him to sail straightaway to Holland. Furthermore, on 16 May he wrote to the King himself pressing him to come to England as quickly as possible, saying that his presence was essential to 'make the people of this distracted country happy'.[49] In London Monck and his wife busied themselves on preparations for the King's return. Mrs Monck began attending to the King's furniture and went around buying him linen while Monck was arranging the ceremonies with which Charles was to be greeted after his arrival at Dover.[50] Rather pathetically Monck had to deal with petitions from prominent republicans, such as Arthur Heslirige and Bulstrode Whitelocke for his protection. Monck was reported to Hyde as saying later that he would make good an earlier promise to save Heslirige's head for twopence; but he would have nothing to do with Whitelocke, who, he knew, had told the Lord Mayor and Common Council that he was plotting to bring back the King six months earlier.[51]

On 14 May Mountagu and his squadron arrived at Scheveningen, the port for The Hague. Writing to Monck at seven in the evening of 23 May, Mountagu said that the Dukes of York and Gloucester had come aboard the warship, the *Naseby*, which was to be renamed the *Royal Charles*, on the previous day. The Princess Royal (widow of William II of Orange) and the Queen of Bohemia paid a visit that afternoon to the fleet when Charles II, having had his last carefree moments at The Hague, came to embark. Monck, seeing that many noblemen with their retinues were riding down in large numbers to Dover to welcome the King, arranged that they should be divided into distinct troops 'for the more conveniency of quartering', as Dr Gumble observed, 'and to prevent quarrels upon that occasion, and that they might have better accommodation'. Monck himself intended only to bring a few of his officers and men with him to Dover and ordered the trusted Colonel Knight to draw up the bulk of his army on Blackheath. The King reached Dover at nine in the morning of 25 May. An express messenger was sent to the General, who was at Greenwich, to tell him that the King refused to come ashore until Monck was with him. As soon as he read the letter Monck made off at great speed, saying he would not sleep till he reached His Majesty.[52]

On that afternoon Charles II landed at Dover pier where Monck duly knelt before him; the King then embraced and kissed him. The mayor and aldermen of the town welcomed Charles with 'a large Bible, with gold Clasps embossed, which they presented'. The chaplain to the Corporation delivered a short speech. 'The Parson,' continued Gumble, who was on the spot, 'would have been longer but the General suggested that Dover was not commodious for such a resort.'[53] Then the King and Monck walked through Dover and got into a coach in which they were driven to Canterbury where they stayed for the weekend. Here Charles was embarrassed by being given a long list of some seventy names of persons whom Monck recommended as Privy Councillors. However, it was discovered that Monck had simply written down all these names in order to get rid of importunate suitors: so his list could be ignored. The King took the opportunity to confer a knighthood of the garter on Monck; the Duke of York and the Duke of Gloucester then hung the insignia of the Order of the Garter around his neck. These ceremonies took place on the evening of Saturday 26 May, the day after the King landed.

On 29 May, Charles II's thirtieth birthday, he arrived at Blackheath where he received a rather tepid welcome from Monck's army. From there he went with his retinue to Whitehall, having been joined and fed by the Lord Mayor of London and his aldermen at St George's Fields. The procession thence was indeed elaborate and impressive, headed by 300 cavalrymen from the City of London militia in silver doublets with five cavalry regiments bringing up the rear under Colonel Knight. Monck rode just ahead of the King and the two royal dukes. The Londoners were beside themselves with enthusiasm. As the General passed them, they cried out 'Hurrah for Honest George Monck!'[54]

16

The Elder Statesman

During the year of the Restoration George Monck received a flow of wealth and offices from the cornucopia of the King's gratitude. That candid contemporary historian, Dr Gilbert Burnet, considered the tide had run so strongly that Charles II would have been restored in any case and that Monck 'only went into it dexterously enough to get much fame and great rewards'.[1] But that was not the way most people felt; the King himself certainly believed otherwise. For a bloodless revolution in his favour was the last thing he expected.

The principal instrument of the Stuarts' return did not remain Sir George Monck, K.G., for long; on 7 July 1660, six weeks after he was knighted, he was created Duke of Albemarle, Earl of Torrington, Baron Monck of Potheridge, Beauchamp and Teyes; his son Christopher was to assume the courtesy title of Lord Torrington, even though jealous people averred that since his father and mother were not married when he was conceived he was a bastard.[2]

The offices that were allotted to Monck included that of Master of the Horse—that sinecure he chose for himself—Gentleman of the Bedchamber, Lord Lieutenant of Devonshire and then of Middlesex and Privy Councillor (one out of its thirty members). On 3 August he received by letters patent under the Great Seal, a commission which made him Captain-General during the royal pleasure. Eighteen days later he was appointed Lord Lieutenant of Ireland, a lucrative post. He was also granted a pension of £7,000 a year to be paid for out of Crown lands, guaranteed to him by a private act of parliament;[3] his Irish lands, confirmed to him by the Act of Settlement of 1662, embodying a declaration of 30 November 1660, were said to be worth £4,000 a year and his estates in Scotland £500.[4] Other gifts awaited him. He was able to buy a country house at New Hall near Chelmsford in Essex; as a major part of his pension he was in February 1661 to receive Theobalds in Hertfordshire, the estate where King James I most loved to hunt, though few stags were now left, and other manors worth altogether above £4,000 a year; in London he lived in the Cockpit on the western side of Whitehall (where the present Treasury building stands) near St James's Park; on 25 March 1663, no doubt because he dwelt in the Cockpit, he became Chief Keeper of St James's Park with the right to appoint his own underlings.[5]

Monck's tastes were modest. Almost his only amusement was breeding horses. Dr Gumble wrote that his temperance was remarkable. When at New Hall he never drank to excess and he was always tough with officers who became drunk; he never ate between meals and on occasions was content with one meal a day. If necessary, he could go without food for thirty hours without grumbling. Possibly his abstemiousness was exaggerated by his appreciative biographer, for the French ambassador noted that, though he was reserved and silent during dinner, 'he usually took delight in the pleasures of the table'. Yet when Pepys saw him at dinner at the Cockpit in April 1667 he remarked on the 'sorry company, his nasty wife, the dirty dishes, the bad meat and the ill dinner'. At any rate he was no gourmet: 'in his Palate he was not curious', as Skinner put it. During his last years, according to Dr Gumble, who wrote that he had 'very good grounds to believe this', he lost all sense of taste.[6] Like Napoleon and Winston Churchill he could manage with four hours sleep a night.

By universal testimony Monck was not a brilliant conversationalist. He was one of those men who keep their thoughts to themselves and prefer to listen carefully as other people do the talking. When he did talk he was abrupt and to the point. One who knew him well wrote 'he was no polite Man in his Address or way of speaking'.[7] The conversational Samuel Pepys thought he was ponderous and slow in his intellectual processes.[8] That may be true, though it is unusual for admirals and generals to be incapable of reaching swift decisions. Nor should Monck's taciturnity be interpreted as meaning that he could not be eloquent on important occasions. Anyone who reads his letters and speeches will discover his clarity of thought. He was no Robert Harley to wrap his ideas up in impenetrable wordiness. All of us have met that type of politician.

Gumble tells us that Monck was an indulgent husband and 'never cast an amorous glance on any other woman'.[9] His health had its ups and downs. Like most gentlemen of his time he suffered from gout; and he became asthmatic. His long-distance sight was poor, but his hearing was excellent. His illnesses did not make him irascible. He never swore; his habit of chewing tobacco was not greatly admired but it kept him placid. As to religion, he was certainly no enthusiast and disliked enthusiasm in others. According to his fellow Privy Councillor, the Earl of Clarendon, he 'had no fumes of religion to turn his head'. He believed in a deity; and, like Oliver Cromwell and the bulk of the Anglicans of his time, he appears to have been a predestinarian. As he rose steadily up the ladder of fame and fortune to reach the top in his early middle age, he was convinced that he had indeed been chosen in advance by God to count his blessings. When he was in Scotland he conferred his patronage on Presbyterian ministers; but it would be inexact to describe him as being a Presbyterian himself. The English Presbyterians thought he had betrayed them.

Both Monck's early biographers, Dr Gumble, who knew him well in Scotland, and Thomas Skinner, who was his physician when he lived at New Hall, regarded it as necessary to apologize for his 'frugality' — the polite name for meanness — while his enemies insisted that he was avaricious and grasping. Lieutenant-General Ludlow — no friend of Monck since he thought that George had betrayed the republican cause — asserted that the office of Master of the Horse, which carried much patronage with it, was 'by the industry of his wife, who having been an Exchange woman, knew how to drive a hard bargain improved to the utmost advantage the sale of offices'.[10] Certainly Anne Monck, elevated by her husband's success to being one of the most influential duchesses in the land, fell over herself in toadying to royalty. Besides looking after the King's linen and furniture before his return, but soon after Charles's declarations from Breda had been received and he had been invited by Parliament to return to England, she wrote to Charles to say that she hoped 'in some measure the King had not succeeded the worse for her tears and prayers' — a pretty extraordinary remark for which she received the royal thanks; later she wrote to Charles's sister, Mary, Dowager Princess of Orange, with expressions of affection and informing her of how she had become a duchess. She also appears to have persuaded her husband to express his willingness to oblige the King's mother, Henrietta Maria.[11]

Gilbert Burnet, who was in Scotland at the time of the Restoration but no doubt picked up plenty of gossip from his friends in London, wrote that the Duke of Albemarle was 'ravenous' and his wife 'a mean contemptible creature' and that 'both of them asked and sold all that was within their reach, nothing being denied them for some time ... '[12] It is fascinating to realize that just as Monck was accused of greed and meanness and his wife of being grasping, so too were a greater general than Monck—John Churchill, Duke of Marlborough, and his wife Sarah over forty years later. In both cases these generals had started life in a modest gentry family and reached the height of their profession by sheer ability and accepted whatever was offered to them by way of reward; it often happens, one is told, that if one has to be careful with money when young, that habit remains ingrained even in a prosperous later life.

Monck and his wife immediately became jealous of Edward Hyde, first Earl of Clarendon who belonged to the same generation as Monck and, like him, came from the west country. Hyde had been unflinchingly loyal to Charles I after he left London in 1642 and to Charles II whom he served assiduously and conscientiously throughout his exile. Edward Hyde was told at the beginning of May 1660 by various correspondents that George Monck was particularly 'unkind' to him and that Anne, though not usually violent against any man, was bitter about him. She inquired about his temper because she had been told that he was 'proud and insolent, contemning all counsel to the King but his own'.[13] It may well have been that Hyde's enemies deliberately tried to arouse Monck's envy but it would not have been unreasonable for the Moncks to wonder whether when Charles II came back to England he would be willing to rely on Monck's advice in preference to that of his old and reliable Minister. In his famous *History of the Rebellion*, written when he was again an exile, Clarendon remarked of Monck that 'it is glorious enough to his memory that he was instrumental in bringing mighty things to pass which he had neither wisdom to foresee nor courage to attempt nor understanding to continue', which was both nasty and untrue. Yet it is significant that in his *Life*, Clarendon, who was always distrustful of soldiers, had nothing critical to say about him. If differences arose between these principal advisers of the monarch it was mainly in regard to foreign policy, for example over a treaty with Portugal and relations with the Dutch Republic.[14] Clarendon was also to criticize Monck's strategy as a general-at-sea in 1666, though of course the Earl knew nothing about the subject. Undoubtedly these two magnificos did not get along very well together. It must have given the Duke of Albemarle some pleasure when the King sent him to Clarendon to demand his seals of office after his disgrace in 1667 because he was blamed for the ill-success of the Dutch War.

Whatever Monck may have felt about Clarendon's influence, the General could scarcely have grumbled about the King's generosity to himself. He was able not only to acquire wealth and prestige, but to secure consideration for his friends and relatives. Before the end of 1660 his brother Nicholas was appointed Bishop of Hereford; his brother-in-law Clarges was knighted; Sir John Grenville became Earl of Bath; Anthony Ashley Cooper, with whom Monck had become close friends after his arrival in London from Scotland, was strongly recommended by him to the King for membership of his Privy Council, a recommendation that was accepted; his old friend, William Morice, was promptly made Secretary of State; finally Monck exerted himself on behalf of officers and men who had been loyal to him in Scotland and during the march to England. He looked after the pay of soldiers who under Major-General Morgan still garrisoned Scotland;[15] he ensured that the soldiers in England, who were in the process of being demobilized, should receive an extra week's pay and that their entry into civilian life was facilitated; and he tried hard, though with limited success, to see that confiscated lands acquired by officers in lieu of pay should be retained by them.

The land question was difficult and disappointing. Before the King's return Monck had drawn up a paper about the confirmation of sales of Crown and other lands. He had proposed that those who were then in service in the army and navy under himself or the generals-at-sea, should be confirmed in possession of their estates for ninety-nine years and not pay more than a sixth of the full yearly value of the property as rent.[16] But in the declaration of Breda Charles left the whole question of the land settlement to parliament, carefully adding that he would also be 'ready to consent' to any act of parliament for the full satisfaction of all arrears due to the soldiers of the army under command of General Monck. Nevertheless, no public legislation was passed on this complicated subject.[17] Broadly, the majority of Royalists who had been compelled to sell part or all of their lands to meet fines managed to get them back before or after the Restoration. A few private acts were passed, actions for trespass successfully obtained against purchasers, or voluntary agreements concluded between purchasers and the original owners. Though a large number of purchasers of Crown and Church lands received no compensation on the grounds that they had already made sufficient profits from them, some compensation was paid by royal commissioners or compensatory leases granted. But it can be said with certainty that Monck's desire that his officers and soldiers should retain the lands they had acquired during the Interregnum was not fulfilled. As, however, agitation over this question was minimal it may be presumed that the majority of Monck's officers were pacified.

What about Monck's former enemies? Charles II had insisted that the regicides, that is to say the judges who had voted for his father's execution, should be punished, but had otherwise left the question of penalties upon Commonwealthsmen to Parliament. After much coming and going between the two Houses of Parliament an act of pardon, oblivion and indemnity was passed in August 1660 by the Convention from which fifty-one men were exempted, but in their trials conducted during the autumn only ten were condemned to death. According to a Royalist report to Hyde early in May, Monck would have been satisfied with just eight executions.[18] While still a member of the House of Commons, Monck had proved himself to be merciful, pressing the House to show favour 'towards some of the most rich and potent of the Rump,[19] As the trial of the exempted men, once having been agreed to by a Grand Jury, was held at the Old Bailey before a commission which included George Monck, he was in a position both to keep his promises and pursue his grudges.

The case of Sir Arthur Heslirige is interesting. He had strongly resisted the Restoration, but equally he had been a former colleague of Monck, for example, during the Dunbar campaign. After he was elevated to the House of Lords, Monck had testified to the Speaker of the House of Commons that when he had arrived in London earlier in the year Heslirige had undertaken to go home and live quietly. In return Monck had promised to secure his life and estate; Heslirige had also refused help to Lambert when he escaped from the Tower and attempted to resist the Restoration. Thomas Clarges had also informed the Commons of Monck's commitment, which was honoured.[20] Nevertheless, Heslirige was imprisoned for life.

Monck was less concerned over Heslirige's former colleague, Thomas Scot, who had vainly attempted as a leader of the Rump to lord it over Monck, when he reached the capital. He remembered how Scot had tried to raise sectarians to oppose his army and how Scot's son had threatened to kill him.[21] Scot was duly executed as a regicide. Another character towards whom Monck felt animosity was the Marquis of Argyll, with whom his dealings in Scotland had been frigid. Argyll came up to London after the Restoration but was arrested and sent back to Edinburgh to be tried for treason. When difficulty was found in proving high treason against him—after all he had crowned Charles II King of Scotland at Scone and had refused to join the Royalist rebellion of 1654—Albemarle sent to the court in Edinburgh what were described as 'private letters' written to him during the Commonwealth period and in consequence Argyll was found guilty and executed. According to Burnet, everyone blamed Monck for his behaviour. But it could reasonably be argued, on the other side, that Argyll's correspondence was official not confidential; and it could have been discovered without Monck's help. Furthermore, Monck testified that when Argyll had appeared at the proclamation of Richard Cromwell in Edinburgh during September 1658 he had done so simply because all the nobility of Scotland had been summoned there.[22] In any case it was felt by many Royalists that Argyll was justly punished by death because of 'the barbarous insolence' with which he had treated the heroic Montrose after he had fought for both the Stuart kings. Still Monck had not a forgiving nature; if historians were allowed to utter moral judgments, none of these men who helped with or survived the Restoration, such as the Earl of Manchester or Edward Mountagu, yet had previously fought against the Stuarts, came well out of being holier than thou when they acted as judges of the regicides and others. It must have been a nauseating performance. Monck himself need not have accepted the office of commissioner at the trials, though it has been argued in his defence that he thus escaped from appearing in the witness box.

The first thing Monck was called upon to do in his somewhat Pooh-Bah-like position* was to disband the army. Charles II was courageous enough to believe that he could rely for his own safety on the loyalty of his subjects rather than upon a standing army, which, despite Monck's efforts, contained a fair number of republicans and might have turned against the monarchy. Eighteen regiments of foot, thirteen regiments of horse and fifty garrisons had to be paid off. The introduction of a poll tax and the imposition of assessments at the rate of £70,000 a month for eighteen months more or less met the cost of the demobilization. Originally it was intended to retain only the life guards of which there were three cavalry troops, the King's, the Duke of York's and Albemarle's. But in January 1661 a rising by Fifth Monarchy Men took place in the City of London whence they marched to Kenwood, between Hampstead and Highgate, where most of them capitulated to a party of cavalry and infantry sent out there by Monck. Though some of these apocalyptic thugs returned to London where they were rounded up and their leader killed after a skirmish with the City militia and the horse guards, this gave Monck an excellent excuse to retain the nucleus of a standing army, for, after all, it is not of much use being a commander-in-chief if one has no army to command. Not only were the Coldstreamers kept in being but also a regiment, raised by King Charles II during his exile in 1656 known as the First Foot Guards, was also retained and was to become familiar to posterity as the Grenadier Guards, the oldest regiment in the British army. In addition the Royal Horse Guards or 'Blues' were put on a permanent footing after the rising of 1661; lastly, the Royal Scots, who had been serving in France, returned to England because of the scare.[23]

The Duke of Albemarle, as he must be called from now on, bent his efforts to ensuring that the soldiers behaved themselves while they awaited disbandment and that the money to meet their arrears of pay was forthcoming. He instructed his officers to administer oaths of allegiance to the new regime and to discharge any soldier who refused to take them. In January 1661 he was complaining to the Privy Council that the proceeds of the assessment and poll tax were coming in too slowly so that not only part of the army, but

* For the benefit of readers who are not familiar with *The Mikado*, Ko-Ko was Lord High Executioner in the Government of Titipu and Pooh-Bah was Lord High Everything Else.

several ships' crews in the navy were still unpaid because of tax arrears. He harried the Privy Council and also took what action he could himself. For example, in his capacity as Lord Lieutenant of Middlesex he asked the Duchess of Somerset to prepare a paper giving the yearly value of her estate within the county so that she could contribute to the assessments.[24]

Other tasks which confronted the Duke of Albemarle as Captain-General were the maintenance of security in Scotland and Ireland; the upkeep of the ports of Dunkirk and Mardyck, which were acquired by Oliver Cromwell from the Spaniards in the Netherlands; and the prevention of disorders in London since apart from the City militia the army was the only police force. In Scotland Monck trusted his old adjutant, Thomas Morgan, to keep the peace; he congratulated him on his success in pacifying Edinburgh.[25] In Ireland he depended on his old friends, Charles Coote, President of Connaught, and Lord Broghill, who commanded in Munster, though they had trouble there with the officers who had expected to be confirmed in their acquisition of lands, as indeed Monck himself had expected. However, a royal declaration of 30 November 1660 did confirm both soldiers and 'adventurers' in estates held by them in May 1659, but there were many exceptions—for example, Church property had to be restored—and opportunity opened for infinite jobbery and corruption, though finally Monck's own property was specially provided for.

Monck's responsibilities as a kind of police commissioner in London were complicated by the fact that many of those who were riotous and unruly there were his own soldiers demoralized because either they were waiting to be paid off or had already been disbanded and were unable to find employment. As early as August 1660 Albemarle had to give orders to his officers and men not to force their way into theatres and playhouses in and around the City of London disturbing gentlefolk and endangering the King's peace. He told them they could only be allowed into places of entertainment with the permission of the owners or doorkeepers. Three months later he instructed Major Anthony Buller, who had earned a reputation as governor of the Scilly Isles and afterwards at the capture of Jamaica, to see that troopers belonging to the Duke of York's regiment patrolled the roads leading into London where a number of armed robberies had been committed. Later he ordered that one of these troops was to provide four cavalrymen to patrol Long Acre, Sr Martin's Lane and the Strand; other troopers were ordered to patrol King Street, Tothill Street, Petty France and Charing Cross.[26] This must have been one of the first occasions when policemen on horseback guarded the west end of London against crime and disorder.

Albemarle's duties as commander-in-chief were otherwise not onerous since the size of the army had been reduced from some 50,000 to 3,000 men. So far as internal security outside the capital was concerned only a number of isolated plots were detected which came to very little. Even the Fifth Monarchy Men, about whom Albemarle had been so perturbed in 1661, were described by him two years later as 'weak though never quiet'.[27] As Master of the Horse Albemarle's duties were nominal, though the King once asked him to arrange that a Turkish horse, a barb and five mares, said previously to have belonged to Oliver Cromwell, should be delivered to the second Duke of Buckingham.[28] In November 1661 he resigned his office of Lord Lieutenant of Ireland; his deputy, Baron Robartes of Truro, who was two years older than himself, refused to go there and instead was appointed Lord Privy Seal. Albemarle with his numerous commitments in London also had no particular wish to go to Ireland again and voluntarily relinquished the post, recommending that his old foe, now Duke of Ormonde, who knew Ireland inside out, should take his place. Albemarle had been seriously ill during the summer of 1661 and the winter of 1661–2.[29] Neither Scotland nor Ireland had agreed with his health and that may well have been one of the factors contributing to his resignation of this valuable but onerous position.

Albemarle dabbled a little in foreign affairs. Before the King's return the Portuguese representative in London had secured an interview with him in which the ambassador advocated an alliance to be sealed by Charles II's marriage to Princess Catherine of Braganza, the daughter of the Queen Regent. The Portuguese motives were obvious. One of the terms of the treaty of the Pyrenees concluded between France and Spain in 1659, ending a war which had lasted twenty-four years, was that France should give no more help to Portugal which was fighting for its independence from Spain. An English diplomatic alliance and the right to recruit professional soldiers in England for service against Spain would to some extent fill the gap caused by the withdrawal of French help. The French Government, still envious of the Spanish empire, strongly favoured an Anglo-Portuguese treaty of alliance. The Spaniards insisted that Catherine was incapable of bearing children; the Earl of Clarendon received the same advice from English merchants in Lisbon. Exactly how Catherine's child-bearing potential was so widely known is obscure; in fact after she married Charles II she had two miscarriages. But Clarendon was doubtful about the match, while Albemarle supported it.[30] That may well have been one of the causes of dissension between two of the King's principal advisers.

Another question of foreign policy in which Albemarle concerned himself was English relations with the Dutch Republic. Although a treaty of peace and alliance had been concluded between the two governments in 1662, a state of undeclared war was in full spate by 1664. Rivalries between the merchants were to be seen in the West and East Indies and along the west coast of Africa. Albemarle, who had fought against the Dutch ten years earlier, was not afraid of their navy and may have been influenced by the view that the prosperity of England would increase if the Dutch were soundly beaten, as they had been in 1654.[31] The same trading companies which had advocated the Navigation Acts of 1651 and 1660 were rabid for war. Much the same causes brought it about as before—disputes over fishing and the right of search by warships and, above all, rivalries over colonies in Africa and America. Neither Charles II nor Clarendon wanted war, but they were pushed into it. The House of Commons voted the unprecedented sum of £2,500,000 to pay for it. James, Duke of York, eager for martial fame, led the royal navy to a notable victory at the battle of Lowestoft on 3 June 1665 while Albemarle acted as his deputy in London harassing the Navy Board with demands for more ships and supplies for his master, though Clarendon remained sour about the whole operations.

War had been officially declared in February 1665 and the Duke of York had taken over his command at the Gunfleet near Harwich on 23 March. But Albemarle was soon to be diverted from his duties as James's deputy. A rumour that a bubonic plague was reaching England from the Middle East by way of Holland had started in the autumn of 1664 and a few cases of deaths from it were reported in London before the end of the year. A hard frost in the winter was followed by a hot summer. By the spring it was sufficiently clear to the Government that the plague had come to London, although the numbers of people dying from it did not attain alarming proportions until midsummer. On 12 May Albemarle was appointed a member of a sub-committee of the Privy Council along with other notabilities and his friend, the Secretary of State, William Morice, 'to consider the best means of preventing the spreading of the infection of the Plague'. But no one was optimistic that anything much could be done. Plagues were believed to be acts of God, which in the past had occurred at fairly frequent intervals and had to be borne with equanimity like earthquakes and thunderstorms. Soon the well-to-do were streaming out of the capital, especially those who lived cheek-by-jowl with the poor in the Westminster slums. The King himself did not leave Whitehall for Hampton Court until late in July and he arranged to hold meetings of the Privy Council at Syon House in Isleworth, which, as it happened, was to be severely hit by the plague. The Duke of Albemarle was left in charge at Whitehall while the Lord Mayor, Sir John Lawrence, helped by his Aldermen who were forbidden to leave, was in control in the City of London. Monck's principal aides were the wealthy Earl of Craven, the friend of Prince Rupert and his mother, and Gilbert Sheldon the Archbishop of Canterbury. Albemarle in the west and Lawrence in the City, wrote the historian of this Plague, were 'the two pillars' upon which the government of London rested. Albemarle was virtually a dictator, but there was little enough he could do except order fires to be lit in the streets with the idea that they would clear the infectious air (this was a recommendation from the College of Physicians), to prohibit anyone except doctors and nurses from visiting infected houses and to have bodies buried in lime. A check was kept on people leaving London so as to prevent the plague from extending into the surrounding countryside. In fact the plague reached several other parts of England, but avoided the city of Oxford where the Court eventually settled. The peak of mortality in London was attained in September 1665; after that the monthly figures fell rapidly and by the end of the year the worst was over.[32]

However, the King did not return to Whitehall until the beginning of February 1666 and his courtiers sheepishly followed. For seven months Albemarle had been in charge there. He had left London for consultations with Charles II at Oxford towards the end of November, but a week later he was back at the Cockpit. By then the King had taken the decision that it was dangerous to allow his heir apparent despite his victory, which was not followed up, to go to sea again. So when Albemarle was in Oxford the Earl of Clarendon informed him that he had been appointed general-at-sea together with Prince Rupert. These two soldierly men had last fought together at the siege of Breda twenty-eight years earlier when Monck was a young captain and Rupert an even younger gentleman volunteer. They had not fought against each other during the first English civil war, but they respected each other's prowess. The Duke of Albemarle was astonished when he heard the news; first, because he felt he could do the King better service by staying in London to cope with the plague; second, because he felt sure his duchess would not want him to go to sea again. But he bowed to the call of duty, though he feared that 'if his wife should come to know of it before he had by degrees prepared her for it she would break into such passions, as would be very uneasy for him'.[33] The first Duke of Marlborough, it may be remarked, was also to be constantly worried over the danger of his wife becoming 'uneasy'. Both wives earned the reputation of being termagants.

It might have been delicate, but it would by no means have been impossible for Albemarle in his fifty-ninth year with health that was none too good and an indignant wife to refuse the generalship-at-sea; after all, Charles II was pretty easy-going. As it was, Albemarle's disbanding of the army, his policing of London, his courageous behaviour in the capital during the great plague and finally his assumption of command during the last stages of the second Dutch war combined to confound the critics who claimed that all he had done was to make himself rich and powerful by restoring the King to his throne when the restoration had become inevitable. In April 1666 Albemarle joined his fellow admiral at the Hope and prepared for his last campaign.

17
The Last Campaign

After the Duke of York's victory off Lowestoft, of which Samuel
Pepys absurdly wrote on 8 June 1666 'a great[er] victory [was]
never known in the world',[1] the excitable Clerk of the Acts hurried
round to see Albemarle at the Cockpit who 'like a man out of himself with content told him all'. But Charles II decided that his
brother's life was too precious to be risked any longer at sea and put
Edward Mountagu in charge of the English fleet. It was Mountagu
who as general-at-sea had conveyed the King back to England in
May 1660 and had by way of reward been created Earl of Sandwich
at the same time as Monck was named Duke of Albermarle. It was
therefore natural that the King should turn to Sandwich to take over
the operations at sea against the Dutch in the summer of 1665 while
his army commander-in-chief, Albemarle, was still in London
struggling with the plague. But these two pillars of the Restoration
did not like or trust one another. Sandwich thought Albemarle a
thick-skulled fool, as he told Pepys several times.[2] Sandwich, however, failed to distinguish himself; an attempt to seize Dutch merchantmen sheltering in the harbour of Bergen in Denmark was a
fiasco while afterwards Sandwich failed to intercept a rich convoy
being escorted home from the East Indies by the Dutch admiral,
de Ruyter. When Sandwich did succeed in capturing a smaller
Dutch convoy he blotted his copybook by sharing some of the
valuable cargo between his flag officers and himself without notifying
his intentions to the Duke of York as Lord High Admiral. Albemarle
threatened to impeach him and Sandwich was saved from disgrace
only by Charles's recollection of his gratitude for the part he had
played in securing his safe return to London. The King then

appointed his cousin, Prince Rupert, and Albemarle as joint generals-at-sea. In spite of their defeat at Lowestoft the Dutch were strongly placed when the campaign of 1666 opened.[3] They had two allies, the Danes and the French. The Danes had been alienated by Sandwich's attack on Bergen; the French had concluded a defensive treaty with the Dutch in 1662; and in January the King's Secretary of State, Lord Arlington, had informed Albemarle that King Louis XIV of France had told his aunt, the Queen Mother Henrietta Maria, that he could no longer delay declaring war on England in fulfilment of his treaty obligations.[4] The only English ally was the warlike Bishop of Munster, whose attack on the Dutch by land was abortive so that by April 1666 he had rapidly withdrawn from the war. Furthermore, much of the money which the English Parliament had voted to pay for the war had been spent or failed to materialize. When Albemarle joined the fleet in the spring he soon discovered that many sailors had received no pay but only 'tickets', that is to say promises to pay. They much preferred working for the mercantile marine or on coal-ships, which paid better and more regularly, than for the royal navy from which the most they could hope was a share of prizes. So seamen had to be pressed into service and rounded up when they deserted their ships. Albemarle also discovered that provisions were scarce and that funds to maintain the sick and wounded were embezzled.[5]

Albemarle and Rupert were not the sort of men to tolerate inefficiency and slackness. They set to work to make good the deficiencies in ammunition, food, beer, fresh water and pay for the crews. Women were ordered to leave the ships as soon as the crews were paid, for among other things they were suspected of bringing in the plague.[6] It is likely that Albemarle with his newly acquired expertise put in hand all necessary precautions to prevent the plague from spreading into the fleet. Overcoming most of these administrative difficulties, the joint generals-at-sea managed by the beginning of May to have assembled a fleet of some eighty warships at the Buoy of the Nore. This compared with a Dutch fleet of eighty-four warships, thirteen frigates and a number of fireships. A French squadron of thirty warships and nine fireships under the command of the Duke of Beaufort was known to be getting ready at Toulon on the French south coast. Thus it was expected that when the French linked up with the Dutch the English navy would be seriously outnumbered. It was this fear which shaped and vitiated English naval strategy at the outset of the campaign.

The intelligence reaching Albemarle and Rupert in the second week of May was firstly that the French naval commander-in-chief, the Duke of Vendôme, with a few frigates was waiting for Beaufort's squadron to leave the Mediterranean and sail through the straits of Gibraltar to join him at Belle Isle; secondly, such news as had been received from spies about Dutch naval preparations suggested that their fleet would not be ready to put to sea for several weeks.[7] On 10 May Rupert wrote to the Duke of York as lord high admiral to say, 'I most humbly ... offer this might be a good time, and whilst the Dutch are not in a condition to come out to attempt the intercepting of ... Mons de Beaufort.' Albemarle must have agreed with Rupert's proposal for on the following day one of the English naval commanders, Sir Edward Spragge, was sent to inform Arlington, as the Secretary of State concerned, of the intelligence received about French movements and intentions saying specifically that Beaufort's squadron was expected soon at Belle Isle and observing that 'if his Majesty will have anything attempted upon it, it will do well to do it speedily and lose no time in it ... '[8]

On receiving Spragge's information the King and the Duke of York decided after much discussion in the Privy Council on Sunday 13 May, that it would be highly desirable to crush the French naval squadron straightaway; but they did not want to make any final resolution before obtaining the advice of Albemarle and Rupert. They therefore dispatched Sir William Coventry, who was the Duke's secretary and in effect in charge of the Admiralty, and Sir George Carteret, who was vice-chamberlain to the King and Treasurer of the Navy, to consult the two generals-at-sea. Coventry and Carteret went on Spragge's pinnace to the Buoy of the Nore where they interviewed Albemarle on board his flagship the *Royal Charles*. Rupert was not there when the King's emissaries arrived on the afternoon of Monday 14 May as he was on shore entertaining himself with shooting. Albemarle, however, told them that he approved of the idea of first attacking the French. When they asked him whether sufficient forces could be spared from the main body of the fleet to carry out the operation, Albemarle retorted 'leave us sixty sail and we shall do well enough'. As eighty ships were available, a list of twenty from them to sail against the French was drawn up and it was arranged that Vice-Admiral Sir Christopher Myngs, a 'tarpaulin' officer so no gentleman, should command the expedition. His ship, the *Victory*, a second-rate carrying seventy-six guns, was chosen as the flagship.

But when Rupert returned from his shooting the plan was changed. Rupert insisted that the *Royal James*, a first-rate, should be the flagship and that the *Victory* should go as well, while he himself, not Myngs, would take the command, as the King had promised it to him, a promise which presumably had tentatively been made when the King and the Duke of York had visited the Buoy of the Nore at the beginning of the month. Albemarle did not demur — after all, the arrangement would leave him in sole charge of the main body of the navy — although he might reasonably have worried because some of his best ships and captains had been selected to go with Rupert.[9] It is true that Coventry and Carteret appear to have assured him that the Dutch would not put to sea for another six weeks;[10] but Albemarle made it perfectly clear to them that he would not be in a position to engage the Dutch fleet while Rupert was away unless he received reinforcements.

Such was the situation in the middle of May 1666. Another week was to elapse before Albemarle and Rupert sailed from the Buoy of the Nore at the mouth of the Thames to the Downs at the south-east corner of England. Meanwhile, both the generals-at-sea were agitating for more ships, ketches (two-masted vessels used for errands), money to meet the claims of the sailors, reinforcements from the Thames, cleaned ships returned from the Mediterranean, and they lamented they had no hospital ship. On 21 May Albemarle wrote to Coventry in the strongest language saying that if victuals did not arrive soon, the fleet would miss the summer service and he protested to the King himself about the behaviour of the victualler.[11] Furthermore, he complained to Coventry that they still had not heard the result of his and Carteret's visit — in other words, whether or not Rupert was to be detached from the main fleet to confront the French believed to be coming from Belle Isle into the English Channel.[12]

Eventually on the night of 25 May the Duke of York's orders reached the fleet which was now off the North Foreland. Rupert was to go, as planned, with the *Royal James* and nineteen other men-of-war in search of the Duke of Beaufort's squadron which was expected to sail eastwards through the Channel to join the Dutch in the North Sea. He was to pick up ten more ships at Portsmouth. Albemarle immediately sent a message to the Duke of York to inform him that when these twenty ships left, he would in fact only have fifty-one himself. He therefore asked for the Duke's instructions whether if the Dutch came upon him before he could make up the fleet to seventy vessels (that is to say with reinforcements from the Thames) he should fight them or not.[13]

Clearly Albemarle was worried over the proposed separation of the fleet; and he was even more concerned when he received a letter from Arlington dated 24 May saying that he had received intelligence that the Dutch 'would very suddenly be out'. In answer to this letter, which for some reason or other did not reach him until 28 May, he told the Duke of York that (as a few ships had joined him from the Thames) he would now have fifty-six ships in the Downs, but added that he still needed seventy ships to be able to face the Dutch main fleet with confidence. He explained that he would be loath to be forced to retreat before it 'being it goes against my stomach to do it'.[14] There spoke the old warrior.

Albemarle was understandably doubtful about Prince Rupert's mission, for two reasons: first, he had received more than one report that the Dutch 'would very suddenly be out'; second, because he had reason to believe that the plan to detach Rupert to the Channel was no longer a secret.[15] Yet Rupert eventually set sail on 29 May. Albemarle implied in a letter he wrote to Coventry the day before that he was surprised that despite the news from Holland the Prince had not been stopped from sailing.[16] Did he mean that he himself disapproved or at any rate had misgivings? It is highly likely that he had; but in the social categories of the seventeenth century the command of the heir to the throne and the wishes of Charles II's cousin obviously counted above those of a mere professional commander who had been born a simple country gentleman. Nevertheless, Albemarle was given a free hand over what he should do with the rest of the fleet. The Duke of York told him that he had spoken to the King about the question whether he should fight the Dutch with fewer than seventy vessels and the King had left the decision entirely to him. But he was advised to change his station from the Downs to the Gunfleet, an anchorage south of Harwich because there he could not be forced by the Dutch to fight if he did not want to, whereas in the Downs he might be obliged to do so.[17] After receiving the Duke's letter on 28 May, Albemarle summoned a council of war consisting of his flag officers which met aboard the *Royal Charles*; there the decision was taken not to go to the Gunfleet but to the Swin an anchorage where he would be able to collect reinforcements from the Thames. Once he had got together his seventy ships his intention was to sail north to Southwold bay in Suffolk ready to fight the Dutch.

But the trouble was, as was soon to emerge, that the strategy for the summer campaign was based on faulty intelligence, though not so faulty as has sometimes been suggested. Louis XIV had indeed ordered Beaufort to sail to Belle Isle and thence to the Channel.[18] But when he learned that an English squadron, which had been operating in the Mediterranean under Sir Jeremy Smith and which Beaufort had been instructed to attack, had returned safely through the straits of Gibraltar to England, Beaufort was ordered to take shelter in the Tagus until he was reinforced, for Louis feared that the English fleet might overwhelm the French squadron if it entered the Channel before the Dutch were ready for action. An English naval captain had erroneously reported that this French squadron had left Lisbon earlier than in fact it did and it was in consequence of this report that Rupert had gone off on what proved to be a wild-goose chase.[19] The second error related to the time when the Dutch fleet was putting out to sea. This had in fact taken place as early as 21 May, but it was not until the evening of 27 May that Albemarle had received the news from Arlington, which took as long as four days to reach him, that the Dutch would 'suddenly be out'. As late as 20 May another English squadron which had been cruising off Holland in search of prizes reported no sign of an imminent departure of the Dutch fleet.[20] That no doubt was why Albemarle acquiesced a week later in Rupert's voyage to the Channel.

While Albemarle was still in the Downs on 30 May he obtained positive news that the Dutch fleet was sailing westwards; he himself then resolved to move north and anchored near the North Foreland protected by the Goodwin sands. The decision he now had to make was whether to fight the Dutch—a question which had been left to his discretion by the Lord High Admiral—or whether he should withdraw his ships into the safety of the Thames. That day a dispatch from the Duke of York informed Albemarle that a message had been sent to Rupert ordering him to return with his squadron from the Channel and that five or six other ships were being sent to join the main fleet. A council of war was held early in the morning. Some of the flag officers were dubious about the wisdom of fighting the Dutch with inferior numbers, but others thought that owing to the heaviness of some of the English ships they would not be able in any case to get away before the Dutch attacked them. After listening to those different views Albermarle resolved to fight for two reasons: first, he thought it was better to confront the Dutch then rather than delay until the French squadron joined them; second, he was afraid that to retreat — even if it was feasible — would undermine the morale of his own sailors. Evidently too he believed that he would be reinforced in good time by Rupert's ships and by reserves, for he reported when his fleet was half way between the North Foreland and Dunkirk on 1 June that the wind was so high that he did not think an engagement could take place that day.[21] He was wrong. In fact the battle, which was to last four days, began in the early afternoon.

The Dutch had been sighted at anchor off Ostend; as soon as the English fleet was spotted sailing towards them, the Dutch warships cut or shipped their cables and got under sail. Albemarle had the weather gauge, but the wind was blowing so fiercely from the south-west that the lower tiers of his guns could not be brought into action. On the other side, the Dutch lying to leeward were able to employ all their cannon, firing, as their custom was, at the masts and rigging on their enemy's ships. Albemarle's van or White squadron at first successfully engaged the Dutch rear squadron commanded by the impetuous Cornelis van Tromp. The fight was fiercely contested and when Albemarle was obliged to tack because his ships were too close to the shore, the other two Dutch squadrons were able to come to Tromp's rescue virtually surrounding the English fleet. Sir William Berkeley, the vice-admiral of the White, now at the rear, was then killed when his ship was boarded and captured. Fireships were sent in by the Dutch and did much damage. Both Albemarle on the *Royal Charles* and Sir Robert Holmes, rear-admiral of the Red, had to anchor in the middle of the battle in order to repair their rigging, but were able to continue the conflict. As one account of the battle that day put it, 'the two fleets contended, the English to maintain the honour they had got, and the Dutch to regain what they had lost last summer; continuing to fight so long as there was light enough to distinguish friends from enemies.'[22]

When the battle was resumed next day, 2 June, much confused fighting took place. The wind had dropped somewhat so that the possession of the weather gauge by Albemarle became more advantageous; on the other hand, he had lost so many ships on the first day that he was now outnumbered by nearly two to one. Therefore, after the two fleets had passed each other three times on opposite tacks, Albemarle summoned his council of war and it was decided to draw off to the English coast near Harwich; his fleet was closely followed by the Dutch with their tails up even after night fell.

On Whitsunday 3 June, the sea became so becalmed that in the morning nothing much happened. In the afternoon Prince Rupert's long awaited squadron returned from its fool's errand and was gratefully spotted. Unluckily some of Albemarle's ships got stuck on the Galloper sands south of Harwich and a warning had to be sent to Rupert lest he suffered the same fate. Albemarle then joined Rupert on board his flagship the *Royal James*, and since the numerical inferiority of the English fleet had now been reduced the two generals-at-sea determined to renew the offensive on the following day.

On the last day of the battle, 4 June, the Dutch enjoyed the weather gauge during most of a day-long struggle when the two fleets passed each other five times firing their broadsides. De Ruyter concentrated his fire on the two English flagships, the *Royal Charles* and the *Royal James*, which fought heroically enough, but some of the English captains failed to play their full part; according to Albemarle, only twenty-two or twenty-three stayed with him.[23] In the end the battle degenerated into a *mêlée* fight even though the English succeeded in breaking through the Dutch line to secure the windward position. The Dutch claimed that the English were saved from complete destruction only by the descent of fog. As it was, their losses were severe. Christopher Myngs, like Berkeley, was killed on board his flagship; Sir George Ayscue, Admiral of the White, was taken prisoner; Albemarle's secretary, Sir William Clarke, to whom historians owe so much, was maimed on the 2nd and died on the 4th; ten English ships were destroyed or captured and 8,000 men lost. Unquestionably the Four Days Battle was an English defeat.

How far was George Monck, Duke of Albemarle culpable? Two accusations have been levelled against him. The first, put forward by a modern professor, is that Albemarle—and Rupert—were distinguished neither 'by great intelligence or much real grasp of the conditions of sea warfare' and they were both to blame for having to fight the Dutch 'with only half a fleet'.[24] But naval historians have praised the high degree of skill and enterprise contributed by George Monck to the English victories in the first Anglo-Dutch war. The late Sir Julian Corbett, for example, gave Monck the credit for introducing the tactic of 'line ahead'; Michael Lewis ascribed to him the achievement on the fourth day of the battle in the second war of one of the most difficult feats in sailing-ship warfare, that is breaking in on the enemy from leeward. As to Rupert, it is odd to suggest that a prince who was a superb linguist, claimed to have invented the process of mezzotint, sailed halfway round the world in an aged and rickety warship and won several brilliant victories on land, as at Lichfield and Newark, was lacking in intelligence. But to revert to George Monck, it is reasonable to suppose that after his great victories over the Dutch in the first war he underestimated his enemy in the second, although in his book he specifically warned his readers against such a mistake. The second accusation against Monck, made by a naval authority, was that he ought immediately to have recalled Rupert as soon as he knew that the Dutch navy was coming in full force against him. But he did not in fact know this for sure until the eve of the battle and on that same day he received a dispatch from his superior, the Duke of York, telling him that the King had already sent directions to Rupert to return.[25] It was not in any case Monck's right or duty to recall the Prince—his fellow admiral— to his aid and it was certainly not his fault that owing to a muddle by Coventry and Arlington the notice of recall reached Rupert only after a delay of a day and a half.[26]

After the recriminations died down each fleet licked its wounds. Albemarle returned to the Buoy of the Nore and thence sent his damaged ships for repair at Harwich, Sheerness and Chatham. Preparations were at once put in hand to renew the campaign. Albemarle proceeded to dismiss several of his captains, telling Arlington that as so many of them had not stuck to him in the hottest part of the engagement before Rupert came he hoped the King would not be displeased with what he was doing. The King may not have been displeased, but the Duke of York was, though he did nothing about it.[27] As to the crews, Arlington was informed that they were now 3,000 men short, even after efforts had been exerted to press fresh recruits and catch deserters.[28] Owing to this shortage it was decided to transfer the crews of some of the smaller warships (fourth, fifth and sixth rates) to larger vessels lest better ships had to be left unmanned and thus become 'a prey to the enemy'.[29] For once in a way repairs were expeditiously carried out, money was received to pay off the seamen's tickets, adequate victuals reached the fleet and hospital ships were provided. By the first week of July the generals-at-sea were able to tell the King that 'all our men seem in hearty and cheerful condition'.[30]

Two lessons had been learnt from the naval defeat. One was that the Dutch had more fireships. This deficiency was rectified so that when the battle was resumed the English had as many fireships as the Dutch. The second was that yet another attempt was made to prevent *mêlée* fighting. On 18 July additional instructions were issued to all flag officers.[31] It was laid down that when the van squadron, having the wind, came within reach of the enemy's rear, it was to wait until the whole line came up before it launched its attack. In the event of the enemy tacking the van must tack first and the whole line follow. In other words, the three squadrons were to keep in line and act in unison. This was an ideal that neither side was to find easy to fulfil.

On 23 July 1666 the refurbished English fleet left the Buoy of the Nore and with the wind blowing south-south-east sailed in the direction of Harwich. Part of the Dutch navy, which was ready to renew the fray, was reported to be at the Gunfleet (between the mouth of the Thames and Harwich). Each side was estimated to have ninety warships and seventeen fireships (which were used somewhat like later torpedoes). The battle began at ten o'clock in the morning of 25 July — St James's day — off Orfordness in Suffolk. The Dutch were ranged in a half-moon, the ships well apart from each other to avoid danger from fireships. The English fleet managed to obey its instructions to keep in line. The squadron to break formation was the Dutch rear commanded by Tromp which attempted to outmanœuvre the English Blue or rear squadron under Sir Jeremy Smith. The battle lasted five hours before the Dutch commander-in-chief, de Ruyter, stood off and ran for home. The English White and Red squadrons chased the main body of the Dutch all the next day as far as the Dutch coast. But there was little wind and both the Dutch White and Red squadrons got safely into the protection of the Wielings followed by their errant rear squadron which at last broke off the fight and got away.

The Dutch had the worst of the battle, losing the admiral of their van squadron and a large number of other casualties, estimated by Dutch naval officers themselves when they were drinking in the taverns afterwards at 8,000 killed and wounded.[32] Apart from the expendable fireships the English lost only one third-rate vessel carrying sixty-eight guns which was burnt. Sir Jeremy Smith was accused of cowardice — among others by his colleague Sir Robert Holmes, rear-admiral of the Red; and Holmes was a close personal friend of Rupert. But Albemarle wrote to the King 'to clear a gallant man's reputation', assuring Charles that 'Smith had more men killed and hurt in his ship than in any of the fleet and that his ship ... received more shot.'[33] In general the two admirals were satisfied that the victory justified the ringing of bells and the lighting of bonfires.

St James's Fight, as it was called, was followed by what later would be known as an amphibious raid.[34] The English fleet followed the Dutch across the North Sea in search of prizes and in the first week of August anchored off Zeeland. Here they were informed by a Dutch traitor that the islands of Vlie and Schelling at the entrance to the Zuider Zee, near which many richly laden merchant ships rode were poorly protected. After holding a council of flag officers Albemarle and Rupert decided that Sir Robert Holmes should be given an opportunity to demonstrate his own bravery by attacking these two islands with a light and mobile force of eight frigates, five fireships and seven ketches manned with twice as many marines as sailors. The operation was to be carried out on 8 August. The expeditionary force was told by the captain of Prince Rupert's 'pleasure boat', named the *Fanfan*, that 150 merchantmen gathered from all over the world lay at anchor off Vlie guarded only by two warships which had escorted a hundred of them back from the Baltic. Holmes resolved instead of landing on the island to destroy this array which was both vast and profitable. Two fireships were launched against the two Dutch warships and both of them burnt. Other fireships were clapped against the sides of the biggest Dutch merchantmen and then Holmes sent in boats to spread the fire by setting alight all the ships they could find but with a strict command that they must not plunder them. The operation lasted most of 9 August. Holmes did not think it worth while immediately to land on Vlie, but the capital of Schelling named Wester Schelling, described as a very fair town with 1,000 houses, was set aflame. Holmes then contemplated a landing on Vlie, but was obliged to return to base on the evening of 10 August. A hundred and fifty ships were said to have been burnt valued with their cargoes at a million pounds sterling. The soldiers who took part in the operation also returned with a gratifying amount of booty. The exploit, to be known as 'Holmes's bonfire', virtually concluded the campaign of 1666. George Monck, not a gambling man, bet Prince Rupert five pieces of silver that the Dutch would not come out again to fight that year.[35] He must have won his bet. As to the English fleet, it reached Suffolk a week after Holmes's bonfire but when it returned to the Dutch coast blistering east winds prevented any fresh operations.

In early September Charles II summoned the Duke of Albemarle back to London. The same winds that had prevented a further attack on the Dutch had spread a fire which had started in a baker's shop in Pudding Lane in the City of London (the site of the modern Monument) and spread right across the City almost as far as the Inner Temple where it was halted. Over 13,000 houses were destroyed apart from St Paul's cathedral, all the city churches and the Customs House on the river; some of the houses had been blown up on the King's orders to prevent the fire from reaching Whitehall and Westminster. Monck had earned a fine reputation by his services during the plague of the previous year and Charles clearly felt that his return from sea would restore confidence in the capital after the new disaster. According to the *London Gazette* he had been called back 'to put his happy and successful hand to the finishing of the great deliverance'. When the King and Duke of York visited the desolated areas he accompanied them. An Italian living in London wrote home to say 'my Lord Monck ... has promised that he will either die or bring home the value of all that has been burned'.[36] This does not sound much like Monck who, though he recognized his own abilities, was hardly a boastful man. What he did was to use his authority to stop as far as he could the theft of property and pillaging among the ruins. His organizing genius was applied to salvage, to the reopening of shops and markets, and to the feeding of victims who had lost their homes. After he had done all he could he returned to the fleet, not coming home finally until the beginning of October 1666.

Charles II now adopted what proved to be a disastrous policy. Although the House of Commons had voted altogether £5,500,000 to meet the cost of the war—an amount four or five times as large as the King's peace-time revenue—the money came in slowly and sometimes stuck on the hands of officials before it reached the navy. So in order to economize the King decided to lay up his bigger ships, that is to say the first, second and third rates, which were mostly kept in the Chatham dockyards, and employ a force of frigates to harass Dutch commerce off Scotland and in the Channel. Meanwhile he hoped to negotiate a peace treaty both with the Dutch and the French. The French had not helped the Dutch much during 1666, but the mere danger of a French squadron joining the large Dutch battle fleet was, as has been noticed, a complication for English naval strategy. Through the personal influence of his mother, a French princess, and his sister Henriette, married to Louis XIV's only brother, Charles hoped to detach the French from the Dutch. If the Dutch themselves failed to agree to a peace treaty, then the bigger English warships, refreshed by their rest in safety, could be brought into action later in the year.

It is not known whether Albemarle approved of that policy. The Duke of York as Lord High Admiral certainly did not, but was overruled. The instigator of the policy was doubtless the senior Secretary of State, Lord Arlington, who persuaded the King of its feasibility. Thomas Skinner wrote: 'of this limber and ductile Contrivance the Duke of Albemarle was neither the Author nor the Promoter.'[37] By this time Skinner was attending the Duke at New Hall and may have collected authentic information about his views. In any case Albemarle was no longer admiral and had other duties to fulfil.

The Duke of York took considerable care to protect the laid-up ships against a Dutch surprise attack. He told the Navy Board that the safety of the first and second rates lying in the Medway was of primary importance.[38] A chain or boom drawn across the river at Gillingham reach, he said, must be strengthened; Commissioner

Peter Pett, who had been appointed a member of the Navy Board largely because a long tradition of fine ship-building was preserved in his family since Elizabethan times, was resident at Chatham and therefore the man mainly responsible for its defence. The other place that the Dutch might be expected to attack was Harwich, which was also vulnerable. During the winter the King and his brother twice inspected the defences at the mouth of the Thames (of which the Medway is a tributary) and particularly the fortress at Sheerness on the Isle of Sheppey.

Unlike the English, the Dutch did not lack the means to make war *à l'outrance*. At the beginning of April a report received from The Hague stated that de Ruyter had a force of fifty-eight ships which were intended to prevent the English coming out of the Thames. Towards the end of the same month a French envoy noted that the Amsterdam admiralty had done even greater wonders than had been hoped in Holland. There was, he thought, no question of de Ruyter remaining on the defensive.[39] But where to attack? It was discovered that only coal-ships were to be found at Harwich so a daring plan, to which Cornelis de Witt, a leading Dutch statesman gave birth, was to be put into effect: this was to raid the Medway and destroy English warships known to be at anchor there. A Dutch expeditionary force consisting of over fifty large warships, a few frigates and fourteen fireships and accompanied by fifteen companies of infantry to serve as marines was seen off from the Texel by Johan de Witt, the Grand Pensionary of Holland and the most important statesman in the United Netherlands, and was accompanied by his brother Cornelis, who had been provided with sealed orders by the States General. De Ruyter, though a seaman of daring, was slightly apprehensive. After all, the news of the Dutch preparations could hardly have been kept secret and its objective was so likely that he assumed the English admiralty had taken every precaution. However, after cruising off Harwich the Dutch fleet reached the approaches to the Thames without interference; de Ruyter learned that even the English frigates were widely scattered; but it was first resolved by the Dutch Council of War on 8 June to send Lieutenant-Admiral van Ghent with a squadron to see if he could capture and destroy the English merchantmen reported to be lying at the Hope reach near Gravesend. Nothing came of this and soon the Dutch took more decisive action. The fort of Sheerness was captured by marines and Queensborough, the chief town on the Isle of Sheppey, raided. Then on 11 June Captain Thomas Tobiasz with a small force of light vessels was sent on reconnaissance into the Medway.[40]

By now the English authorities were duly alarmed. Charles II ordered the Duke of Albemarle to go with plenipotentiary authority to Chatham and Prince Rupert was sent to Woolwich arsenal. In fact Albemarle first visited the Tower of London to see what guns were available and arrived at Gravesend on the evening of Monday 10 June, the date when the Dutch captured Sheerness fort.[41] He found that the fort on the Kent side of Gravesend had few guns mounted. Therefore, he ordered the governor, Sir John Griffith, to mount as many guns as he could, repair the fortifications and resist the Dutch if they came up the Thames. He reached Chatham on the morning of Tuesday 11 June where he discovered that everything was in disarray. At eleven o'clock at night he summoned a conference to discuss the defensive arrangements. Broadly they were as follows: five small ships were to be sunk at the Mussel bank where the Medway began to narrow. Higher up at Gillingham reach, the chain protecting the waterway to Chatham was to be strengthened, batteries were to be erected on both banks of the river and guardships stationed on each side of the chain. One guardship, the *Unity*, was on the southern side of the river beneath the chain and two others the *Charles V* and the *Matthias* positioned above the chain. Furthermore, three fireships were to be collected and sunk near the chain, although one of them was grounded before it could be brought there. Edward Gregory, who was a naval clerk at Chatham, managed to arrange for the ships to be carried there and to be sunk on Wednesday morning, though he had not received his instructions until late the previous night. Commissioner Pett was less helpful. One thing that Albemarle wanted done urgently was for the *Royal Charles*, once a proud first-rate in Cromwell's navy, to be taken farther up the river so as to be, if possible, beyond the grasp of the Dutch raiders. For even if they broke through the chain at Gillingham reach, they still had to negotiate the river flowing past Upton fort where it was narrower than at Gillingham. Pett said he could not spare the boats and crews to shift the *Royal Charles*, as Albemarle needed them all to carry ammunition to the makeshift batteries. Nevertheless, the Duke assured the authorities in London that the great ships in the river were safe against assault and pressed the King for an immediate £10,000 to pay men working in the shipyards. But later he changed his mind because he discovered that many of the men to whom wages were owing had deserted rather than face the expected Dutch assault.

Albemarle was utterly determined that the Dutch should not pressure their way through and capture or destroy the larger vessels moored in the river. But all his efforts were in vain. On 12 June, largely through the heroism of one of the Dutch captains, the chain was broken and the guardships sunk. During the night of 12 June after the enemy had thrust past the chain and captured the *Royal Charles*, which had too small a crew and too few guns, Albemarle decided that he and his gentlemen volunteers, who were armed only with pikes, should board one of the ships and make a last stand. But he was persuaded that such a gesture, although heroic, would serve no useful purpose; and, in fact, the Dutch withdrew because the cannonade from Upton castle had been effective, and all their fireships had been expended while many ships known to have been sunk by Albemarle's orders higher up the Medway, and much debris drifting about, was making the return journey to the open sea perilous. So the Dutch bravely and carefully moved down the Medway towing the *Unity* and *Royal Charles* with them and got back safely to Holland. Altogether the Dutch captured or destroyed eight valuable warships for the loss of some hundred men and their fireships. It has justly been said that 'But for the defence hastily organized by Albemarle, and ably seconded by trained bands, volunteers and a few seamen, the English Navy might well have been completely destroyed.' As it was, this was the Pearl Harbour of seventeenth-century England.

Of course Albemarle made mistakes. As Edward Gregory pointed out at the time, the sinking of ships at Mussel bank was a waste of effort; Captain Tobiasz had little difficulty in clearing a channel there for the larger Dutch ships to get through. Also it is arguable that Albemarle would have been wiser to employ his resources in sending the *Royal Charles* higher up the river out of reach of the Dutch than in manning the batteries at Gillingham reach which failed to halt the Dutch progress, although had it not been for the bravery of one Dutch captain in boarding the *Unity* and breaking the chain the Dutch advance might have been repulsed by Albemarle at Gillingham reach.

The importance of the Dutch exploit can be exaggerated, but it caused panic in London and facilitated the conclusion of peace, which Charles II was able to announce when he addressed his long Parliament on 29 July. When this same Parliament met in the autumn it asked for an explanation of 'the miscarriages in the late war' both from Albemarle and Rupert. The defeat in the Four Days Battle was attributed by Albemarle chiefly to unreliable and belated intelligence, while Rupert launched an attack on the Navy Board for not furnishing sufficient provisions. As to the Dutch raid on the Medway, Albemarle placed the blame squarely on Commissioner Pett. He accused him, for example, of using boats essential for the defence to carry his own goods to safety. Albemarle also stressed the panic which assailed the dockyard workers in the King's pay saying that he found scarcely a dozen men out of 800 doing their duty and these were 'so distracted with fear that I could have little or no service from them'. This was also indirectly a criticism of Pett who was in charge there. For good measure he pointed out that he had experienced difficulty in obtaining tools from Pett to set up the batteries and in the end had been obliged to break into his stores. Pett had already been suspended from duty. He was imprisoned in the Tower of London and threatened with impeachment. In effect the whole Navy Board was justly condemned for mismanagement. The Commons were convinced that Albemarle himself was in no way to blame for the setbacks in the second Anglo-Dutch war; even before they heard his and Rupert's reports they voted thanks to them both for their 'eminent merit in the late war'.

18

Death
and Retrospect

The end of the second Dutch war was a watershed in the reign of Charles II. Not long before peace was concluded by the treaty of Breda on 21 July 1667, the Lord High Treasurer, the fourth Earl of Southampton, an old and honest servant of the King and a contemporary of Albemarle, died; Charles then decided to put the Treasury into commission; Albemarle was to be its head, but most of the work was done by his friend, Anthony Ashley Cooper, now Lord Ashley, who had been Chancellor of the Exchequer under Southampton.[1] On 25 July, the same day on which Parliament was recalled by the King, Charles sent Albemarle to demand from his Lord Chancellor, the Earl of Clarendon, the Great Seal, the emblem of his office.[2] Charles knew perfectly well that the House of Commons would be crying out for vengeance upon his Ministers — not upon his admirals — for the failure to win the war, culminating in the public affront of the Dutch raid up the Medway. Just as Pett was the scapegoat for the shortcomings of the Navy Board, Clarendon was certain to be the chief culprit selected for the defeat in the war, simply because he was, and prided himself in being, the King's leading adviser, although in fact he had been opposed to waging the war and had little or no responsibility for the way in which it was conducted. According to Edmund Ludlow, that staunch republican, who was writing his memoirs in the safety of Switzerland, Albemarle 'embraced the occasion of revenge with joy'. His story is that the Lord Chancellor had blamed Albemarle for launching an attack on the Dutch fleet while Rupert's squadron had been separated from him in 1666. It is possible that Clarendon did utter some critical remarks in the Privy Council which might easily and reasonably have riled Albemarle. Clarendon refused to surrender his Seal to

241

Albemarle, but gave it up later when the King sent a warrant under his Sign Manual. To save the former Chancellor's life and property the King ordered him into exile. At the end of November he left England never to return.

So Albemarle remained the last senior statesman of the older generation (apart from the Duke of Ormonde in Ireland), while a group of younger men were filling or clamouring for important posts. It must have been hard work for Albemarle during the second half of 1667. The King, either because he genuinely feared a Dutch invasion or to impress the rulers of France and the United Netherlands with his military strength, had ordered the enlistment of several new infantry regiments. As late as April of the following year Albemarle was inquiring of the ordnance commissioners on behalf of the King how much it would cost to raise a regiment of foot containing a thousand soldiers of whom two-thirds would be musketeers and one-third pikemen.[3] But even the King's most loyal supporters in the House of Commons were opposed to any increase in the size of the army lest it became an instrument of tyranny. As soon as Parliament opened again, which was on the first anniversary of Albemarle's victory over the Dutch at sea, the members of the Commons unanimously agreed to petition the King to dissolve any new regiments that had been formed.[4] Four days later Charles summoned the Commons to his presence in the House of Lords to assure them that he did not intend to govern by a standing army. 'I am more an Englishman', he added 'than so [to do].'[5] After explaining that new regiments had not been recruited 'until the enemy was landed' — presumably on the Isle of Sheppey — he said that they would promptly be disbanded once the peace was signed. In fact it had already been concluded, but the King did not then reveal the somewhat humiliating terms of the treaty and instead adjourned the Houses until the beginning of October so as to allow tempers to cool.

Albemarle must have been extremely busy raising and disbanding regiments and seeing in his capacity of treasury commissioner that they got paid. He was particularly concerned over the widowed and destitute. For example, before he became treasury commissioner he had written to the navy commissioners from the Cockpit asking that tickets (promises to pay) should be made available to widows and parents of Devonshire seamen who had died fighting against the Dutch.[6] By the end of same year he was writing to Sir Robert

Holmes telling him about a seaman who had received no tickets for serving at sea on board the warship *Defiance* and requiring that the man who had lost the use of one of his arms should receive what was due to him.[7] Once on the treasury commission Monck was strongly placed to see that his sailors and soldiers were paid their arrears. It was typical of his Poo-Bah situation that he signed warrants in conjunction with his friend Ashley for sums of money 'towards paying his Majesty's marching forces', which he commanded himself.[8]

But in the winter of the same year ill health, which had struck him down in 1661–2, compelled him to leave London for his estate at New Hall, hoping that the rest and fresh air might cure him.[9] According to Dr Skinner, he was suffering from 'dropsy' and shortage of breath, which suggests to a modern physician, congestion of the heart.[10] For a time he thought he had been cured by some pills given to him by a young doctor who had once served under him. He began to sleep better; but when he was put on a diet he failed to adhere to it. At any rate it must have been extremely pleasant on the estate; he was able to occupy himself with building a stone wall around it and by entertaining visitors. John Evelyn, who later when he became commissioner for sick and wounded seamen and prisoners of war and was to be on friendly terms with Monck, had visited New Hall in 1656 to note, as an amateur of architecture and landscape gardening, the features of this extensive estate. It originally had been acquired by King Henry VIII, who was responsible for the gate house, and assigned as a gift to Oliver Cromwell after his victory at Worcester although when he became Lord Protector, he exchanged it for Hampton Court.[11] Evelyn remarked in his diary on the noble hall, the wide staircase and the handsome gate house, but was particularly excited by the gardens and park, filled with deer, and an avenue nearly a mile long planted with stately lime trees.[12]

We are fortunate that during the summer of 1669 when Monck was hopefully convalescing after his illness, he received a visit from Cosmo III, Grand Duke of Tuscany, who recorded his impressions in his memoirs.[13] He described Monck as a man of middle size, stout and squarely built with a complexion 'partly sanguine and partly phlegmatic' and a fair if somewhat wrinkled face. He did not think highly of the duchess—a lady 'of low origin' who allowed her former station to show itself 'in her manner and her address, she being in no way remarkable for elegance or gentility'. The Duke received his

Italian guest in his dressing gown since he was obliged by his complaint 'a confirmed dropsy' (perhaps he was just overweight?) to keep to the house and retire from the Court into the country. Like Pepys, Cosmo did not think much of Monck's taste in food, for he was 'ushered into a room where refreshments were prepared, which had, however, more the appearance of a parsimonious collation than a handsome dinner'. Like Evelyn, he admired the delightful gardens with their spacious walks, sheets of water and hedgerows of fruit trees. Cosmo thought Albemarle lived in the style of a nobleman — why not? He was a nobleman — on an annual income of £20,000 a year. It must have been a curious ménage.

Among George Monck's visitors at New Hall were the Archbishop of Canterbury, Gilbert Sheldon, and Dr Thomas Gumble, who had now become one of Albemarle's chaplains. Both of them were seriously concerned about the Duke's health — he was in his sixtieth year — and showered him with spiritual advice. On the prompting of the Archbishop, Gumble asked Monck if he had made his will and settled his estate. The Duke said he had done so. Nevertheless, his chaplain suggested to him that he might consider putting part of his estate in trust so that if his heirs male should die out, the money could be dedicated to building and maintaining a hospital for former serving officers who were down on their luck. What Gumble must have had in mind was not a hospital in the modern sense of the word, but a superior alms-house where men who had fought for their country but had small means, could live on a reasonable scale of comfort and be adequately looked after.[14] In retrospect one can imagine another Chelsea hospital endowed by George Monck instead of by Nell Gwyn. For Gumble was perceptive. The heirs male did die out and many unworthy persons fought law suits to obtain a share of the Albemarle estate.

It is uncertain from Gumble's narrative whether or not the idea appealed to Albemarle; at any rate he did nothing about it. His will was short and simple and devoid of complicated provisions for future eventualities.[15] It was dated 8 June 1665; he told Gumble rather inexactly that he made it before he last went to sea; it must in fact have been drawn up during the plague when the danger of death loomed up and given into the charge of the Earl of Craven who had stayed with Albemarle in London when the rest of the Court had fled the capital. Everything was left to his son Christopher. Monck's 'beloved wife' Anne was given half his plate and all his jewels, but these were entailed; after her death they too were to go to Christopher. The Duke, however, also made a deed of trust, as he informed Dr Gumble. He confided the 'tuition and breeding' of his son, who was not yet seventeen (though already a member of parliament for Devonshire) to Anne and no fewer than eight of his friends including the Earl of Craven, Sir William Morice, Sir John Maynard, an eminent barrister, and Sir Edward Turner, at that time Speaker of the House of Commons. One name is significantly missing from the list, that of Sir Thomas Clarges. Both the Duke and Duchess had quarrelled with him apparently because he gave himself airs to which they thought he was not entitled.[16] The deed of trust does not appear to have survived, but it is reasonable to assume that in it he made proper provision for his wife and left some tokens of esteem to his friends and servants.

One wonders whether, apart from his ill health and approaching death and despite his riches and sinecure offices, Monck felt contented during the last two years of his life. The death of the Earl of Southampton and the absence of the Duke of Ormonde left him isolated in the centre of government. There is a story that in 1667 the Duke of Albemarle related how some republicans told him before the Restoration that by bringing in the King he would put the country under pimps and whores and that all would 'decline into Infamy and Decay'; then, so the anecdote continues, 'the good old man said with some Resentment he found them the truest Prophets he ever met in his Life'.[17]

In the autumn of 1669 Monck resolved to return to Westminster, but clearly recognized that he had not long to live. Breathing became increasingly difficult for him; according to Dr Skinner, 'he could not lye down in his Bed, but entertained himself only with some Sleeps in his Chair.' The Bishop of Salisbury said in his funeral oration on Monck that 'in twelve months space he very seldom slept or took any rest within his bed but suffered all that while an internal painful strangulation.'[18] He tried hard to carry on his public duties, but evidently could not leave the Cockpit. There he was visited by the King and the Duke of York, Lord Arlington, who had also called upon him at New Hall, the Earl of Bath and the inevitable Gumble.[19] Albemarle's only remaining wish was to see his son married. In December he managed to conclude a marriage treaty between his son and the fifteen-year-old Elizabeth Cavendish, daughter of Lord Ogle, who was later to become the second Duke of Newcastle. Once the dowry (£20,000) and jointure had been settled the young people were married on Thursday 30 December 1669. The dynast would have been distressed to foresee that his estates were to fall to pieces in the hands of an insane octogenarian while rival claimants squabbled over the proceeds.

On the morrow of New Year's Day 1670 Monck must have remembered or been reminded that this was the tenth anniversary of the date when he left Coldstream on his march to London to restore the King. Between eight and nine on the following morning he died 'like a Roman general' sitting up erect in his chair. His bedchamber was open as if it were a tent and many of his officers were with him. He showed neither fear nor pain and once he smiled.[20] The old soldier had won his last victory and faced the unknowable with his usual intrepid courage.

Anne Monck, Duchess of Albemarle, was not to live to witness her husband's funeral; in fact she was buried in Westminster Abbey before he was. A fortnight after her husband's death she was reported to be dangerously ill; she died on 29 January and was buried on 28 February.[21] It was thought that she had lost all taste for living.

After a post-mortem Monck's body had been embalmed and then, following the precedents established by the treatment of James I's and Oliver Cromwell's bodies, an effigy in armour with a golden baton in its hand was prepared; it surmounted the coffin and was placed in Somerset House where for a period of three weeks hundreds of people came to pay their respects. The King had undertaken to meet the cost of the state funeral which took place on 30 April 1670.[22] The procession left Somerset House and moved along the Strand, the streets being lined by two regiments of the City militia; it was headed by the Duke of York's troop of horse guards and followed by that of the King. Then came a regiment of foot guards (the Grenadiers) and Monck's own regiment led by his friend the Earl of Craven (the Coldstream Guards). Towards the tail of the procession were the Duke of Albemarle's favourite horse and his grooms. The chief mourner was Albemarle's son Christopher or Kit. Other great men who attended the funeral included the Duke of Ormonde, the Earl of Sandwich (what was he thinking?), Lord

Arlington, Lord Ashley and Sir Thomas Clifford; a young ensign, John Churchill, destined to be Monck's military successor, was also there. Most of the mourners were admitted to the Abbey where, after the funeral service had been read, Seth Ward Bishop of Salisbury delivered a short but eloquent sermon in which he praised Albemarle's 'deep Prudence and an impregnable Taciturnity', his courage and care for his soldiers and of course his restoration of the King with all that it entailed. The title given to the sermon when it was printed and published by the King's order was *The Christian's Victory over Death*.

Monck's only surviving child, Christopher, was given the vacant Garter immediately after his father died and was appointed a Gentleman of the King's Bedchamber. He led an extremely extravagant life, as he could afford to do, starting after he reached his majority with the purchase of the first Earl of Clarendon's house in Piccadilly. He and his wife entered into the spirit of Charles II's Court where they gambled, gave parties and patronized plays. Christopher became Chancellor of Cambridge University on the recommendation of Charles II, fought against the Duke of Monmouth, and having entertained James II at New Hall, where they killed stags together, he was made Governor of Jamaica in November 1686; there a tropical disease carried him off on 6 October 1688 at the age of thirty-five. His wife went insane and lived to be eighty. They were both buried in the Monck vault in King Henry VII's chapel of Westminster Abbey. The title of Albemarle, though sought after by the Earl of Bath, lapsed.[23]

The Restoration is the act by which George Monck is best remembered. In an epithalamium printed in both Latin and English after his death, the poet wrote:

> The Tyrant being dead, the Gen'ral came
> And saw th' succeeding Rage, then Overcame
> Not by the Noise of Arms, but by the Deep
> Silence of Counsels which he knew to keep;
> Strange kind of Conq'ring this, and almost New
> in one Dayes space three kingdoms to subdue ... [24]

It is doubtful if Monck thought of the Cromwellian Protectorate as a tyranny; at least no evidence exists to prove it. But the real interest of the Restoration is the how and the why.

Posterity has received a slanted portrait of Monck because two of the most widely read writers of his time, Samuel Pepys and the first Earl of Clarendon, disliked him. Pepys pictured him as ponderous and rather stupid; Clarendon thought that he had been extremely lucky to be in the right place at the right time, for which he was unduly rewarded. Yet Pepys gave the show away when he wrote towards the conclusion of his diary, 'the blockhead Albemarle hath strange luck to be loved, though he be the heaviest man in the world, but stout and honest to his country,'[25] while Clarendon admitted his bravery during the Great Plague. Monck reciprocated their dislike, in the case of Pepys because he suspected him of being corrupt, although this is a dangerous word to use in the context of the seventeenth century—and also inefficient. The insufficiency of the provisions for the navy in the second Dutch war and the self-seeking, cowardice and incompetence of the dockyard workers at Chatham in 1667 shocked him. As to Clarendon, he thought that he monopolized the King's counsels disadvantageously and it may well have been that Monck blamed the Lord Chancellor for drawing up the declaration of Breda in such a way that the officers and men who served under Monck in Ireland and Scotland had difficulty in retaining lands granted to them in place of substantial arrears of pay. Even Monck himself lost estates that he acquired in Ireland, though he was compensated.[26]

Gilbert Burnet, a rather underestimated contemporary historian, was puzzled by Monck's behaviour before the Restoration because 'he kept himself under such reserve';[27] one of his guesses about it was that he 'had no settled design any way, and resolved to do as occasion should be offered him' is about the best, although that was his attitude after he had already made up his mind that the monarchy must be reinstated; he was not a mere opportunist. Writing in the middle of the eighteenth century the philosopher David Hume, like Burnet, another Scotsman pretty cocksure in his opinions, cautiously observed: 'His soldiers usually called him honest George Monck ... he was remarkable for his moderation in Policy ... his established character for truth and sincerity stood him in good stead.'[28] But Professor J. D. Reid D.D. of the University of Glasgow, describing the Presbyterian Church in Ireland at the length of three volumes a generation after Hume's *History of Great Britain* appeared thought nothing of Monck's character for truth and sincerity. 'This adventurer,' he observed, 'whose name has justly become a byeword for perfidy and dissimulation ... [was] peculiarly well fitted by his consummate address and duplicity to watch over the interests of parliament.'[29]

As often happens, an impartial, detached, view comes not from a British but a foreign historian, François Guizot, a statesman of experience and wisdom; he believed that Monck was always a Royalist at heart and 'had no fixed principles, no strong passions, no great political ambition'.[30] Fixed principles are rarely the stock-in-trade of statesmen, but Guizot was surely right in thinking that Monck was not personally ambitious. Guizot wrote in the first half of the nineteenth century, while Sir Julian Corbett, Monck's most enthusiastic biographer, wrote in the second half. His conviction was that Monck was 'lovable' and 'misunderstood', the victim of servile historiographers who failed to appreciate his greatness.[31] Unfortunately Sir Julian's short book is marred by a contrast he draws between his hero and the despotic Cromwell who used Monck for his own ends and at the same time feared his uprightness.

Leaving 'servile historiographers' on one side, one sees clearly that the portrait of honest simple-minded George Monck, accepted by so many writers in modern times, cannot survive serious scrutiny. Another legend which has found its way into history books is that Monck was inflexibly opposed to the taking of oaths as a point of principle. In fact not only did he take several oaths himself, for example to uphold the Covenant, which he took twice, but he imposed oaths on his own soldiers both when he was in Scotland and when he arrived in London in 1660. Of course he learned from his own experience of life that oaths were more frequently broken than kept; they were amusing antics devised by politicians. When on inconvenient occasions, as in February 1660, he was confronted with demands for an oath from himself and solemnly asserted that taking any oath at all was against his conscience, that imperturbable countenance must have been hard to keep straight.

However he manœuvred during the crises in his career, Monck's portrait, if he sat for it, would not be too hard to paint in words. Of course no man is, or can be expected to be, completely consistent. Yet it may be suggested that George Monck was not unlike loyal regular officers in our own times. He believed in order and hated anarchy. Initially he was ready to obey Parliament because he thought that it stood for the interests of landed gentlefolk such as were his own family and friends. But neither the Assembly of Saints nor the remnants of the Rump in fact did so. Some of their members, like Heslirige, were, it is true, country gentry, but both at the centre and in the English counties were to be found men of what it is now fashionable to call 'the middling sort' who would not normally have been thought to belong to the governing classes. To that extent they were not representative, as Monck realized in 1660. Yet he was loyal to authority so long as the authority was clearly identifiable as it was when Oliver Cromwell was Lord Protector and Charles II was King. Also he expected loyalty to himself from his own officers and therefore came down hard on those of them who fomented unrest for political reasons. Above all, as King Charles II recognized, he was an Englishman who loved his country.

One thing is absolutely certain. Monck was a man of immense courage. We think of him fighting his way to the top of the horn-work at Breda while some of his own troops were deserting him; we recall him awaiting the attack of a large Irish force with a handful of infantry protecting the fords by which his own cavalry would be returning from the heart of hostile country; we remember how he set an example at Nantwich to demoralized troops from Ireland by defying the victorious Fairfax with a pike in his hand; how he directed the English infantry at the battle of Dunbar with a third as many men as those commanded by the Scots; how he won the battle of Southwold bay after his fellow admiral had been shot dead at his side; how he confronted the Dutch again thirteen years later with only just over half the number of his enemy's warships at his disposal and in the end fought them to a standstill; how he remained at Westminster during the plague after nearly all the other courtiers had fled the stricken town; we remember too his coming back to the capital in 1666 to soothe the frightened Londoners robbed of their homes by the Great Fire; and, finally, we think of the devoted and by no means useless efforts with which in his sixtieth year he resisted the Dutch incursion up the Medway to protect the English navy from destruction when, as Clarendon recorded, he was ready to die brandishing his sword and surrounded by his volunteers.

It is scarcely surprising that King Charles II regarded George Monck as a father figure or that, as Pepys admitted, he was generally loved. He was as tough towards his enemies as he was generous to his friends. His letters are full of concern for the wounded and widows and for men cast out of the armed services without adequate compensation. Like any good officer, he did all he could for the welfare of his soldiers and sailors, seeing to their food, their beer, their clothes and their pay. He badgered the King himself about the shortcomings of the victualler appointed by Samuel Pepys; and he, like Prince Rupert, was rightly angry when Pepys had the impertinence to contend that these two fine admirals had brought back the navy in an ill condition from the high seas.

To turn from Monck as commander, is it right to say, with all deference to historians of the calibre of Gilbert Burnet and François Guizot, that he was a statesman of no fixed principles? Everyone has to learn from experience, but surely what Monck came to value most was peace at home, stability, discipline and order. That was why he fully supported Cromwell as Lord Protector. The kind of statesmen he admired were men of the middle including Broghill, Oliver St John and John Thurloe. He was incapable of understanding the great mind of a poet and thinker like John Milton who dedicated to him in 1660 one of his last political treatises.[32] For, as with the political philosophers, Hobbes and Filmer, Monck dreaded anarchy following rebellion, a dread that was central to the thinking of most educated seventeenth-century Englishmen.

Unlike Cromwell, George Monck was not obsessed by the idea of an all-wise Providence directing every turn in his own and his country's fortunes; he was probably a deist and to some degree a determinist, but he recognized that a man's own strength of character can swing the odds. In Scotland he came to be Presbyterian in sympathy because he was convinced that religious uniformity under the control of the civil government was a factor in securing peace and order in the land. In England he was an Anglican, but Anglicanism in those days was much the same as Presbyterianism without the presbyters. He had little use for sectarian extremists who demanded toleration and were themselves intolerant. His character did influence events just as, say, George Washington's refusal to accept defeat and his magnanimity afterwards shaped the American war of independence and its consequences. No doubt because of the ever-creeping anarchy Charles II would ultimately have been restored to his throne if George Monck had never lived. The devious means that he employed to attain his ends can be condemned; certainly to write of honest, stupid old George is a caricature. But without these means would the Restoration have been bloodless and revenge restrained?

George Monck's fixed principles may be alien to the Europe that exists three centuries since he died. For rebellion is endemic and peace, order, patriotism and personal discipline can be called dirty words. But whatever his faults may have been, George Monck was cast in a heroic mould.

Appendix
A Note on Monck's Income

A precise estimate of the value of all the Duke of Albemarle's properties in England, Scotland and Ireland and of his pay and perquisites would need prolonged and difficult research.

The King granted to the Duke by letters patent lands to the annual value of £7,000. The most important of these were the palace and estate of Theobalds in Hertfordshire and neighbouring estates including Cheshunt estimated to be worth £4,066 18s. 4d. a year; the next in value were various properties in the duchy of Lancaster, including the collectorship of rents in the forest of Blackburn etc, estimated at £1,477 7s. 1¼d. Other properties with smaller yields were in Middlesex (Enfield Park which included fee farm rents and profits on fairs), Derbyshire (Clewer), Yorkshire (New Park) and Berkshire (Mote Park, worth £274 a year). The gross value of these lands, including fee farm, tithes and other rights, appears to amount to £7,666 11s. 8½d, but these were subject to various complicated deductions.[1]

In Ireland Charles II granted Albemarle 211 acres in Galway, 470 acres in Athlone and Roscommon and 2,887 acres in county Mayo, but of the latter only about 1,200 Irish acres were profitable. These had a 500-year lease. All were in Connaught.[2] Furthermore, he was granted 19,542 acres in county Wexford, but the grant was subject to a 'saving' of rights decreed to Lawrence Esmond, which may have reduced Albemarle's estates there.[3] Clarendon thought Albemarle's lands in Ireland were worth £4,000 a year. On one occasion before the Restoration Monck spoke of retiring to his estates in Ireland. Albemarle was also granted a share of the Bahama Islands and is known to have been involved in the Royal Africa Company.

Although New Hall was once a royal palace, Albemarle purchased the house and estate from the second Duke of Buckingham in 1662; the reversion of other property in the parish of Boreham where New Hall was situated, valued at £58 13s. 11d, was granted by the Crown to the Duke in April 1664.[4] The value of the family property in Devonshire and Exeter was over £2,000. He may also have saved money when he was in Scotland and received some money from the Rump, though almost certainly not the sum of £20,000 that was voted to him.

Albemarle would have been paid as commander-in-chief something of the order of £4,000 (Oliver Cromwell was paid £10 a day as commander-in-chief) and would also receive fees and perquisites from his other offices such as Master of the Horse and Gentleman of the Bedchamber and also as Commissioner for the Treasury. It is usually stated that Albemarle left £15,000 a year in income and £60,000 in property.[5] One would have thought that the Duke of Tuscany's statement that Albemarle's income was £20,000 a year was nearer the mark. This was not excessive by the standard of other dukes.

Bibliographical Note

1 Unpublished material

I have never been an enthusiastic participator in *la fureur de l'inédit* and it would be an exaggeration to say that I have made any sensational discoveries except possibly the letter from Monck to Fairfax which I have quoted on p. 62 from the Clarke Papers. I am grateful to the Provost and Fellows of Worcester College, Oxford, for allowing me to examine the Clarke Papers and to quote from them. Monck's order book (Clarke MSS. 49) is of particular interest. In the Bodleian Library, Oxford, I have found letters by or to Monck bearing on his career, especially Carte MSS. xxiv and lxvii, Rawlinson A195, Tanner lv and Misc. D180; in the British Library, notably Egerton MSS. 2618; in the National Library of Scotland among the Phillips MSS. and the Advocates MSS.; and documents in the National Maritime Museum, Greenwich. I have also studied the journals of the Common Council of the City of London in the Guildhall Library, which are illuminating on Monck's activities immediately before and after he reached London from Scotland. Detailed references will be found in the Notes on pp. 259ff.

2 Biographies

The best biography of Monck written in a white heat soon after his death is by Dr Thomas Gumble, *The Life of General Monck* (1671). Gumble was first chaplain to the Council of Scotland and afterwards Monck's own chaplain. Although Skinner became Monck's physician, Thomas Skinner's *Life of General Monk*, ed. W. Webster (1723), has justly been described as 'a mere compilation', largely a rephrasing of Gumble, but contains a little additional material about the last years of Monck's life. The biography of Monck by the distinguished French statesman and historian, F. P. G. Guizot, trans. A. R. Scoble with the title *Monck or the Fall of the Republic* (1851), is largely based on Gumble and the dispatches by the French ambassador in London, Antoine de Bordeaux. It is to be noticed that fuller versions of these dispatches and additional ones are in *The History of Richard Cromwell and the Restoration of Charles II*, also by Guizot, trans. A. R. Scoble (1856). Sir Julian Corbett's *Monk* (1889), a short biography in the 'Men of Action' series, is the work of an able military and naval historian, concentrating on his career as an officer; it is over-favourable to Monck at the expense of Cromwell and others. Two biographies of Monck were published in 1936: Oliver Warner, *Hero of the Restoration* and J. D. Griffith Davies, *Honest George Monck*. Mr Warner was an excellent naval historian; his book contains sixteen illustrations including the only known portrait of Monck's wife. Mr Griffith Davies's book is particularly useful because he prints in full several of Monck's most important letters and the Bishop of Salisbury's funeral oration. Neither of these two biographies, both good of their kind, contain detailed references or were based on detailed research.

3 Letters

Most of Monck's letters are in print scattered between various volumes. John Toland, *A collection of several letters and declarations sent by General Monck to Lord Lambert* (1660 and 1714); C. H. Firth (ed.), *Clarke Papers*, four vols (1891–1901); C. H. Firth (ed.), *Scotland and the Commonwealth* (Edinburgh, 1895), and *Scotland and the Protectorate* (Edinburgh, 1899). Sir Charles Firth was an impeccable editor and missed little of value. Other letters by Monck are to be found in the Historical Manuscript Commission's report on the Hastings Family, vol. II (1930) and in the Leyborne-Popham MSS. (1899). Some of Monck's official correspondence during the Interregnum is in vols III–VII of the *Thurloe State Papers*, ed., T. Birch (1742), and during the reign of Charles II in the *Calendar of State Papers (Domestic)* which are complete for this period. For Monck's correspondence as admiral see section 5 below.

4 Scotland

In addition to the two books edited by C. H. Firth referred to in section 3 above, I used C. S. Terry, *The Cromwellian Union* (Edinburgh, 1902), and the *Diary of Sir Archibald Johnston of Warriston*, three vols (Edinburgh, 1911–1940).

5 Ireland

The most important sources are J. T. Gilbert (ed.), *A Contemporary History of Affairs in Ireland 1641–1652*, three vols (Dublin 1879); James Lord Audley, Earl of Castlehaven, *Memoirs 1624–1651*, ed. C. O'Connor (Waterford, 1753); and Sir Richard Bellings, *History of the Irish Confederation and war in Ireland 1641–1649*, ed. J. T. Gilbert (Dublin, 1891). A good modern account of the Confederation is T. L. Coonan, *The Irish Catholic confederacy and the Puritan Revolution* (New York, 1954). R. Bagwell, *Ireland under the Stuarts*, three vols (reprinted 1962), is still useful.

6 Monck as Admiral

Monck's correspondence during the two Anglo-Dutch wars in which he took part will be found in C. T. Atkinson (ed.), *Letters and Papers relating to the first Dutch War 1652–1654*, vols IV–VI (1910–30) and J. R. Powell and E. K. Timings (eds), *The Rupert and Monck Letter Book 1666* (1969). H. T. Colenbrander, *Bescheiden uit vremde archiven omtrent de groote Nederlandsche zeeoorloegen* (The Hague, 1919), contains valuable material.

7 The Restoration and After

The diaries of John Evelyn and Samuel Pepys are of value (I used Esmond de Beer's superb edition of Evelyn but kept to H. B. Wheatley's edition of Pepys), though Pepys did not much care for admirals except for his patron, the Earl of Sandwich. The Earl of Clarendon's *History of the Rebellion and Civil wars in England*, ed., W. D. Macray (Oxford 1888), and *The Life of Edward Earl of Clarendon*, two vols (Oxford, 1857), are indispensable but Clarendon did not like Generals. Professor W. L. Sachse has edited the *Diurnal of Thomas Rugg 1659–1661* (1961) from Add. MSS. 10116–7 in the British Library. Godfrey Davies, *The Restoration of Charles II 1658–1660* (Oxford, 1955) and David Ogg, *England in the Reign of Charles II*, vol. I (Oxford, 1955) continue the standard histories by S. R. Gardiner and C. H. Firth on the Interregum. More bibliographical detail will be found in the following references in which these abbreviations are used:

Add. MSS.	Additional Manuscripts in the British Library
B.L.	British Library
Cal. Clarendon S.P.	*Calendar of the Clarendon State Papers* (five vols, 1869–1932)
C.J.	*Journals of the House of Commons*
C.S.P. (Dom)	*Calendar of Papers (Domestic)*
C.S.P. (Ireland)	*Calendar of State Papers relating to Ireland*
D.N.B.	*Dictionary of National Biography*
E.	Thomason Collection of tracts in the B.L.
H.M.C.	Historical Manuscripts Commission reports
P.R.O.	Public Record Office
Thurloe S.P.	A collection of State Papers of John Thurloe Esq., Secretary first to the Council of State and afterwards to the two Protectorates.

Notes

Chapter 1, Ancestry and Early Life

1 Bishop's transcripts of parish registers of All Saints, Merton, in Devon County Record Office at Exeter.

2 The entry reads '*Jacobi Sexto 1608 duodecimo die Maii baptista est arma fil ... Richard Skinner qui fuit peregrinus. Eodem anno undecimo die Decembri baptista est Georgius Monck filius Thomas Monck equitus.*' Parish register of Holy Trinity, Landcross.

3 J. E. D. Gover, A. Mawer and F. M. Stenton, *Place-names of Devon*, English Place-name Society (1931), vol. VIII, p. 100. Previous biographers have wrongly stated that Potheridge was a contraction of pon-the-ridge. Presumably Puda was an Anglo-Saxon.

4 Cf. W. G. Hoskins, *Devonshire* (1972), pp. 434–5. At the time of writing, Potheridge was tenanted by a farmer and his family who have been there for many years; it is owned by the Clinton Trust.

5 Oswald J. Reichel, *The Hundreds of Devon*, extra vol. published by the Devonshire Association (1928), p. 542.

6 The name of William Le Moyne is recorded in the pipe rolls of 1183 and 1185 as being the tenant in possession of Potheridge. He also owned two virgates of land at Stockleigh. Reichel, *The Hundreds*, p. 565.

7 John Prince, *Worthies of Devon* (1810), p. 586. I am sceptical about this story, but it is entertaining and possible.

8 Even J. H. Round, who was critical of many claims of Norman descent, admitted that the Moncks were a very ancient family. See his *Family Origins* (1930), p. 164.

9 G.E.C., *Complete Peerage*, VIII (1932), p. 67; *D.N.B.* under 'Plantagenet'.

10 See 'George Monk's Pedigree', in Thomas Skinner, M.D., *The Life of General Monk*, ed. William Webster (1723), pp. xcvii, xcviii.

11 I am grateful to Professor Hoskins for this information. Sir George Smyth's will is in the probate department of the Public Record Office,

PRO 11/133/209. Although Smyth left various legacies to his sons and sisters he left nothing to George Monck or George's mother who had of course a settlement and a dowry. According to her husband, on marriage his children were barred from making claims on the estate. But that did not prevent Sir Thomas from expressing the hope that his wife's marriage portion would be made equal to that of Sir George's other children. H.M.C. Exeter Records, p. 162.

12 E.g. J. D. Griffith Davies, *Honest George Monck* (1936), p. 3.

13 John Giffard, son of Thomas and Margaret Giffard, and his wife Alice were seised of the manor of Landcross and on 14 August 1621 enfeoffed it to their son, Antony, for his life. G. Wrottesley, *The Giffards*, William Salt Archaeological Society publications, vol. V, N.S. (1902) pp. 36–7.

14 Cf. *Devonshire Association Reports and Transactions*, vol. 34 (1902), p. 652 n. 2. The church at Landcross is about 7 miles from Potheridge while the church at Merton is some 2½ miles from Potheridge, so it is a question of deciding whether a newly born baby could have been carried over either of these distances. If not, Professor Hoskins suggests that George's mother might have been prematurely delivered at her sister's house.

15 Margaret Monck married Thomas Giffard in the reign of Henry VIII and had 19,500 acres settled on her. Wrottesley, *The Giffards*, p. 32. Another Margaret Monck (George Monck's aunt) married another Thomas Giffard in 1600. *Devonshire Association Reports*, vol. 34, p. 652. Catherine, wife of Thomas Monck, died on 2 November 1595 and was buried at Parkham church in Devon; Roger Giffard of Halsbury, the second son of John Giffard of Brightleigh, 'turned her tomb over and on the reverse side inscribed the names of two of his wives and his daughter'. Fourth Report of H.M.C. (1874), p. 469.

16 There used to be a saying in Budleigh Salterton that the captains only talked to the colonels, the colonels only talked to the generals, and the generals only talked to God.

17 *D.N.B.* under 'Lewis Stukely'. The Giffards also intermarried with the Stucleys. Sir Lewis's daughter, Audrey, was the first wife of Roger Giffard of Brightleigh. Wrottesley, *The Giffards*, pp. 36–7.

18 W. G. Hoskins, *Exeter Freemen 1266–1967* (1973), p. 113. Sir George Smyth arranged this. H.M.C. Exeter Records, p. 162.

19 W. G. Hoskins (ed.), *Exeter in the 17th Century* (1957), p. 8. The suburb was St Sidwell; the rate, the highest in the parish, £6, was paid by George Monck in 1629. I assume that he acquired the property either from his father or mother.

20 Skinner, *Monk*, p. 10, says flatly, 'In his Youth he was brought up at a School in the Country [county].' Professor Hoskins has told me that if

George Monck lived at Old Matford he would certainly have gone to the Exeter grammar school.

21 A. L. Rowse, *Sir Richard Grenville* (1937), pp. 15–16.

22 The chief primary sources for this campaign are Sir Edward Cecil's own *Journal* (1627) and John Glanville, *Journal of the Voyage to Cadiz*, ed. A. B. Grosart for the Camden Society (1883); the fullest secondary account is in vol. II of Charles Dalton, *Life and Times of General Sir Edward Cecil Viscount Wimbledon* (1885) where many of Cecil's letters from the State papers are printed in full.

23 The story of why Monck first went to sea in 1625 given by Thomas Gumble in *The Life of General Monck* (1671), pp. 2–4 has been accepted by Sir Charles Firth in his article on Monck in the *D.N.B.* and by all Monck's previous biographers starting with Skinner. The story is that when King Charles I visited Plymouth for ten days in September 1625, Monck's father, Sir Thomas Monck, as a leading Devonian gentleman, would naturally have expected to be among those who welcomed the King, but he was afraid that a judgment might be laid against him on account of his debts while the King was there. To avoid such an embarrassing situation he dispatched his son George to Exeter to bribe the under-sheriff of Devon not to do so. Although the under-sheriff accepted the bribe he broke his word and 'in a most treacherous manner seized the person of Sir Thomas Monk, upon an Execution in the face of the whole Country [county] convened to receive his Majesty'. Angry at this betrayal, George chastised the under-sheriff. In order to avoid punishment for the escapade, Monck's friends and relatives persuaded Sir Richard Grenville to take him to sea. The arguments for accepting the story are first that it is circumstantial and second that Gumble implied that he had heard it from George Monck himself, though Gumble's book was not published until after George's death. Gumble did not meet Monck until 1655 and Monck was notoriously a reserved man. I find it odd that a gentleman of Sir Thomas's high standing in the county should think it necessary to bribe an under-sheriff. It is also curious that he should have sent George on this errand instead of his eldest son, Thomas. There is no independent confirmation of Gumble's story, so I feel it is non-proven.

24 See Glanville, *Journal*, p. 33; Cecil, *Journal*, p. 13; and instructions to Sir Edward Cecil printed in full in Dalton, *Wimbledon*, II, pp. 159ff.

25 This is stated in Dalton, *Wimbledon*, II, p. 196, on the authority of F. P. G. Guizot, *Life of Monck* (1838), p. 5. But what Guizot said related not to the Cadiz expedition but to the attack on the isle of Rhé in 1627. Of that, wrote Guizot, Monck 'en avait conservé un souvenir amer, et l'exprimait souvent en racontant les événements de sa jeunesse'. Presumably that was Guizot's version of a short remark in Gumble,

Monck, p. 4, referring to the expedition to Rhé and La Rochelle in 1628 that Monck '(young as he was) would often relate with grief the ill Conduct of that Affair, by which the English reaped nothing but Reproach and Dishonour'. Thus there is no evidence that Monck said what Dalton made him say about the Cadiz expedition. Nevertheless, the failure at Rhé was so remarkably similar to that at Cadiz that it is likely enough that he felt bitterly about both the first campaigns in which he took part.

26 Sir Edward Cecil to Lord Conway, 8 Sept. 1625: 'the Troupes ... are better fedd than taught'. Dalton, *Wimbledon*, II, pp. 129–30.

27 In fairness to Cecil, however, it must be pointed out that in a letter to the Duke of Buckingham dated 6 Sept. 1625, he wrote that he had inquired into the defects of the fleet 'especiallie in the matter of victuall, the foundacon of this and all expeditions' and asked for more money for revictualling the ships. Dalton, *Wimbledon*, II, pp. 129–30.

28 S. R. Gardiner, *A History of England 1624–1628* (1875), ch. XIII.

29 Dalton, *Wimbledon*, II, pp. 398–9. It is not clear to whom this long memorandum was addressed; it was meant to reach Buckingham.

30 Richard Grenville, *Two Original Journals* (1724) 1, 2, p. 60.

31 Griffith Davies, *Honest George Monck*, pp. 15–16.

32 Skinner, *Monk*, p. 14, specifically says that Monck came back from Rhé in 1628. Neither Skinner nor Gumble are precise about Monck's part in these campaigns.

33 Gumble, *Monck*, p. 4.

34 Ibid., pp. 4–5.

Chapter 2, The Rising Soldier

1 One receives the impression from various letters calendared in *C.S.P.* (*Dom*) *1637–1638* that the regiments were disbanded pretty promptly as there are various complaints that they had not been paid their arrears.

2 Cf. Clements, R. Markham, *The Fighting Veres* (1888) pt II.

3 This was the pay of an ensign on both sides in the English civil wars. C. H. Firth, *Cromwell's Army*, ed. P. H. Hardacre (1962), p. 186; Peter Young and Richard Holmes, *The English Civil War* (1974), p. 51. I assume that the Dutch paid much the same rate less one-third for the cost of food.

4 Henry Hexham, *A Journal or Brief Relation of the taking of Venlo, Roermont, the memorable siege of Maastricht* (1633), pp. 15ff. Hexham does not mention Monck's name, but the Earl of Oxford's regiment took a leading part in the siege.

5 Viscount Strafford to the Earl of Carlisle, 7 Oct. 1633, *The Earl of*

Strafford's letters, ed. W. Knowler (1739), I, p. 119; the Earl of Cork to Lord Goring, 20 Feb. 1634, Add. MSS. 19832, f. 36v.

6 John Dinley to Sir Francis Nethersole, 19/29 Nov. 1633, *C.S.P.* (*Dom*) *1633–1634*, p. 292.

7 Monck's earlier biographers imply that it was the nineteenth Earl of Oxford's regiment that was bought for Goring. It was not: it was one of Lord Vere's regiments which had been commanded by Sir John Holles, who was related to the Veres, at Maastricht. Holles was Monck's superior officer in Goring's regiment.

8 C. R. Markham, *Life of Fairfax* (1870), p. 17. Monck's brother-in-law, Thomas Clarges, told the French ambassador in London, M. Bordeaux, in 1660 that Monck was 'in want of the French tongue'. *The History of Richard Cromwell and the Restoration of Charles II*, trans. A. R. Scoble (1851), I, p. 188.

9 Lord Dungarvan to the Earl of Cork, 16 Apr. 1634, *Lismore Papers* (1886–8), II, 3, pp. 197–8.

10 Queen of Bohemia to Archbishop Laud, 4/14 Feb. 1637, ibid., p. 422.

11 George Goring to Lord Goring, 4/14 Feb. 1637, ibid., p. 421.

12 A good account of the character of seventeenth-century fortified towns before the changes made by Vauban, is in George A. Rotrock's introduction to S. L. de Vauban, *A Manual of Siegecraft and Fortification* (1968), pp. 4ff. A useful list of terms employed in fortification is given on pp. 201–3 of Reginald Blomfield, *Sebastien Le Prestre de Vauban* (1938). A map of the fortified town of Breda is to be found in Markham, *The Fighting Veres*, opposite p. 162.

13 Henry Hexham, *A True and Brief Relation of the famous Siege of Breda* (1637), pp. 17ff.

14 Ibid., p. 20.

15 Ibid., pp. 21–2.

16 Ibid., pp. 27–8.

17 Ibid., p. 28.

18 Ibid.

19 Thomas Gumble, *The Life of General Monck* (1671), p. 8.

20 C. R. Boxer, *The Dutch Seaborne Empire 1600–1800* (1965), pp. 32–4. English historians sometimes write of Dordrecht and sometimes Dort; they are the same place.

21 I.e. from 1631 to 1638.

22 Gumble, *Monck*, p. 9.

23 Cf. C. V. Wedgwood, *The King's Peace* (1955), Bk II.

24 According to Gumble, *Monck*, p. 15, Leicester was Monck's cousin; this is repeated by John Prince, *Worthies of Devon* (1810), p. 587, but I have not been able to verify it.

25 The Earl of Newport was a friend of Goring; it was to him that Goring

first revealed the 'Army Plot' in 1641. Sir Philip Warwick, *Memoirs* (1701), p. 180, called him 'the silly and faithless Earl of Newport'.

26 Young and Holmes, *The English Civil War*, p. 31.

27 Hamilton to Charles I, 7 May 1639. *Hamilton Papers*, ed. S. R. Gardiner (1880), p. 78.

28 Edmund Verney to Ralph Verney, 1 Apr. 1639, Peter Verney, *The Standard Bearer* (1963), p. 132.

29 C. V. Wedgwood, *Thomas Wentworth* (1961), p. 273.

30 Robert Reid to Sir Francis Windebank, 13 Jan. 1640, *C.S.P.* (*Dom*) *1639–1640*, p. 332.

31 Cf. Gumble, *Monck*, p. 19: 'And when the Earl of Strafford General of the Army moved the King instead of treating further with such insolent Rebels to give him Leave to charge them Lieutenant-Colonel Monck was one of those few that earnestly urged a Battle ... ' That sounds like a meeting of the full council of war.

32 Viscount Strafford to Cottington, 24 Aug. 1640, *C.S.P.* (*Dom*) *1640*, p. 627.

33 Wedgwood, *King's Peace*, p. 347.

34 Thomas Skinner, M.D., *The Life of General Monk*, ed. William Webster (1723), p. 19; Gumble, *Monck*, p. 10.

35 Sir Henry Vane to Sir Francis Windebank, 10 Sept. 1640, cited in S. R. Gardiner, *History of England* (1899), IX, pp. 203–4.

36 Skinner, *Monk*, p. 19.

37 Wedgwood, *King's Peace*, p. 353.

Chapter 3, Campaigns in Ireland

1 Judicious accounts of the origins of the Irish rebellion will be found in R. Bagwell, *Ireland under the Stuarts* (1909), I ch. XIV and W. E. H. Lecky, *A History of Ireland in the Eighteenth Century* (1892), I, ch. 1.

2 *The Earl of Castlehaven's Review or his Memoirs of his Engagement and Carriage in the Irish Wars* (1684), p. 16.

3 Castlehaven, *Review*, p. 10.

4 Mary Hickson, *Ireland in the Seventeenth Century* (1884), contains a selection from the thirty-two volumes of depositions now in Trinity College, Dublin, about the so-called massacres which she used to prove that they were authentic and widespread. Modern historical opinion, however, refuses to accept that view. As Thomas L. Coonan justly observed in his book *The Irish Catholic Confederacy and the Puritan Revolution* (1954), p. 115: 'No question connected with Irish history has been discussed with greater acrimony and less profit.'

5 R. W. Blencoe, ed., *Sydney Papers* (1825), pp. xviii–xxii.

6 Monck to the Earl of Leicester from Chester, 21 Jan. 1642, John Nalson, *Impartial Collection of Great Affairs of State* (1683), II, pp. 919–20.

7 See *C.S.P. (Ireland) 1633–1647*, pp. 783, 788, 791ff.

8 Quoted from a letter in the Longleat MSS. written by one of Monck's captains, in Julian Corbett, *Monk* (1889), pp. 24–5.

9 Richard Bellings was to become Secretary to the Irish Confederation. His history is printed in J. T. Gilbert (ed.), *History of the Irish Confederation and War in Ireland 1641–1649* (1882–91), seven vols, I, pp. 1–164. The quotation is on p. 80.

10 Corbett, *Monk*, p. 26.

11 Leicester to Ormonde from London, 20 May 1642, in Gilbert, *History*, 2, p. 43.

12 Sir Richard Cox, *Hibernia Anglicana* (1690), p. 107.

13 Oath of association in Castlehaven, *Review*, pp. 31ff.

14 C. V. Wedgwood, *Thomas Wentworth* (1961), p. 223.

15 Clarendon, ed., *History of the Rebellion and Civil Wars* (1826), II, p. 585 and III, p. 482.

16 T. Carte, *The Life of James Duke of Ormonde* (1851), III, p. 38.

17 Captain William Tucker in his Journal, printed in Gilbert, *History*, II, pp. 170ff, mentions Monck's presence on 8 and 9 Nov. 1642.

18 Ibid., p. 174.

19 Gilbert, *History*, I, p. 149.

20 Ibid.

21 Bellings in Gilbert, *History*, I, p. 91.

22 Ibid., p. 25.

23 Castlehaven, *Review*, p. 35. Tucker said Preston had 1,200 foot and 160 horse; Monck returned with 600 foot and 100 horse.

24 Castlehaven seems to imply that Monck relieved Ballynekill in October, ibid., p. 35, but it is clear from Tucker's journal, in Gilbert, *History*, II, p. 177, that it was in December. Monck attended the Council of War in November and Tucker says he returned to Dublin on 18 December after defeating Preston.

25 Tucker in Gilbert, *History*, II, p. 180.

26 Ibid., pp. 190ff.

27 'This day Coronell Monke acquaints them with the designe of the Lord Lisle to take Ross and Wexford if God bless them.' Tucker in Gilbert, *History*, II, p. 198.

28 Official account of warfare in Leinster, where Ormonde won a victory near the towns of Ross and Wexford on 18 Mar. 1643, written by George Creichton, the chaplain to his regiment, ibid., pp. 248–50.

29 Ibid., pp. 257ff.; Bellings in Gilbert, *History*, I.

30 Ibid., p. 258.

31 Cited in Coonan, *The Irish Catholic Confederacy*, p. 93.

32 Lords Justices to Colonel George Monck, 26 June 1643, from Dublin castle, Gilbert, *History*, II, p. 271.
33 Ibid., p. 272.
34 Belling, in Gilbert, *History*, II, pp. 160–61.
35 S. R. Gardiner, *History of the Great Civil War* (1886), I, p. 264.
36 Castlehaven, *Review*, p. 42; Bellings in Gilbert, *History*, I, pp. 161–2; Cox, *Hibernia Anglicana*, p. 132.
37 Colonel Monck and officers at Trim to Lords Justices, 12 Sept. 1643. Ibid., II, p. 364. See also ibid., II, p. cx. Monck to Lords Justices, 13 Sept. 1643, Carte, *Life of Ormonde*, VI, p. 294.

Chapter 4, In the Tower of London

1 George Digby to Ormonde, 10 Nov. 1643, T. Carte, *The Life of James Duke of Ormonde* (1851), III, p. 37.
2 Ibid., p. 96.
3 H. M. C. Ormonde, N.S., II, pp. 343–4. L. Crawford, *Ireland's Ingratitude to the Parliament of England*, 3 Feb. 1644. E. 33 (28).
4 Carte, *Ormonde*, III, p. 104.
5 Thomas Skinner, M.D., *The Life of General Monk*, ed. William Webster (1723), p. 23.
6 J. D. Griffith Davies, *Honest George Monck* (1936), p. 44, wrote: 'Certainly Charles was at some pains to placate the irate colonel', but that is guesswork. After all Monck had refused to take an oath which every other colonel except Crawford had done.
7 They derive from Thomas Gumble, *The Life of General Monck* (1671), pp. 17–18.
8 Byron to Ormonde, 30 Jan. 1644 from Chester, J. R. Phillips, *Memoirs of the Civil War in Wales and the Marches 1642–1649* (1874), II, p. 130, says that Prince Rupert gave Monck a commission to raise a regiment. This must be wrong as Rupert was not at that time commander-in-chief, but only General of Horse and this was presumably an infantry regiment. The story that Monck was to be appointed Major-General of the Irish brigade is in Skinner, *Monk*, p. 25. It is unlikely that the King intended Monck to supersede Byron immediately, but it is possible that as Monck was well-known to the regiments sent over from Ireland the King meant to give Byron another post and to put Monck in charge of all the forces from Ireland after they had arrived.
9 Fairfax stated that he had 2,500 foot and 28 troops of cavalry and he estimated the Royalists at 3,000 foot and 1,800 horse. Fairfax to Essex, 29 Jan. 1644, from Nantwich, Phillips, *Civil War in Wales*, II, p. 126. In his *Short Memorial of the Northern Actions 1642–1644* (1699),

Fairfax says he had 1,800 horse and 3,000 foot, exactly equal to the Royalists. Byron says he had 1,500 foot and was equal to the Roundheads in horse. Byron to Ormonde, 30 Jan. 1644, from Chester, Phillips, *Civil War in Wales*, II, p. 129. If Fairfax had 1,800 horse in 28 regiments they would have been almost up to strength, which was rarely the case. My guess is that the Royalists were inferior in foot and superior in horse.

10 A good account of the battle of Nantwich is in C. R. Markham, *Life of Fairfax* (1870), pp. 129–31.

11 Byron to Ormonde, Phillips, *Civil War in Wales*, II, p. 130.

12 Julian Corbett, *Monk* (1889), p. 39.

13 Markham, *Fairfax*, p. 130.

14 Griffith Davies, *Honest George Monck*, p. 48, says Fairfax 'took Monck and Warren back with him to Yorkshire and imprisoned them in Hull'; this cannot be right because after the battle of Nantwich Fairfax was ordered to go to Lancashire to besiege Lathom House.

15 Skinner, *Monk*, p. 25.

16 *C.J.*, III, p. 554.

17 Cf. A. L. Rowse, *The Tower of London* (1972). Dr Rowse does not generalize about the way in which distinguished prisoners were treated, but one gathers this from what he writes about Overbury and others.

18 Gumble, *Monck*, p. 20.

19 George Monck to Thomas Monck, 6 Nov. 1644. Skinner, *Monk*, pp. xix–xx.

20 Corbett, *Monk*, p. 43.

21 Monck, *Observations upon Military and Political Affairs* (1671), p. 1.

22 Ibid., pp. 145–6.

23 Ibid., p. 4.

24 Ibid., p. 3.

25 Ibid., p. 9.

26 Ibid., pp. 11–12.

27 Sir James Turner, *Memoirs* (1829), p. 14.

28 Monck, *Observations*, p. 12.

29 Ibid., p. 93.

30 Ibid., p. 119.

31 Ibid., p. 25.

32 Ibid., p. 18.

33 Ibid., p. 38.

34 Ibid., ch. 2, pp. 23–4.

35 For example, Henry Hexham laid down that besiegers should choose 'a Bulwark rather than a Curtain to be battered with your Ordnance' *Principles of the Art Military* (1643 edn), p. 40.

36 Ibid.

37 Monck, *Observations*, p. 101.

38 Ibid., p. 151.

39 Gervase Markham, *The Souldier's Accidence; or an Introduction to Military Discipline* (1625); Robert Norton, *The Gunner* (1628); William Bariffe, *Military Discipline* (1635); Hexham, *The Principles of the Art Military* (first published in 1637).

40 *D.N.B.* under 'Sir Thomas Clarges'. According to this article neither the story that Anne Clarges was the daughter of a farrier nor the story that her brother was an apothecary, is true. The sources for Anne's parentage include Aubrey, Clarendon and Hearne, but none of them are to be trusted without confirmation. The date on which Thomas Ratsford died is not known. Estelle Frances Ward in her book *Christopher Monck Duke of Albemarle* (1915), p. 7, quoting a letter from Frances Monck to her brother George dated 8 Nov. 1646 from H.M.C. Buccleuch, 15th Report, pp. 308-9, stated that Monck must have been married before then, presumably because Frances Monck refers to his 'wife'. Through the kindness of the present Duke of Buccleuch I examined the original of this letter. The date certainly reads 1646 but on the endorsement says that it was addressed to General Monck in Scotland. In 1646 Monck was a prisoner in the Tower, while 'Captain Clarke' referred to in the letter did not become Monck's secretary until 1654. Therefore, I feel sure the date was a slip of the pen. In any case the word 'wife' was loosely used in the seventeenth century. For example, Lucy Walter was often called Prince Charles's wife, though when he became King Charles II he swore that he had never married her. See Maurice Ashley, *Charles II: the Man and the Statesman* (Panther edn 1973) pp. 38-9, 250. There is no reason to suppose that George Monck married before the date recorded in the register of St George's, Southwark. No doubt he decided to do so once he knew that Anne was enceinte. She gave birth to Christopher on 14 Aug. 1653.

Chapter 5, Ireland Again

1 R. Bagwell, *Ireland under the Stuarts* (1906), vol. 2 remains the most useful secondary account. Thomas L. Coonan, *The Irish Catholic Confederacy and the Puritan Revolution* (1954), gives the Irish point of view. J. T. Gilbert (ed.), *A Contemporary History of Ireland 1641-1652* (1880), three vols, T. Carte, *The Life of James Duke of Ormond* (1851) and Richard Bellings in J. T. Gilbert (ed.), *History of the Irish Confederation and war in Ireland 1641-1649* (1882-91), seven vols all contain valuable documentary material. For Monck's relations with the Scots in Ulster, see also J. S. Reid, *History of the Presbyterian Church in Ireland* (1867), II, chs XIII and XIV.

2 Thomas Gumble, *The Life of General Monck* (1671), p. 22; T. Carte *The Life of James Duke of Ormond* (1851), III, p. 270.

3 B. Whitelocke, *Memorials* (1853), under 13 Nov. 1646.

4 *C.S.P.* (*Ireland*) *1648–1660*, p. 726, under 17 Nov. 1646.

5 Cf. Thomas Skinner, M.D., *The Life of General Monk*, ed. William Webster (1723), p. 30, who says Lisle left London on 28 Jan. 1647.

6 Monck was put in command of the counties of Down and Antrim and those parts of Ulster not under the command of Sir Charles Coote.

7 *C.S.P.* (*Ireland*) *1648–1660*, p. 761 under 11 Aug. 1647.

8 In a letter dated 12 Oct. 1647 the House of Lords was told by Colonel Jones that Monck had joined him with 1,500 foot and 600 horse, *C.S.P.* (*Dom.*) *1647–1648*, p. 593. These presumably were reinforcements brought over by Monck; he himself seems to have reached Lisburn by early November, *Lords Journals*, IX, p. 508. H.M.C. Hastings, II, p. 352.

9 J. F. Taylor in *Owen Roe O'Neill* (1896) described him as 'a greathearted man of genius'; Elizabeth O'Neill in *Owen Roe O'Neill* (1937) said he 'fought for Ireland and failed'. The latter is the more readable biography of the two, but neither carries great conviction and Elizabeth O'Neill slurs over O'Neill's dealings with Monck.

10 Derby House Committee to Monck, 4 Oct. 1648, *C.S.P.* (*Ireland*) *1648–1660*, p. 31. Cf. Monneries to Mazarin from Kilkenny, 2 Oct. 1647, Gilbert *Contemporary History*, VII, p. 337.

11 Derby House Committee to Monck, 4 Oct. 1648, *C.S.P.* (*Ireland*) *1648–1660*, p. 30.

12 Cf. Inchiquin to Ormonde from Cork, 29 Jan. 1649, Bellings in Gilbert, *History*, VII, p. 238.

13 Monck to officers of regiments under his command, 21 Mar. 1649, H.M.C. Hastings, II, p. 356.

14 Ibid.

15 Ibid., p. 357; Reid, *Presbyterian Church*, p. 101, n. 15.

16 Ibid.

17 Ibid.

18 Council of State minutes, 26 Mar. 1649, *C.S.P.* (*Dom*) *1649–1650*, p. 52. As late as August 1649, one of Monck's officers informed the Speaker that Monck's men were in extreme want of money so that they could not go into the field, H.M.C. Portland, I, p. 495.

19 Derby House Committee to Monck, 8 Nov. 1659, *C.S.P.* (*Ireland*) *1648–1660*, p. 35.

20 I found this letter in Clarke MSS. (Box 3) at Worcester College Library in Oxford. It is undated but in view of the references to Ormonde and Inchiquin and to the return of Sir George Monro to Ireland, it may have been written about March. The alternative is late May or early June

since Jones in his letter to Cromwell of 6 June speaks of Monck coming to his assistance. Carte MSS. 118 f. 44 v.–f. 45.

21 Cited in Gilbert, *Contemporary History*, II, 2, pp. vi–vii.

22 E. Ludlow, *Memoirs*, ed. C. H. Firth (1894), I, pp. 228–9. Gilbert, *Contemporary History*, II, 2, i, p. 207.

23 On 10 April 1649 Ormonde told King Charles II that though negotiations with O'Neill were continuing, 'it may be doubted whether at the rate he sets upon himself his friendship or his enmity is most to be wished for'. Carte MSS. xxiv, ff. 405–6.

24 Monck to O'Neill, 29 Mar. 1649, Carte MSS. lxviii, f. 176; but it is not absolutely certain whether this was the first approach or whether it was in reply to an approach from O'Neill.

25 Clarke MSS. lxviii, f. 176.

26 *C.S.P. (Ireland) 1648–1660*, pp. 364–5. The Calendar misdates this letter which was a reply to O'Neill's of 25 Apr.

27 John Bradshaw to Monck, 23 Apr. 1649, Carte MSS. xxiv, f. 493. As the copy of this letter is among the Ormonde papers, I assume it was intercepted.

28 *The True State of the Transactions of Colonel George Monck with Owen-Roe-mac-Art-O'Neal*, cited in Gilbert, *Contemporary History*, II, 1, p. ix. *Perfect Occurrences 27 July–3 August 1649*, E352.

29 Michael Jones to Cromwell, Carte MSS. cxviii, ff. 44–5. I think Cromwell must have received this letter as it would have been difficult to intercept it.

30 Whitelocke, *Memorials*, p. 416; Bellings in Gilbert, *History*, VII, p. 126.

31 Gilbert, *Contemporary History*, II, 1, p. xi.

32 Cf. Council of State minutes, 6 Aug. 1649, *C.S.P. (Dom) 1649–1650*, p. 263.

33 Ibid., p. 264.

34 Ibid., p. 263.

35 *The True State*, in Gilbert, *Contemporary History*, II, 1, pp. 4–5.

36 The battle of Rathmines took place on 2 August; the news appears to have reached London on 11 August, the day after Monck was condemned. See *A Perfect Diurnall*, no. 315, and *The Kingdom's Faithfull and Impartiall Scout*, B.L., no. 19.

37 *The True State*, in Gilbert, *Contemporary History*, II, 1, p. 5.

38 *The True State* is dated 15 Aug. 1949, E.509 (11).

39 Council of State minutes, 15 Aug. 1649, *C.S.P. (Dom) 1649–1650*, p. 278.

40 W. C. Abbott, *Writings and Speeches of Oliver Cromwell* (1939), II, pp. 99–100, printed the summary of an alleged letter from Cromwell to the Council of State dated *c.* 4 Aug. 1649 given in Clement Walker, *The Complete History of Independency* (1661), II, p. 230, and appeared

to accept this as being genuine, though later he qualified his view. Antonia Fraser, *Cromwell Our Chief of Men* (1974), p. 323, accepts the letter without question. The story first appeared in Julian Corbett, *Monk* (1889), pp. 64–5, and was refuted by S. R. Gardiner, *History of the Commonwealth and Protectorate 1649–1660* (1894), I, pp. 93–5 and notes.

41 *C.S.P. (Dom) 1649–1660*, p. 118.
42 H.M.C. (Hastings), II, p. 353.
43 Skinner, *Monk*, pp. 33–4.
44 Corbett, *Monk*, p. 51.
45 H.M.C. (Hastings), II, p. 356.
46 Monck to Colonel Rawdon at Lisnegarvy (Lisburn) from Exeter, 16 Dec. 1649, ibid., p. 361.

Chapter 6, *The Dunbar Campaign and After*

1 See n. 9 to ch. 1 above.
2 The date of Thomas Monck's death is usually assigned to the summer of 1649, but Monck in a petition to the Committee for Compounding dated 3 May 1649 says that his brother had been dead for two years. *Calendar of Committee for Compounding 1643–1646*, p. 1367.
3 Thomas had been fined for delinquency in acting as a commissioner for the King. This might have been because he had been a commissioner of array but more probably because he was one of the commissioners appointed by the King who sat in the chapter house at Exeter and constituted the ultimate Royalist authority in Devon and Exeter. E. A. Andriette, *Devon and Exeter in the Civil Wars* (1971), ch. 7.
4 Thomas Monck's fine for being a delinquent was at one-sixth of the value of his estate and amounted to £323, afterwards reduced to £161 10s. because of his mortgages. Another estate, Clawton Manor, was omitted from the declaration to the Committee for Compounding, but it was discharged from any fine in 1653 under the terms of the Act of Pardon, *C.S.P. (Compounding) 1643–1646*, p. 1368.
5 Ibid.
6 Ibid.
7 The letter from Frances Monck to her brother discussed in note 40 to ch. 4 makes it clear that at some date when George Monck was in Scotland Anne Ratsford was living at Great Potheridge.
8 See n. 17 to ch. 1.
9 After the Restoration Monck is known to have owned 1,200 acres of profitable land in county Mayo. See appendix. On 30 Dec. 1650 the Council of State issued a warrant to permit some goods of Colonel

Monck to be shipped to Ulster free of Customs *C.S.P. (Dom) 1650*, p. 568. This and Monck's letter to Colonel Rawdon from Exeter on 16 Dec. 1649 (see p. 95 above) strongly suggest that he had acquired property in Ulster before the Restoration. When he went to Wicklow in the late summer of 1643 it was said that he had acquired property there (see p. 40 above) but that is more doubtful.

10 Several critics of Cromwell's action at Drogheda have exaggerated the number killed. The garrison consisted of 2,000 infantry and 300 cavalry. Ormonde to Prince Rupert, 11 Sept. 1649, Carte MSS. xxv, f. 516. But a number of these escaped. See Maurice Ashley, *The Greatness of Oliver Cromwell* (1957), p. 231.

11 See Maurice Ashley, *Charles II: The Man and the Statesman* (1971), pp. 320–21.

12 Monck, *Observations upon Military and Political Affairs* (1671), p. 108.

13 H. Cary, *Memorials of the Great Civil War* (1842), II, p. 224.

14 W. C. Abbott, *Writings and Speeches of Oliver Cromwell* (1939), II, p. 224.

15 *Memoirs of Captain John Hodgson* (1806), p. 139.

16 *C.S.P. (Dom) 1650*, pp. 258, 283. Godfrey Davies, *Early History of the Coldstream Guards* (1924), ch. III.

17 *Relation of the Fight at Leith near Edinburgh*, quoted in note to Hodgson, p. 130.

18 W. S. Douglas, *Cromwell's Scotch Campaigns* (1898), chs. III and IV.

19 Douglas, *Campaigns*, p. 75.

20 Ibid., p. 84.

21 Cited by Douglas from *Several Letters*, E.612 (8).

22 Douglas, *Campaigns*, p. 102.

23 Cromwell to the Speaker, 4 Sept. 1650, Abbott, *Cromwell*, II, p. 323.

24 Ibid., II, p. 323.

25 Thomas Gumble, *The Life of General Monck* (1671), p. 34.

26 Hodgson, *Memoirs*, pp. 144–6.

27 Gumble, *Monck*, p. 38. According to one account when Monck's advice was sought by Cromwell he said: 'Sir, the Scots have the numbers and the hills; these are their advantages. We have discipline and despair, two things that will make soldiers fight: these are ours. My advice, therefore, is to attack immediately, which, if you follow, I am ready to command the van.' This quotation is used both by Griffith Davies and Oliver Warner in their biographies, but I have not been able to discover its source. It is, however, consistent with the views expressed by Monck in his own book.

28 Hodgson, *Memoirs*, pp. 145–6.

29 Abbott, *Cromwell*, II, p. 324.

30 John Buchan, *Oliver Cromwell* (1934), p. 376.
31 Abbott, *Cromwell*, II, p. 324.
32 Douglas, *Campaigns*, ch. V.
33 Maurice Ashley, *Cromwell's Generals* (1954) ch. 1. In my chapter on Dunbar in this book I now consider I gave too much importance to Cadwell's relation in *Ormonde Papers*, I, p. 381, and insufficient to Hodgson who states that he attended the Council of War held on the eve of the battle.
34 Abbott, *Cromwell*, II, p. 372.
35 Douglas, *Campaigns*, p. 216.
36 *Mercurius Politicus*, no. 52, p. 838.
37 Burntisland surrendered on 29 July 1651. *Collections by a Private Hand* in J. Maidment's *Historical Fragments* (1833).

Chapter 7, Subduing the Scots

1 W. C. Abbott, *Writings and Speeches of Oliver Cromwell* (1939), II, pp. 443–5.
2 C. H. Firth, *The Regimental History of Cromwell's Army* (1940) 2 vols, *passim* for details about these regiments; cf. also the list of regiments in Scotland in Jan. 1653. Of these Twistleton's, Fairfax's and Saunders's did not return to Scotland from England until 1652. C. H. Firth (ed.), *Scotland and the Commonwealth* (1895), pp. 114–15.
3 Cromwell to the Council of State, 21 Aug. 1651 from Doncaster. Abbott, *Cromwell*, II, p. 451.
4 *Scotland and the Commonwealth*, pp. 20, 29, 335.
5 C. H. Firth (ed.), *The Journal of Joachim Hane* (1896), introduction.
6 *Scotland and the Commonwealth*, p. 2.
7 Ibid., p. 4.
8 Clarke MSS. XIX, f. 104 v.
9 Lumsden to Monck, 26 Aug. 1651 from Dundee, *Several Proceedings in Parliament*, 4–11 Sept. 1651.
10 Colonel Okey to the (?) President of the Council of State (?) *Perfect Diurnall*, 8–15 Sept. 1651.
11 *Scotland and the Commonwealth*, p. 12.
12 Monck to the President of the Council of State Sept. (?) 1651, ibid., pp. 17–18.
13 Proclamation of 15 Sept. 1651, *Mercurius Scoticus*, 16–23 Sept. 1651.
14 Okey to the President of the Council of State, 19 Aug. 1651 from Stirling, *Several Proceedings in Parliament*, 21–28 Aug. 1651.
15 'A Brief Relation' in *Scotland and the Commonwealth*, pp. 21ff.
16 Ibid., p. 333.
17 Ibid., p. 24.

18 These regiments were Cobbett's, Pride's and Gibbons's.
19 Firth, *Regimental History*, p. 510; *Scotland and the Commonwealth*, p. 28
20 H. G. Tibbutt, *Colonel John Okey 1606–1662* (1954), pp. 47–8.
21 Monck to the Council of State, 31 Oct. 1651, *Scotland and the Commonwealth*, p. 337.
22 Proclamation by Monck, 27 Oct. 1651, ibid., p. 336.
23 Ibid., p. 15 and notes.
24 Ibid., p. 16n.
25 John Nicoll, *Diary of Public Transactions and Other Occurrences, chiefly in Scotland*, ed. D. Laing (1836), p. 29.
26 National Library of Scotland 849.
27 National Library of Scotland 8291, f. 10.
28 Order of 13 Nov. 1651, Clarke MSS. XX, f. 48.
29 Order of 7 Oct. 1651, H.M.C. Sixth Report, p. 685b.
30 Clarke MSS. XX f. 3.
31 Report from Dundee, 2 Nov. 1651, Clarke MSS. XX.
32 Captain T. Thompson to the Navy Commissioners, *C.S.P. (Dom) 1650*, p. 262 misdated in the *Calendar*.
33 Letter from Aberdeen, 10 Jan. 1652, *Scotland and the Commonwealth*, p. 335.
34 Ibid., pp. 348–57.
35 Instructions to commissioners sent to Scotland, 4 Dec. 1651, Egerton MSS. 1048, f. 142.
36 Newsletter from Dundee, 8 Jan. 1652, *Scotland and the Commonwealth*, p. 334.
37 Nicoll, *Diary*, p. 80.
38 William Clarke to the Speaker from Dalkeith, 14 Feb. 1652, *Scotland and the Commonwealth*, p. 33.
39 A letter from General Monck, 31 Oct., ibid., p. 337.
40 Colonel Edward Conway to Major George Rawdon, 8 Apr. 1652 from Kensington, H.M.C. Hastings, II, pp. 361–2.
41 Monck to all officers and soldiers to whom it may concern, 26 May 1652, National Library of Scotland 849, no. 22.
42 Newsletter from Dundee, 16 Oct. 1651, Clarke MSS. XX.

Chapter 8, General-at-Sea

1 For the origins of the war see S. R. Gardiner, *Commonwealth and Protectorate 1651–1654* (1897), ch. XXI and his introduction to the *Letters and Papers relating to the first Dutch war 1652–1654*, ed. C. T. Atkinson (1899), I, pp. 48–53.
2 Cf. *C.S.P. (Dom) 1651–1654*, pp. 381, 398. Monck was in Yarmouth during Aug. 1652.

3 Blake to the Council of State, 1 Dec. 1652 cited in J. R. Powell, *Robert Blake: General at Sea* (1972), p. 196. Monck was officially notified of his appointment by the Council of State on 3 December.

4 For Vane and the Admiralty see Violet Rowe, *Sir Henry Vane the Younger* (1970), chs VII and VIII.

5 Ibid., appendix E, p. 274.

6 There is a letter from Monck at Chatham asking that any letters that shall come for him shall be sent down when any messenger of state is coming to see them. Document at the National Maritime Museum Greenwich.

7 *Letters and Papers*, III, pp. 274, 284.

8 For the battle of Portland 18 Feb. 1653 see Powell, *Blake*, ch. 16, *Letters and Papers*, IV and Gardiner, *Commonwealth and Protectorate*, pp. 157–61.

9 The three generals-at-sea to the Speaker, 27 Feb. 1653, *Letters and Papers*, IV.

10 Thomas Gumble, *The Life of General Monck* (1671), p. 57.

11 Powell, *Blake*, p. 216.

12 *Fighting Instructions 1530–1816* (1905). Navy Records Society, pp. 99ff and introduction, p. 96. *Letters and Papers*, IV, pp. 262–6.

13 Powell, *Blake*, p. 225. Corbett on the other hand, wrote that although 'Monck's was the only new mind that was brought to bear on the subject. Yet it is impossible to credit him with introducing new tactics.' I do not see why. However, Michael Lewis, *Navy of Britain* (1948) p. 441, suggests that a rough-and-ready line ahead was tried out before the time of the Spanish armada.

14 Deane's and Monck's instructions to Vice-Admiral William Penn, 29 and 30 Mar. 1653, *Letters and Papers*, IV, pp. 273–6, 282.

15 Deane and Monck to Admiralty Committee, 4 Apr. 1653, ibid., p. 299.

16 Deane and Monck to Admiralty Committee, 10 May 1653, ibid., V, p. 35.

17 Powell, *Blake*, pp. 236–9 *Letters and Papers*, V, account by a flag officer who took part in the battle. Gumble, *Monck*, pp. 65–8.

18 Monck to Admiralty Committee from the *Resolution* fourteen leagues from North Foreland at six in the morning, 3 June 1653, ibid., V, pp. 72–3.

19 J. R. Powell (ed.), *The Letters of Robert Blake* (1937), p. 215.

20 *Letters and Papers*, V, pp. 248–58.

21 Monck to Admiralty Committee, 23 and 27 July 1653, *Letters and Papers*, V, pp. 313–14, 328–30.

22 Cited in Powell, *Blake*, p. 245.

23 *Parliamentary History*, XX, p. 193.

24 Monck to the Lord President of the Council, 1 Aug. 1653, *Letters and Papers*, V, pp. 351–2.

25 Monck to Admiralty Commissioners, 3 Aug. 1653, ibid., pp. 374–5.

26 Monck to Willoughby, 18 Sept. 1653 from the *Resolution* at Aldburgh, ibid., VI, p. 73.

27 Monck to Admiralty Commissioners, 17 Nov. 1653 from the *Swiftsure* in the Hope, ibid., V, p. 180.

28 *Letters and Papers*, IV, p. 360.

29 *C.J.*, VII, p. 328.

30 Gumble, *Monck*, pp. 75–7.

31 Lilburne to Cromwell, Nov. 1653, *Scotland and the Commonwealth*, pp. 262–87.

32 Lilburne had evidently been informed of Monck's appointment by the middle of January 1654. Cf. Lilburne to Monck, 21 Jan. 1654 from Dalkeith, *Scotland and the Protectorate*, ed. C. H. Firth (1899), pp. 209–13.

Chapter 9, Monck's Defeat of the Scottish Royalist

1 Major-General Deane's proclamation, 9 June 1652, C. H. Firth (ed.), *Scotland and the Commonwealth* (1895), pp. 45–6.

2 Articles of agreement, 19 Aug. 1652, pp. 48–9, 57–60. Willcock, *The Great Marquess* (1903), p. 280.

3 *Several Proceedings in Parliament*, 25 Nov.–2 Dec. 1652.

4 'Memoranda on the Rising in Scotland' in *Scotland and Commonwealth*, p. 137.

5 Cf. ibid., pp. 161ff.

6 The General Assembly was dissolved on 20 July 1653. Cf. ibid., p. 162; John Nicoll, *Diary of Public Transactions and Other Occurrences, chiefly in Scotland*, ed. D. Laing (1836), p. 110; Lilburne to the Protector, 28 Mar. 1654, Clarke MSS. I, f. 24.

7 Lilburne to Lambert, 29 Dec. 1653, Clarke MSS. LXXXVI, f. 37.

8 *Thurloe S.P.*, II, p. 222.

9 Lilburne to Cromwell, 14 Jan. 1654 from Dalkeith, *Scotland and the Protectorate*, ed. C. H. Firth (1899), pp. 19–20.

10 Lilburne to Lambert, 3 Jan. 1654; Lilburne to Cromwell 1 Apr. 1654, ibid., pp. 8, 66–8.

11 Lilburne to Lambert, 11 Apr. 1654, ibid., pp. 81–3.

12 Commission to Monck, 8 Apr. 1654, *Thurloe S.P.*, II, p. 222.

13 Instructions to General Monck, 6 Apr. 1654, *Scotland and the Protectorate*, 81–3.

14 Sir A. Johnston to James Guthrie, H.M.C. (Laing), p. 292.

15 Lilburne to Monck, 21 Jan. 1654 from Dalkeith, *Scotland and the Protectorate*, pp. 20–21.

16 Monck to Lambert, 27 Apr. 1654, ibid., p. 96.

17 *Thurloe S.P.*, II, pp. 216–62.

18 Monck to Cromwell, 22 Apr. 1654, *Scotland and the Protectorate*, pp. 90–91, 93–4.

19 Ibid., pp. 97–8 etc. It is not clear in what capacity Lambert was addressed by Monck, but it seems that after Cromwell became Protector, Lambert was recognized as his deputy commander-in-chief. Monck wrote deferentially to him as 'My Lord'. Cf. W. H. Dawson, *Cromwell's Understudy* (1938) chs X and XI.

20 Monck to Cromwell, 25 Apr. 1654, *Scotland and the Protectorate*, pp. 93–4.

21 Ibid., pp. 105–6 letter of 14 May 1654.

22 Monck ordered a fort to be built there, which was subsequently replaced by Fort William, named after King William III. The troops from Ireland were stationed mainly at Inverlochy where Loch Lochy joins the sea.

23 Monck to Cromwell from Ruthven in Badgenoth, *Scotland and the Protectorate*, pp. 143–4.

24 Monck to Cromwell, 17 July 1654 from camp at Glen Dowart, ibid., pp. 145–6. In a letter of news from England in the *Cal. of Clarendon S.P.*, II, p. 379 it is stated that Monck had been compelled to send for more men, raising his army to twelve infantry regiments and seven cavalry regiments plus dragoons, which must have been roughly correct.

25 Monck to Cromwell, 21 July 1654 from camp near Weems castle; Morgan to Monck from camp near Ruthven, 22 July 1654; *Mercurius Politicus* 27 July–3 Aug. 1654. The battle of Dalnaspidal was fought on 19 July 1654.

26 Monck to Cromwell, 29 July 1654 from Stirling, *Scotland and the Protectorate*, pp. 148–53.

27 Ibid., pp. 154–5.

28 Ibid., pp. 186–7.

29 Monck to Cromwell, 24 Aug. and 29 Aug. from Dalkeith, ibid., pp. 161–2, 165. Letter of 26 Sept. re Montrose, ibid., p. 190. Letters of 13 and 14 Aug. re Earls of Atholl, Tullibardine and the Earl of Perth Advocates MSS. 9752, ff. 1–3.

30 Monck to Cromwell, 14 Sept. 1654, ibid., pp. 176–7.

31 Monck to Lord Cardross, National Library of Scotland 3420f. 195.

32 *Scotland and the Protectorate*, p. 218.

33 Ibid., pp. 154–5.

34 Ibid., pp. 161–2. Cf. Nicoll, *Diary*, p. 134.

35 Ibid., p. 174.

36 Monck to Cromwell, 19 Aug. 1654 from Stirling, ibid., pp. 155–6.

37 Monck to Army Committee, 28 Oct. 1654, ibid., pp. 201–3.

38 Monck to Cromwell, 19 Aug. 1654; Monck to Treasury Commissioners, 10 Nov. 1654, ibid., pp. 155–6, 212–13.

39 Downing to Monck, 30 Sept. 1654, Egerton MSS. 2618, f. 46.

40 Monck to Cromwell, 26 Oct. 1654 from Dalkeith, *Scotland and the Protectorate*, pp. 201–2.

41 Monck to Cromwell, 12 Dec. 1654, ibid., pp. 225–6.

42 Ibid.

43 Monck to Cromwell, 21 Dec. 1654, ibid., pp. 225–6.

44 Ibid., pp. 157–8.

45 Ibid., pp. 161–2.

46 Monck to Cromwell, 16 Sept. 1654, ibid., pp. 184–5.

47 Monck to Lambert, 28 Sept. 1654, ibid., pp. 190–91.

48 Monck mentions this in the letter referred to in n. 45 above. Thomas Gumble, *The Life of General Monck* (1671), p. 88, also states that Cromwell 'had written to Monck about this Design, and glanced at an inclination that he had, for to give him the Command which certainly had produced great Effects'.

Chapter 10, Military Governor of Scotland

1 Clause I of The Instrument of Government. The text is printed in *The Constitutional Documents of the Puritan Rebellion*, ed. S. R. Gardiner (1906), pp. 405ff.

2 *The Cromwellian Union 1651–1652*, ed. C. Sandford Terry (1902), pp. lii–liv.

3 Ibid., introduction by Professor Terry.

4 *Thurloe S.P.*, III, pp. 423, 701; John Nicoll, *Diary of Public Transactions and Other Occurrences, chiefly in Scotland*, ed. D. Laing (1836) p. 159; *C.S.P. (Dom)* 1655, p. 303; *Scotland and the Protectorate*, ed. C. H. Firth (1899), pp. 550–52, 362.

5 Monck to Cromwell, 8 March 1655, Firth, *Scotland and the Protectorate*, pp. 253–4.

6 Nicoll, *Diary*, pp. 124–5; Monck to Lambert, 4 May 1654, Firth, *Scotland and the Protectorate*, p. 100.

7 *Thurloe S.P.*, vi, p. 444.

8 Monck to Lambert, (?) Mar. 1655, ibid., p. 260.

9 Cf. Maurice Ashley, *Financial and Commercial Policy under the Cromwellian Protectorate* (revised 1962), pp. 90–91.

10 Monck to Cromwell, 23 Nov. 1654, Firth, *Scotland and the Protectorate*, pp. 213–14.

11 Ibid., pp. 308ff.

12 C. H. Firth and R. S. Rait, *Acts and Ordinances of the Interregnum* (1911), II, p. 898.

13 Nicoll, *Diary*, pp. 81–3. *The Cromwellian Union*, pp. xxi–xxiii.

14 W. C. Abbott, *Writings and Speeches of Oliver Cromwell* (1939), IV, p. 826.

15 Monck to the Sheriffs, 29 Sept. 1654; Dickson and Douglas to Monck, 29 Oct. 1656, Firth, *Scotland and the Protectorate*, pp. 191–2, 332–3, *C.S.P. (Dom) 1654*, p. 368; Nicoll, *Diary*, pp. 138, 186; *Mercurius Politicus*, 26 Oct.–2 Nov. 1654.

16 *The Letters and Journals of Robert Baillie*, ed. D. Laing (1842), III, p. 252.

17 Ibid., p. 244.

18 *Clarke Papers*, III, p. 22. Nicoll, *Diary*, p. 152.

19 Firth, *Scotland and the Protectorate*, pp. 186–7.

20 For an enlightening essay on Scotland in this period see Hugh Trevor-Roper, 'Scotland and the Puritan Revolution' in his *Religion, the Reformation and Social Change* (1967), ch. 8.

21 For a character sketch of Overton see Maurice Ashley, *Cromwell's Generals* (1954), ch. VIII.

22 Monck to Cromwell, 28 Sept. 1654, Firth, *Scotland and the Protectorate*, pp. 192–3.

23 Monck to Cromwell, 10 Nov. 1654, ibid., pp. 211–12.

24 See Maurice Ashley, *John Wildman: Postmaster and Plotter* (1947), ch. VII.

25 Newsletter of 19 Dec. quoted by H. G. Tibbutt, *Colonel John Okey 1606–1662* (1954), p. 69. The text of the petition of the three colonels is printed in ibid., pp. 64–8.

26 Nicoll, *Diary*, p. 145.

27 Monck to Cromwell, 28 Nov. 1654, Firth, *Scotland and the Protectorate*, p. 216.

28 Monck to Cromwell, 16 Jan. 1655, ibid., p. 238.

29 Abbott, *Writings and Speeches of Oliver Cromwell* (1939), III, p. 557. *Thurloe S.P.*, III, p. 65.

30 Ashley, *Cromwell's Generals*, pp. 146–7; Monck to Cromwell, 25 Jan. 1655, Firth, *Scotland and the Protectorate*, pp. 242–3.

31 Ibid., p. 243.

32 Monck to Lambert, 30 Jan. 1655, Firth, *Scotland and the Protectorate*, pp. 245–8.

33 Monck to Cromwell, 20 Mar. 1655, ibid., pp. 256–7.

34 In April 1975 I myself was nearly stranded in a motor car during a snowstorm in the Cairngorms. The road between Stirling and Braemar had to be closed for four days.

35 Monck to Cromwell, 21 Apr. 1655, Firth, *Scotland and the Protectorate*, pp. 266–7.
36 Monck to Cromwell, 8 May 1655, ibid., p. 268.
37 Ibid.

Chapter 11, Monck and the Cromwells

1 Monck to Cromwell, 18 and 21 Aug. 1655; Monck to Lambert, 21 Aug. 1655. C. H. Firth (ed.), *Scotland and the Protectorate* (1899), pp. 298–300; *Thurloe S.P.*, VI, p. 472.
2 Monck to Lambert, 3 July 1655, Firth, *Scotland and the Protectorate*, p. 289.
3 Monck to Cromwell, 25 Aug. 1655, ibid., pp. 300–1.
4 Monck to Broghill, 31 July 1655, ibid., pp. 294–6.
5 Monck to the Council of State, 11 Feb. 1658, *C.S.P.* (*Dom*) *1657–1658*, pp. 284–5.
6 Monck to Cromwell, Aug. 1655 and 15 Oct. 1657, ibid., pp. 296–7, 367–96.
7 Establishment 21, Dec. 1657, Clarke MSS. 51 f. 42; *C.S.P.* (*Dom*) *1657–1658*, p. 186. Monck to Council of State, 5 Dec. 1657, Firth, *Scotland and the Protectorate*, pp. 371–3.
8 Monck to Lambert, 12 May 1655; Monck to Cromwell, 21 Apr. 1655, ibid., 266–7, 269.
9 Humble Address of the Officers in and about the Headquarters to Monck, 6 June 1655, Clarke MSS. ff. 27ff., 740ff. Monck to Cromwell, 14 July 1655, Firth, *Scotland and the Protectorate*, pp. 290–91.
10 Lord Cranston to Monck, 8 Apr. 1657; Colonel Thomas Lyon to Charles II, 29 Jan. 1655; Charles II to the Earl of Leven, 2 Aug. 1655, ibid., pp. 352–3, 245, 297–8.
11 Monck to Cromwell, 1 Aug. 1654, ibid., pp. 153–4; Cromwell to Monck, 20 May 1654 and 10 July 1654. W. C. Abbott, *Writings and Speeches of Oliver Cromwell* (1939), III, pp. 305, 368; writing on 25 May 1654 one of Monck's officers described how 'some of the worst of the prisoners were ordered to the Barbados and escaped out of prison and are gone'. *Letters from Roundhead Officers from Scotland* (1856), p. 71.
12 Nicoll, *Diary of Public Transactions and Other Occurrences, Chiefly in Scotland*, ed. D. Laing (1836), p. 147, Mann to Monck, Mar. 1657 and 16 July 1657. *Thurloe S.P.*, V, pp. 136, 145, 162, 208, 215, 241. Firth, *Scotland and the Protectorate*, pp. 350, 351, 352, 362–3. Monck to Cromwell, 21 Mar. 1657, Clarke MSS. 51, f. 5.
13 Nicoll, *Diary*, pp. 159–61, 163–4. *Thurloe S.P.*, VI, pp. 423, 716, *C.S.P.* (*Dom*) *1654*, pp. 108, 255.

14 Monck to Cromwell, 11 July 1657, Firth, *Scotland and the Protectorate*, pp. 360–61, 364.

15 Monck to Thurloe, 5 and 30 Aug. 1656, *Thurloe S.P.*, V, pp. 366–367.

16 The commission of the Council of Scotland was dated from 24 June 1655 and the Council was appointed for three years. When the commission was renewed, Samuel Desborough became president. *C.S.P. (Dom) 1655*, pp. 108, 255; *Thurloe S.P.*, VII, p. 94. The Council was given the task of appointing commissioners for Customs and excise and supervising the levying of the assessments in Scotland.

17 Thomas Burton, *Diary* (1828), IV, p. 168.

18 Nicoll, *Diary*, p. 183.

19 Cromwell to Wilkes, Jan. 1655, *Clarke Papers*, II p. 239.

20 Monck to Thurloe, 8 and 20 Nov. 1655. *Thurloe S.P.*, pp. 161, 221. Thomas Skinner, M.D., *The Life of General Monk*, ed. William Webster (1723), p. xlviii, printed a letter from Charles II dated 12 Aug. 1655 which he says was addressed to Monck. This was accepted by Guizot and by Sir Charles Firth in his article on Monck in the *D.N.B.* But in n. 2 on p. 123 of his second vol. of *The Last Years of the Protectorate* (1909), Firth shows that from letters printed in *Thurloe S.P.*, IV, pp. 162ff., it is clear that this letter was not addressed to Monck at all but to the Earl of Atholl. I am indebted to Miss Frances Dow for drawing my attention to this reference, as I was misled by Skinner or rather by his editor.

21 Tobias Bridge to Thurloe, 27 Dec. 1655, *Cal. Clarendon S.P.*, III, pp. 4–5.

22 Monck to Thurloe, 3 July 1658, *Thurloe S.P.*, VII, pp. 232–3.

23 Monck to Thurloe, 25 Dec. 1655 and 26 May 1656, *Thurloe S.P.*, III, p. 342; Monck to Dr William Stone, 1 Jan. 1657, Clarke MSS. 51 f. 1; Monck to Cromwell, 22 May 1657; Monck to officers of regiments in Scotland, 22 May 1657, *Scotland and the Protectorate*, pp. 354–5.

24 Monck wrote to Thurloe, 2 June 1657, that he was 'very glad to hear that his Highness hath given consent to the humble petition and advice *under the title of Protector* which I doubt not will be for the good and the peace of these nations'. *Thurloe S.P.*, VI, p. 329 (my italics).

25 Monck to Thurloe, 23 Dec. 1658, ibid., VII, pp. 479, 583.

26 Thomas Gumble, *The Life of General Monck* (1671), p. 94.

27 *C.S.P. (Dom) 1657–1658*, p. 333.

28 Monck to Cromwell, 7 May 1655, Clarke MSS 47; Monck to Cromwell, 28 Sept. 1657, *C.S.P. (Dom) 1657–1658*, pp. 128, 284.

29 Monck to Cromwell, 24 Sept. 1657. This is printed in full in J. D. Griffith Davies, *Honest George Monck* (1936), appendix B. It is wrongly stated in this book that the letter was concerned with parliamentary

representation of the Scottish burghs. I am grateful to Miss Frances Dow for this information.

30 *C.S.P. (Dom) 1657–1658*, p. 266.

31 Morgan to Monck, 31 Aug. 1657, Egerton MSS. 2618, f. 53. Lieutenant-Colonel Hughes to Monck, 15 May 1658, *Clarke Papers*, III, p. 150 etc.

32 Charleton to Leveson, 6 Mar. 1658. H.M.C. Duke of Sutherland, p. 166.

33 *Thurloe S.P.*, VII, pp. 322–3.

34 *Scotland and the Protectorate*, pp. 383–4; Robert W. Ramsey, *Richard Cromwell Protector of England* (1935), chs. I and II.

35 Monck to Thurloe, 25 and 27 Sept. 1658, *Thurloe S.P.*, VII, pp. 422, 435.

36 Gumble, *Monck*, pp. 94–5.

37 *Thurloe S.P.*, VII, pp. 387–8.

38 Godfrey Davies, *The Restoration of Charles II* (1955), ch. III.

39 Clarges to Henry Cromwell, 19 Oct. 1658, *Thurloe S.P.*, VII, p. 452.

40 Monck to Thurloe, 21 Dec. 1658, ibid., p. 475.

41 Monck to Thurloe, 23 Dec. 1658, ibid., pp. 479, 583.

42 Burton, *Diary*, IV, pp. 112–14.

43 Monck to Samuel Desborough, 24 Mar. and 19 Apr. 1659, *Scotland and the Protectorate*, pp. 411, 414.

44 Fleetwood to Monck, 23 Apr. 1659, H.M.C. Leyborne-Popham, p. 116.

45 This letter has not survived; it is referred to by Bordeaux in his dispatch to Mazarin of 5/15 May 1659. F. P. G. Guizot, *The History of Richard Cromwell and the Restoration of Charles II*, trans. A. R. Scoble (1856), p. 381.

46 Cf. R. Baker, *A Chronicle of the Kings of England* (1733), p. 570.

47 Fleetwood and officers to Monck, 3 May 1659 from Wallingford House, *Clarke Papers*, IV, pp. 4–6.

48 This is what Gumble implies and Gumble was with Monck at the time. Gumble, *Monck*, p. 97. Baker, *Chronicle*, p. 570; Davies, *Restoration*, p. 99 and n. 49; Firth, introduction to the *Clarke Papers*, IV, pp. ciii–ix.

49 Monck to Parliament, 12 May 1659, *C.J.*, VII, p. 658; Monck to Fleetwood, 12 May 1659, *Thurloe S.P.*, VII, pp. 669–70.

50 Broderick to Hyde, 16 Dec. 1659. *Cal. Clarendon S.P.*, III, p. 628.

Chapter 12, Monck Decides

1 Mason and Sawrey to Monck from London, 3 May 1659. H.M.C. Leyborne-Popham, p. 116.

2 For detailed accounts of Pride's Purge see David Underdown, *Pride's Purge* (1971), and Blair Worden, *The Rump Parliament* (1975).

3 Godfrey Davies, *The Restoration of Charles II* (1955), p. 97.

4 Committee of Safety to Monck, 10 May 1659, Monck to Committee of Safety, 17 May 1659, *Clarke Papers*, IV, pp. 9–10.

5 Monck to Fleetwood, 12 May 1659, *Thurloe S.P.*, VII, pp. 669–70.

6 *Clarke Papers*, IV, pp. 11–15.

7 Monck to the Speaker, 18 June 1659, ibid., pp. 22–3.

8 Monck to the Speaker, 2 June 1659, ibid., pp. 16–17; Nicholas to Marces, 9 July 1659, *C.S.P. (Dom) 1659–1660*, p. 18.

9 See Davies, *Restoration*, pp. 106–9 quoting *C.S.P. (Dom) 1659*, pp. 375ff.

10 *C.J.*, VII, pp. 677, 680; R. Baker, *A Chronicle of the Kings of England*, continued by E. Philips (1733), p. 670. It has been accepted that for the period 1658–60 Philips based his narrative on the papers of Thomas Clarges, Monck's brother-in-law; Thomas Gumble, *The Life of General Monck* (1671), p. 101.

11 Ibid., p. 101. According to an account of the fall of Richard Cromwell among the Clarke Papers, 160 officers, mostly Cromwellians, were dismissed as early as 14 June, *Clarke Papers*, IV, p. 21. Davies, *Restoration*, p. 110, says only one change was made in Monck's cavalry regiment, Monck's protest being read to the Committee of Safety on 9 Sept. 1659 and referred to Parliament, *C.S.P. (Dom) 1659–1660*, p. 183. The proposed changes are given in *Clarke Papers*, IV, pp. 39–40. For the history of Saunders and his regiment see C. H. Firth, *The Regimental History of Cromwell's Army* (1940), I, pp. 288ff. Whitelocke, as the president of the Council of State, wrote to Monck announcing the Rump's approval of the new establishment on 12 Aug. 1659.

12 *C.S.P. (Dom) 1659–1660*, pp. 19, 31, letter of 10 July 1659.

13 *Diary of Sir Archibald Johnston of Wariston* (1911–40), III, p. 124.

14 E. Ludlow, *Memoirs*, ed. C. H. Firth (1894), II, p. 112. It was stated in a letter written from T. Ross in Brussels to Gervase Holles in Amsterdam: 'Monck is very refractory in Scotland and refuseth to send a regiment into England as desired.'

15 Booth's rising has been thoroughly analysed. The latest account, which I have followed, is in J. S. Morrill, *Cheshire 1630–1660* (1974), ch. 8. See also David Underdown, *Royalist Conspiracy in England 1649–1660* (1960), ch. 12; R. N. Dore, 'The Cheshire Rising of 1659' in *Transactions of the Lancashire and Cheshire Antiquarian Society*, vol. 69 (1659) and J. R. Jones, 'Booth's Rising of 1659' in *Bulletin of the John Rylands Library*, vol. 39 (1957).

16 Thomas Skinner, M.D., *The Life of General Monk*, ed. William Webster (1723), p. 103.

17 Baker, *Chronicle*, pp. 573–4.
18 John Price D.D., *The Mystery and Method of His Majesty's Happy Restoration Laid Open to the Public View* (1680); Maseres Tracts (1815) II, pp. 695ff. Price says that Atkins served with George Monck in Ireland but I have been unable to confirm this.
19 Gumble, *Monck*, p. 107.
20 Cf. Nicoll, *Diary of Public Transactions and other Occurrences, chiefly in Scotland*, ed. D. Laing (1836), pp. 244–5.
21 Monck to Ralph Knight, 13 Aug. 1659, H.M.C., XIII, 6, p. 3.
22 Gumble, *Monck*, pp. 107ff; Price, *The Mystery*, pp. 708ff; Baker, *Chronicle*, p. 575.
23 Baker, *Chronicle*, p. 576; Gumble, *Monck*, pp. 110–11.
24 Price, *The Mystery*, p. 726.
25 Davies, *Restoration*, p. 140, n. 92; cf. *Complete Prose Works of John Milton*, VII (1974), introduction by Austin Woolrych, p. 134, n. 2.
26 Price, *The Mystery*, p. 722.

Chapter 13, The Break with the Army in England

1 Monck to Lenthall, 2 Sept. 1659, Z. Grey, *Impartial Examinations* (1739), IV, pp. 160–61.
2 Wariston to Monck, 14 July 1659, H.M.C. Leyborne-Popham, p. 118. On 12 August twelve Scots including David Leslie were arrested for refusing the engagement. *Clarke Papers*, IV, p. 41; proceedings of the Committee of Safety, 9 Sept. 1659. C.J., VII, p. 89; *C.S.P.* (*Dom*) *1659–1660*, p. 183; Council of State to Monck, 20 Sept. 1659, *Clarke Papers*, IV, p. 56; warrants of Council of State, 23 July and 8 Aug. 1659, *C.S.P.* (*Dom*) *1659–1660*, p. 87.
3 Cf. Godfrey Davies, *The Restoration of Charles II* (1955), ch. IX.
4 Colonels Mitchell, Sankey and others to Monck from Derby, 25 Sept. 1659, H.M.C. Leyborne-Popham, pp. 122–3.
5 Lambert and other officers to Monck and his officers, 5 Oct. 1659, E.1000 (22). Davies, *Restoration*, p. 149.
6 *Declaration etc*, 12 Oct. 1659. B.L. 669 f. 21 (75); *Account of events in London*, 3 Nov. 1659, *Clarke Papers*, IV, pp. 91ff.
7 Monck to the Speaker, 13 Oct. 1659, B.L. E.1000 (6). Davies, *Restoration*, p. 151; Clarke MSS. 32 f. 17.
8 Monck's order book, 19 Oct. 1659, *Clarke Papers*, IV, pp. 64ff.
9 Ibid., pp. 67–8. Monck to Speaker, Fleetwood and Lambert, 20 Oct. 1659, *Toland's Collection of Monck's Letters* (1712), pp. iii–vii.
10 *Clarke Papers*, IV, p. 69.
11 Ibid., pp. 70ff; Bordeaux to Mazarin, 24 and 27 Oct. 1659, F. P. G.

Guizot, *The History of Richard Cromwell and the Restoration of Charles II*, trans. A. R. Scoble (1856), II, p. 279.

12 Monck to Nobility, Gentlemen, Sheriffs and Justices of the Peace from Edinburgh, 15 Nov. 1659, *Clarke Papers*, IV, p. 114.

13 Monck to Johnston of Wariston and to Lambert, 3 Nov. 1659, *Clarke Papers*, IV, p. 88.

14 Ibid., pp. 96–9.

15 Monck to Robert Lilburne, 3 and 4 Nov. 1659; *Clarke Papers*, IV, p. 89; to Fleetwood, 3 Nov. 1659, Clarke MSS. 52, f. 7; to Johnston of Wariston, 5 Nov. 1659, *Clarke Papers*, IV, pp. 100–101; Commissioners for the Army in Scotland to Monck, 6 Nov. 1659 from Durham, ibid., pp. 103, 104.

16 Monck to Lambert, 8 Nov. 1659, ibid., p. 107.

17 R. Baker, *A Chronicle of the Kings of England* (1733), p. 586. For a detailed account of Monck's relations with Fairfax see Austin Woolrych, 'Yorkshire and the Restoration' in *Yorkshire Archaeological Journal* (1958). This story is accepted by Davies, *Restoration*, p. 179 and notes. Morgan arrived in Edinburgh almost certainly on 7 November (cf. extracts from Monck's order book of 8 November telling Morgan to visit Linlithgow, Stirling and Fife, to ensure the loyalty of the officers there to Monck, *Clarke Papers*, IV, p. 108). Cf. Monck to Morgan, 13 Nov. 1659. Bodleian Miscellaneous letters, D.180, f. 68. It is interesting that at this very time John Evelyn published the first edition of his effective *Apology for the Royal Party* while Whitelocke made a speech (see note 24 below) warning the Mayor and Common Council of London against Monck.

18 Monck's speech to some from the Scottish shires, 16 Nov. 1659, Clarke MSS. 32, f. 101; Scottish commissioners to Monck from Edinburgh, 16 Nov. 1659; Monck to Lords, Gentlemen and Burgesses of Scotland from Edinburgh, 17 Nov. 1659, Clarke MSS. 32 f. 100; Monck to Scottish Burghs, 18 Nov. 1659, H.M.C. 6th Report, p. 616.

19 It must be remembered that while the commissioners from the army in Scotland were negotiating with the Wallingford House party in London during the first half of November, Monck had sent his brother-in-law, Clarges, to interview Lord Fairfax at Nunappleton. Fairfax had told Clarges that 'if General Monck had any other designs than to restore Parliament and settle the nation upon its ancient government I will oppose him; but otherwise I will heartily join with him'. Later Fairfax's cousin, Brian, recorded that Fairfax told Monck when he saw him in Yorkshire at the beginning of January that 'there was no peace nor settlement in England but by a Free Parliament, and upon the old foundations of monarchy'. Though Monck did not commit himself to Fairfax he was hardly startled at the suggestion. But as was his custom he kept his

thoughts to himself. Brian Fairfax, 'Iter Boreale' in *Fairfax Correspondence*, IV, pp. 153ff.

20 Monck to Lord Mayor of London, 12 Nov. 1659. *Old Parliamentary History*, XXII, p. 46; Newsletters of 14 Nov. and 6 Dec. 1659 in *Clarke Papers*, IV, pp. 112–13, 165–6, 167, 188 etc. Common Council Journals of 23 Nov., 22, 28 and 29 Dec. 1659. City Journal 41. ff. 211v–212, 214v, 216v and 217. The City authorities were highly embarrassed by Monck's communications because the last thing it wanted to be involved in was a quarrel between two armies. However, once the Rump was restored on 26 Dec., the Common Council appointed a sub-committee to consider how to answer Monck's letter of 12 Nov.; on 28 Dec. the sub-committee on the peace and safety of the City of London was ordered to prepare an answer which was agreed to on 29 Dec., but before it was dispatched Monck was known to have left Scotland. So the City sent its reply by its Swordbearer to meet him on his way south.

21 The agreement was signed on 15 Nov. 1659, Clarke MSS. 51 f. 17. Cf. Guizot, *Richard Cromwell*, II, p. 289; *Clarke Papers*, IV, pp. 116–120; Baker, *Chronicle*, p. 588; Lambert to Monck, 21 Nov. 1659, *Clarke Papers*, IV, pp. 124–5.

22 Monck and officers in Scotland to the three commissioners in London, 24 Nov. 1659, *Clarke Papers*, IV, pp. 126ff. Bordeaux to Mazarin, 25 Nov. 1659, Guizot, *Richard Cromwell*, II, p. 293.

23 Commissioners to Monck, 16, 17, 24 and 26 Nov. 1659, ibid., pp. 132–40; Lambert to Monck from Newcastle, 29 Nov. 1659, ibid., pp. 148–51; Monck to Commissioners, 25 and 28 Nov., pp. 140–41. Bordeaux to Mazarin, 1 Dec. 1659, Guizot, *Richard Cromwell*, II, pp.293–7; Fleetwood to Monck, 1 Dec. 1659, *Clarke Papers*, IV, p. 162; Colonel Samuel Atkins to William Clarke, 1 Dec. 1659, H.M.C. Leyborne-Popham, pp. 130–31; Nicholson to Colepeper, 19 Nov. 1659, *C.S.P.* (*Dom*) *1659–1660*, p. 209.

24 Speech by Whitelocke on 8 Nov. 1659, E.1010 (5); Monck to Commissioners, 28 Nov. 1659, *Clarke Papers*, IV, p. 163.

25 Fleetwood to Monck, 1 Dec. 1659, ibid., p. 162; Bordeaux to Mazarin, 8 Dec. 1659, Guizot, *Richard Cromwell*, II, pp. 300–304; Whitelocke's speech as above, n. 24.

26 Monck to Vice-Admiral Goodson from Edinburgh, 29 Nov. 1659, B.L. 669, f. 22 (20).

27 Monck and fifty-six officers in Scotland to the Commissioners in London, 25 Nov. 1659, *Clarke Papers*, IV, pp. 126ff; Monck to Fleetwood, ibid., pp. 129–31; Nicholas to Colepeper, 19 Nov. 1659. *C.S.P.* (*Dom*) *1659–1660*, p. 269; Bordeaux to Mazarin, 5 Dec. 1659, Guizot, *Richard Cromwell*, II, p. 300.

28 Owen to Monck, 19 Nov. 1649; Monck to Owen, 29 Nov. 1659, *Clarke Papers* pp. 121ff, 151–4.

29 Monck to Lambert, 24 Nov. 1659, ibid., pp. 131–2.

30 Major Yaxley Robson to Monck, 21 Nov. 1659. H.M.C. Leyborne-Popham, p. 128; Robson to Monck, 1 Dec. 1659, *Clarke Papers*, IV, 160–61; Joseph Witter to Monck from Dunbar, 1 Dec. 1659, National Library of Scotland, 33/7/15; Monck's orders to Morgan, 8 Nov. 1659, *Clarke Papers*, IV, p. 108; Monck to Morgan, 13 Nov. 1659, Misc. letters D.180, f. 68 (Bodleian); Colonel Miles Mann to Monck from Inverness, 12 Nov. 1659, H.M.C. Leyborne-Popham, p. 126; Gumble, *Monck*, pp. 100ff.

31 Council of State to Monck, 24 Nov. 1659, Clarke MSS. 52, ff. 51–2.

32 Bordeaux to Mazarin, 5/15 Dec. 1659. Guizot, *Richard Cromwell*, II, p. 300.

33 Fleetwood to Monck, 6 Dec. 1659, *Clarke Papers*, IV, pp. 168–71.

34 Broderick to Hyde, 16 Dec. *Cal. Clarendon S.P.*, III, p. 628.

35 Price, *The Mystery*, pp. 730ff; Gumble, *Monck*, pp. 151ff.

Chapter 14, The March to London

1 There is a curious reference to Monck's Royalism in a memorial written by Sir John Hinton, one of Charles II's doctors, for the King's benefit. It states 'The day before General Monk went into Scotland [presumably in 1654] he dined with me ... after dinner he called me into the next room and after some general discourse, taking a lusty glass of wine, he drank a health to the Black Boy, as he called your Majesty, and whispered to me that if ever he had the power, he would serve your Majesty to the utmost of his life.' This memorial was written in 1679, eight years after Monck's death and so was not liable to be contradicted. It seems a little out of character. On the other hand, it is not clear why Hinton should have made up the story. H. Ellis, ed., *Original Letters illustrative of English History*, third series (1846), IV, p. 307.

2 On 23 Nov. 1659 the Common Council agreed to a day of humiliation because 'the very foundations of the Government are rased'. On 18 December a sub-committee was appointed to confer with Fleetwood from time to time about the City militia and the need for the nation to be ruled in a parliamentary way. Journal, 41. ff, 211v–12.

3 *Fairfax Correspondence*, IV, p. 146.

4 On 27 Dec. the London Common Council decided to petition the restored Rump to admit the secluded members and to convene a free parliament. Journal, 41, f. 216.

5 R. Baker, *A Chronicle of the Kings of England* (1733), p. 592. Cf. Godfrey Davies, *The Restoration of Charles II* (1955), p. 185 and n. 87.

6 *C.J.*, VII, p. 797.

7 Ibid.; *Clarke Papers*, IV, pp. 222–3; the same messenger from the Rump brought the orders for Lambert's forces to return to the positions they occupied on 20 Oct. 1659.

8 John Price, *The Mystery and Method of His Majesty's Happy Restoration Laid Open to the Public View* (1860), p. 750.

9 Thomas Gumble, *The Life of General Monck* (1671), pp. 196–7.

10 *Clarke Papers*, IV, pp. 237–8.

11 *Diary of Sir Archibald Johnston of Wariston* (1911–40), III, p. 158.

12 Lambert to Monck from Newcastle, 10 Dec. 1659, *Clarke Papers*, IV, pp. 179–83; 'News from Berwick', 8 Dec. and 'News from Coldstream', 9 Dec. in ibid.

13 Monck to the Governor of Stirling, 15 Dec. 1659, ibid., pp. 194–5; Commissioners from the Scottish shires to Monck, 13 Dec. and 17 Nov. 1659, ibid., pp. 190–91, 121. Baker, *Chronicle*, p. 590.

14 Monck to Lambert, 14 (?) Dec. and 16 Dec. 1659, H.M.C. Leyborne-Popham, pp. 133–4; *Clarke Papers*, IV, pp. 195–6.

15 *C.S.P.* (*Dom*) *1659–1660*, pp. 87, 121. He was also given permission at this time to raise an excise on salt.

16 Monck to Sir Hardress Waller, 28 Dec. 1659; to the Council of Officers in Ireland, 28 (?) Dec. 1659; Monck to Commissioners of Parliament, 29 Dec. 1659, *Clarke Papers*, IV, 225–9, B.L. 669 f. 21 (39). Waller had been commander-in-chief in Ireland after the fall of the Cromwells, but was superseded by Ludlow on the orders of the Rump. Like Ludlow, he had been a regicide. Although he declared for the restoration of the Rump, Monck distrusted him. C. H. Firth, *The Regimental History of Cromwell's Army* (1940), vol 2, pp. 445–8.

17 W. H. Dawson, *Cromwell's Understudy* (1938), ch. XXV, but the account of Lambert's actions and motives is unsatisfactory. An excellent account of how Fairfax seized York from Robert Lilburne is that by A. H. Woolrych, 'Yorkshire and the Restoration', *Yorkshire Archaeological Journal* (1958).

18 Monck to Overton from York, 14 and 16 Jan. 1660; Overton to Monck, 13 Jan. 1660, *Clarke Papers*, IV, pp. 244–7. Overton had been restored by the Rump to the governorship of Hull on 13 July 1659.

19 Monck to Morgan, 13 Jan. 1660, ibid., p. 247. *C.J.*, VII, p. 799. On 22 Jan. Monck belatedly thanked the Council of State for his commission as commander-in-chief dated 24 Nov. 1659 notified to him by Clarges, *Clarke Papers*, IV, pp. 256–8.

20 Price, *The Mystery*, p. 746.

21 H.M.C. Leyborne-Popham, p. 152. Coote had allied himself with Hardress Waller against Ludlow and in February declared himself in

favour of admitting the secluded members. Cf. E. Ludlow, *Memoirs*, ed. C. H. Firth (1894), II, pp. 209, 229.

22 Z. Grey, *Impartial Examinations* (1739), p. 163; *Clarke Papers*, IV, pp. 253–5.

23 Monck to Chief Justice St John, 21 Jan. 1660, ibid., pp. 249–50.

24 White Kennet, *A register and chronicle* (1728), p. 20 for the petition to the Speaker. Monck to Mr Rolle, 23 Jan. 1660, *Toland's Collection of Monck's Letters* (1712), XVIII; *Clarke Papers*, IV, pp. 258–9. Monck to William Morice, 23 Jan. 1660, ibid., p. 260. E. Ludlow, *Memoirs*, ed. C. H. Firth (1894), II, p. 208.

25 Bordeaux to Mazarin, 23 Jan. 1660. F. P. G. Guizot, *The History of Richard Cromwell and the Restoration of Charles II*, trans. A. R. Scoble (1856), II, p. 333.

26 Ibid.

27 Gumble, *Monck*, p. 220, H.M.C. Leyborne-Popham, pp. 207ff.

28 Baker, *Chronicle*, p. 595.

29 Ibid., p. 596; Clarke MSS. 52 f. 65v. The letter was carried to the Rump by Colonel Lydcote.

30 A copy of this forgery is in a volume of material relating to George Monck now in the National Maritime Museum at Greenwich.

31 Most of the petitions and declarations were printed and are in B.M. 669 f. 23 and f. 25. *Declaration of 5,000 gentlemen of Oxford to Monck at his headquarters at the Glasshouse in Broad Street*, C.S.P. (*Dom*) *1659–1660*, p. 361; City Journal, 41 f. 218ff. and for the apprentices' petition, *C.S.P.* (*Dom*) *1659–1660* p. 345. Address of the knights of Buckinghamshire to Monck, ibid., p. 341. B.M. 669 f. 23 for petitions from Warwickshire and Bedfordshire, and from Cheshire, Shropshire and Staffordshire.

32 Add. MSS. 10166 f. 52v, under date 28 Jan. 1660.

33 *The Diurnal of Thomas Rugg 1659–1661*, ed. W. L. Sachse (1966), pp. 29–31.

34 Nicholas to Mordaunt, 28 Jan. 1660, *C.S.P.* (*Dom*) *1659–1660*, p. 334.

35 Henry Booth to Nicholas, 25 Jan. 1660, ibid., p. 324.

36 Mordaunt to Charles II, *Cal. Clarendon S.P.*, III, p. 651.

37 Council of State to Monck, 2 Feb. 1660; apprentices and young men of London to Monck, 2 Feb. 1660, *C.S.P.* (*Dom*) *1659–1660*, pp. 344–345. Rugge, *Diurnal*, pp. 34–5; Thomas Skinner, M.D., *The Life of General Monk*, ed. William Webster (1723), pp. 219–20.

38 Rugge, *Diurnal*, p. 35. John Watkins to Edward Wilcox in Bristol, H.M.C. Leyborne-Popham, p. 144; *C.J.*, VII, p. 834.

Chapter 15, The Restoration of Charles II

1 *Diary*, ed. H. B. Wheatley (1893–99), I, p. 91.

2 *Fairfax Correspondence*, IV, p. 195.

3 Monck to Weaver, 21 Jan. 1659 from Nottingham, *Clarke Papers*, IV, pp. 250–51.

4 H.M.C. Portland, VII, p. 11.

5 Monck to Morice, 25 Jan. 1659 from Market Harborough, ibid., p.260.

6 C. H. Firth, *The Regimental History of Cromwell's Army* (1940), two vols., II, pp. 507–8, I, pp. 333–5. Fagge married Morley's sister, Mary.

7 Thomas Gumble, *The Life of General Monck* (1671), pp. 229–34 who prints Monck's speech in full; Thomas Skinner, M.D., *The Life of General Monk* (1723), ed. William Webster, pp. 225–6; Baker, *Chronicle*, pp. 596–7.

8 R. R. Sharpe, *London and the Kingdom* (1894), II, pp. 358–64.

9 Nicholas to Lipse, 10 Dec. 1660, *C.S.P. (Dom) 1659–1660*, p. 280.

10 Monck to the Lord Mayor of London, 6 Jan. 1660 from Newcastle. *Parliamentary History* (1863), XXII, pp. 50–52; R. Baker, *A Chronicle of the Kings of England* (1733), p. 595; Sharpe, *London and the Kingdom*, II, p. 366.

11 Godfrey Davies, *The Restoration of Charles II* (1955), p. 278 and authorities quoted in n. 5.

12 E.g. Gumble writes: 'The City ... in the Common Council resolved "To pay no publike Taxes till the House was filled up with equal Representatives".' *Monck*, pp. 234–5; William Prichard to William Canne, 7 Feb. 1660, H.M.C. Leyborne-Popham, pp. 142–3. I fell into this trap in my recent book on Charles II.

13 E. Ludlow, *Memoirs*, ed. C. H. Firth (1894), II, 219. Another version is that Heslirige said: 'Now, George, we have thee, body and soul.'

14 Price, *The Mystery and Method of His Majesty's Happy Restoration Laid Open to the Public View* (1860), p. 763.

15 Ludlow, *Memoirs*, II, p. 218.

16 Price, *The Mystery*, p. 763.

17 Gumble, *Monck*, p. 236.

18 Monck to the Speaker, 9 Feb. 1660 from Guildhall and Parliament's resolution of the same date, *Parliamentary History*, XXII, pp. 92–3; Bordeaux to Mazarin, 12 Feb. 1660, F. P. G. Guizot, *The History of Richard Cromwell and the Restoration of Charles II*, trans. A. R. Scoble (1856), II, pp. 347–53.

19 Baker, *Chronicle*, p. 598; Monck and officers to the Speaker, 11 Feb. 1660 from Whitehall. *Toland's Collection of Monck's Letters* (1712), XXII; *The Diurnal of Thomas Rugg 1659–1661*, ed. W. L. Sachse (1966), p. 39.

20 Pepys, *Diary*, I, pp. 51–3; Rugg, *Diurnal*, p. 40.

21 Various letters from Charles Fairfax, Thomas Morgan and Lord Fairfax to Monck, 11–18 Feb. 1660 in H.M.C. Leyborne-Popham, pp. 146–164; Richard Elsworth to Monck, 25 Feb. 1660 from Bristol; Major Thomas Izard to Monck from Bristol, 29 Feb. 1660; Coote to Monck, 16 Feb. 1660 from Dublin, ibid., pp. 161, 164, 152–3.

22 Monck to Council of State, 13 Feb. in answer to President of Council of State to Monck, 12 Feb. 1660, *Clarke Papers*, IV, pp. 261–2; *C.S.P. (Dom) 1659–1660*, p. 358; Council of State to Monck, 13 Feb. 1660, p. 360; Monck to Council of State, 14 Feb. 1660 from Drapers Hall, *Clarke Papers*, IV, p. 263. Monck to Heslirige, 13 Feb. 1660, Clarke MSS. 51, f. 73v.

23 Heslirige to Monck, 12 Feb. 1660, *Clarke Papers*, IV, pp. 260–61; Monck to Heslirige, 13 Feb. 1660, *Cal. Clarendon S.P.*, III, pp. 678–679; Monck to Heslirige, 15 Feb. 1660 from Drapers Hall, *Clarke Papers*, IV, p. 264.

24 Lord Fairfax to Monck, 14 Feb. 1660; Monck to Lord Fairfax and gentlemen of Yorkshire, 18 Feb. 1660, H.M.C. Leyborne-Popham, pp. 149–55.

25 The evidence for this derives from Anthony Ashley Cooper. K. H. D. Haley, *The First Earl of Shaftesbury* (1968), p. 131. The account was written long after the events but, Professor Haley says, 'there is no good reason to doubt its accuracy'. Bordeaux to Mazarin, 16 Feb. 1666, Guizot, *Richard Cromwell*, II, p. 355. Much of what Bordeaux wrote about Monck was guesswork.

26 *Parliamentary History*, XXII, pp. 140–43 for text of speech. Baker, *Chronicle*, p. 600; Price, *The Mystery*, p. 772; Rugg, *Diurnal*, p. 43.

27 Haley, *Shaftesbury*, pp. 130–31 and n. 2; Ludlow, *Memoirs*, II, p. 235; Woolrych, *Complete Prose Works of John Milton*, VII (1974), pp. 174–5. I agree with Professor Woolrych to whom I owe the suggestion about the attitude of the Speaker. For Monck and the baptism of Lenthall's grandson, see Rugg, *Diurnal*, p. 58.

28 Baker, *Chronicle*, p. 601.

29 Bodleian English hist. MS. C.487, f. 11v.

30 Christopher Cornwell to Monck, 25 Feb. 1660 from Ipswich; Humphrey Warner to Monck, 28 Feb. 1660 from Bury St Edmunds; Richard Ingoldsby to Monck, 29 Feb. 1660, H.M.C. Leyborne-Popham, pp. 158, 162–3, 165–6, 226; Rugg, *Diurnal*, p. 46; Major Thomas Izard to Monck, 29 Feb. 1660 from Bristol; Okey to Monck from Bristol, 25 Feb. 1660, ibid., pp. 158–64; H. G. Tibbutt, *Colonel John Okey* (1954), pp. 120–2; Price, *The Mystery*, pp. 779–81; Garrison of Hull to Monck, 28 Feb. 1660, H.M.C. Leyborne-Popham, p. 167; Monck to Governor of Hull, 4 (?) Mar. 1660, Clarke MSS. 57,

f. 76; Council of State to Overton, 4 Mar. 1660, *C.S.P.* (*Dom*) *1659–1660*, p. 381; Monck to Lord Fairfax, 5 Mar. 1660. Clarke MSS. 49, f. 121v; Baker, *Chronicle*, p. 602 for Monck's letter to Okey. *Clarke Papers*, IV, pp. 264–6 and notes for details about Okey's replacement.

31 Monck to Colonel Bennett, 12 Mar. 1660, Clarke MSS. 49, f. 122.

32 Monck to officers commanding regiments, 17 (?) Mar. 1660, *Clarke Papers*, IV, pp. 266–7.

33 Charles Fairfax to Monck, Feb. 1660, H.M.C. Leyborne-Popham, p. 159.

34 Price, *The Mystery*, pp. 781–2; Baker, *Chronicle*, pp. 603–4; Tibbutt, *Okey*, pp. 122–3; Sheriff Ellison to Monck, 27 Feb. 1660 from Newcastle; Major Jeremiah Tolshurst to Monck, 29 Feb. 1660 from Carlisle; Captain W. Richardson to Monck, 25 Feb. 1660 from Durham, H.M.C. Leyborne-Popham, pp. 159–61, 162, 165, 176, 179; Bordeaux to Mazarin, 27 Feb. 1660. Guizot, *Richard Cromwell*, II, p. 371; Sir William Lockhard to Monck, 17 Apr. 1660 from Dunkirk, ibid., p. 176.

35 Rugg, *Diurnal*, p. 62.

36 In his *Restoration* Davies does not explain very clearly the sudden appearance of the House of Lords. For Monck's reluctance to allow it to meet see C. H. Firth, *The House of Lords during the Civil War* (1910), ch. IX.

37 Rugg, *Diurnal*, pp. 73, 75.

38 Davies, *Restoration*, ch XVI; *Huntington Library Quarterly* (1952), p. 211ff.

39 Price, *The Mystery*, pp. 793–4.

40 Bordeaux to Mazarin, 8 Mar. 1660, Guizot, *Richard Cromwell*, II, pp. 375–8.

41 Price, *The Mystery*, pp. 784–6.

42 *Cal. Clarendon S.P.*, IV, p. 620.

43 Charles II to Monck, 4 Apr. 1660, Gumble, *Monck*, pp. 369–72. See also ibid., pp. 289–91; Price, *The Mystery*, p. 791.

44 *C.J.*, VIII, p. 8.

45 Marcês to Hyde, 13 May 1660, *Cal. Clarendon S.P.*, V, p. 32; Monck to Knight, 3 May 1660, H.M.C., XIII, p. 4. Bordeaux to Mazarin, 3 May 1660, Guizot, *Richard Cromwell*, II, p. 422.

46 Burnet, *Own Times*, I, p. 151; *Cal. Clarendon S.P.*, III, p. 32.

47 Ibid., pp. 746–7.

48 Colonel Fairfax to Monck, 11 May 1660 from Hull, H.M.C. Leyborne-Popham, p. 186.

49 Monck to Charles II, 16 May 1660 from St James's, Clarendon MSS. 72, f. 396.

50 Bordeaux to Mazarin, 11 May 1660, Guizot, *Richard Cromwell*, II,

pp. 427–9; Gumble, *Monck*, pp. 381–2. *Cal. Clarendon S.P.*, III, p. 739.

51 Heslirige to Monck, 30 Apr. 1660, *Clarke Papers*, IV, p. 268; Broderick to Hyde, 7 May 1660. *Cal. Clarendon S.P.*, V, p. 21; Ruth Spalding, *The Improbable Puritan* (1975), p. 295 quoting Longleat MSS. Whitelocke wrote to Monck asking for clemency as early as 28 January.

52 Mountagu to Monck, Egerton MSS. 2618, f. 77; Gumble, *Monck*, p. 382; Langley to Leveson, 24 May 1660, H.M.C., V, p. 207; Monck to Knight, 23 May 1660, H.M.C., XIII, VI, p. 4.

53 Gumble, *Monck*, p. 384.

54 Griffith Davies, *Honest George Monck* (1936), p. 239.

Chapter 16, The Elder Statesman

1 G. Burnet, *Own Times*, p. 152.

2 Pepys, *Diary*, 17 Nov. 1667.

3 These are listed in Clarendon MSS. 88, ff. 20–22. The private act is listed in *Statutes of the Realm* (1810), V, p. 43. See Appendix.

4 Clarendon, *The Life of Edward Earl of Clarendon* (1857), II, pp. 53–4; Bagwell, *Ireland under the Stuarts*, III, pp. 16, 229 and notes; *C.S.P. (Ireland) 1660–1662*, p. 128. In the Act of Settlement clause CXXXV houses and lands in Galway in the possession of Sir Thomas Clarges were to be disposed of by the King; the way he disposed of them was to grant them to Albemarle. I have been unable to work out precisely the nature of Albemarle's holdings in Ireland. The Act of Settlement confirmed by clause VII that the English officers and soldiers who enjoyed estates in Ireland conferred on them in payment of arrears, as on 7 May 1659, might retain them. Furthermore, commissioned officers serving there before 5 June 1649 (who included Monck) were to receive compensation for arrears of pay out of forfeited lands. By clause XV lands granted to Monck for his arrears and service in Ireland and also lands purchased by him in lieu of arrears now in his possession were specifically confirmed to him. A private act was also passed in 1665 securing several lands, tenements and hereditaments to him. *Irish Statutes*, II, pp. 248, 253; III, p. 138. See also Appendix above.

5 *C.S.P. (Dom) 1660–1685*, p. 295.

6 Thomas Gumble, *The Life of General Monck* (1671), p. 468; Thomas Skinner, M.D., *The Life of General Monk*, ed. William Webster (1723), p. 419; Pepys, *Diary*, 4 Apr. 1667.

7 R. Baker, *A Chronicle of the Kings of England* (1733), p. 652. I assume the continuator had this from Clarges.

8 Pepys, *Diary*, 28 Dec. 1663.

9 Gumble, *Monck*, p. 469. Estelle Francis in her biography of Christopher Monck, pp. 64ff suggests that George Monck had an illegitimate son Thomas; the evidence is extremely tenuous and even if the argument is accepted, Thomas must have been the son of Anne Ratsford by Monck before she left her husband. A series of law suits about the ultimate disposal of Monck's estates are described in the above book.

10 Gumble, *Monck*, pp. 468ff. Skinner, *Monk*, p. 424; E. Ludlow, *Memoirs*, ed. C. H. Firth (1894), II, p. 284.

11 Mrs Monck to Charles II, 6 May 1660; Charles II to Mrs Monck, 11 May 1660. *Cal. Clarendon S.P.*, V, pp. 18, 29; Princess of Orange to Duchess of Albemarle, Egerton MSS. 2618, f. 79; F. P. G. Guizot, *The History of Richard Cromwell and the Restoration of Charles II*, trans. A. R. Scoble (1856), II, pp. 427–9.

12 *Own Times*, p. 168.

13 Lady Mordaunt to Hyde, Thomas Dowde to Hyde, Colonel Robert Philipp to Hyde, Dr Morley to Hyde, 4 May 1660, *Cal. Clarendon S.P.*, V, pp. 12–14.

14 Sir George Downing to Clarendon, 10 Feb. 1665, *Cal. Clarendon S.P.*, V, p. 468.

15 Cf. Morgan to Albemarle, 2 Dec. 1661 from Leith, H.M.C. Leyborne-Popham, p. 191.

16 T. H. Lister, *Life and Administration of Edward first Earl of Clarendon* (1838), III, pp. 500–3. This paper was dated 9 May 1660. It is in the handwriting of Sir Philip Warwick and was sent by him to Hyde on that date, *Cal. Clarendon S.P.*, V, p. 25. It was thus sent to Charles II more than a month after the declaration of Breda had been signed in which the King had handed over the land settlement to parliament. On 21 July 1660 Monck ordered his officers commanding regiments of horse, to collect particulars of Crown lands purchased by officers and soldiers including their values and the dates when they were bought. It looks as if Monck left his demands on this question until it was too late.

17 The clearest discussion of this complicated question is Joan Thirsk, 'The Restoration Land Settlement' in *Journal of Modern History*, vol. 26 (1954), pp. 315–28.

18 Broderick to Hyde, 3 May 1660, *Cal. Clarendon S.P.*, V, p. 7.

19 W. Smith to J. Langley, 23 June 1660, H.M.C. Sutherland, p. 173.

20 Heslirige to Monck, 30 Apr. 1660, *Clarke Papers*, IV, p. 265; Broderick to Hyde, 7 May 1660, *Cal. Clarendon S.P.*, III, pp. 739–40; Albemarle to Sir Edward Turner, 4 July 1660, *Clarke Papers*, IV, p. 302; H.M.C. Eighth Report, I, p. 212; *Parliamentary History*, XXII, p. 447. It appears to have been generally known in the House of Com-

mons that Albemarle had promised that Heslirige's life should be spared. Cf. ibid., p. 444. Ludlow declares that Monck had also promised to intervene on behalf of Colonel Francis Hacker. But as Hacker supervised Charles I's execution, Albemarle must have realized he could not save him from the scaffold.

21 Certificate by Albemarle that one William Carre in 1659 was examined by the Council of State about a plot against the army with a blank commission signed by Thomas Scot, President of the Council, for raising several Anabaptists to oppose the army. Scot's son vowed to kill Monck at that time, Clarke MSS. 49, f. 163.

22 Certificate by Albemarle, 7 Dec. 1660, Clarke MSS. 49. Burnet, *Own Times*, I, pp. 207–13; Baker, *Chronicle*, p. 627; Julian Corbett, *Monk* (1889), pp. 197–9 and notes; Willcock, *Argyll*, ch. XIX.

23 C. Walton, *History of the British Standing Army 1660–1700* (1894), ch. 1; J. W. Fortescue, *History of the British Army* (1914) I, pp. 291–4.

24 *Cal. Clarendon S.P.*, V, p. 76; Albemarle to the Duchess of Somerset, 14 Oct. 1662. Add. MSS. 32096, f. 11; Albemarle also wrote to the Earl of Huntingdon, a minor, who does not appear to have had property in Middlesex, H.M.C. Hastings, II, p. 141; on 14 Mar. 1660 he wrote to the commissioners for the assessment in Exeter to hasten their work, H.M.C. Exeter Records, p. 211; and there are other instances of this activity.

25 Monck to Morgan, 14 July 1660, English Letters, D.180 in the Bodleian.

26 Albemarle's orders of 28 Aug. and 19 Nov. 1660 in Clarke MSS. 49.

27 Albemarle to the Earl of Winchelsea, 28 Dec. 1663 from the Cockpit, H.M.C. Finch, I, p. 294.

28 Charles II to Albemarle Master of Our Horse, 13 May 1662, Egerton MSS. 2618, f. 97.

29 In Wheatley's edition of Pepy's *Diary* an entry under 28 Dec. 1663 is 'went and spoke with the Duke of Albemarle about his wound at New Hall, but find him a dull heavy man, methinks by his answer to me'. Wheatley wrote (III, p. 392) 'it is a pity that Pepys instead of hazarding this absurd remark did not tell us more about the Duke of Albemarle's wound'. The new transcription of the diary shows that the word was not 'wound' but 'wood'.

30 Baker, *Chronicle*, p. 629; E. Prestage, *The Diplomatic Relations of Portugal with France, England and Holland* from 1640 to 1668 (1925), pp. 139–41 and p. 140 n. 2; David Ogg, *England in the Reign of Charles II* (1955), ch. I, pp. 183–5 based on English records.

31 For the origins of this war see Charles Wilson, *Profit and Power* (1957), chs VII–IX. Professor Wilson (p. 107), quotes Monck as saying

apropos the causes of the war: 'What we want is more of the trade the Dutch now have.' This is based on A. T. Mahan, *The Influence of Sea-power on History* (1890), p. 107. Monck was ill at this time and according to Gumble, *Monck*, p. 410, he 'scarce declared himself in it till Parliament had voted to adhere with Lives and Fortunes'.

32 This paragraph is based on W. G. Bell, *The Great Plague in London* (1924). See also Charles Creighton, *A History of Epidemics in Britain* (1891), ch. XII. Clarendon, *Life*, II, p. 404 pays tribute to Monck and Craven.

33 Ibid., II, pp. 484–8.

Chapter 17, The Last Campaign

1 Pepys, *Diary*, 8 June 1666.

2 Ibid., 3 May 1660.

3 Good accounts of the campaign will be found in David Ogg, *England in the Reign of Charles II* (1955), ch. VIII; R. C. Anderson, introduction to *The Journals of Sir Thomas Allin* (1941); *The Rupert and Monck Letter Book*, ed. Rev. J. R. Powell and E. K. Timings (1969), pp. 185–95.

4 Arlington to Monck, 21 Jan. 1666, Egerton MSS. 2618, f. 123.

5 Letters from Rupert and Albemarle to William Coventry and others in *Letter Book*, pp. 13–52.

6 Rupert and Albemarle to Sir Thomas Allin, Sir George Ayscue, Sir Christopher Myngs and Sir James Jordan, 16 May 1666, *Letter Book*, pp. 13, 48.

7 Rupert and Albemarle to Arlington, 11 May 1666, *Letter Book*, p. 200.

8 Rupert to Duke of York, 10 May 1666; Rupert and Albemarle to Arlington, 11 May 1666 from Buoy of the Nore, ibid., pp. 200–201.

9 Coventry's recollections, ibid., p. 202; cf. ibid., p. 185–6.

10 This is what Albemarle told the House of Commons on 31 Oct. 1667. Coventry's recollections dated 15 May 1666, denied that he and Carteret had delivered any intelligence about the Dutch not coming out. Rupert in his narrative of the same date as that of Albemarle merely says that the plan to separate the two fleets 'was encouraged' by other intelligence that 'the Dutch were not likely to come abroad in some weeks'. Rupert's letter to the Duke of York of 10 May shows that Rupert had received the intelligence before the visit of Coventry and Carteret on 14 May. On the other hand, in Coventry's notes for an answer to Prince Rupert and the Duke of Albemarle, presumably written in Oct. 1667, he wrote: 'The information given by Sir George Carteret and myself that the Dutch would not come out in six weeks. Desire

to avoid disputing that matter of fact.' Albemarle was a pretty good liar, but Rupert was not. It seems likely that Carteret and Coventry did say what was attributed to them by Albemarle about the Dutch fleet. But Rupert might also have learnt about the Dutch delay in coming out from naval intelligence and from Arlington or Morice. The fact is that everybody concerned believed that the Dutch would not set sail as early as they did. All the relevant documents are printed in the *Letter Book*, the originals being in *C.J.*, VIII and Add. MSS. 32094.

11 Albemarle to Coventry, 21 May 1666 and to the King on the same date, *Letter Book*, pp. 208–10. The victualler was Dennis Gauden who had originally been given a contract to supply the Tangier garrison. On 27 Oct. 1665 Pepys was appointed Surveyor of Victualling in addition to his other posts for which he received £500 a year. Gauden who had the contract to supply the navy in the second Anglo-Dutch war paid Pepys £300 a year for the concession; he also presented him with two flagons worth £100 and an extra payment of £500 when he obtained this contract. It is clear therefore that Pepys was responsible for the victualling out of which he made a fair amount of money. No wonder he did not care for Albemarle who kept on prodding him about the shortage of victuals. See Arthur Bryant, *Pepys: the Man in the Making* (1933), pp. 221, 222, 274.

12 Albemarle to Coventry, 23 May 1666 from the *Royal Charles* in the Downs. This crossed a letter from the Duke of York dated 22 May in which he announced the King's approval of the decision to separate the fleet. *Letter Book*, p. 215.

13 Albemarle to Coventry, 26 May 1666 from the *Royal Charles* off the South Foreland, ibid., p. 221.

14 Albemarle to Arlington, 28 May 1666 from the Downs, ibid., p. 223.

15 Albemarle to Coventry, 26 May 1666 off the South Foreland; Albemarle's narrative of 31 Oct. 1667, *Letter Book*, p. 222; Albemarle to Coventry, 27 May 1666 from the Downs, *Letter Book*, pp. 217, 283, 222.

16 Albemarle to Coventry, 28 May 1666, ibid., p. 224. This letter refers back to Coventry's letter of 26 May, ibid., p. 217. I think this date should be 25 May, but perhaps it was received on 26 May. The significant sentence reads: 'it [i.e. Coventry's letter] told the Lord General [i.e. Albemarle] the Dutch would very suddenly be out yet that altered not Prince Rupert sailing.' Is this a flat statement of fact or is it an implied criticism of Coventry and/or Rupert?

17 Duke of York to Albemarle, 28 May 1666, ibid., pp. 224–5.

18 Louis XIV to Beaufort, 30 Apr./10 May 1666 and 5/15 May 1666, H. T. Colenbrander, *Bescheiden uit Vreemde Archiven omtrent De Groote Nederlandsche Zeeoorlogen 1652–1676*, I, pp. 306–7.

19 Introduction to pt II of the *Letter Book*, p. 187.

20 Ibid., p. 186.

21 Albemarle to Coventry forenoon, 1 June 1666 from the *Royal Charles* half-way between the North Foreland and Dunkirk, ibid., p. 231.

22 Anderson, introduction to *Thomas Allin*, II, pp. xxiii–xxvi and *Letter Book*, pp. 189–92.

23 Albemarle to Arlington, 9 June 1666 from the Nore, *Letter Book*, p. 257.

24 Charles Wilson, *Profit and Power* (1957), pp. 135–6. Professor Wilson, it seems to me, relied overmuch on Pepys and what Coventry told Pepys. But Pepys and Coventry certainly contributed largely to the defeat by not supplying the two generals-at-sea with sufficient ships and supplies to meet their needs while Coventry was responsible for misleading intelligence: see note 10 above. Incidentally Rupert joined Albemarle on the third day of the battle, not, as Professor Wilson says, on the second day.

25 Roland A. Shelley in vol. 25 of the *Mariner's Mirror* wrote 'at his [Albermarle's] door 90 per cent at least of the blame should be laid'.

26 Duke of York to Albemarle, 31 May 1666 in which he says he dispatched at midnight on 30 May the order to Rupert to return with his squadron. Rupert received this order at Portsmouth at five o'clock in the afternoon of 1 June and thence sailed to the Downs, although by then Albemarle was at the Gunfleet. *Letter Book*, pp. 229, 286. Mr Shelley argued that no time was lost in dispatching the order to Rupert, but it could have arrived at Portsmouth on 31 May if Coventry had sent it off after the meeting of the Privy Council on 30 May. On 30 May Albemarle received a report from Captain Thomas Ewer that he had met a Swedish merchant ship whose captain told him that 93 Dutch warships had set sail on 21 May. Understandably, Albemarle was dubious about this second-hand intelligence though he passed it on. He did not receive confirmation until 31 May by which time he had learnt of the King's recall of Rupert.

27 Albemarle to Arlington, 9 June 1666, *Letter Book*, p. 257; Pepys, *Diary*, 13 June 1666.

28 Rupert and Albemarle to Arlington, 24 June 1666, ibid., p. 261.

29 Rupert and Arlington to the King, 17 July 1666, ibid., pp. 102–3.

30 Rupert and Albemarle to the King, 5 July 1666, ibid., p. 264.

31 These instructions were discovered by the editors of the *Letter Book*, pp. 104–5 and are not in in J. Corbett's *Fighting Instructions*.

32 Nieuwsbericht uit Vlissingen, 17 Aug. 1666, Colenbrander, *Bescheiden*, I, p. 461.

33 Albemarle to the King, 14 Aug. 1666, *Letter Book*, p. 270.

34 The official account was entitled *A True and Perfect Narrative of the*

Great and Signal Success of a Part of His Majesty's Fleet (1666), which was based on a letter from Sir Robert Holmes to Arlington, S.P. 29/167, f. 77. A full up-to-date account is in Richard Ollard, *Man of War* (1969), ch. XIII.

35 Thomas Clifford to Arlington, 16 Aug. 1666, *Letter Book*, p. 281.

36 Albemarle arrived in London on Fri. 7 Sept., W. G. Bell, *The Great Fire of London* (1920), p. 323.

37 Clarendon *Life*, III, p. 199; Thomas Skinner, M.D., *The Life of General Monk*, ed. William Webster (1723), pp. 406–7.

38 Duke of York to the Navy Board, 4 Apr. 1667, Colenbrander, *Bescheiden*, I, p. 529.

39 Wicquefort to Frederik III of Denmark, 23 Mar./2 Apr. and 20/30 Apr. 1666, ibid., pp. 528–30.

40 P. G. Rogers, *The Dutch in the Medway* (1970), ch. VII.

41 Albemarle's own account of his movements was given in his report to the House of Commons *C.J.*, IX pp. 10ff. According to Pepys, Albemarle wrote on Wed. 12 June that 'all is safe to the great ships against any assault—the boom and chain being fortified'. *Diary*, 12 June 1667. Pepys did not like Monck but presumably he did not make this up, though he may have simplified what Albemarle wrote.

Chapter 18, Death and Retrospect

1 The new appointments were made on 24 May and included besides Albemarle and Ashley, Sir Thomas Clifford, Sir William Coventry and Sir John Duncombe. Cf. Evelyn, *Diary*, III, p. 427 n. 7. George Monck had been a commissioner in 1660 before Southampton took over.

2 E. Ludlow, *Memoirs*, ed. C. H. Firth (1894), II, p. 406; Pepys, *Diary* 26 Aug. 1667.

3 H.M.C. Bath, II, p. 151 dated 6 Apr. 1668.

4 *The Diary of John Milward, Sept. 1660–May 1668*, ed. C. Robbins (1938), p. 84.

5 Ibid., pp. 84–5.

6 Albemarle to the Navy Commissioners, 20 Apr. 1667, *C.S.P. (Dom) 1660–1685*, p. 176.

7 Albemarle to Sir Robert Holmes, 4 Dec. 1667 from the Cockpit. National Library of Scotland 591, no. 1812.

8 Warrant signed by Albemarle and Ashley, 2 Dec. 1667. In May 1661 the officers at Dunkirk had written: 'You having been a father to your country would', they were sure, 'not let them be disbanded without payment of their arrears'.

9 Thomas Skinner, M.D., *The Life of General Monk*, ed. William Webster (1723), pp. 408-9; Thomas Gumble, *The Life of General Monck* (1671), pp. 453-4. Skinner says 'fresh air', Gumble 'good Air and Diet'. My guess is that the diet was half the trouble; Monck appears to have eaten indiscriminately.

10 I owe this suggestion to Dr Bethel Solomons.

11 According to W. C. Abbott, *Writings and Speeches of Oliver Cromwell* (1939), I, p. 622, II, pp. 495, 535 and notes, Parliament bought the property for Cromwell and sold it to him for five shillings.

12 John Evelyn, *Diary*, II, pp. 179-80 and notes.

13 *Travels of Cosmo the Third Grand Duke of Tuscany through England in 1669* (1821), pp. 468-71.

14 Gumble, *Monck*, pp. 456-7.

15 His will is in PRO 11/332/11. The other trustees named in the will were Sir William Doyley of Yarmouth, Robert Scowen of Cornwall, John Powell of Devon and Thomas Stringer of Middlesex.

16 E. F. Ward, *Christopher Monck Duke of Albemarle* (1915), p. 24 quoting a statement of Christopher's sister-in-law, Frances Cavendish, in the Portland MSS.

17 R. Baker, *A Chronicle of the Kings of England* (1733), p. 646.

18 Skinner, *Monk*, p. 412; funeral oration printed in J. D. Griffith Davies, *Honest George Monck* (1936), pp. 348-50.

19 Gumble performed the office appointed by the Church for the Visitation of the Sick and administered the sacrament early in the morning of 1 Jan. 1667.

20 *The Monckton Papers, Miscellanies of the Philobiblion Society* XV, ed. E. Peacock, contains an account by Sir Philip Monckton, who was present, of Monck's last moments.

21 Newsletter from Whitehall, 18 Jan. 1670, H.M.C. Hastings, II, p. 316.

22 An account of the funeral is in Add. MSS. 10117, f. 237v. It is printed in full as well as the funeral oration by Griffith Davies, *Honest George Monck*, pp. 284-8.

23 Some of Christopher Monck's correspondence and that of his wife is summarized in H.M.C. Portland, vols. I, II and VIII. I have followed the account of their lives in Ward, *Christopher Monck*; the author examined the Portland papers at Welbeck.

24 Bodleian Vet A 1 a 2 (2).

25 Pepys, *Diary*, 24 Oct. 1667.

26 See Appendix.

27 G. Burnet, *Own Times*, I, p. 144.

28 Hume, *History of Great Britain* (1841), V, p. 426.

29 Reid, *Presbyterian Church*, II, pp. 54-6.

30 F. P. G. Guizot, *History of Richard Cromwell and the Restoration of Charles II*, trans. A. R. Scoble (1850), II, p. 5.
31 Julian Corbett, *Monk* (1889), p. 220.
32 In March 1660 Milton wrote a 'letter to Monck' entitled *The Present Means and Brief Delineation of a Free Commonwealth Easy to Put into Practice and Without Delay*. In this tract, which is lost, Milton aimed to bring up to date his *Readie and Easie Way to Establish a Free Commonwealth* which was written during the first three weeks of February 1660. The letter to Monck, Austin Woolrych thinks, was a draft and never reached the General. *Complete Prose Works of Milton* VII (1974), pp. 189–92.

Appendix, A Note on Monck's Income

1 This paragraph is based on Clarendon MSS. 88, ff. 20–2.
2 Ibid., f. 21; *Books of Survey and Distribution* published by the Irish Manuscripts Commission, volume concerned with Mayo, states that Monck had 1,200 profitable Irish acres, but nothing in Roscommon or Galway so perhaps he sold these. I owe this information to Dr J. G. Simms.
3 *Irish record commissioners report 1821–1825*, p. 144. I also owe this reference to Dr Simms.
4 Clarendon MSS. 88, f. 21.
5 These are the figures given by E. F. Ward, *Christopher Monck Duke of Albemarle* (1915), pp. 46–7 who states that Albemarle's son had estates or profits from estates in twelve different counties.

Index